INLAND AND COASTAL
NAVIGATION

REVISED
SECOND EDITION

DAVID BURCH

STARPATH®

Seattle, Washington

ISBN 978-0-914025-40-5

Published by
Starpath Publications
3050 NW 63rd Street, Seattle, WA 98107
Manufactured in the United States of America
www.starpathpublications.com
10 9 8 7 6 5 4

Cover map: Imagery © 2013 TerraMetrics, Map data © 2013 Google
America's Cup photo: © ACEA / PHOTO ABNER KINGMAN

Contents

Preface to the first edition

This book has been used for many years in classroom courses on small craft navigation. It is equally applicable to power or sailing vessels, kayaks or ships. The fundamental principles of marine navigation are the same to all, just as the Rules of the Road apply to all vessels. The subject matter is described as small craft navigation simply because we cover techniques and routes that do not apply to large ships.

These days GPS is the mainstay of the navigation of any vessel, but it is both legally and practically not prudent to rely on just this one source for navigation. Furthermore, the GPS cannot tell you the safest, most efficient route from where you are to where you want to go. That you must decide yourself, taking into account the lay of the charted waterway, the depth of the water, the wind, currents, sea state and visibility, the Navigation Rules, the time of day, the performance of your vessel, the crew on board, and more. In short, choosing the best route takes the knowledge presented in this book.

Another value of this background in the traditional methods of hands-on navigation is the ability it then gives you to easily spot check the GPS as you proceed. These position checks, along with good logbook and plotting procedures, will keep you on top of the navigation at all times. The continuous process of GPS checking not only assures your safety, but also keeps you in tune with your environment. With this process, you will know the names of landmarks around nearby, you can identify features on the distant horizon, you know who has the right of way as you approach another vessel, you know ahead of time that the current will start setting you strongly to the right, and so on. The GPS cannot answer these things; you must rely on your knowledge.

A thorough background in navigation fundamentals will also make your time on the water more enjoyable as it removes unnecessary anxiety, and adds another dimension to your sport. You then remain in command and are not dependent on electronics. Modern marine electronics are generally very dependable, but they are not guaranteed. The hallmark of good seamanship is to look ahead and be prepared.

Preface to the second edition

The second edition has been fully updated to include new resources now available, as well as changes in terminology and even such basics as the types of nautical charts we now use—or will very shortly. The important new role of mobile devices and electronic chart systems in general is addressed as well as ways to keep up to date with anticipated developments.

We have also taken the opportunity to readdress the main topics of traditional navigation throughout the book with a new outlook in some cases. Contact information for the several federal agencies we count on for navigation data were updated, and we have established an online link for further updates, as they will certainly change again.

There have also been changes in terminology over this period related to electronic navigation. The technology of typical marine and handheld GPS receivers has improved over the past several years, but the risks of relying on GPS alone have not changed.

For our powerboater and paddler readers, please do not be distracted by our use of the word "sailing." We use it in its basic maritime sense of any vessel underway—as when the *Navigation Rules* refer to Steering and Sailing Rules, or as standard navigation references are called Sailing Directions. When matters specific to sailboats are addressed, we refer to "when under sail." This book does contain information specific to navigation under sail, but the vast majority of the content applies to "any description of watercraft used for transportation on the water."

We have also redone the Glossary completely, adding the terms to the end of the chapters in which they first appear. This should facilitate both home study and classroom use.

Contact with the author, further resources, and news related to the text can be found at starpath.com/navbook. Comments and suggestions are always appreciated.

Revised edition

Sections of Chapter 8 were updated to account for NOAA's 2021 discontinuation of the official *Tide Tables* and *Tidal Current Tables*, notably rendering outdated the Table 2 corrections for subordinate stations included in each. The primary source of tidal data now is tidesandcurrents.noaa.gov where users can create their own annual tables. Many navigators also obtain tidal data digitally from dedicated apps, after confirming their validity. Thus throughout the book we have replaced "*Tide Tables*" and "*Tidal Current Tables*" with "tide predictions" and "current predictions" to reflect these important changes. Copies of Table 2 still in print (reproduced from the 2020 editions) should be used with caution as many of the entries are incorrect.

The brief Chapter 12 section on WAAS satellites was also updated to account for new satellite numbers and locations.

Acknowledgments

It is a pleasure to once again thank Starpath instructor Larry Brandt for his careful review of the text, which led to many helpful suggestions. This book has benefited greatly from his insights into both the practice and the teaching of navigation, as well as from his sharp eye as an editor.

Many illustrations from the first edition were drawn by Stephen Davis. Several of these have been adapted from the originals. Many new illustrations have been added to the second edition by Tobias Burch, who also did the book and cover design. I remain grateful for his skill and good work on this book and others.

Context

This book concentrates on traditional navigation using log and compass and paper charts. In early 2021 NOAA began transitioning to all electronic navigational charts (ENC) and discontinuing traditional paper charts. By the end of 2024, all traditional paper charts will be discontinued. These will be replaced with a new concept in nautical charts called NOAA Custom Charts (NCC), which are user defined paper charts with the ENC format, discussed briefly in Chapter 12. The way we use these new paper charts for navigation, however, will be essentially the same as what we teach in this book for traditional charts. The knowledge and skills you gain here are not affected by these chart format changes.

CHAPTER 1
THE ROLE OF NAVIGATION

1.1 Introduction

Navigation means knowing where you are and choosing a safe, efficient route to where you want to go. These two skills are mandatory for long trips into unknown waters and are often valuable for shorter trips in well-known waters. For the most part, navigation skills learned and practiced in one area apply to other areas as well; the fundamental techniques of navigation are universal. Safety, efficiency, and enjoyment are the main reasons to learn navigation. As opposed to wilderness hiking or ocean sailing—where actually getting lost might be a safety concern—inland navigation focuses more on avoiding hazardous areas that could be an immediate threat to a boater's safety: waters with strong currents, strong winds, big waves, or big ships. Discerning these hazards and knowing how to avoid them is part of navigation.

All boat trips must be planned. A proposed trip must fit into the number of days you have allotted, and a day's run must fit into a day. If you do not make your destination by nightfall or in time for favorable currents at the anchorage, the arrival could be more of an adventure than you want at the end of a long day. In extreme cases it could be dangerous. A wrong turn made when sailing downwind might take a long hard sail against the wind to correct. Poor navigation can turn a relaxed sightseeing outing into an adventure. With the basic navigation skills of nautical chart reading, keeping track of position, and predicting currents, an itinerary can be set up and checked off underway that will help keep the experience in line with your intentions. Under any circumstances, however, the key to good navigation during the trip is thorough navigation planning before the trip.

Once underway on a well-planned route, navigation consists of keeping track of where you are along that route. The challenge of this task depends on prevailing conditions. When sailing along a shoreline on a clear day, keeping track means little more than just looking around. As one headland is passed, the next comes into sight. By identifying the next headland on the chart, you know where you are (see Figure 1-1). After passing a few prominent points, and noting the time it took to get from point to point, it is easy to figure out how fast you are actually progressing (regardless of what your knotmeter might say) and decide how far or how long to continue on that day.

At night, in the fog, or when crossing large open waters, there is much less to see. Under these conditions, the value of practiced navigation skills is more apparent. If the only visible landmarks are far off, they will not help much in locating your position. In these cases, course direction must be read from a compass, and progress along that course reckoned from knotmeter speed and predicted current flow. It is indeed true that these skills are not often called upon for much of our daily boating (especially with a functioning GPS), but your time on the water will always be more relaxed if you are confident that you can navigate this way if need be. It pays to prepare for fog, significant currents, or nighttime sailing.

Even thorough planning, however, cannot cover all the navigational decisions a mariner confronts underway, even on a simple route along a shoreline. Should you, for example, sail point to point, straight across each bay you meet or follow the longer but less exposed concave route along the shoreline? And how should the point itself be approached: close in along the beach, or passed wide well away from waves and currents at the point? These and many other important decisions ultimately must be made underway, in the prevailing conditions of wind, waves, and current. Although navigation covers a broad range of topics, all navigation decisions depend on knowing where you are. You cannot pick the best route to where you want to go without knowing where you are at the time. Good navigation and the safety it affords always boil down to knowing where you are at all times—and from a practical point of view, that means being able to look at a chart and point to your position on it.

...In Depth

12 Special Topics

Throughout this book you will find these ...In Depth links or references to sections in Chapter 12. They present details or side topics related to the present discussion.

Please take a look at Chapter 12 to see how these are organized. In the paper edition, these are just references; in the electronic version of this book, they are links.

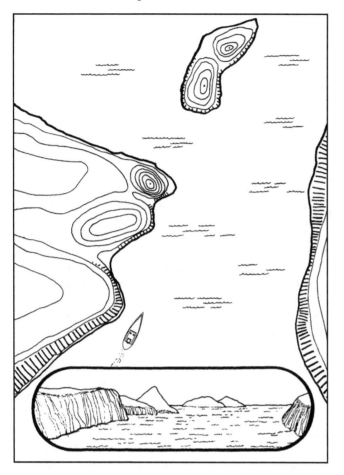

Figure 1-1. *Navigation from point to point. The inset shows the perspective from an elevated view. From the lower perspective of the cockpit of a small boat, the bases of the land masses appear more along a single straight line because the close horizon blocks the true view of the shorelines (see inset Figure 2-8).*

Crossing a shipping lane is one obvious example of how important it is to know where you are. Some waterways routinely traveled by large ships are divided into inbound and outbound lanes, which all large shipping traffic must follow. Although clearly marked on charts, the lane boundaries are not at all discernible from the water. They are effectively mile-wide invisible streets, which might lie a mile or more off the shoreline. If you detect an approaching ship while crossing the lanes, you have a quick navigation decision to make, but any choice of action must start with knowing where you are relative to the lane boundaries. These days, we have various aids such as radar, GPS and electronic charting that might make this an easy observation in some cases, but the prudent navigator will always know how to do these things without these aids if need be.

1.2 Types of Navigation

Finding and keeping track of position is done by one of two ways: piloting or dead reckoning. Piloting is the formal name for the usual way of getting around, using known landmarks. Sailing past a buoy, you know where you are as soon as you can find that buoy on the chart. The same is true near any prominent landmark.

Well away from landmarks, on the other hand, it is not as simple to pinpoint your position on the chart by just looking. To find position with only one distant landmark in sight requires a compass direction to the landmark and a measure of how far away it is. With two charted landmarks in sight, position can be found from the intersection of the two compass bearings plotted on the chart. This and other piloting techniques are explained later.

With no identifiable landmarks in sight, position must be figured from speed, course, and time. The procedure is called *dead reckoning*. It is an unusual name, but it was commonly used and listed in nautical dictionaries in the 1600s. To navigate by dead reckoning, a present position is deduced from the distance and the direction sailed away from a known location. Sailing at a rate of 6 miles per hour toward due north, you can deduce that in 30 minutes you should be 3 miles north of where you started. With the known starting point shown on the chart, you can draw this route on the chart and point to where you think you are.

Although it may not be thought of in these formal terms, the navigation of any trip proceeds as a sequence of piloting fixes, with navigation by dead reckoning between the fixes (see Figure 1-2). Starting from a known position, you set off in the direction of your destination at some estimated speed. From this you can deduce how long the trip should take and where you should be at various intermediate times. Once underway along this route, whenever you suspect that winds or currents or any other factor might be influencing your progress, you take a position fix using piloting. Sometimes this takes no more than a careful look around and a quick note on the chart.

Other times it might require compass bearings and drawing a few lines on the chart. In any event, once you find out where you are, you mark it on the chart with the time of the fix and then figure the route that will take you from there to where you want to go. The several steps of this process are the subjects of this book.

...In Depth

12.1 Traditional Skills in the Satellite Age

There is a tendency in these modern times to think that GPS and other high tech electronics have taken all the vinegar out of navigation... see here why this is not the case and what to do about it. This is a key article on how to relate what we are learning here with other instrumentation and daily procedures.

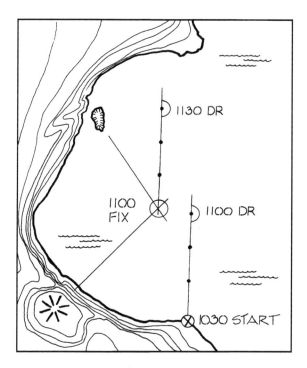

Figure 1-2. *Navigation by dead reckoning (DR) and piloting. Using estimated speed, compass course, and time underway, the navigator thought he was at the 1100 DR position shown. He was actually located at the 1100 fix position as found from compass bearings to the island and peak.*

Navigation skills are often distinguished by the waters sailed. Offshore navigation usually refers to navigation out of sight of land, as opposed to inshore navigation, which refers to navigation in sight of or in close proximity to land and to established aids to navigation. The terms, however, are relative to vessel size and weather conditions. The centers of large bays, straits, or inland sounds can present conditions similar to those many miles offshore in the ocean, despite the visibility of land on either side. The distinction fades even more at night and in the fog. Furthermore, in sight of land is relative to the height of the land, as explained in Chapter 6. A low coastline will slip below the sea horizon at a few miles offshore, whereas a coastal mountain range might be seen at 30 miles off on a very clear day.

For practical matters of small craft navigation and seamanship, a vessel is effectively offshore in any waters whenever the nearest land is more than a few miles off; this is, in part, because from this distance off, many lights, buoys, and other aids designed for the inshore navigation of larger vessels are simply not in view from the low perspective of many small craft. On the other hand, only skippers of smaller vessels can usefully distinguish the region of *close-inshore* navigation, meaning right along the shore in and out of off-lying rocks and shoaling—a water realm of unique navigation and often unique joys—reserved for small shoal-draft vessels (see Figure 1-3).

1.3 Navigation as a Hobby

There are two distinct aspects to navigation: knowing where you are and choosing the best route to where you want to go. The fundamental task of finding position is more or less straightforward. The techniques of piloting and dead reckoning are readily learned and mastered with little practice. Planning the best route through various waterways and conditions, on the other hand, is not always so easy. This distinction is even more dramatic when using the electronic aids covered in Chapter 7. With them, determining accurate position is simply a matter of pushing a button and reading a dial, whereas practical route selection is scarcely benefited at all from that information.

The elusive factors that boaters must always bear in mind when route planning are wind and current and their effects on waves. Big steep waves are potentially dangerous to a vessel, and strong winds make big waves. Current flowing against waves steepens them even more, a lot more. So not only do adverse winds and currents hinder progress along some routes, their interactions are often an even larger threat to progress and safety.

Planning the best route, therefore, involves more than choosing the shortest distance between two points on the chart. You must consider which way and how strong the wind is blowing, now and later in the day, and which way and how strong the currents are flowing, now and later in the day. You must consider how winds are influenced by the shape of the land, and how currents are influenced by the shape of the waterway. You must learn how waves are made by the wind and how the shape and depth of the waterway affect its waves. Getting from one place to another in a small vessel is often as much a question of the oceanography and meteorology of the area as it is a question of

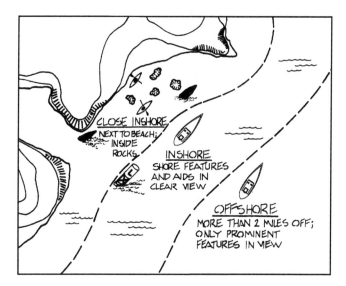

Figure 1-3. *A way to distinguish navigation regions in terms of the available aids to navigation. The terms and associated safety and navigational considerations are relative to the nature of the waterway and shore as well as the prevailing visibility and the size of the vessel.*

simple geographic navigation. This diverse but interrelated knowledge is best obtained by treating navigation and all it entails as part of boating itself, rather than something that must be learned in order to go boating.

Add a new dimension to the sport—a knowledge of the wind and the sea and the orientation skills that good navigation practice instills. Treat navigation itself as a hobby, not just the means of getting from point A to point B. Take pride in finding out where you are by different navigation methods. Practice it as a game in clear weather from a known position. Figure how long each leg of a trip should take and check your work, even when there is no need to predict the times. Predict the currents in all waters you cover, and check your work. Practice listening to weather reports, and watch the skies to compare surface winds with cloud patterns. Then, when you need these skills, and they are not a game, you are prepared.

Keep notes of what you learn on each outing. Navigation skills progress much faster with a notebook. With good records, you can learn in one season what it takes years to learn without keeping records. On each trip, a navigator is exposed to a barrage of navigational experiences and details. But it takes written records to remember more of these than you forget. Eventually, local knowledge compiled from individual trips begins to jell. Lessons learned in one place can be applied to another, and the watery part of the world accessible to you begins to expand.

1.4 How to Navigate Today

This course covers the traditional methods of navigation by chart and compass and log, as if we did not have any electronics at all, but the reality is that it is almost negligent these days not to have a GPS, at least an inexpensive hand-held model. Not only does it make your navigation easier and more accurate, but it can be used to learn skills needed to navigate without it.

With that in mind, please at this point, skim through Section 12.1 on the role of what we are learning and how it will fit into our actual navigation in practice. You can come back to that article for a more in-depth reading later on, but it will be helpful to know what is there and where we are going. Several of the tricks and procedures we study later are outlined in the article.

Later on, we will discuss the concept of waypoints and how to use them, but you can also at this point take a look ahead to Section 12.2 on Keeping Track of Course and Position Underway. It will also show where the skills we will learn here fit into the overall navigation practice, with more specific discussion of their application in an actual voyage.

The content of these two articles should give you a way to start practicing some of the basic ideas and procedures right away, without having to wait till we have covered each topic in detail.

Both of these sections are still in the In-Depth category because they include terms and ideas that we have not yet covered in this Chapter 1. You can be confident, though, that these ideas will be explained in the later chapters of this course book.

1.5 What is a Small Craft?

In the past, small craft was defined as vessels under 65 ft, which can probably be traced to the 20-meter length limit used in some of the Rules of the Road. But this definition is rarely used now as it is way too general when it comes to weather and navigation. The National Weather Service (NWS) solves the problem (after stating there is no precise definition) with this nugget: "Any vessel that may be adversely affected by Small Craft Advisory criteria should be considered a small craft."

A 16-foot skiff, or a 25-foot cruiser is definitely a small craft, but a high-powered 25-footer may be much less challenged by some navigation situations than is a 74-footer with low power. Typical sailing vessels are usually small craft, and generally in most navigation situations, vessels up to 70 feet or so would be considered small craft.

Sailboats in light air are all effectively small craft. They are low-powered in these conditions, and they are very susceptible to the wind and current conditions we cover. There is, however, not really a distinction between power and sail when it comes to basic navigation, and for that matter, most of the standard or traditional navigation skills are the same in a kayak as they are in a ship. The main distinction has to do with what equipment you have and what power is available—and it will depend on the circumstances.

The vast majority of the material in this book would apply to the navigation of any vessel, although we concentrate on the equipment available on smaller boats. We do not, for example, cover use of gyro compasses, but what any navigator might do with the bearing data once obtained by gyro would be pretty much the same if obtained with an inexpensive bearing compass. On the other hand, we do devote more detail to the effects of current and wind, because these are far more important more often to low-powered small craft than they are to ships or other large vessels.

...In Depth

12.2 Keeping Track of Course and Position

Once underway on a well-planned route, navigation reduces to keeping track of where we are along that route. This note covers some of the ways to do this.

Chapter 1 Glossary

bearing. The numerical value of the direction to an object (0° to 360°). It can be specified as relative to true north, magnetic north, or the bow of the boat.

charts. Maps of the waterways used for navigation. They include depth data, topographic features of the shoreline, and magnetic variation, as well as aids to navigation such as lights and buoys.

close-inshore. Close to beach, in and out of rocks and surf and pocket bays. In oceanography, called the littoral zone.

compass. Instrument to measure direction, usually using the magnetic field (mechanical or electrical) or on some large ships, using a gyro.

current. Horizontal flow of the surface water, can be driven by the tides or other sources.

dead reckoning. Estimating your position based on distance (log) and direction (compass) run from your last known position, corrected for current, leeway, and helm bias as needed.

GPS. Global Positioning System, a worldwide, all-weather satellite navigation system that provides highly accurate position on land and sea. From these accurate positions, course and speed over ground can be derived.

gyro. An electronic device used on larger vessels to determine accurate vessel heading. It is based on gyroscopic principles and does not depend on the earth's magnetic field.

inshore. Not far from the shore, in sight of land in clear weather, usually in 100 fathoms of water or less, but away from the hazards of the close-inshore region.

knotmeter. A boat's speedometer, it measures speed in knots, usually by means of a spinning propeller below the hull.

log. (1) A boat's odometer, counts miles through the water, usually using the same propeller as the knotmeter. (2) To record something in the logbook. (3) Another name for the logbook itself. (4) The process of covering some distance underway, as "We logged 10 miles this morning."

navigation. Finding and keeping track of your position on a chart and from there figuring a safe efficient route to where you want to go.

Navigation Rules. (1) The international set of rules and regulations designed to prevent collisions at sea. Also called COLREGS (Collision Regulations). Canada and the United States each have modifications to the International COLREGS that apply to their inland waters. (2) The book published by the United States Coast Gaurd (USCG) that presents the Rules.

offshore. Ocean or coastal location, out of sight of land, usually without soundings.

piloting. Finding or keeping track of position using charted landmarks for references, such as compass bearings. Piloting can be relative, such as following a channel or point to point along a shore, or used specifically to determine a position fix on the chart.

position fix. A known position of the vessel on the chart at a particular time determined by some form of piloting or by electronic navigation using GPS or radar.

radar. An electronic navigation aid that measures line-of-sight range and bearing to landmarks or other vessels. It can be used for piloting, position fixing, or collision avoidance.

Rules of the Road. A common name for the *Navigation Rules*.

sailing. (1) To make way in a sailboat under the power of the wind. (2) More generically, the movement of any vessel, as used in Sailing Directions, or referred to in the *Navigation Rules*, Part B, Steering and Sailing Rules, that apply to all vessels, power and sail. (3) A routing option based on map projections and other factors, such as rhumbline sailing, great-circle sailing, mid-latitude sailing. The full set of options is referred to as the sailings.

shipping lanes. Official or unofficial routes taken by commercial traffic through a waterway. Official lanes controlled by the USCG are referred to as Vessel Traffic Safety (VTS) lanes. Rule 10 in the *Navigation Rules* addresses navigation in or near VTS lanes.

shoaling. Means shallow water. Also called shoals or shoal water.

small craft. An unofficial term meaning a vessel, whose size or design limits its performance in some conditions. At one time it was considered to be all vessels less than 66 feet (20 meters), but this definition is no longer used. The *Navigation Rules* apply to "Any description of watercraft used for transportation on the water," so vessels such as sail boards, paddle boards, kayaks, rowboats, dinghies, and jet skis would also be in this category, just as a 100-ft houseboat might be, or a 70-ft yacht could be as well.

waypoints. Specific checkpoints (Lat and Lon) on a chart that are chosen to mark progress points or turning points along an intended route. They are best chosen to be points that are easily identified (visually or with radar) by prominent nearby landmarks or aids to navigation such as buoys or lights.

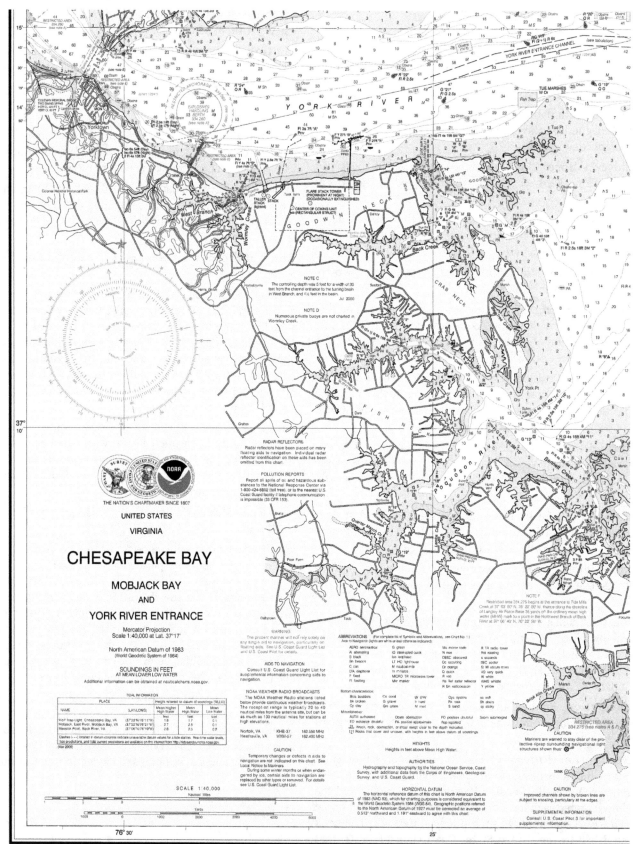

Figure 1-4. *Section of a NOAA PDF chart (free online downloads), showing correction dates as well as a print scale. Bottom left line should be 6" long when printed to proper scale.*

CHAPTER 2
NAUTICAL CHARTS AND CHART READING

2.1 What is a Nautical Chart?

The first step in navigation is having the proper nautical chart on board. Nautical charts are maps of waterways designed specifically for marine navigation. They show water depths, shoreline composition, extent of the tidal range on the shore, inshore rocks, aids to navigation (lights, buoys, daymarks), the direction that compasses point to in the charted area, and other aids to navigation such as shoreside buildings, structures, and terrain that are visible from the water. Most mariners distinguish the name chart from map when referring to these, but this is certainly not important—it is a maritime tradition similar to calling a rope a line when it is on a boat.

Charts come in various sizes (some are big sheets, some are smaller sheets), and they are made to various scales, although US issues cost the same regardless of these distinctions. Areas covered by individual charts range from single bays to entire oceans. Two charts of the same sheet size that depict areas of different sizes must have different scales. The most detailed charts cover single bays or harbors. A harbor chart scale of 1 to 10,000 (written 1:10,000) means that 10,000 inches of the harbor appears as 1 inch on the chart. It takes some trickery, however, to interpret 10,000 inches.

Considering a handspan to be just over 7 inches, chart scales can be converted to nautical miles per handspan to get a quick feeling for what they mean. A 1:10,000 scale is equivalent to 1 mile per handspan. Chart scales of 1:40,000 cover 4 miles for each handspan on the chart. To figure miles per handspan for any scale, drop the last four digits of the scale factor, and what is left is the number of miles per handspan. To calibrate your handspan for this purpose, stretch your hand out along the mile scale of a 1:40,000 chart to see what fingertip is 4 miles from your thumb tip. This handspan is then the one to use to interpret all chart scales.

The terms "large scale" and "small scale" are frequently used to describe charts. As with high and low gears on a bicycle, however, the logic of the names is not apparent. "Large" refers to the chart scale written as a fraction: 1/10,000 is larger than 1/80,000. Consequently, large-scale charts cover small areas; small-scale charts cover large areas. A specific island, for example, would appear large on a large-scale chart and small on a small-scale chart. Ocean chart scales might be as small as 1:1,200,000. The handspan trick keeps this in perspective. On this chart, a handspan is 120 miles. For the purposes of small craft navigation, large scale means 1:40,000 or larger.

2.2 Choosing Charts

Nautical charts are readily available for all navigable waters of the United States and most other parts of the world as well. Charts of American waters are prepared by the National Ocean Service (NOS), a division of the National Oceanic and Atmospheric Administration (NOAA)—see nauticalcharts.noaa.gov. American charts of foreign and international waters are published by the National Geospatial-Intelligence Agency (NGA). The larger NOS chart dealers will also carry the NGA charts. Many countries have charting services of their own, which are usually coordinated by a hydrographic office. Some of these foreign charts are carried by American dealers, but most are not. See any chart catalog for specific information on obtaining charts. Of special interest to North American sailors are the excellent charts of Canadian waters produced by the Canadian Hydrographic Service.

The best way to select charts for American waters is through NOAA's Nautical Chart Catalogs (see Figure 2-1). These free pamphlets (also available online) show maps of the cataloged region with the individual charts available outlined on it. Each chart has a specific name, number, and scale. The catalogs also list authorized chart dealers in the region. Authorized dealers are obligated to sell only the latest editions and charge only the official price. Canadian and NGA chart catalogs are similar.

Close maneuvering in small anchorages, for example, calls for the most detailed (largest scale) charts available. Hazards close to the shoreline such as rocks, shoaling (that might enhance waves or currents), kelp beds, and details of the shore itself (sand or rocks, steep or flat) are not discernible from small-scale charts. Access to the shore through off-lying rocks can only be judged, if at all, from detailed charts. A small island on a large-scale chart can appear as a rock on a small-scale chart (see Figures 2-2a and b).

For close inshore navigation, the larger the chart scale, the better. As a rule, 1:40,000 is the smallest scale useful for reading features needed for landing or navigation along a rocky shoreline. One to 20,000 or larger would be even better, but they are not always available or more detailed. On the other hand, long trips call for some compromise in chart selection since a 1:20,000 chart can be just 10 miles across. The series of large-scale charts needed for a long trip makes an unwieldy stack of paper. Furthermore, long trips require at least one small-scale chart (1:80,000 or smaller) for planning the overall route—to locate, for example, the public lands in the area. It is tedious, at best, to plan long

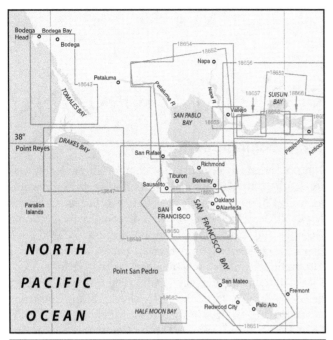

Chart Number	Title	Scale
18643	Bodega and Tomales Bays	1:30,000
18647	Drakes Bay	1:40,000
18649	Entrance to San Francisco Bay	1:40,000
18650	San Francisco Bay—Candlestick Point to Angel Island	1:20,000
18651	San Francisco Bay—Southern part.	1:40,000
	Redwood Creek	1:20,000
	Oyster Point	1:20,000
18652 SC	San Francisco Bay to Antioch	1:40,000; 1:80,000
18653	San Francisco Bay—Angel Island to Point San Pedro	1:20,000
18654	San Pablo Bay	1:40,000
18655	Mare Island Strait	1:10,000
18656	Suisun Bay	1:40,000
18657	Carquinez Strait	1:10,000
18658	Suisun Bay—Roe Island and Vicinity	1:10,000
18659	Suisun Bay—Mallard Island to Antioch	1:10,000
18660	San Joaquin River—Stockton Deep Water Channel	
	Antioch to Medford Island	1:20,000

Figure 2-1. *Section of a NOAA Nautical Chart Catalog. Each chart has a unique number, name, and scale, although some charts contain large-scale insets of specific areas, as indicated in the list of chart titles. This chart catalog is also online.*

routes across several charts. Also, once underway, it is difficult to identify islands on the horizon and other distant features when they are not on the same chart you are using. This is one potential disadvantage to NOAA's special folio charts, called small craft (SC) charts, or to the commercial chart packets available for some areas.

Whenever possible, it is best to select charts by actually looking at them at the chart dealer. This way you can compare different scales of the same areas to see if the extra information provided on the large-scale charts is required for your intentions in the area. If you are only transiting a featureless shoreline, the larger-scale charts might not add significant detail to justify the extra expense and gear.

Unfortunately, chart agents with a large stock of optional charts for you to peruse might soon be a thing of the past, as NOAA is switching in 2014 to all print-on-demand (POD) charts, which already account for about 75%

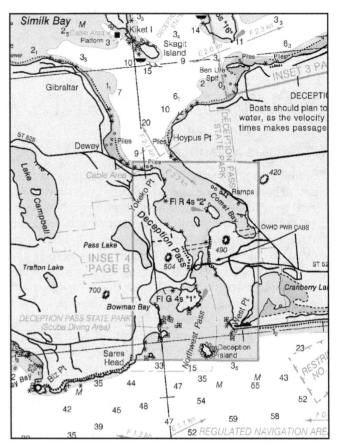

Figure 2-2a. *Sections of two charts of the same area having different scales. The smaller scale (2.2a) is 1:80,000; the larger scale (2.2b) is 1:25,000. Each is from a small craft chart that has north to the left of the page.*

of paper chart purchases. Fortunately, however, the NOS nautical chart website is excellent, making it easy to find the charts available, with convenient viewers that can be zoomed in to see details. They also now offer new options in charting such as the BookletCharts, which break up the chart into individual panels, as well as new high-resolution PDF images of the full chart. Charting and chart distribution are changing at the moment, so we need to keep an eye on the options and how the agents and other commercial outlets will be responding.

...In Depth

12.17 POD and NCC Printed Charts

NOAA discontinued printing traditional lithographic charts in April, 2014, after which all paper charts are Print-on-Demand. This note discusses that transition with pros and cons to look out for. (By 2025 NOAA will in turn have discontinued all traditional paper charts replacing them with ENC and NCC.)

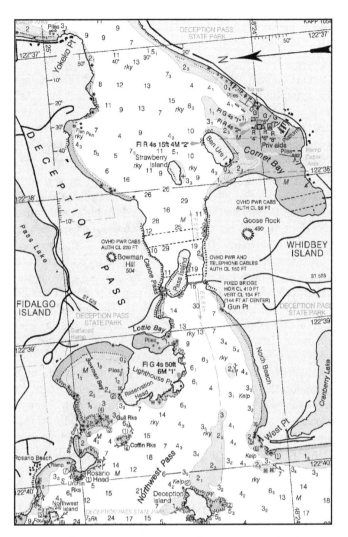

Figure 2-2b. *Sections of two charts of the same area having different scales. The smaller scale (2.2a) is 1:80,000; the larger scale (2.2b) is 1:25,000. Each is from a small craft chart that has north to the left of the page.*

2.3 Electronic Charting

Nautical charts and topographic maps are available online. They can be viewed online in convenient viewers or downloaded to be viewed in your own electronic charting software. US nautical echarts are all free. Some topographic maps are free; others are commercial products. See starpath.com/getcharts. There are two basic formats for nautical charts, vector charts (called ENC for electronic navigation charts) and raster charts (called RNC for raster navigation charts). The latter are direct reproductions of the paper charts into digital images and usually the preferred format when you have the option.

The NOAA chart site has a list of free echart viewers. These programs have convenient, versatile display options and let you lay out and plan a trip completely on the screen. You can enter waypoints with the click of a button, label them, and then have the program label the course line for each leg of the voyage with the distance and compass bear-

ing between waypoints. The annotated chart segments of interest can then be selected, cropped, and printed out in full color for a trip. Whatever method you might use to protect your paper charts can be applied, including lamination, which is often very inexpensive.

Navigation with an echart program using GPS input to track your position across the chart is generally referred to as using an electronic chart system (ECS), and the associated software can be called ECS software. Several of these programs include very convenient tide and current options, so you can not only visualize the trip on any chart scale you choose at the click of a button, but also display and print both the tide height and the current speed and direction in that region. With practice, ECS is certainly the most convenient and thorough means of planning a trip, but you should still spot-check a few of its results the old-fashioned way, by using paper charts and plotting tools. And, needless to say, this computerized approach to navigation planning will not appeal to all sailors. If it fits your lifestyle and resources, then it will be a boon; if not, you can always do this the tried and tested way that it has been done for hundreds of years with chart and pencil.

Bear in mind that, as with much wonderful new technology, you often must go backward for a while before going forward. And this is just as true with the ECS revolution. There is a learning curve to crawl up before the fun ride down the other side. It could well take longer to carefully plan a trip by computer than by hand the first couple times you do it, but if you do a lot of extended sailing that calls for navigation, then this equipment and approach to planning will prove to be very worthwhile. It could be especially valuable to schools and clubs that are providing trip planning for their members.

Many commercial and recreational vessels use ECS not only for planning but also underway with direct input to the computer from their GPS satellite navigation system. This arrangement then shows their precise position right on the nautical chart (on the computer screen or mobile device) at all times and leaves a trail of dots showing where they have been. If they are drifting off course into danger, it is obvious at a glance. With a simple mouse click, they can take ranges and bearings to charted landmarks, or compute new a course to any destination.

With mobile devices like smartphones and tablets, we have to address the waterproofing issue, but there are numerous options on the market. We have just seen one popular mini-tablet come out in a waterproof version, and there will likely be more, and there are many companies making protective covers.

Also, many modern radars now include a plotter option that is directly linked to the GPS. With these you can watch on the same screen a chart view, radar view, both views side-by-side, or one overlaid on top of the other.

In any event, these types of developments can indeed be hazardous to navigation, since with their amazing convenience there is a tendency to not learn basic navigation, or to get so many things showing on the screen that it is confusing—so we let this topic go for now, and get on with learning the basics that we must ultimately depend upon.

2.4 Latest Editions and Corrections

The date on a chart does not always tell whether it is the latest edition of that chart. Some charts are reissued every year, others only every 3 or 4 years. The decision to reissue a chart depends on the number and seriousness of the changes that must be made. The latest issue of a chart can be checked by contacting the Coast Guard or any authorized chart dealer. They in turn will refer to a quarterly USCG publication called *List of Latest Editions*. A chart with the present year's date is probably the latest edition. One dated more than 4 years ago is probably outdated. The *List of Latest Editions* is online or available from official chart dealers.

The important things that are likely to change on new chart issues are locations of buoys and lights, flashing characteristics of lights, locations of shipping lanes, and the layout of structures on land. Much of the remainder of what charts show does not change with most new issues, but this cannot be counted on. Valuable shoreline information obtained from recent surveys might be missed if you go with outdated charts. Old charts can often be updated adequately by hand after comparing them with new ones or with lists of known chart corrections discussed below. Nighttime navigation calls for up-to-date data since it relies on proper light identification.

The latest chart data, including temporary as well as permanent chart alterations and other news of interest to marine navigation, are compiled weekly in the Coast Guard's Local Notice to Mariners (see Figure 2-3). These are kept on file at Coast Guard offices, marinas, chart dealers, and some libraries, and they are all online for very convenient review. A long trip into unfamiliar waters with planned nighttime sailing, or any other anticipated dependence on charted navigation aids, calls for going this extra mile in chart preparation. A quick survey of recent notices could reveal interesting information. Buoys can be dragged away by currents or collisions with ships; the only light for miles might be temporarily out of order; or an announced

Navy bombing run might clarify what is meant by a Restricted Area marked on the chart. Important notices also are broadcast daily on VHF marine-radio frequencies.

Once a year, all permanent chart changes that pertain to lights, buoys, and other aids to navigation are compiled and printed in another Coast Guard publication called the *Light List*. If a *Light List* is newer than the latest issue of a particular chart, the data it contains supersedes that printed on the chart.

For example, suppose, early some August, you plan a trip for the end of the month. The most recent chart of the area you plan to visit is 2 years old. This chart claims the Cape Hazard Light flashes every 6 seconds and can be seen from 12 miles off. Your current *Light List*, however, states that this same light flashes every 4 seconds and can be seen from 10 miles off. The *Light List* supersedes the chart, so its information is what to expect and what should be written in ink on this chart next to that light. Checking the latest Local Notice to Mariners (dated August 2), you discover that this light is reported to be "operating at reduced intensity," meaning it cannot be seen from as far as it should. This calls for a pencil note on the chart and a check on the next several notices when available. It might even take a telephone call to the Coast Guard or a check of their Web site just before leaving to verify the status of this light. The visible range of lights and how this is determined from the *Light List* and charted light data are fundamental to nighttime navigation. US and Canadian Light Lists are online.

This level of preparation might seem excessive when compared with navigation practice in hiking or driving. You would not, for example, call the Highway Department before a cross-country drive to verify whether the street light in Podunk was working. The difference lies in the consequence of a wrong turn. A wrong turn in Podunk will not lead to a roller coaster ride that eventually turns the car over and fills it with water. A wrong turn in a boat in some places can rain on your parade—not often, but possibly.

2.5 Symbols and Soundings

Chart reading takes practice. There is a wealth of information on nautical charts, much of which is presented in symbolic or abbreviated terms. Once the symbols and conventions are learned, a nautical chart becomes a wonderful resource that is easy to use. If a picture is worth a thousand words, a chart is worth a book.

The primary guide to the interpretation of chart symbols is an inexpensive booklet called *Chart No. 1* (see Figure 2-4) published jointly by NOAA and NGA and available as a free PDF and in print editions. *Chart No. 1* lists all chart symbols and their meanings, although quite tersely at times. Rock and shoreline symbols, especially important to small craft navigation on close-in routes, are explained below, but the booklet should be referred to for further details and practice. To learn the symbols, pick any chart and use

...In Depth

12.26 How to Fold Charts

For longer trips that require multiple charts, it is almost impossible to stress how important it is to have your charts organized...

U. S. COAST GUARD
LOCAL NOTICE TO MARINERS

I. SPECIAL NOTICE

SPECIAL WARNING NO. 69 - WEST COAST OF AFRICA - WESTERN SAHARA -

1. Unprovoked attacks on shipping off the coast of the Western Sahara by Polisaro front guerrillas using machine guns, grenades, and mortars continue to occur resulting in the loss of life and property. Polisario spokesmen have been quoted as stating that any vessel in Western Sahara territorial waters, which the Polisario considers to be a war zone, would be the target of attack.

II. DISCREPANCIES - DISCREPANCIES CORRECTED

The following is a list of aids to navigation that are not watching as advertised in the Light List Volume VI, Thirteenth District section:

LL #	Aid Name	Status	Chart	BNM	LNM
755/16135	Strait of Juan de Fuca Traffic Lane Separation Lighted Buoy J	Off Station	18400	0174-87	5/87
9120	Coos River Channel Light 8	Damaged/TDBN	18587	2194-85	1/86
9935	Clatsop Spit Lighted Bell Buoy 8	Missing	18521	0155-87	4/87
9970	Clatsop Spit Lighted Whistle Buoy 14	Improper characteristic	18521	0257-87	7/87
10050	Astoria Pier 3 East Light	Extinguished	18521	0222-87	6/87

III. TEMPORARY CHANGES - TEMPORARY CHANGES CORRECTED

The following is a list of aids to navigation that have been temporarily changed as advertised in the Light List Volume VI, Thirteenth District section:

LL #	Aid Name	Temporary status	Chart	BNM	LNM
None	Columbia River Entrance Test Lighted Buoy	Established	18521	1042-86	27/86
		Relocated		0130-87	4/87
9100	Coos River Entrance Light 1	Discontinued	18587	0959-86	25/86
None	Coos River Entrance Temporary Daybeacon 1T	Established	18587	0959-86	25/86

VI. ADVANCE NOTICE OF CHANGES IN AIDS TO NAVIGATION

OREGON AND WASHINGTON - COLUMBIA RIVER - HARRINGTON POINT TO CRIMS ISLAND - Aids to Navigation - Changes -
Pancake Point Dike Light 59 (LLNR 10480) will be discontinued.
Pancake Point Temporary Lighted Buoy 59T, a green buoy show a flashing green light every 6 seconds with a nominal range of 4 miles, will be permanently established in approximate position 46°08'58.8"N. 123° 22'20.5"W.
Chart 18523.

VIII. GENERAL

OREGON AND WASHINGTON - COLUMBIA RIVER - NAVIGATION LOCKS - Closures -
The navigation locks at Bonneville, The Dalles, John Day and McNary Dams across the Columbia River at river miles 145, 191, 216, and 292 (respectively) will be closed to navigation from 0700 local 8 March 1987 until 0800 local 22 March 1987 for annual maintenance.
Charts 18531, 18533, and 18535.
LNM CG Seattle 1, 2, 3, 4, 5, and 6 of 1987.

Figure 2-3. *Sample contents of the Local Notice to Mariners. Such notices are published by each US Coast Guard District and they are online at the USCG web site. There are samples of US and Canadian notices in the Chart Problems book.*

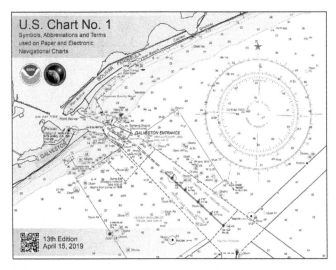

Figure 2-4. *Cover of the pamphlet called* Chart No.1, *which lists all nautical chart symbols and abbreviations. See Section 12.5 for more discussion of this publication and related products.*

Chart No. 1 to identify symbols at random. Any marking on the chart that is not listed in *Chart No. 1* is probably an actual structure built in the shape of the mark, or the work of a passing insect. Canadian chart symbols are similar to American ones, but there are enough minor distinctions to justify having a copy of the Canadian counterpart (also called *Chart No. 1*) when using Canadian charts, although the US edition does have columns defining international symbols (Figure 2-4a).

The numbers scattered across the waters on charts are actual measurements of water depths called soundings. The units of the soundings vary from chart to chart. They will be either feet, fathoms, or meters. One fathom is 6 ft. One meter is just over 3 ft (3.28). The international trend is to convert all charted depths and heights to meters, but NOAA is not rushing into this, and there are few complaints about it. Canadian charts are in meters. Depth units on US charts are noted in bold purple print on the chart border.

With one exception, the same units are used for all soundings on any one chart. The exceptions occur in the shallower depths of some charts that use fathoms. A sounding with a subscript on these charts, such as 3_2, is a mixed notation meaning 3 fathoms and 2 ft, or 20 ft. When this convention is used, the chart is labeled "SOUNDINGS IN FATHOMS—FATHOMS AND FEET TO 11 FATHOMS." Other charts using fathoms do not follow this convention, but instead mark this same depth with a $3_{1/3}$, meaning 3 and one-third of a fathom. On charts using meters for soundings, the symbol 3_2 means 3.2 meters.

It is important to know what is meant by these charted depths. They cannot represent the actual depth of the water at all times, since depths change 10 or 20 ft each day in some places as the tides rise and fall. At any point on the chart, the tides go up and down twice a day, and books are available that tell the height of the tide at any time at that place. Tide books are made by the same agency (NOS/NOAA) that makes the charts, so they use the same reference level for both, and that reference level is the one marked on charts by soundings and shoreline boundaries.

Suppose a tide book states that at noon today the tide height at Seal Rock will be 5 ft. This means the depth of the water at noon at Seal Rock will be 5 ft above the reference level printed on the chart. If charted soundings around Seal Rock all read 20 ft (meaning the sea bottom is 20 ft below the reference level), the depth to expect at noon at Seal Rock is 25 ft. The depth of the water at any point on a chart is just the charted depth plus the tide height at that time read from a tide book.

The reference level (officially called the chart datum) could be at any height above the sea bottom, but the actual level used is not chosen arbitrarily. It is always taken to represent the depth of the water at the average value of the lowest tides. In other words, charted depths represent the shallow end of the tidal range at any particular spot. This means that tide heights listed in tide books are mostly positive numbers, and the actual water depth at any point

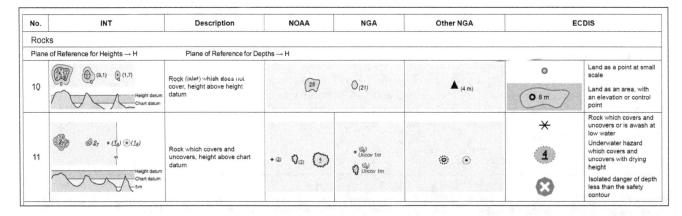

Figure 2-4a. Chart No. 1 *column structure. For NOAA paper charts we care only about the one column headed "NOAA." INT are for paper charts from other nations; NGA are US Navy and NATO paper charts; and ECDIS (electronic chart display and information system) is a nicknamed column of symbols used on electronic navigational charts (ENC), which by definition meet IHO standard S-52. The plane of reference direction to Section H (actually H-20) shows the notable fact that islet elevations are relative to MHW, whereas spot elevations and elevation contours are relative to mean sea level.*

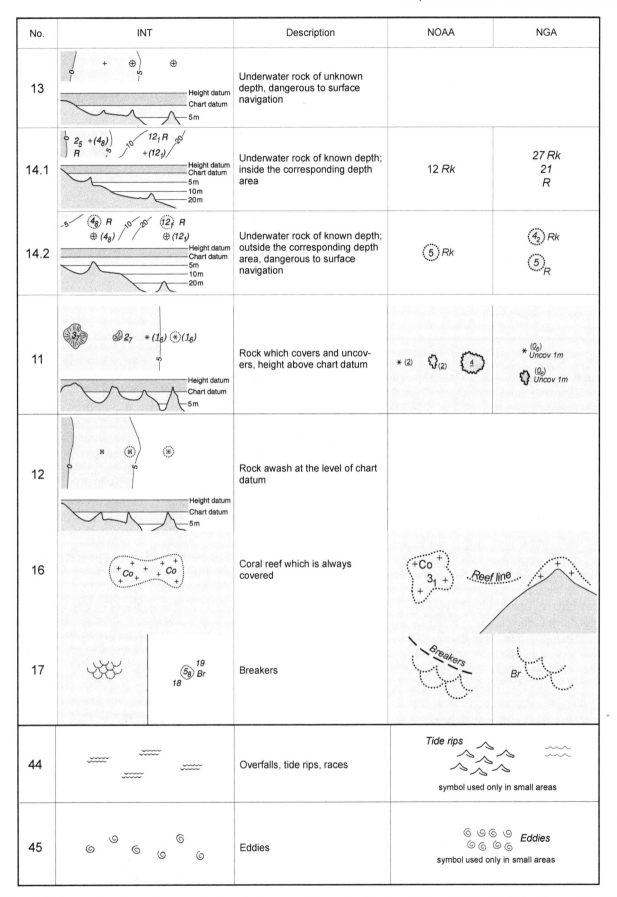

Figure 2-5. *Composite of sample paper chart symbols representing navigation hazards from Sections H (Tides, Currents) and K (Rocks, Wrecks, Obstructions, Aquaculture) of* Chart No. 1. *Three right-side columns not shown.*

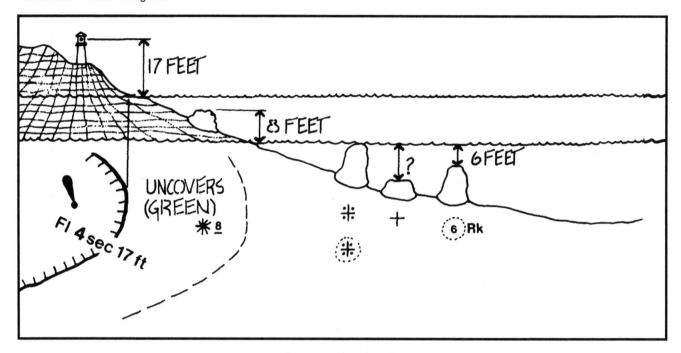

and time will most likely be greater than that printed on the chart. The only time the water will be shallower than charted is during a negative tide—meaning the tide height printed in tide books is prefaced with a minus sign (-). From a practical point of view, this occurs only for a few hours each month, and even during these periods it is rare to find a tide more than 1 or 2 ft negative. Canadian tide tables use a slightly lower chart datum (*lowest normal tides*), which results in fewer negative tides than US tables.

To a chart-reading navigator in some waterways, however, the tide's effect on the exposed shore is more important than it is on the actual water depths. For some shoal-draft vessels, a small change in tide height can open or close water routes over low-lying lands. Areas with large tidal range can appear remarkably different at high and low water. A broad beach can turn into a cliff; a single large island can turn into a group of small islands. This information is read from a chart by the color of the shore adjacent to the water. The foreshore—that part of the shoreline that covers and uncovers with the tides—is green on charts. Shallow water is blue on charts and dry land is yellow (tan), so it makes sense to show the mixture as green.

When the tide height is zero, land should begin where the green meets the blue. As the tide rises, the foreshore shrinks, and when the tide height reaches the average high water level for that area, land should begin where the green meets the yellow. The level of the tide must often be considered in order to identify what is in view from what is shown on the chart. Samples of shoreline chart symbols are shown in Figure 2-7.

2.6 Rocks

The symbols used to describe rocks—from boulders to islands—pose a special challenge in chart reading. This part of chart reading is fundamental to all mariners. A rock the size of a room can appear on the chart as a simple asterisk (*) or a tiny plus sign (+). The symbols themselves are small, and some that are only slightly different in appearance have very different meanings. But there is tremendous information in these symbols, and it pays to learn them well.

All chart symbols and notations must be interpreted literally. The notation "(6)" beside an asterisk, as opposed to the notation "(6)," for example, can mean the difference between seeing and not seeing the same rock. An underlined number "(6)" means the top of the rock is 6 ft above the water whenever the tide height is precisely zero. This rock will be out of sight underwater whenever the tide height is over 6 ft. A number "(6)" with no underline means the top of the rock is 6 ft above the water whenever the tide height is equal to the average high-water level of the tide in that area (mean high water). This rock stays in view above the surface at all times. The first notation is a drying height; the second is an elevation. In other words, the latter "rock" was an islet, too small to be distinguished as such on that chart scale. The parentheses distinguish the rock-height information from nearby water depths.

Elevations are measured from the mean-high-water level to the top of the land surface unless the elevation appears with a line over the top of it instead of underneath it, in which case it is measured to the treetops on the land. Rock symbols and notations are illustrated in Figures 2-5 and 2-6. Please take special note of Figure 2-6. This is a graphic explanation of these important symbols. The key

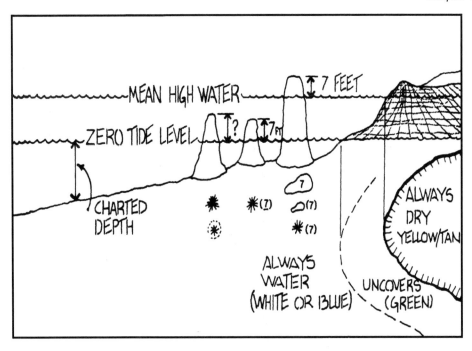

Figure 2-6. *Schematic definitions of rock symbols. Underlined numbers are drying heights relative to a zero tide level; numbers without underlines are elevations. Drying heights and elevations printed among soundings are placed in parentheses.*

The basic rocks are the "asterisk rock", the "plus sign rock" and the "plus sign with 4 dots." It is fundamental to know the distinctions among these three and how their visibility is tied to the tide height.

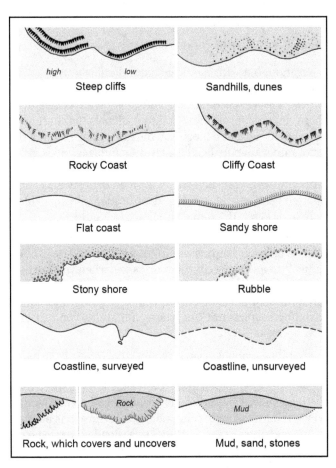

Figure 2-7. *Composite of samples of shore and foreshore symbols from* Chart No. 1. *Technical definitions of stones, rubble, and the like are given in Table 2-8, in Section 2.13.*

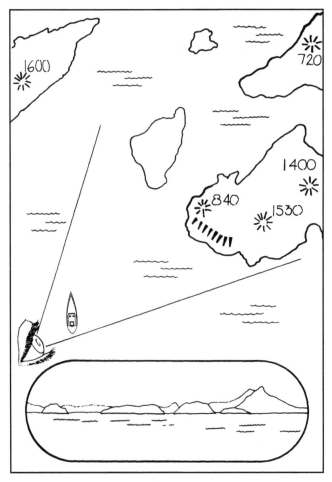

Figure 2-8. *The sailor's perspective of a chart section (inset). Without local knowledge, it is often necessary to use compass bearings to identify the terrain.*

here is knowing the value of mean high water (MHW) for the region you care about. This important datum is listed on every nautical chart in a table printed somewhere on the chart. The most common type of rock symbol one will see is the simple "asterisk rock"—a rock that covers and uncovers. This rock must be visible when the tide is zero or less, and it must be covered and not visible when the tide is higher than the mean high water for that region.

The submerged rock or simple "plus sign rock" will be covered even when the tide is zero. Unless there is a specific sounding associated with the symbol, you will not know how deep the rock is.

In a sense, the most dangerous kind of rock is the "plus sign with four dots rock," one dot in each quadrant of the plus sign. Referring to Figure 2-6, note that this type of rock is right at the surface at zero tide. Every vessel of any class can hit this type of rock at zero tide. They appear as just a ripple on the surface near zero tide.

For practice, look over your chart of choice and pick out various types of rocks, and also look for the values of mean high water on several charts. You can also go to the NOAA chart webpage and use their online chart viewer to practice in various waters around the country. Some places have more rocks than others.

2.7 Terrain and Perspective

Wilderness canoeing and backpacking develop skills of interpreting the lay of the land from elevation contours on maps, which is good training for nautical chart reading. This aspect of map reading is equally important in marine

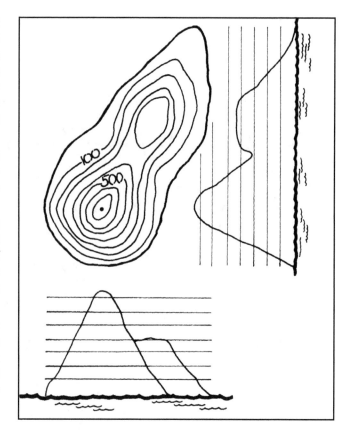

Figure 2-10. *A charted island as seen from the east and the south.*

navigation, but with nautical charts there is a twist to the problem. On many charts, only the outline of the land is shown, with very little specific information on its height. In these circumstances, the task is to read from the chart what you should see based mostly on the horizontal extent of the land, rather than its height. Elevation information is given in many cases, but the more frequent challenge is to get by without it or to rely heavily on isolated data such as a few charted peak locations or the identification of a steep bluff here and there. An example is shown in Figure 2-8.

Along a shoreline with many curves and headlands and islands or other landmasses in the background, it is often difficult to locate specific bays or passes when you are new to the area. In complex waterways, such as areas with many large rocks or small islands, much navigation time can be saved by keeping track of where you are as you sail into new horizons.

Another element of chart reading that differs from backcountry map navigation—where you are free to climb to a higher elevation for a better view—is the low perspective of the land viewed from the cockpit of a small craft. Much of what is charted simply cannot be seen because it is blocked by the curvature of the earth. A large island with two peaks might appear as two islands from some distance off, or a bluff well inland from the charted shoreline might appear as the edge of the land when viewed from a distance. In some cases, the only way to identify the various features in sight is to take compass bearings to them.

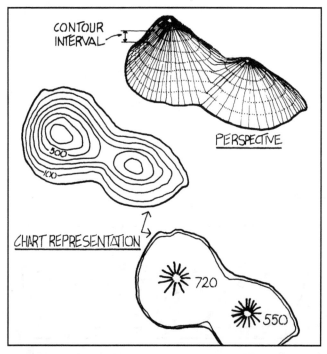

Figure 2-9. *The contour and hachure representations used on nautical charts. Elevations are always in the same unit throughout the chart and are relative to mean sea level.*

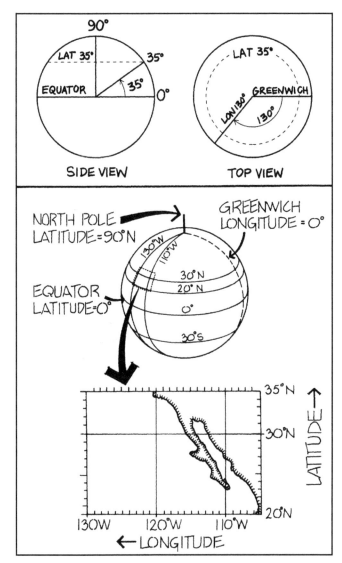

Figure 2-11. *Latitude and longitude as they appear on the globe and on nautical charts. Top section shows how latitude and longitude angles are defined.*

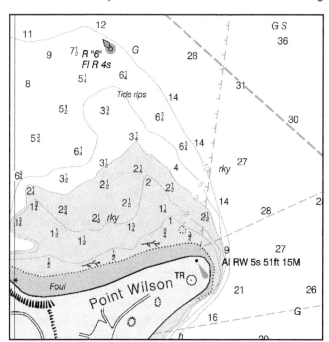

Figure 2-12. *A navigation light and buoy as represented on nautical charts. The* Light List *description of these is given in Figure 2-13.*

relative to mean high water. Mean sea level, to a good approximation, is halfway between mean low water and mean high water.

2.8 Latitude, Longitude, & Nautical Miles

Cities are sometimes designed with streets running north-south and avenues running east-west. An address might be the intersection of 47th Street North and 122nd Avenue West. The street-avenue grid is a convenient way to specify precise locations in a city.

Latitude and longitude designate a similar, though invisible, grid on a global scale used for specifying locations anywhere on earth. The latitude of a place tells how far it is north or south of the equator. Its longitude tells how far it is east or west of the Greenwich meridian (see Figure 2-11). Latitude and longitude are expressed in degrees and minutes because they correspond to angular distances on the globe. I am now sitting, for example, near the intersection of latitude 47° 40' North and longitude 122° 23' West.

Angles are subdivided just as time is: 1 degree (1°) equals 60 minutes (60') and 1 minute (1') equals 60 seconds (60"). To avoid confusion, caution is required with these units and notations. The only standard notations for angular minutes (') and seconds (") are optional notations for feet (1 ft = 1') and inches (1 in = 1"). This can lead to confusion, so navigators should use only "ft" and "in" when abbreviating these lengths, and avoid the other notations. Also, even though one can write 30' of angle as "30 arc minutes," it is never abbreviated 30 min, nor is 30 minutes of time ever abbreviated 30'. The same is true with seconds

When given, the height of the land visible from the water is charted as elevation contours similar to those on topographic maps or as isolated hachure symbols that mark only the peak locations and their height (see Figure 2-9). The hachure symbols often imply that a peak or plateau is conspicuous, although when several appear in the same direction, they must be identified from their relative heights, which can be misleading when some are farther away than others. Elevation contours must be interpreted, as illustrated in Figure 2-10. In areas where the elevation contours are very complex, it is often helpful to outline a particular high contour on the chart with a colored highlight marker in order to identify peaks and valleys from various perspectives.

Charted elevation contours and spot elevations are relative to mean sea level, in contrast to the charted heights of lights, bridge clearances, and islet heights, which are

(1) No.	(2) Name and Location	(3) Position	(4) Characteristic	(5) Height	(6) Range	(7) Structure
			WASHINGTON - Thirteenth District			
	Strait of Juan De Fuca					
16465	McCurdy Point Buoy 4	48-08-41.761N 122-50-40.019W				Red nun.
16470	Point Wilson Lighted Buoy 6	48-09-10.994N 122-45-37.635W	Fl R 4s		3	Red.
	ADMIRALTY INLET AND PUGET SOUND TO SEATTLE (Chart 18441)					
	Admiralty Inlet					
16475	Point Wilson Light	48-08-38.969N 122-45-17.197W	Al RW 5s 0.1s R fl 4.9s ec. 0.1s W fl 4.9s ec.	51	W 18 R 15	White octagonal tower on fog signal building. 51

Figure 2-13. *The* Light List (Vol. 6) *entry for the aids shown in Figure 2-12.*

of angle and time. You will see this done on TV sometimes, but you should never see it in the nav station.

The latitude-longitude grid is printed on all nautical charts, and in modern navigation we will use it frequently. It is used for setting up waypoints to define a navigation route, and it will be used for transferring a GPS position from the electronic readout to a paper chart. Near land, however, it is always valuable to keep track of your position (in your mind and logbook) relative to prominent landmarks, such as 2 miles north of Lookout Point. This is less prone to errors and provides a far more realistic vision of where you actually are.

Latitude-longitude positions are also used when locating specific reference stations for tidal current predictions, and when confirming the identity of a specific light or buoy. It is absolutely fundamental to learn how this grid is printed on charts and to practice reading the latitude and longitude of some light or buoy (see Figure 2-12). Use the *Light List* to check your answer. It lists the precise latitude and longitude of all lights and buoys (see Figure 2-13).

Beyond locating positions, however, the latitude scale is useful for measuring distances between points. The north-south distance between consecutive latitude degree lines on any chart of any place on earth is always 60 nautical miles, because this is the way the nautical mile is defined.

One nautical mile is the distance you must travel north or south to change your latitude by 1'. A nautical mile is just over 6,000 ft, or approximately 15% longer than a statute mile. The official definition of a nautical mile is 1,852 meters, exactly. An official linear definition is required because the earth is not precisely spherical, so the practical definition in terms of latitude does not withstand fine scrutiny.

Nautical miles (abbreviated nmi) are the standard units of distance in navigation, and they are also used to define the standard units of speed (knots). A speed of 1 knot is a speed of 1 nmi per hour. The unit *knots* derives from

the historical sailing practice of measuring boat speed by streaming a line, with precisely spaced knots along it, over the stern and counting the number of knots that pass by in a particular time.

It is easy to appreciate the usefulness of the nautical mile in navigation. It makes the latitude scale on nautical charts into a miles scale (see Figure 2-14) and helps interpret the separation of places on the basis of their latitude alone. It helps navigational thinking in general, even when

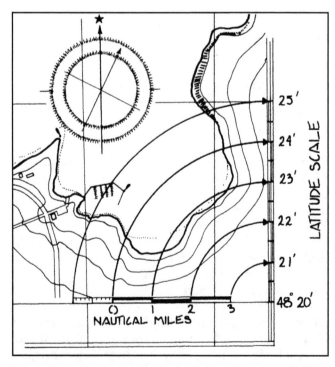

Figure 2-14. *The equivalence of latitude minutes and nautical miles (sea miles). Charts with scales of 1:80,000 or larger will have a miles scale printed on them, but smaller-scale charts will not. When no miles scale is shown, use the latitude scale, which is often more convenient, even when a miles scale is available.*

not applicable to a particular voyage. You know immediately, for example, that Cape Flattery, Washington (at latitude 48° North), is 600 miles north of San Francisco, California (at latitude 38° North), and that Hawaii (at latitude 20° North) is 1,200 miles north of the equator. Or, that Cape Chelyuskin, Russia, the northernmost point of Asia, at 77° 43' North, is just 737 miles (12° 17') from the North Pole.

Approximate latitude increments are shown in Table 2-1, which is helpful in understanding the precision of a latitude we read from a chart or GPS screen.

Bear in mind, however, that even though 1° of latitude always equals 60 nmi, the distance between consecutive longitude degree lines is not constant because these lines converge at the poles. Only at the equator is 1° of longitude equal to 60 nmi. At higher latitudes, the separation between longitude lines decreases, and the higher the latitude, the faster they converge. Longitude increments for various latitudes are shown in Table 2-2.

You cannot just subtract longitudes to figure the east-west separation of two places; this distance must be read from a chart. This is also the reason that the latitude-longitude grid on nautical charts is not square, but rectangular. Charts of the tropics (at low latitudes) show almost square grids, but those for Alaska (at high latitudes) are narrow rectangles, longer in the north-south direction than in the east-west (see Figure 2-15). Nautical miles per 1° of longitude can be approximated by 60 × Cos (Lat).

To be formally correct, 1° of latitude is called 60 *sea miles*, but this unit does not have a fixed length; its average is 6,080 ft. A cable is one tenth of a sea mile. The distinction between sea miles and nautical miles is rarely made in American parlance.

2.9 Reading Distances

Charts are made with all geographic features shown to scale. If two headlands are shown 4 inches apart on a 1:20,000 chart, the distance between them should be 80,000 inches, or 1.1 nmi (after some math). This method would work for

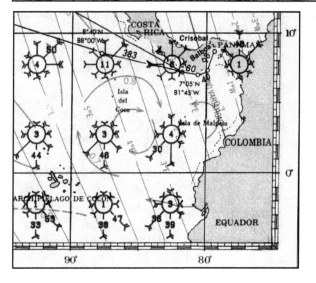

Figure 2-15. *A comparison of the latitude-longitude grid shapes at high and low latitudes from Pilot Charts.*

Table 2-1. Latitude Increments	
Latitude Minutes	*Approx. Feet*
1.0'	6000 ft
0.1'	600 ft
0.01'	60 ft
0.001'	6 ft
Latitude Seconds	*Approx. Feet*
30"	3000 ft
20"	2000 ft
10"	1000 ft
5"	500 ft
1"	100 ft

Table 2-2. Longitude Increments		
Latitude North or South	*Feet per 0.1' of Longitude*	*Nmi per 1° of Longitude*
0°	608 ft	60.1
10°	600 ft	59.2
20°	572 ft	56.5
30°	528 ft	52.1
40°	467 ft	46.1
50°	392 ft	38.7
60°	305 ft	30.1
70°	209 ft	20.6

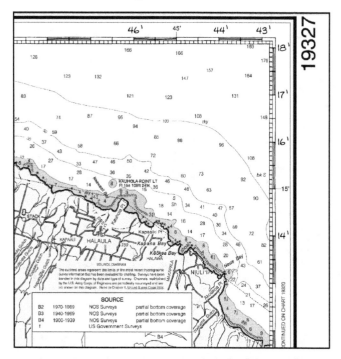

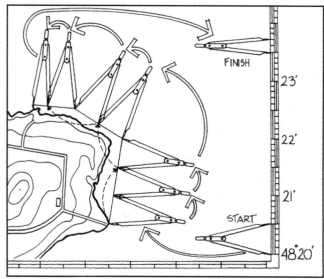

Figure 2-17. *Walking dividers across a chart to measure distance. The distance shown is 3.2 nmi, measured in half-mile steps.*

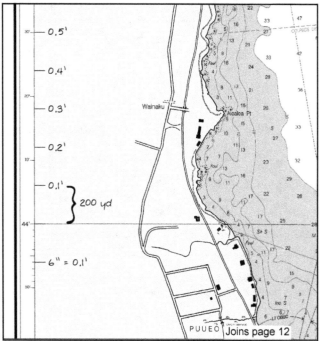

Figure 2-16. *Preparing a chart with prominent and convenient distance scales.*

any chart, but it is not practical. A simpler approach is to lay the 4 inches along the special distance scale printed somewhere on the chart, and read off the answer directly. These scales show distances in nautical miles, yards, and sometimes meters. But there is typically only one of these on each chart, and it may be under a fold in the chart when you need it.

A better and more common method is to use the latitude scale printed on the left and right borders of each chart.

Because 1' of latitude always equals 1 nmi, the latitude grid can always be used for a distance scale. To find the distance between two points using the latitude grid, measure the distance between the two points in any convenient units (inches, finger widths, or a handspan) and then transfer this length to the latitude scale. If the measured length spans 5' of latitude, the two points are 5 nmi apart. Latitude grids on charts with scales 1:40,000 or larger are divided into angular minutes and seconds, so this still takes a quick conversion to figure equivalent distances. For each chart used, or each exposed section of a folded chart, it is best to label some section of the latitude scale in miles or yards using the conversions given below, as shown in Figure 2-16. This saves doing the arithmetic each time it is used.

Table 2-1 includes a few convenient conversions (the values in feet are rounded off).

The actual way a distance measurement is performed depends on where and when it is done. Reading chart distances is best done using a pair of dividers—a standard drafting tool with two pointed legs that are hinged so they can be set at any desired separation. The hinge is stiff enough that the dividers hold their settings as you move them from one place to another, as shown in Figure 2-17. If the two locations of interest are farther apart than the dividers will extend, set the dividers to some convenient interval (like 1 nmi) on the latitude scale, then walk the dividers between the two points, and count the number of steps. The last step will be some fraction of a mile, which can be read from the labeled part of the latitude scale and added to the sum. This is also the way to measure crooked routes around land masses. Videos of these operations are shown in the Starpath Chart Trainer program.

Sometimes in the cockpit of a small craft, we might not use dividers and just improvise distance measurements for a quick answer. Two fingers used as dividers, two marks on a piece of paper, or a thumb held on a ruler's edge to mark the length will transfer a distance to the latitude scale adequately for occasional measurements. Besides, divider points are a definite hazard if you happen to be navigating from an inflatable. For dinghy excursions or even some small craft operation, we might want to navigate as much as possible by eye and hand alone, and this is best accomplished by careful planning and chart preparation before departing. This includes laying out routes and noting distances along them on the chart. With good planning, most numbers needed underway should already be noted on the chart.

When planning a long trip using a chart with a scale smaller than 1:80,000, you will notice that the special distance scale is missing, leaving no option to the latitude scale for measuring distances on these charts. Because of the mathematical way the spherical earth is projected onto the flat paper of a nautical chart, there cannot be a single distance scale that represents the entire chart of a very large region. One consequence of this projection was mentioned earlier: the rectangular latitude-longitude grid grows narrower at higher latitudes. When the chart covers a large latitude range, this grid contraction is apparent on a single chart, and a latitude interval is longer at the top of the sheet than it is at the bottom. It is still true that 1' of latitude equals 1 nmi everywhere on the chart, but because the latitude grid is expanded at the top, the number of inches per mile will be larger at the top of the chart than it is at the bottom.

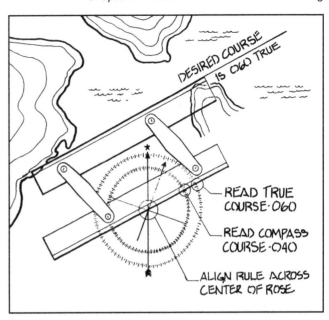

Figure 2-19. *The use of parallel rulers to read the direction of a compass course. A pencil rolled from the course line to the compass rose is a makeshift alternative method. The use of various plotting tools is covered in Chapter 6.*

To find the distance between two points at the top of a small-scale chart, use the latitude scale at the top of the chart. For points near the bottom, use the latitude scale at the bottom of the chart. Again, this is a concern only when reading distances from charts with scales smaller than 1:80,000. The absence of a separate distance scale on a chart is the sign that this procedure is required. When a distance scale is given, any part of the latitude scale can be used for any part of the chart.

2.10 Reading Directions

Nautical charts are made (mathematically projected) the way they are so they can be used to find the direction from one point to another. To appreciate the problem on a global scale, imagine two points, A and B, marked on the skin of an orange, which you then peel and squash flat. Because north is not a unique direction on the peel, it is nearly impossible to tell from the flat peel how to get from A to B. It is not even easy with the peel in place on the orange. Nautical charts solve this problem, and the only price to be paid

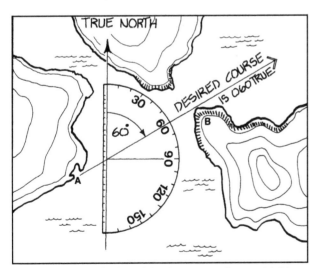

Figure 2-18. *The definition of the true course from point A to point B. True north is toward the top of the chart in all charts except some small craft folio charts. Instead of taking a protractor to the line between A and B, the more traditional approach is to take the line to a protractor. Circular protractors oriented toward the north, called compass roses, are printed several places on each chart for this specific purpose. As with measuring distances, the actual way the line of interest is transferred to the compass rose depends on when and where it is done.*

...In Depth

12.4 Navigation Tools

No two navigators will agree on what constitutes the minimum number of tools necessary for navigation, but over the years we have found that these are optimum for small craft navigation...

is the unusual way that distances must be measured on charts of larger areas, as mentioned earlier.

On all nautical charts (outside of the polar regions), north is a unique direction everywhere on the chart, and on almost all charts this direction is straight up, toward the top of the page. The only exceptions are small craft folio charts and river charts, which are oriented in whatever direction best matches the run of the waterway to the shape of the page.

Going back to the basics, finding the direction from some point A to some point B means finding out how many degrees to rotate away from north when standing at A, in order to face toward B. One way to read this from a chart is to draw a line straight north from point A and another line that runs from point A to point B, and then use a protractor to measure the angle between these two lines (see Figure 2-18). With this procedure you might find, for example, that point B lies 60° to the right of north. But this is more a principle than a practical method.

When planning a trip and for navigation underway, another special plotting tool called parallel rulers are one convenient way to transfer lines to and from the compass rose without changing their orientation. A typical application is to draw the route you intend to follow on the chart as a series of straight-line segments, and then use parallel rulers and a compass rose to determine what a compass should read when sailing along each leg of the route, as shown in Figure 2-19. Details and examples are given in later sections.

Most charts have three circular scales on each compass rose (see Figure 2-20). The outer scale is a true scale oriented toward geographic (true) north. The middle and inner scales are *magnetic scales* oriented toward magnetic north. The middle scale is the one used almost exclusively, because it is the one that shows what compasses should read. There is little call for the true direction given by the outer scale, because a typical small craft's only practical reference for steering and position fixing is the compass.

The innermost scale is also on the magnetic orientation, but it is divided into *compass points*, not degrees. Compass points mark the cardinal and intercardinal directions such as (for the northeast quadrant) north, north by east, north-northeast, northeast by north, and northeast. This scale remains on charts mostly for the sake of maritime tradition. Each compass point is 11.25°. The salty phrase "Ship ho!, Two points on the starboard bow," means "Look, a ship is in sight, about 22.5° to the right of the front of the boat."

When dealing with chart and compass directions in navigation—of kayaks or ships—it is best to use specific numerical angles on a 0 - 360° scale, rather than relative angles or descriptive labels. When asked the direction to steer, the answer "340" is less likely to cause confusion than "north-northwest" or "20 west of north." Furthermore, isolated phrases like "due east" or "north-northwest" always imply true directions unless otherwise specified. Another valuable custom is to preface directions that are numerically less than 100 with a zero. When telling the direction to steer, say 075 (zero seven five or "oh" seven five), rather than just 75 (seventy-five). These customs minimize confusion in communications and record keeping.

Figure 2-20. *A compass rose. The outer scale is used for true directions; the middle scale is used for magnetic compass directions; the innermost scale is a magnetic scale marked off in compass points (not used in modern navigation). The variation is West and the change is East, so it is getting smaller with time. In 2015, the variation would be 32' less, or 3° 43' W.*

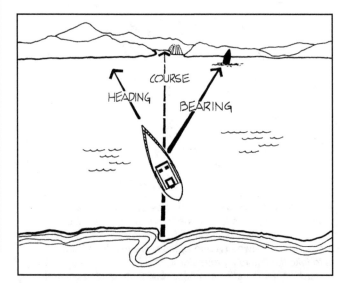

Figure 2-21. *Heading, course, and bearing directions. Distinctions among these terms are important in navigation. Course over ground (COG) and course made good (CMG) are illustrated in Chapter 7.*

Strangely enough, of all the directions used in navigation, none is called a "direction." Standard navigation practice calls for the definitions shown in Table 2-3.

For example: "As a helmsman steers the compass course 050, the *heading* might oscillate between 040 and 060 with passing waves, but the *bearing* to Lookout Point remains 135 magnetic." "They were steering course 060 according to the chart, but because the current was strong, their actual *course over ground* was about 080, so the inlet was not in sight when they got across." "We steered course 030 from 7 A.M. till 10 A.M. and then turned to steer 050 until noon, and when the fog lifted, we were right at Seal Inlet, so our *course made good* was 060 as planned."

There are other directions in navigation with special names, but these are the fundamentals that others are based upon (see Figure 2-21).

2.11 Aids to Navigation

In marine navigation, there is a distinction between *navigational aids* and *aids to navigation*. Anything used on board to assist navigation is called a navigational aid. Examples include charts, books, compasses and other instruments, plotting tools, binoculars, and even special procedures. Things external to a vessel that assist with navigation are called *aids to navigation*. These include lights, buoys, daymarks, foghorns, and various radio transmissions. The distinction in terminology often clarifies the context of American writings on navigation, although this distinction is not made in British usage.

Table 2-3. Directions and their meanings	
Direction	*Meaning*
Heading	Direction the boat is pointed
Course	Direction you want to go
Bearing	Direction to some landmark
Course Over Ground	Direction you are actually moving
Course Made Good	Direction from where you started to where you ended up

All aids to navigation are listed in the Coast Guard's annual publication *Light List*. The terms *lights* or *lighted aids* mean those specifically placed along a waterway as aids to navigation. Their positions and descriptions are included on charts and in the *Light List*. Most are maintained by the Coast Guard, but others are *private aids* maintained by other organizations to aid local boating or commercial operations. In contrast to lighted aids, the lights carried on vessels to identify their type and motion are in a separate category with separate definitions and rules. Vessel lights are not discussed in the *Light List*; they are covered in the Coast Guard's *Navigation Rules*.

2.12 Lights

The size and brightness of lighted aids vary from a simple bulb on the end of a post, barely visible from 1 mile off, to giant structures housing the brightest lights in the world, some of which can be seen from more than 25 miles off. The brightest lights are located in conspicuous places such as a point of land or a prominent place along a cliff. They are valuable landmarks even when they are not lighted, so it is important to be able to identify them from their charted or tabulated descriptions. Lights are on from sunset to sunrise, although most are operated automatically by light-sensitive switches so they do come on during daylight hours in the reduced visibility of fog and rain. Unfortunate-

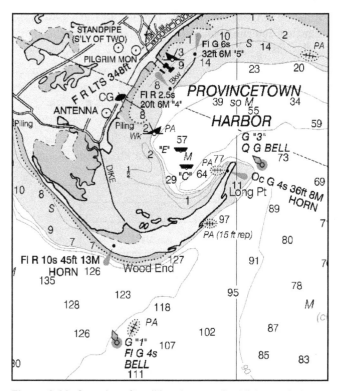

Figure 2-22. *Samples of traditional paper chart light symbols.*

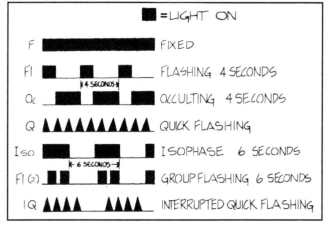

Figure 2-23. *Samples of light patterns used on aids to navigation. A complete list is in the introduction to the* Light List.

Table 2-4. Light identification	
Label	*Meaning*
F	White light, always on
F R 25ft	Red light, always on, positioned 25 ft above MHW
Qk Fl	White light. flashes on once a second
Fl 4s	White light, flashes once every 4 seconds
Fl G 6s "3"	Green light, flashes once every 6 seconds, with the number 3 on the structure
Iso 6s 80ft	White light, on 3 seconds and off 3 seconds, positioned 80 ft above MHW
Al	Alternating colors

Table 2-5. Structure prominence by nominal range	
Not prominent structures	*Lighthouse or tower*
Fl 6s 27ft 10M	Gp Fl (2) 6s 40ft 14M
I Qk Fl 15ft 6M	Fl 5s 39ft 15M
Fl 6s 21ft 11M "1"	Alt Fl W & R 10s 27ft 16M
Iso 6s 30ft 6M	Gp Fl (3) 10s 27ft 19M

ly, a bulb on a post and a giant lighthouse or tower have the same chart symbol: a small purple teardrop (meant to represent a light flash) emanating from a black dot placed at the precise location of the light (see Figure 2-22).

The prominence of the structure housing the light is best determined from its *Light List* description, although it can often be judged from the light's characteristic noted on the chart beside its symbol. Simple lights without prominent structures have charted labels such as those listed in Table 2-4.

The abbreviations used to describe lights and their meanings are given in the *Light List* (see Figures 2-13 and 2-23). These and similar notations next to the teardrop imply the light has a simple mounting: on a post, on the end of a pier or breakwater, or on some relatively plain concrete, steel, or wooden structure on shore or in the water. The only part of this notation that might help identify the light as a landmark is the height of the light when given. When not given on the chart, the height is usually given in the *Light List*. These notations do not represent lighthouses, but they must be fixed to land as opposed to a buoy or other floating structure—lighted buoys do not use the teardrop symbol, and their charted notations are in italics, as are the descriptions of all floating aids. Although these labels do not represent bright lights, the actual brightness of these

lights cannot be deduced from their labels or symbols, nor can their range of visibility from the deck of any vessel be deduced from these data alone. The visible range of these lights must be figured from the brightness and height of the light given in the *Light List*.

When the structure of the light must be guessed from a chart without a *Light List* available, the charted clue that a light might be a lighthouse or conspicuous tower is an additional notation of its brightness following the other characteristics of the light. A light's brightness is specified by its *nominal range* (in nautical miles) with a notation such as "10M" following the other data on the light. The nominal range of a light is how far it can be seen in clear weather when the observer's view of the light is not limited by the curvature of the earth. See Table 2-5.

It is important to remember, however, that this charted range is not how far you are able to see the light from your vessel; it is just a measure of the brightness of the light and a clue to the type of structure you might look for to use the light as an unlit landmark in daylight. From the low perspective of typical small craft, the curvature of the earth limits the range of visibility, so it is usually the height of the light that determines how far it can be seen, not the actual brightness of the light.

As a rule of thumb, any light listed with the nominal range of 14 miles or more is probably a lighthouse or other large tower, often painted in a conspicuous pattern.

The nominal range, however, is only a guideline to the type of structure; a few simple flashing lights that are very bright are on quite plain structures. A light in

Table 2-6. Light List Classification of Light Types	
Classification	*Sample*
Primary seacoast lights are in upper case in boldface	**NORTH HEAD LIGHT** Gp Fl W 30s 194ft 26M
Secondary lights and large navigational buoys are upper and lower case in boldface:	**Point Bonita Light** Occ W 4s 124ft 18M
River, harbor, and other lights are all upper case:	ANITA ROCK LIGHT Qk Fl W 20ft 6M
Lighted buoys are in italics	*Blossom Rock Lighted Bell Buoy* BR I Qk Fl 6M
Unlighted fixed aids and unlighted buoys are in upper and lower case	Village Rock Daybeacon 12 Deep River Channel Buoy 8

Hawaii, for example, labeled "Fl W 15sec 169ft 24M" is on a plain skeleton tower 20 ft tall. A complex flashing pattern is another clue to a prominent structure because these patterns require large rotating lenses that need large structures to house them. With a *Light List*, however, you need not guess the form of the structure from its charted label; the structure type of each light is included in the light's description. The Coast Guard further classifies each aid in the *Light List* by type style, as shown in Table 2-6.

Whenever lights are numbered, the numbering follows the same sequence used for neighboring buoys described in the following section. The latest edition of the *Light List* is available online as a PDF download.

2.13 Buoys and Daymarks

Buoys are used to mark waterways much as street signs are used along highways. Buoys, however, convey their information with their shape, color, sound, and numbering rather than with the use of words and arrows. It is rarely necessary for a sailor to know the fine details of the various buoyage systems used throughout the world, because the purposes of buoys are usually clear from their charted locations. Mariners might, in some special areas, follow buoys as they would street signs, but they are far more

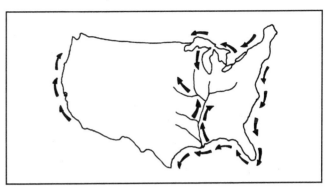

Figure 2-25. *US conventions on the* returning *direction for coastal waters. Buoy and daymark numbers increase in the directions shown.*

commonly used as reference marks in piloting rather than guides to the proper route.

Remember, however, that buoys might not be precisely where the chart shows them to be. They are fixed to the bottom only with an anchor structure, and the anchor can be dragged in strong current or wind (or from collisions with vessels that pull them off station). Those susceptible to drag are also occasionally repositioned in search of more stable locations, and these changes might not be shown on the latest chart edition. Piloting with buoys must be done with caution. Some buoys at river bars and other inlets are used to mark shifting sandbars. These are often not even charted because their positions change frequently.

Buoys are also used to mark dangerous shoaling—of interest to low-powered vessels because of the influence of shallow water on current flow and sea state. Yellow or yellow-and-white buoys are used for special purposes such as marking temporary dangers and restricted areas.

The meanings of specific buoys and conventions of the various buoyage systems used in specific areas and countries are explained with diagrams in the backs of the *Light List* and *Chart No. 1*. The primary use of buoys is to mark the safe boundaries of channels or other waterways, although safety in this sense is relative to the size of the vessel. If a shoaling, for example, extends out to near the middle of a waterway, the end of it would be marked with a buoy. In this situation, the waterway viewed from a vessel might look much the same on either side of the buoy, so a mariner approaching this buoy must either look at the chart (to see what the buoy marks and from this know

○			Approximate positon of buoy
⚲	⚲	⚲	Light buoy
⚲ BELL	⚲ BELL		Bell buoy
⚲ GONG	⚲ GONG		Gong buoy
⚲ WHIS	⚲ WHIS		Whistlebuoy
⚲ C	⌂		Can or Cylindrical buoy
⚲ N	⌂		Nun or Conical buoy
⚲ SP	⌂		Spherical buoy
⚲ S	*I*		Spar buoy
⚲ RW	⚲ BW		Fairway buoy (RWVS; BWVS)
⚲ RW	⚲ BW		Midchannel buoy (RWVS; BWVS)
⚲ R "2"			Starboard-hand buoy (entering from seaward-US waters)
⚲ "1"	⚲ "1"		Port-hand buoy (entering from seaward-US waters)

Figure 2-24. *Samples of buoy and beacon symbols*

...In Depth

12.5 Notes on the Nav Station

How to optimally organize an underway navigation station, whether for racing or cruising. Oftentimes, the convenience and design of our workspace make a big effect on our overall work.

which side to pass it on) or be able to interpret this instruction from the buoy itself.

Buoys that mark channel boundaries are red on one side of a channel and green on the other side. The most common rule for interpreting buoys in *US and Canadian waters* is "red right returning." The rule is a reminder that vessels traveling toward more inland waters ("proceeding from seaward") should pass buoys in such a way as to keep red ones on their right (starboard) side and green ones on their left (port) side. When headed toward the sea, the reverse is true: A vessel approaching a red buoy anywhere within a waterway that leads toward the sea should steer right of the buoy, so the buoy passes on the left side of the boat. If it were a green buoy, the vessel would steer to the left of it, leaving the buoy to the right. For boaters, this rule is valuable for predicting the routes of larger vessels seen approaching buoys, so that they can keep clear of them. Along coastal routes or on inland waters where the returning direction is uncertain, the conventions illustrated in Figure 2-24 are used to define this direction for the purpose of buoy placement and numbering.

Nevertheless, buoy numbering can still be unique to a region. In some parts of the world, the returning direction is the same as the flood current direction, and the leaving direction the same as the ebb direction. But even that does not help in all cases. Along the 10-mile-long Swinomish Channel that passes La Conner, WA, for example, the buoy and light numbers increase to a point near La Conner from either the North or South entry to the channel.

Besides the color of the buoy, which might not be discernible in twilight or when viewed toward the sun, buoys are also distinguished by their shape, number, and sound signals, as listed in Table 2-7.

When the color of a buoy is uncertain, its shape might identify its type. The can shapes and the truncated cone shapes (called *nuns*) are illustrated in Figure 2-24. The whistles, bells, and gongs placed on some buoys are activated by wind and waves. The bell and gong sounds are similar

if heard separately, although bells are higher pitched. Bells can be distinguished from gongs because each device has several clappers. The several bells all have the same tone, whereas the several gongs have different tones. If a buoy heard in the fog makes different tones, it is a gong buoy. If it makes all the same tone, it is a bell buoy. There is no consistent convention for which sound signal is used on which buoy. Relatively few buoys have sound signals; buoys with sound signals are usually lighted.

Buoys are numbered sequentially, with the numbers increasing in the *returning direction*, toward more inland waters—which is usually, but not always, the direction of the tidal flood. New sequences begin at new channels and at the intersections of waterways. Occasionally, the numbers are out of order or a number is skipped (permanently or temporarily, during repairs), but they will always be odd-numbered on the left side and even-numbered on the right side. Buoys marking the sides of channels are solid colors (green or red), and all are numbered. A few have numbers and letters such as 2D or 8A.

Solid-color buoys in Canada, on the other hand, do have numbers and letters. The letters are area designators as defined in the Canadian *Light List*. The odd-even numbering convention, increasing toward more inland waters, is the same, however. Details on all Canadian aids and conventions are listed in *The Canadian Aids to Navigation Systems*, Canadian Coast Guard Publication TP 968. There is also a Canadian *Chart No. 1*.

Buoys marking the entrances, middles, or junctions of channels are painted two colors (white with orange or red; or red and green). These buoys are lettered rather than numbered. The letters are often chosen from the initials of the name of the buoy: Blossom Rock Buoy is lettered BR, the Yaquina Bay entrance buoy is labeled Y. Sequential letters are used on sequences of buoys: the sequence of Vessel Traffic Service (VTS) buoys that leads south to Seattle, Washington, along Puget Sound is labeled SA, SB, SC, and so on. Proceeding farther south, they switch to a Tacoma sequence: TA, TB, TC. Some buoy lettering, however, has no apparent significance.

There are numerous chart symbols for buoys, but the most common is a diamond extending from a dot that marks the location of the buoy. The diamond color matches the buoy color. A lighted buoy has an additional purple dot (or halo) overlaying the position dot and part of the triangle. Notations next to a buoy symbol include its light characteristic, letters or numbers that name the buoy (those actually painted on the buoy are inside quotation marks), and sometimes letters to specify the shape and color of the buoy. Examples are shown in Figure 2-26.

To prepare for buoy identification when planning a trip, it is best to check the *Light List*, using *Chart No. 1* as a guide. In foreign waters, check the local equivalent of these publications when available, or refer to the International Association of Lighthouse Authorities (IALA) Mari-

Table 2-7. Buoy identification	
In the returning direction	
Left-side	*Right-side*
Solid Color	Solid Color
Green	Red
Can-shape	Nun-shape
Odd numbers	Even numbers
White or green lights	White or red lights
Mid-channel or junction buoys	
Striped, two-colors, or solid yellow (VTS)	
Various shapes	
Letters without numbers	
Red, green, or white lights	

time Buoyage Systems A and B explained in the *Light List* and in *Chart No. 1*. The "red right returning" rule, used in the United States and Canada, for example, is part of the IALA-B system; most other countries use the IALA-A system, where the rule is "red left returning."

In shallow inland waters, daymarks (also called daybeacons) are used much as buoys are to mark the waterway. They are unlighted signs on posts or other structures in the water or on shore. Their chart symbols are small triangles or squares corresponding to their actual shape. Letters beside the chart symbols for daymarks are coded to give the purpose, color, and shape of the mark. The code is given in the *Light List* and in *Chart No. 1*. Daymarks are named with numbers and letters similar to the way buoys are. Examples are shown in Figure 2-26. Daymarks usually have reflective borders, which might help in locating them with a bright flashlight at night.

Although modern mariners rarely drop a weight with wax on it over the side to check the bottom as was done in the past, it can still be useful in chart reading and anchoring or beaching your vessel to know the bottom characteristics listed in Table 2-8.

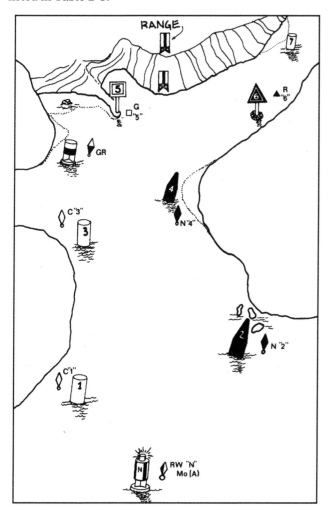

Figure 2-26. *Buoys and daymarks along a channel. Associated chart symbols are shown next to each aid. Complete definitions are in* Chart No. 1 *and in the buoy sections of the* Light List.

Table 2-8. Bottom and stone characteristics used on nautical charts	
Charted name	Particle diameter (millimeters)
Mud (silt, clay)	smaller than sand
Sand	0.06 to 2
Stones	
Gravel	2 to 4 (buckshot to marbles)
Pebbles	4 to 64 (marbles to golfballs)
Cobbles	64 to 256 (golf balls to soccer balls)
Boulders (rocks)	bigger than cobbles

Chapter 2 Glossary

aid to navigation (ATON). Lights, buoys, daymarks, and electromagnetic broadcasts used to assist in marine navigation.

buoys. Floating aids to navigation that vary in size from little more than a stick to huge structures. Some are lighted, most are labeled.

Chart Catalog. An online PDF that lists and depicts graphically the existing charts for a particular region. Print a copy to keep with your charts.

chart datum. The reference tide level used to assign a tide height on nautical charts. MLW and MLLW are examples.

Chart No. 1. NOAA booklet listing chart symbols and abbreviations.

compass points. One thirty-second of a full circle. One point = 11.25°.

compass rose. A 360° protractor diagram on a nautical chart, often relating true north to magnetic north.

course. The direction of intended travel, from the last waypoint to the next.

course made good (CMG). The direction from a one known position on the chart to a later known position, independent of the route between the two.

course over ground (COG). The present value of the CMG over the past few seconds derived from the GPS.

daymarks. Aids to navigation in the form of a flat sign, the shape and color of which provides specific information. If in the water, they are fixed permanently to the ground below it.

dividers. A navigator's plotting tool used to measure the distance between two points.

echart. An electronic version of a nautical chart viewed on some electronic device, either in the form of a raster image or a vector drawing.

ECS (electronic chart system). A GPS connected to an electronic device that displays echarts showing the present and past positions of the vessel. ECS usually include ways to measure range and bearing between points, waypoints and routes, and displays of other navigational information.

ENC (electronic navigation charts). A vector echart, which means the chart is drawn on the screen as it is viewed by a set formulas and a database of coordinates. The results are a series of line segments and symbols. Colors, lettering, and other display options can be user adjusted. The IMO standard format is called S-57.

heading. The direction the boat is pointed at any one time.

Latitude. Distance of a point on the chart north or south of the equator, measured in degrees, from 0° at the equator to 90° N or S at the poles. 1° of Lat = 60 nmi. Lines of constant latitude are called parallels.

Light List. USCG annual list of all aids to navigation, with their properties and locations.

Local Notice to Mariners (LNM). Weekly USCG publication that includes chart changes and other information crucial to safe navigation in the region covered. They are available in print, online, and they are broadcast on VHF. See also Notice to Mariners.

Longitude. Distance of a point on the chart east or west of the meridian running through Greenwich, England, measured in degrees, from 0° to 180°, E or W from Greenwich. 1° of longitude = 60 nmi x cos (Latitude). Lines of constant longitude are called meridians.

magnetic variation. The angular difference between true north and magnetic north, labeled East when the latter is east of the former, and West otherwise.

meridian. A line of constant longitude, running north-south on a chart. 0° Lon is called the Prime Meridian. 180° Lon is called the International Date Line.

nautical mile (nmi). Distance unit used in marine navigation defined as exactly 1852 meters. It is equivalent to 1' of latitude on a spherical earth, but varies slightly from this on the real earth, depending on the latitude. For most practical applications we can approximate it as 6,000 ft.

nav station. The place on the boat where the navigation tools, instruments, and charts are located and where much of the navigation is carried out.

NGA (National Geospatial-Intelligence Agency). An agency of the US Dept. of Defense. Their marine navigation resources were historically identified as NIMA, DMA, and HO.

NOAA (National Oceanic and Atmospheric Administration). An agency of the US Dept. of Commerce. Services under them of interest to mariners are the NWS and NOS.

NOAA Custom Charts (NCC). A new form of user-designed nautical chart based on the ENC format.

nominal range. The brightness of a navigation light expressed as clear-weather visible range in nautical miles.

NOS (National Ocean Service). A NOAA division responsible for charts, tides, currents, and Coast Pilots.

Notice to Mariners (NTM). Same as Local Notice to Mariners, but produced by NGA to include those for international waters as well.

parallel rulers. A plotting tool designed to transfer a line or direction parallel to itself across the chart.

PDF. Portable document format is a file type that can be read on a computer or tablet and most smartphones. The free reader required is available from adobe.com.

Pilot Charts. Climatic wind, weather, and current atlas charts of the oceans from the NGA, which include magnetic variation and great circle routes. Also produced by the British Admiralty in the UK.

RNC (raster navigation charts). An echart made from the graphic image of the printed paper charts.

rock awash. A rock that is just at the water level when tide height = 0.

soundings. Depths of the water shown on nautical charts (relative to 0 tide height) that represent actual measurements made at some time.

sunrise, sunset. The time the upper edge (limb) of the sun first appears or disappears over the visible horizon. These times are listed in Tide Tables and in the *Nautical Almanac*.

track. (1) The path a vessel makes across the chart. (2) The line between two waypoints that is assumed in the ECS output called "cross track error."

VHF. Very high Frequency. (1) The most common type of marine radio used for short range communications between vessels and to shore based stations. (2) The radio electromagnetic frequency spectrum from 30 MHz to 300 MHz, with corresponding wavelengths of 1 to 10 meters.

CHAPTER 3
OTHER NAVIGATION AIDS

3.1 Overview

Nautical charts are the primary source of navigation data for boat trips, but they do not contain all of the pertinent navigation information you will need. In addition to tide and current references, several other sources should be consulted when planning a trip. This preparation takes time and effort, but it is worthwhile. Other than specific tour guides, these additional references are not always intended for small craft navigation, so it takes time to ferret out the relevant parts: isolated notes on winds and currents, hazards and havens, or other bits of local knowledge—the mariner's catchall phrase for any information that aids navigation in a specific area.

Once you get there, local knowledge accumulates in the usual way, by direct experience. Good navigators, however, obtain as much of this knowledge as possible ahead of time. They know the sources and do the work to check them—which takes some running around because these references are rarely found in the same store or library.

3.2 *Coast Pilot & Sailing Directions*

Coast Pilots (US), *Pilots* (UK), and *Sailing Directions* (US & Canada) are titles that various government agencies use for similar publications. They include the same types of information, in the same format. Pilot means guide, and these are guidebooks to the waterways they cover. Beyond this, the titles are misleading. *Coast Pilots* cover inland waters as well as coastal, and *Sailing Directions* have very little to do with sailing these days.

These publications are required reading for larger vessels because they include specific rules and regulations on shipping as well as navigation, weather, and current data. *Coast Pilots*, for example, show where shipping lanes must be followed in certain areas, or where international right-of-way rules change to inland right-of-way rules. They are required reading for recreational sailors as well, because these books include the bulk of navigational information not presented on charts. Again, much of their content is not pertinent to sailing, but certain parts are essential to all mariners, in any craft. The *U.S. Coast Pilot* (see Figure 3-1) will be used as an example of these references; the content and use of others listed below are similar. *US Coast Pilots* are all online. Find the links at starpath.com/navpubs.

The U.S. *Coast Pilots* cover all U.S. waters in nine volumes, including inland waters such as the Great Lakes (volume 6), Puget Sound (volume 7, chapter 13), and San Francisco Bay and connecting waters (volume 7, chapter 7). Each volume has an introductory chapter on general information that applies to the waters of the entire volume. These are general discussions of navigation (specialized to specific areas) that should be read as a supplement to this book. The introduction is followed by chapters that divide the region into sections. Each section lists the pertinent chart, and then proceeds, point to point, along the shoreline on that chart discussing the areas. A map at the front of each volume shows the chapter sections outlined in it.

The appendix to each volume is an extensive list of all relevant navigation publications and where they can be obtained, as well as the addresses of relevant agencies including all Coast Guard and National Weather Service (NWS) offices in the region covered. It also lists shore stations that provide medical advice by marine radio on request. The appendix is followed by a set of tables that include extensive marine weather statistics and various conversion tables.

Coast Pilots are published annually, but unlike tide and current tables or the *Light List*, an outdated *Coast Pilot* is

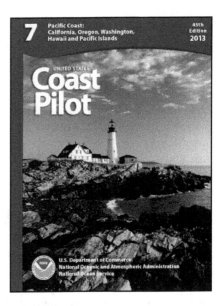

Figure 3-1. *Cover of a U.S.* Coast Pilot. *The appendix to each* Coast Pilot *contains a complete listing of addresses and telephone numbers of all agencies that provide navigational and related information for mariners.*

still valuable. Piloting information relevant to small craft navigation does not change from year to year. Mariners should check these volumes for weather, current, local hazards, and prominent landmarks in the area. Facilities for boaters also are listed, but this information is sparse and may be outdated.

Weather data are listed in three places in each volume of the *Coast Pilot*: the tables section at the back of the book, the separate introductions to each chapter, and in each section of each chapter covering specific areas. All three should be checked. The tables list climatic statistics that help plan the time of a trip and tell what wind, sea state, and water temperature to expect during each month. A sample is shown in Figure 3-3. Text sections warn of local weather such as unusual storm patterns, hazardous afternoon sea breezes, and the probability of fog. Sections on the Hawaiian Islands, for example, might warn that the windward side of an island has frequent rain (often obscuring visibility), whereas the leeward side is dry. Individual sections also tell where to find shelter from certain winds, although some small craft might well find shelter in other places as well.

Information on currents in the individual sections is mostly a reminder of what you will find by checking the NOAA current predictions or current charts, but in a significant number of other cases, this *Coast Pilot* information is unique. Often enough, you will find current information here that does not appear in any other reference: rough rules on when currents turn relative to tides, the locations of large consistent eddies, the likelihood of tide rips, the average current speed at headlands or secondary passes not included in NOAA predictions, as well as other details such as wind-driven currents. Maximum currents in major channels reported in the *Coast Pilot* are sometimes significantly larger than those predicted by NOAA. This apparent discrepancy—an important note for sailors—can occur whenever the precise location of the NOAA reference station is not at the narrowest part of the channel.

Coast Pilots also list other matters of interest to boaters. These include the likelihood of deadheads (nearly submerged logs floating vertically), locations of kelp beds, commercial fishing practices in the area, locations and descriptions of public shoreline lands, restrictions near wildlife preserves, and customs procedures at the Canadian and Mexican borders. There is also extensive discussion of passageways into harbors or temporary shelters. When the *Coast Pilot* describes a passageway as hazardous to small craft, it is referring to vessels up to 65 ft in length or longer. There is no specific definition. Very small boats can sometimes negotiate such passes more readily than larger vessels, but nevertheless, these warnings should be noted. Study the chart and current predictions carefully to decide whether specific *Coast Pilot* warnings apply to small craft as well. If there is shallow water along the edges, it can usu-

Chart 18480. For 5.5 miles from Destruction Island to Hoh Head, the coast trends in a general NW direction. The cliffs are 50 to 100 feet high, and many rocks and ledges extend 1.2 miles offshore in some places.

Abbey Islet, 3.5 miles NE of Destruction Island, is over 100 feet high and covered with trees. It is 200 yards off the cliffs. Many rocks are close S of it, the most distant of which is **South Rock**, 46 feet high, 1 mile S, and 0.5 miles offshore.

At the mouth of **Hoh River**, 2 miles SE of Hoh Head, is a broad sand beach; the absence of cliffs for 0.5 mile is noticeable for a considerable distance offshore. In smooth weather the river can be entered by canoes, but the channel shifts. An Indian village is on the S bank at its mouth.

Hoh Head, 200 feet high, is a bright yellow cliff covered with a dense forest. It projects a little over 0.5 mile from the general trend of the coast. A large cluster of rocks is off the S cliff of the head and covered rocks extend to about 1.6 miles offshore between the head and North Rock. A rock covered 2 1/4 fathoms lies 1.8 miles WNW of Hoh Head.

Middle Rock, **North Rock**, and **Perkins Reef** are other dangers within 1.5 miles off Hoh Head. Middle Rock, 65 feet high and black with vertical sides, is 0.8 mile off the mouth of Hoh River. North Rock, a mile S of Hoh Head, is 107 feet high and grayish in color, with steep sides; in the afternoon sun this rock shows white, which makes it a very distinct land-mark. Perkins Reef is a long, bold, and jagged islet, 1.1 miles W of Hoh Head. This area has numerous other rocks, covered and bare.

The coast continues rugged and rocky from Hoh Head to La Push, 11 miles to the NW. The cliffs are 100 to 120 feet high, broken here and there by small streams. Several rocky islets, 25 to 120 feet high, and covered ledges extend in some places as much as 2 miles offshore.

Alexander Island, 121 feet high, is 2 miles NNW of Hoh Head and a mile offshore. It is covered with low vegetation and is flat-topped with steep sides. The island is prominent in hazy or smoky weather. A covered rock, 1.8 miles WNW of Alexander Island, is the outermost known danger in this vicinity.

Figure 3-2. *Sample text from the* Coast Pilot *that describes the region shown in Figure 3-5.*

Table 3-1. Navigation Reference Books		
Publication	*Source*	*Waters covered*
U.S. Coast Pilot	USA (NOAA)	American
Sailing Directions	USA (NGA)	foreign
Sailing Directions	Canada	Canadian
Admiralty Pilots	British	worldwide

ally be used to avoid strong currents and rips, but if the edges are steep and rocky, they may be even more dangerous than midstream.

An equally important part of the *Coast Pilot*'s data is its tips on fair-weather navigation. Often it is difficult to identify peaks and valleys from charted elevation contours alone, especially from an uncertain position. Much of the *Coast Pilot*'s text is devoted to descriptions of the land as seen from the water (see Figure 3-2). It points out prominent landmarks useful for piloting fixes, and it warns of features that are deceiving when viewed from the water, such as one island that appears as two from certain perspectives, or a peak on a headland that appears as a separated island. Pictures and drawings of the coastline are included. It also tells the colors of hills and which structures near towns are conspicuous, in addition to other pieces of local knowledge that cannot be read from chart symbols.

Pilots and *Sailing Directions* for the same area produced by different agencies could have more or less detail of interest to boaters. The only way to know is to check all sources. When planning a trip to British Columbia, for example, the *U.S. Coast Pilots* would not be applicable because their coverage stops at the border. The *U.S. Sailing Directions* (No. 154) covers this area, and it is these that should be read along with the Canadian *Sailing Directions*, the primary reference in this case. For sailing along the west coast of Mexico, the U.S. *Sailing Directions* (No. 80) and the British *Pilots* would be the primary references. The latter are very expensive books, but deserving of the high esteem they have worldwide.

Coast Pilots are big books, and it is neither practical nor necessary to carry them on board in all cases. Pertinent notes can be made directly on the charts to be used, or photocopies of the pertinent sections can be carried along instead of the volume. Quick-print shops can drill holes in a *Coast Pilot* or a *Canadian Sailing Directions* and then cut off the binding so it can be ring-bound in selected parts. *U.S. Sailing Directions*, originally printed in loose leaf, are now also in bound volumes. And, again, they are available online as PDFs, and could be carried in a smart phone.

Do not avoid doing this research for a second trip even if nothing relevant was found when you looked for an earlier trip to another location. Some remote places that boaters go to are not mentioned at all in pilots, and some descriptions of other areas do not suit boaters. In the long run, however, time spent going through these books will improve your navigation—even in those cases when it does

not aid particular trips. Several volumes of the NGA (National Geospatial-Intelligence Agency) *Sailing Directions* are also online, and they clearly show what a wonderful resource this can be—although these are only for foreign waters. The various resources are summarized in Table 3-1.

3.3 The *Light List*

The Coast Guard publication called the *Light List* (see Figure 3-4) was mentioned in Chapter 2 as an annual source of corrections to charted light and buoy data. But it is more than that. It includes information about lights and buoys that is not on charts, and the general information section of the *Light List* is comparable to that of *Coast Pilots*. At some point, it should be read as a supplement to this book for details of navigation by lights and buoys. It includes all definitions and conventions used in navigation by lights, as well as practical guidelines and technical details that are often crucial to understanding notes in other sources for navigation at night.

The bulk of the *Light List* text consists of details on each light, buoy, and daymark in the region covered by the volume at hand. A sample section is shown in Figure 2-13. Each lighted aid has a unique *Light List* number. All are listed, although those located near intersections of major waterways may take longer to locate in the book because of the way it is organized. It breaks the covered region up into separate sections for seacoasts, rivers and harbors, and secondary channels, and then lists the lights sequentially along each subsection. A light at the mouth of a river might be listed in both the seacoast section and the river section, or it could be in just one of these sections. Sometimes both must be checked to find it. The same search might be required for lights at the mouth of a secondary channel onto a river.

The *Light List* is most important for navigation at night or in the fog, because it provides uncharted information on the visible range of lights and the bearings from which they are obscured. For daytime navigation, it tells of privately maintained aids (both lights and buoys) that are sometimes not shown on charts. It also describes locations and mounting structures of daymarks, which help with their identification.

...In Depth

12.7 Sailing the West Coast

Here is a sample of a magazine article that summarizes local knowledge and experience along with *Coast Pilot* data to present what is effectively a set of *Sailing Directions* for the West Coast...

WEATHER ELEMENTS	JAN	FEB	MAR	APR	MAY	JUN	JUL	AUG	SEP	OCT	NOV	DEC	YEARS OF RECORD
METEOROLOGICAL TABLE – COASTAL AREA OFF NORTH BEND, OR Between 42°N to 44°N and 124°W to 127°W													
Wind > 33 knots [1]	6.5	5.8	4.0	2.4	1.6	2.3	2.1	1.3	1.4	1.8	4.5	5.6	2.9
Wave Height > 9 feet [1]	11.9	11.4	9.8	5.5	5.4	4.7	5.2	3.2	3.3	4.9	11.3	12	6.5
Visibility < 2 nautical miles [1]	6.3	6.9	4.5	5.0	4.5	4.9	7.7	14.8	8.7	9.8	5.9	7.1	7.4
Precipitation [1]	18.7	17.7	15.9	10.1	7.6	5.7	3.6	4.0	4.6	6.8	15.2	18.2	9.3
Temperature > 69° F	0.0	0.0	0.0	0.1	0.3	0.7	1.3	1.5	1.2	0.4	0.1	0.1	0.6
Mean Temperature (°F)	49.7	50.0	50.3	51.5	53.6	56.5	58.9	59.3	59.8	57.0	54.0	51.1	55.0
Temperature < 33° F [1]	0.1	0.2	0.0	0.0	0.0	0.0	0.0	0.0	0.0	0.0	0.0	0.2	0.0
Mean RH (%)	83	82	82	81	82	84	86	87	86	85	83	83	84
Overcast or Obscured [1]	42.9	43.2	39.4	34.0	33.6	37.0	37.6	43.6	32.9	34.4	41.4	40.4	38.0
Mean Cloud Cover (8ths)	5.7	5.7	5.6	5.2	5.1	5.3	4.8	5.2	4.4	4.7	5.5	5.6	5.2
Mean SLP (mbs)	1018	1017	1017	1019	1019	1019	1019	1017	1016	1018	1018	1018	1018
Ext. Max. SLP (mbs)	1037	1051	1039	1043	1042	1046	1040	1037	1038	1050	1050	1045	1051
Ext. Min. SLP (mbs)	969	973	984	980	988	995	997	992	985	982	976	961	961
Prevailing Wind Direction	S	S	S	N	N	N	N	N	N	N	S	S	N
Thunder and Lightning [1]	0.4	0.7	0.1	0.2	0.2	0.1	0.1	0.1	0.3	0.3	0.6	0.5	0.3

[1] Percentage Frequency
These data are based upon observations made by ships in transit. These ships tend to avoid bad weather when possible thus biasing the data toward good weather samples.

Figure 3-3. *Sample of the weather statistics from a* U.S. Coast Pilot.

When planning a trip, the *Light List* should be checked to verify charted aids and to find uncharted ones to add. Once in the right section of the book, it is easy to run down the list to make chart notes as the tabulation follows the shoreline in each section. Again, notes or copies are all that are needed on a trip, not the book itself. If there is a bright light in the region, it can usually be found in the index from the name of its location. The index gives the *Light List* number of the light (not a page reference), from which the light can be located in the book. If no such light exists, the names of prominent points or capes in the area might be found in the index, and they can guide you to the proper place in the book. Links to *Light Lists* are at starpath.com/navpubs.

3.4 Tour Guides and Other References

The best source of local knowledge for boating is other boaters who have been to where you want to go. Numerous books are available that cover specific regions along with more general guide books that also discuss experiences in various areas. These should be checked for information about a planned boat trip. It pays to follow a few known routes that such books describe before breaking new ground on your own, but try not to rely on any single reference when it comes to predicting conditions at a particular area. Whenever possible, check several references to a particular area and note the dates of the trips. Then check the weather statistics in the *Coast Pilot* to see if the writers' experiences were typical for the season and to learn what conditions could be present at the time you plan to go. Idyllic coastal coves in calm air can be hellholes when exposed to strong winds and big seas.

Sailing and boating magazines can be sources of local knowledge in some cases. Sailor's travelogues or cruising guides are another potential source of local knowledge for nearly all waters of the globe. Again, there are many options. The best bet is to look through a good nautical bookstore once you have planned a trip to a specific place. Some of these resources are very informative, especially with regard to shoreside attractions (or distractions), prominent landmarks, and occasionally with winds and sea states.

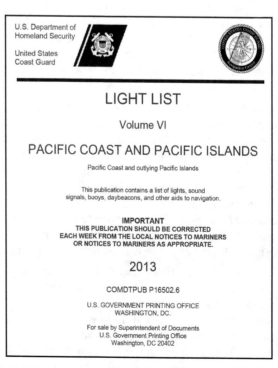

Figure 3-4. *Cover of the* Light List.

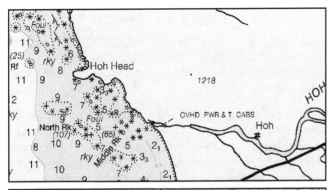

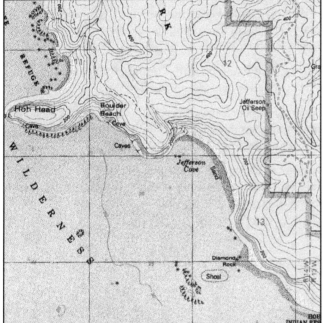

Figure 3-5. *Section of a 7.5' topographic map (middle) and at the top, the only nautical chart available (1:76,253) for the region. In isolated coastal examples such as this one, topographic maps might provide more information on the waters and shoreline. The two sources do not agree on the positions of coastal rocks, as is often the case. On the bottom is the same view captured from Google Earth (Image © 2013 DigitalGlobe, Map data © 2013 Google). Several echart programs offer the option to switch to this type of satellite image for navigation. Figure 3-2 contains the* Coast Pilot *description for this region. Jefferson Cove beach is 0.5 mile long.*

A new resource is the growing presence of online travelogues and sailor's blogs. Again, we risk generalizing specific descriptions we might read, but often, there is a way to contact the authors and talk to them. A prime example of this resource is activecaptain.com, which is an interactive cruising guide for boaters worldwide.

3.5 Topographic Maps

Topographic quadrangle maps produced by the U.S. Geological Survey are used by hikers to find their way around the back country. They show detailed elevation contours and the locations of towns and roads. They are made in three scales, named by the latitude extent of the map. The two that might be of interest to small craft navigators are the 7.5' series (scale of 1:24,000) and the 15' series (scale of 1:62,500). As with nautical charts, dividing the scale factor by 10,000 gives the number of nautical miles per handspan on topographic maps, although distance scales and mile markers along major rivers are given in statute miles on these maps. Similar maps from other countries use different scales. As with charts, scales larger than 1:40,000 or so are of most value to navigation.

Topographic maps can be valuable to shoal-draft vessels exploring inshore waters. They show locations of roads, streams, swamps, houses, structures, hiking trails, and the shape of the terrain near shore are presented much more thoroughly on topographic maps than on nautical charts. River expeditions usually call for topographic maps, as nautical charts are only available for large rivers that are accessible to large vessels. For coastal trips, topographic maps show more clearly than charts how to get back to civilization by land in the event of an emergency—or how to be reached from land after reporting an emergency by marine radio.

Because topographic maps always show terrain contours clearly (whereas nautical charts vary significantly in this aspect), they are often a better guide to shelter from wind near shore. A topographic map might help locate adequate shelter downwind of a small hill on a spit, which would not be discernible from a nautical chart. And because wind is usually focused and accelerated in valleys, wind flow on inshore waters (or over a campsite at night) can often be more readily predicted from maps than from charts.

For actual navigation on inshore waters, topographic maps will not often be the primary reference, but there are exceptions. For some remote coastal regions, topographic maps show more detail along shore than their nautical counterparts (see Figure 3-5). The same is true in a few cases on inland waters. Some quadrangle maps (then called topographic-bathymetric maps) are made in conjunction with National Ocean Service/National Oceanic and Atmospheric Administration (NOS/NOAA) and consequently show depth contours and inshore rocks in some detail. But even in these special cases where quadrangle maps add much to navigation preparation, they do not replace nautical charts as required equipment. Topographic maps do not show navigation lights and buoys. They are not dependable for soundings or inshore rock locations. They do not warn of tide rips and other hazards, and very few can match the foreshore information given on large-scale nautical charts. If appropriate in light of the notes above, check these maps when planning a trip, but compare them carefully with nautical charts of the same area before deciding they alone might be adequate.

Topographic maps do not show compass roses, so marine compass navigation with them is not as simple as it is with charts. See usgs.gov for sources, or check out the remarkable map and terrain viewer at viewer.nationalmap.gov, and be sure to check out all the display options in the side panel and the tools in the menu bar.

Chapter 3 Glossary

Coast Pilots. Annual NOS publications that cover important navigation, weather, current, logistics, and legal data not included on nautical charts. They cover US coastal and inland waters.

local knowledge. Information related to navigation in some specific waterway and not readily available from standard sources. The presumption in this use of the word "knowledge" is that this information is valid, as opposed to hearsay or anecdotes that might not be dependable.

NWS (National Weather Service). A division of NOAA responsible for gathering, analyzing, and distributing weather information.

Pilots. The name of British Admiralty sailing directions that cover all waters worldwide.

Sailing Directions. Annual NGA publications of similar information as in Coast Pilots but for international waters. Also available from Canada and the UK (called Pilots).

topographic maps. Land maps of the terrain, with elevation contours. Occasionally useful as supplements to nautical charts in special locations.

CHAPTER 4
COMPASS USE

4.1 Introduction

Every mariner in any vessel on an extended trip will eventually need to rely on a compass to some extent. But even when it is not essential, a good marine compass mounted so it is always in view is a valuable aid for many aspects of small craft navigation, and this value increases with usage. Although it is quite possible to cover many safe and happy miles with little more than an occasional glance at the compass, getting by without much compass use should not distract from the benefits of practiced compass use. Good navigation calls for frequent use of a good compass.

Compasses are used for steering, finding position, identifying landmarks, and monitoring the effects of wind and current. Within each of these broad categories are numerous specific applications. The primary use of a compass is to tell which way to go when it is not apparent from just looking around. When circumnavigating a large island, for example, a boater faces new horizons at every corner. Often there are so many bays, headlands, and other islands in the background that the course to the pass around the next corner is uncertain (see Figure 4-1).

To solve this common problem, locate your position on the chart, and read the compass bearing from there to the pass using the chart's compass rose. Point the boat in that direction using a compass, and the target should be dead ahead. From then on, you could steer toward the target and not rely on the compass, although it still pays to keep an eye on the compass. After steering toward the target for some time you might discover that the boat's compass heading has changed, even though the target has not left the bow. This means that current is pushing the boat off the original line to the target (as shown in Figure 4-2), which is another example of compass use: compass readings have told you something about your position and motion, independent of its use as a steering guide.

Compass use in clear weather and daylight is often more a matter of efficiency than safety. In rare cases, a mistaken target could lead to dangerous waters, but such errors usually only lead to more work, not danger. Eventually the mistake becomes apparent, as does the extra distance that must be sailed to correct it. But if you are caught offshore when darkness or fog is setting in, it is essential to take a compass bearing to your destination while it is still visible. That bearing is the only way to get to your destination after landmarks fade away. As pointed out in the last example, it is equally important to know of any currents in the area

and how to adjust the compass course to compensate for their effects. Without the target in view, the effect of current on your course line will not be detectable (see Figure 4-3).

A compass is frequently required on long crossings. In some areas, for example, large open waters can be hazardous on summer afternoons when thermal winds (sea breezes) build to 25 knots or more. Such waters are usually calm in early morning, which makes this a good time to cross. But in the early hours of daylight, radiation fog that builds up overnight may not have burned off. A small craft navigator might face a choice between following a compass course in calm water and fog, or waiting for clear weather and risk being caught on open water as the wind builds.

When relying on a compass, it is important to know what it reads, what affects the reading, and how to check the reading. A compass error of 6° causes a boat to slip sideways off its intended course line by 10% of the distance sailed (see Figure 4-4). Sailing at 3 kts, this compass error would take a boat off course by 0.3 mile each hour. Such a large compass error, however, would have an even worse effect on locating a position or judging current flow from compass bearings.

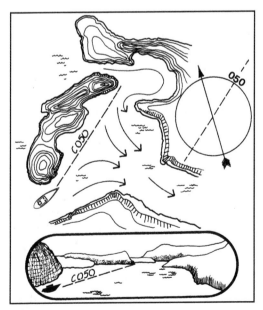

Figure 4-1. *Use of a compass to identify landmarks.*

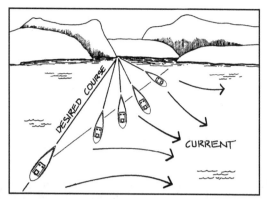

Figure 4-2. *A boat set off course by current with bow kept on a constant heading toward the target.*

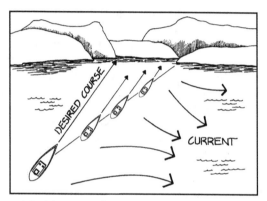

Figure 4-3. *A boat set off course by current with bow kept on a constant compass heading.*

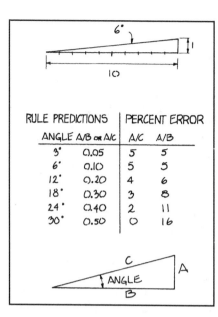

Figure 4-4. *The Small Angle Rule. To a good approximation, the height of an angle of 6° is one tenth of the length of either side. The rule can be extended as shown to larger or smaller angles using multiple of 6°.*

RULE PREDICTIONS		PERCENT ERROR	
ANGLE A/B or A/C		A/C	A/B
3°	0.05	5	5
6°	0.10	5	5
12°	0.20	4	6
18°	0.30	3	8
24°	0.40	2	11
30°	0.50	0	16

It is also fundamental to remember that the compass heading of a boat tells which way the boat is pointed, *not which way the boat is moving*. In the example of a boater headed for the corner of an island (Figure 4-2) the helmsman kept the boat headed toward the pass, and the compass course changed as current pushed the boat off the original course line. Had the pass been obscured by fog as the helmsman maintained a constant compass (Figure 4-3), they would not have noticed that the pass moved off the bow as the current pushed the boat off course, and thus would not have gotten there on that heading.

4.2 How a Compass Works

The earth's magnetic field flows northward like a prevailing wind, and compass needles align with this magnetic field as wind vanes align with the wind. The direction of magnetic field flow at any location is called *magnetic north*, but the name is misleading. This is not a unique direction worldwide. The field flow meanders around the magnetic terrain of the earth as it moves northward. In New England, magnetic north is toward a true direction of 346; in the Pacific Northwest, it is toward 016.

The difference between magnetic north and true north at any location is called the magnetic variation of the place—in contrast to navigation on land where the same

thing is called *declination*. Magnetic variation is labeled east (E) or west (W) depending on whether magnetic north lies to the east or west of true north. Magnetic variation along the Pacific Coast of North America is easterly, up to 16° E near the Canadian border. Along the Atlantic Coast it is westerly, increasing to about 16° West in Maine. The (2013) line of zero variation runs northward through the center of the Gulf of Mexico. For the latest data along with historical values and precise calculators, see ngdc.noaa.gov/geomag/geomag.shtml.

Magnetic variation is given on all nautical charts, in the center of each compass rose (see Figure 4-5) along with the year it was valid and the annual change. The additional note telling how it changes with time, such as "annual decrease 6'," is usually of little practical interest. It takes many years for the variation to change a full degree. By the time this correction reaches a degree or two, the chart would be far outdated. On some very old charts, this can even be dangerous. We have seen cases in Alaskan waters where correcting the compass variation on 1970s charts according to the prescription gave us variations in 2002 that were off by 3 or 4 degrees.

...In Depth

12.8 How to Check a Compass

Charts show magnetic directions; compasses show compass directions. With no deviation, these directions are identical, which is what every mariner wants. With deviation, they are different, which adds an extra step to navigation with compass heading. This note explains how to determine whether you have deviation and what it is if so...

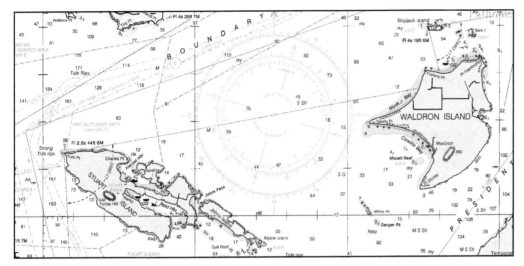

Figure 4-5. *A compass rose can be used for converting true to magnetic directions or vice versa. The line showing the boundary of the obscured sector of Turn Point Light has a true bearing of 260 and a magnetic bearing of 238. Accidentally, this line passes through the center of the compass rose on this chart.*

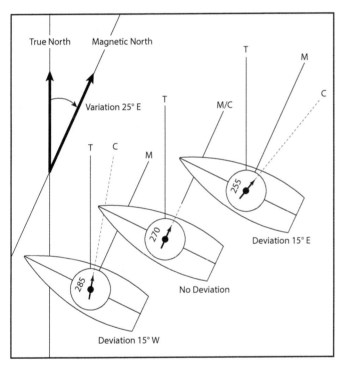

Figure 4-6. *Compass heading versus true and magnetic headings. When a compass has deviation, the compass needle does not point to magnetic north, as it should.*

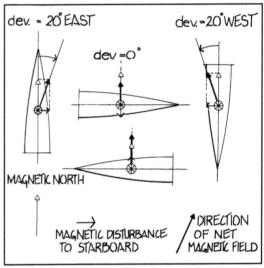

Figure 4-7. *How deviation changes with boat heading. The boat has a magnetic disturbance to starboard, which rotates relative to the earth's magnetic field as the boat turns. Compass needles point in the direction of the net magnetic field.*

A standard marine compass is a magnetized needle attached to a circular floating card graduated in degrees. The north-seeking end of the needle is attached at the 000 position on the card. The card is balanced on a jeweled pivot within a dampening liquid. The 000 point on the card stays oriented toward magnetic north as the boat turns under it. The compass heading of the boat is read directly from the compass card using an index mark on the compass housing attached to the boat. The line drawn through this index mark and the compass card pivot point is called the *lubber line*. To read the proper compass heading, the lubber line must be parallel to the boat's centerline (bow to stern).

When a boat's magnetic heading is 050, the boat is pointed 50° to the right of magnetic north. If magnetic north in the area lies 20° to the right of true north (variation 20° E), the boat is pointed 70° to the right of true north. With this magnetic variation, a magnetic heading of 050 means a true heading of 070. The general rule for finding true directions from magnetic directions is to add the variation to the magnetic reading when the variation is east, or subtract the variation from the magnetic reading when it is west. "Correcting add east" is the standard reminder of this rule.

This correction of magnetic directions to get true directions, however, is not often required in typical small craft navigation—especially in nonsteel vessels. Nautical charts show magnetic directions explicitly on the magnetic scales of compass roses, so there is no need for true directions. All inshore navigation can be, and usually is, best done with

37

magnetic directions alone. If conversions between magnetic and true directions must be made, they can be read from a compass rose without knowing the rules, as shown in Figure 4-5. Tidal current flow and the directions from which lighthouses are obscured are given in reference books as true directions. These can be converted to magnetic directions with a compass rose.

To read proper magnetic directions, however, the compass needle (000 on the compass card) must always point toward magnetic north, which means the earth's magnetic field at the compass site must not be disturbed by magnetic objects on the boat. Consider the wind vane analogy: If a wind vane is aligned with the natural wind and a fan is directed toward it, the vane will shift off the natural wind direction and point to whatever direction the true wind and fan wind add up to. A compass needle behaves the same way when equipment on the boat produces a disturbing magnetic field at the compass site. If a compass needle does not point to magnetic north, the compass is said to have *deviation* (see Figure 4-6).

When a compass has deviation, the compass heading it shows is not the proper magnetic heading of the boat. Nautical charts show magnetic directions; compasses show compass directions. With no deviation, these directions are identical, which is what every boater wants. With deviation, they are different, which is bad news for navigation. Furthermore, because a magnetic disturbance is from something in the boat, when the boat turns, the direction of the net magnetic field turns, which means the needle orientation depends on the boat orientation (see Figure 4-7). Consequently, a compass with deviation error on one heading will have different errors on other headings. A compass that reads 15° low when headed north could read 10° high when headed east. These errors cannot be predicted; they must be measured for each heading.

Compass deviation is a nuisance to any navigator, but it can be especially troublesome for small craft with deck mounted or bulkhead mounted compasses. We have seen cases where bulkhead mounted compasses worked fine, provided the gooseneck light on the other side of the bulkhead was in place. Move the light, and you move the compass. Or deck mounted compasses that did not work when the quarter berth below was filled with canned goods.

Fortunately, it is easy to determine what will influence the compass, so the boat can be packed or equipment installed in such a manner that the compass is not disturbed. The primary troublemakers are metal objects containing iron. Potential sources of iron that pose a problem to a marine compass are steel ammunition boxes (popular for waterproof and crash proof stowage of cameras and radios); large knives, axes, and stoves for camping; steel battery casings in flashlights; tin cans (which are actually made of steel); magnets in radio speakers; guns; or portable Freon air horns (an effective way to attract attention in traffic). A more subtle problem is the metal nickel, often used in

metal plating as a base substrate. Chrome-plated brass (both nonmagnetic) might contain a thin layer of nickel, which could disturb a compass. Most stainless steels, on the other hand, do not cause magnetic disturbances, even though they contain both iron and nickel. The alloy structure alters its magnetic properties.

To test any object for magnetic disturbance, bring it up to the compass while closely watching the compass needle. If the needle does not move with the object touching the compass, the object is not a problem. If an object is a magnetic disturbance, like a weather radio, this test should show that the object must be kept at least three or four times its bulk dimension away from the compass to avoid shifting its reading. When checking a compass indoors with steel folding chairs nearby, the chairs should be moved three or four times the size of the chair away from the compass.

To learn compass terms, muse on the analogy that God makes variation and man makes deviation.

4.3 Types of Compasses

Compasses commonly used on small craft include deck-mounted, bulkhead mounted, or binnacle mounted marine compasses, as well as hand-bearing marine compasses. Those new to boating may be familiar with the handheld hiker's compasses, but marine compasses are designed for boats, so they work better in all circumstances than hiker's models.

An important distinction between hiking and marine compasses is the way they are read. Marine compasses have the circular scale of numerical directions attached to the needle; hiking compasses have this scale attached to the compass housing on a ring that can be rotated around the needle. When a marine compass turns (attached to a boat or held by hand), the numbers remain stationary, and the index mark on the housing circles the numbers to mark the compass direction. On hiking compasses, the numbers turn with the compass, so they must be rotated into alignment with the needle by hand before a compass can be read.

Marine compasses are dome shaped, so the card can be read at large tilt angles as the boat rolls and pitches in a seaway, whereas thin, flat, hiking compasses tend to stick when tilted. A permanently mounted marine compass can be read in a seaway without touching the compass, whereas a hiking compass must be kept level by hand as the numbers ring is rotated to align 000 with the needle position. Smartphone digital compasses must also be kept level to read, and latest versions include a 2-D level in view with the compass to monitor this.

There are also significant differences among marine compasses. Larger, well-damped compasses can be read to within a few degrees in calm water; smaller ones swing back and forth through many degrees in the best condi-

Figure 4-8. *Types of marine (nonelectronic) compasses. A, Binnacle mount. B, Deck mount. C, Binnacle mount with Flinders spheres for metal vessels. D, Bulkhead mount. E, hockey puck style bearing compass. F, Handheld bearing compass, with mount for deck use.*

Figure 4-9. *Electronic compasses. A and B are sample sensor units. C, D, F are sample remote displays, where C and F include a digitally created analog display. E is an iPhone display, with level indicator (read only when the cross hair is centered). Heading sensor data can also be used in the radar and electronic charting displays.*

tions. Larger models have the further advantage that they can be read from farther away or from an angle. Samples are shown in Figure 4-8.

Compasses are meant primarily for steering. They are always in view, so the helmsman need not be interrupted to read a compass heading. This type is much preferable to a hand-bearing compass whenever a compass course must be followed with no landmarks in sight. Bearings to landmarks can be taken with steering compasses by sighting over the compass or, in some cases, just pointing the boat at the mark.

Hand-bearing compasses are stowed on the boat or navigator's pocket and only removed for occasional sights, either to choose a course or take bearings for a position fix. Beware of small flat compasses used for dinghy racing. These are no more than hikers' compasses that mount on the boat. This style usually has a compass face marked off in quadrants of alternating colors. These are not intended for steering or taking bearings. They are just a questionable means of recording relative wind directions when racing small sailboats.

Hand-bearing compasses differ as much as steering compasses do. Some can be read to within one half of a

degree, others to within only five degrees. Some have good dampening, others do not. There are two basic types. One is held by a handle at arm's length; the other is held up to the eye as the bearing is read through a lens and mirror from an internal scale. The latter style is more accurate and compact. Nighttime bearing sights require models with internal lights. Some hand-bearing compass lights are battery operated; others utilize photoluminescence.

High-quality steering compasses include internal magnets that can be adjusted to cancel out any deviation that might be present. These adjustments are important for larger vessels, but less often on nonsteel small craft—larger steel vessels often require external adjustments as well called Flinders spheres (Figure 4-8, C).

On nonsteel vessels, the internal adjustments can cause more harm than good if not set to zero—effectively adding deviation to an otherwise accurate compass. If your compass has these adjustments, the first step is to check that they are set to their neutral position, and if not, to do so .

The adjustment screw on the fore-and-aft axis of the compass (sometimes extending through the housing and accessible from either end) usually controls east-west errors; the one perpendicular to it on the side of the compass controls north-south errors. If you have the compass in hand—as opposed to already installed on the boat—you can use this method to check their adjustment: set the compass on a table, well away from magnetic materials, and draw a line on the table oriented toward 000 according to the compass. Then turn the compass around facing the other direction on the line. If the north-south adjustment is set to neutral, the compass should now read 180. If not, turn the north-south screw one eighth of a turn, and make the check again, repeating the process until opposite readings are achieved. Then do the same on a 090-270 line using the other screw. Then double-check the north-south line again. The neutral position of the adjustment screw usually corresponds to vertical or horizontal alignment of the screw slots.

An electronic compass is a heading sensor with a remote display. Samples are shown in Figure 4-9. These compasses all include a mode and procedure for an internal automatic correction for deviation, which usually involves driving the vessel slowly in a full circle, called *swinging ship*.

4.4 Steering a Compass Course

When circumstances require you to follow a particular compass course that is read from a chart or chosen by other means, you must steer the boat in such a way that the compass always reads this particular value. This is called steering by the compass, but the name is misleading and it makes learning to do it well more difficult. In practice, when steering by the compass you rarely look at the compass, but instead concentrate on various reference marks on the horizon in front of the boat. These references could be landmarks, distant cloud formations, stars, or just a slight change in the shading of the sky.

The procedure is to bring the bow in line with the desired compass heading and note what reference mark lies dead ahead or just to one side of the bow. Then steer to keep that reference mark at the same place on the bow. When a wave or passing trough leads you off course, you will detect it by noting that your reference mark is no longer where it was, relative to the bow. Steer the boat toward the mark, and when your mark is in place, the compass will read properly. You need only check the compass occasionally to verify that the mark is still a good one for the course, or whether its proper place on the bow should be adjusted. All such marks must be considered temporary when following a compass course—some might last hours, others only a few minutes. When one mark is no longer useful, choose another that is on line, and steer toward it.

On the other hand, if you try to follow the compass card itself, your heading will swing erratically, and could pose control problems in a seaway, until you get the feel of it. Even in waves where the course must be altered temporarily at each wave, you turn back to your mark to set up for the next wave, and only then check the compass. If you rely on the compass reading when course adjustments must be

fast, you might turn the wrong way; the card might have overshot the mark on the last swing and be way off at the time you look at it.

Bearing these cautions in mind, whenever your mark is lost in the waves or the fog is too thick to see anything at all, or it is simply pitch black at night, there is no choice but to steer directly by the compass card. In these circumstances, it will help to have some other aid, such as wind direction, which can often be an asset. As for relying on the compass alone, if you are looking at the whole top of the compass card, think of your course number as your mark. Remember that in principle, the card is not moving at all, the boat is turning under it. So you turn the boat toward the number if it is off the index. After practicing with the same compass, it becomes automatic.

4.5 Checking a Compass

Hand-bearing compasses never include internal adjustment magnets, and they are typically (except for on metal vessels) not influenced by external disturbances because they are held far from these when used. Generally, it is safe to assume they read properly once the reading location has been checked. Bulkhead or binnacle mounted compasses, however, have more frequent and varied uses in navigation, and these are susceptible to error and must be checked by one of the following methods. If doubts do arise about a hand-bearing compass, it could be tested with these same methods.

Since a compass with deviation error on one heading will have different errors on other headings, the only way to know whether the compass works right is to check it on all headings. In practice, this reduces to checking it on the four cardinal headings, because a typical marine compass on nonsteel vessels that works right on these headings should work right on others.

Before checking for deviation, however, it pays to check the compass card's pivot point. With the boat stable or on land, note the precise compass heading, then briefly place a radio speaker or other magnetic object near the compass to purposefully move the card off its rest position. Then watch its motion as it returns to rest when the disturbance is removed. The card should swing back smoothly, slightly overshooting its original position, and return to where it started from. If it does not, or if its motion is jerky, the pivot jewel is probably worn, and the compass may not be dependable. Expensive compasses can be repaired; inexpensive ones must be replaced.

Next check that the lubber line of the compass is parallel to the boat's centerline. This can usually be done by eye alone to within an accuracy of a few degrees using the axis of the compass housing or its mounting holes as a guide. If the lubber line is skewed 3° off the centerline, the compass will read 3° too high or too low on all headings, depending on the misalignment direction. Although this is generally not a serious problem—the compass can be read to the left or right of the index pin to correct for this—it is still best to mount the compass as straight as possible because the most versatile method of checking a marine compass will not reveal this error. The mounting should be secured solidly so the alignment cannot change underway.

The quickest way to check the steering compass on a small craft is to compare its reading with another compass that is not in doubt. Point the vessel toward north magnetic (000) according to the steering compass, and stand behind the helm with a hand-bearing compass to check the heading of the bow. Then repeat the check with the boat headed 180, 090, and 270. If the hand-bearing compass confirms the steering compass on these headings, the steering compass is probably okay. It is unlikely that the hand-bearing compass will be off. The only things that might affect it are steel in eyeglass frames, a flashlight held too close to it at night, or, possibly, wristwatch batteries.

If you know fairly precisely where you are, another quick method is to read the magnetic bearing to a distant landmark from a chart and then point the boat toward it to see if the boat's compass agrees. But since this requires a prominent landmark (2 or 3 miles off) to be both in view and on the same chart you are on, the method is not always possible.

Closer landmarks can be used if two are in sight that form a line from your perspective. Such lines are called *natural ranges*. They are extremely valuable to piloting because it is easy to tell when you are on the line. You might, for example, steer between two charted rocks, keeping one on the bow and the other on the stern, or steer along the extension of the line between two rocks, which lie ahead or astern of the boat. Then compare the compass heading when on the line to the magnetic bearing between the rocks read from a chart (see Figure 4-10). The same can be done sailing along a breakwater or straight toward a charted street visible from the water. Charted buoys are not dependable for this application because they could be far enough off station to give false range bearings.

When using any of these methods, it is important to compare the compass heading to the charted magnetic bearing headed in both directions, toward the mark (or up the line) and away from the mark (or down the line). If the compass checks out on both directions, it is right on those two headings. If the compass reads high (or low) by the same amount on both directions, then either the lubber line is skewed off the centerline by the difference found, or the charted bearing was read improperly by this amount. In either case, the magnetic environment of the compass is not the problem.

If the compass reads high when headed in one direction and low *by the same amount* when headed in the opposite direction, then the compass has deviation, and the magnetic environment of the compass—or setting of internal adjustment magnets—is likely to be the problem. Check the area around the compass by testing each questionable item

as it is removed. If the compass has internal adjustment magnets, these may be the source of the problem, not the rest of the boat or equipment near it. They should be adjusted to neutral, as explained earlier. If compass errors are found, but they are neither equal nor equal and opposite on reversed headings, then you have a combination of the above problems. Check the lubber-line alignment and the internal magnets, and do the compass checks again.

The above ways to check a compass require a second compass or a chart and special circumstances. When neither of these conditions is met, a compass can still be checked using that fundamental principle of compass errors: they should be equal and opposite on reciprocal headings, as illustrated in Figure 4-7. This method requires no special aids, and it can be at the dock or underway. It is prudent to know how to do it.

To apply this method, pick some reference direction that you can align the boat with, put the boat on that line, and read the compass. It can be a natural range or the direction to a distant landmark—*f*or low star, if all done fairly quickly. After you have done this, swing the boat around, headed the opposite direction on the line. The compass should read exactly 180° different. If it does, the compass is right on both those headings. Next, check it the same way in a direction perpendicular to the one just used. If it also checks on this heading, it is likely to be right on all others. If the toward and away readings are not exactly 180° different, the compass has deviation.

As an example (Figure 4-11), say it reads 340. Turn to head directly away from the landmark and read the compass again. Now suppose it reads 130. If the compass had no error on this heading, it should have read 340 minus 180, which is 160, but it reads 130, so there is deviation error on both headings. The actual error can be found from the equal-and-opposite principle of deviation errors, namely, on opposite headings, the errors should be opposite. This principle implies that the correct magnetic heading away from the mark is always halfway between what you get and what you expect.

In this example you got 130 and expected 160; and halfway between these two is 145. Since 145 is correct and you read 130, the compass reading away from the mark was 15° too low. The equal-and-opposite principle tells us that the reading toward the mark must be 15° too high. When the

...In Depth

12.9 Compass checks with the Sun

Though other aspects are not needed, it is one part of celestial navigation that is valuable on inland waters...

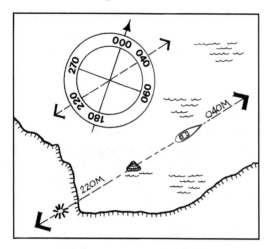

Figure 4-10. *Checking a compass by sailing a natural range. The compass error is the difference between the compass reading when on the range and the proper magnetic direction between the rock and peak, which is measured from the magnetic scale of the compass rose.*

compass read 340, the correct reading was 325. All compass readings on headings near 340 will be too high by 15°. On different headings, however, the error will be different, and the test must be repeated.

Taking the back bearing on some vessels will call for some ingenuity. Choose any structure that is parallel to the centerline for an accurate orientation, such as the edge of a cabin top, boom tied to the centerline, etc.

When traveling in a convoy with other cruisers, or buddy boating around somewhere, it might be of interest to compare compass readings at some point. It can also be useful to note your compass heading at some location near your marina and to keep an eye on it each time you use the boat.

Figure 4-11. *Checking a compass on reciprocal headings. Point toward a distant object or along a range and read the compass; then point away from the object and read the compass. The compass error is half the difference between the compass reading on the away course and the reciprocal of the compass reading on the toward course, or vice versa. No chart is required for this method.*

One might think that a compass could be checked using the electronically determined course over ground from a GPS. To do this, however, you must be certain that wind or current is not causing the boat to move in a direction different from its actual heading, which is not easy to discern without careful study, especially since you cannot use the compass in this case to help the evaluation.

A typical marine compass is a rugged and reliable instrument. If it worked right once, and nothing near the compass has changed, it is safe to assume it still works right. When questions arise about where you are or what you see, believe your compass. It should be the last thing to blame for discrepancies in navigation.

4.6 Compass Conversions

We have stressed that it is not often that one needs to make conversions between compass heading and true headings using variation and deviation, but it does come up, and any course on navigation should cover the subject, so we do. Certainly any navigation test would have questions on the topic.

Our own preference is just use "correcting add east" as explained, and let it go at that, but this may not be best for all navigators. A popular approach to this type of problem is to use a table structure shown in Table 4-1 and just fill in the known data and compute the unknown with specific guidelines.

Table 4-1. Compass Conversion Form		
TRUE heading		
Variation E or W		↑ +E, -W
MAGNETIC heading		
Deviation E or W		↓ -E, + W
COMPASS heading		

One way to remember the order of the table from bottom to top with first letters is this well known saying from navigation schools: Can Dead Men Vote Twice? At Elections (for Add East, going up). To use the table, follow the procedure below.

(1) Fill in the known values, marking Dev or Var E or W as appropriate. Then choose from below for what you want to find, and fill in the table as you compute it.

(2) To find Var, you need to know T and M:

If T > M, Var = T - M and it is East

If M > T, Var = M - T and it is West

(3) To find Dev, you need to know M and C:

    If M > C, Dev = M - C and it is East

    If C > M, Dev = C - M and it is West

(4) To find True, you need to know Magnetic and Variation:

    True = Magnetic + Var E

    True = Magnetic - Var W

(5) To find Magnetic from True, you need to know True and Variation:

    Magnetic = True - Var E

    Magnetic = True + Var W

(6) To find Magnetic from Compass, you need to know Compass and Deviation

    Magnetic = Compass + Dev E

    Magnetic = Compass - Dev W

(7) To find Compass from Magnetic, you need to know Magnetic and Deviation

    Compass = Magnetic - Dev E

    Compass = Magnetic + Dev W

In short, the difference between True and Magnetic is Variation, and the difference between Compass and Magnetic is Deviation. The correcting direction is compass to magnetic, and magnetic to true, and in the correcting direction, the rule is add East for the variation and deviation.

Here are some practice problems. After doing a few, the use of the table will become more automatic. Answers shown in parenthesis.

(1) True = 235, Mag = 220, what is Variation?

TRUE heading	235 T	
Variation E or W	(15 E)	↑ +E, -W
MAGNETIC heading	220 M	
Deviation E or W		↓ -E, + W
COMPASS heading		

(2) Mag = 135, Variation = 20 E, what is True?

TRUE heading	(155 T)	
Variation E or W	20 E	↑ +E, -W
MAGNETIC heading	135 M	
Deviation E or W		↓ -E, + W
COMPASS heading		

(3) True = 200, Var=10 W, what is Magnetic?

TRUE heading	200 T	
Variation E or W	10 W	↑ +E, -W
MAGNETIC heading	(210 M)	
Deviation E or W		↓ -E, + W
COMPASS heading		

(4) Compass = 355, Mag = 005, what is Deviation?

TRUE heading		
Variation E or W		↑ +E, -W
MAGNETIC heading	005 M	
Deviation E or W	(10 E)	↓ -E, + W
COMPASS heading	355 C	

On this one and others, you can ask yourself, how did I get from 355 to 005? Answer: I added 10, which is going up, which means the label is E.

4.7 Deviation Tables and Interpolation

A list of compass deviations for various compass headings is called a deviation table. This is where you record your study of the compass errors, or you pay a professional to swing the compass and provide you with a table. (The phrases "swinging the compass" and "swinging ship" to adjust the compass mean the same thing.)

A sample is shown in Table 4-2. The example shows typical values we might measure on a nonsteel vessel, but a professional adjuster would typically have the errors removed to a much lower level than this. For steel vessels, the pattern would likely be more complex. The in-depth *Handbook of Magnetic Compass Adjustment* from the National Geospatial-Intelligence Agency (NGA) is online (starpath.com/navpubs).

If you end up using a deviation table then you will inevitably get some practice with interpolation. For example, if the wind has me steering 030 C, then I can tell at a glance that my magnetic course is 026 M. But if that compass course were 050 C, then I need to make some estimates, that is, guess the correction is about 3 W, or work out the proper interpolation.

This is how we go about it: we see that going from 30 to 60 the deviation drops from 4.0 to 2.5, so it is changing at a rate of 1.5° deviation for each 30° of heading, so for a 20° change in heading the deviation changes by (1.5/30) × 20 = 1°. Applying this change to the 30° value we get 4.0 - 1.0, which is 3.0, so our guess was pretty good.

Likewise, if you decide from chart work that you need to steer a course of 200 M, then looking at the table you see the correction would be about 4 E, so you would steer 196 C

—double checking in your mind with "correcting add east" that 196 + 4 = 200 so you applied the correction properly.

Alternatively, there are slick mobile apps that do all kinds of interpolations to aid the navigator. An example is shown in Figure 4-12. These tools can be very handy for more complex interpolations, which come up more frequently in celestial navigation and marine weather.

Table 4-2. Deviation Table		
Compass Heading	*Deviation*	*Magnetic Heading*
000	5.0 W	355
030	4.0 W	026
060	2.5 W	057.5
090	0.0	090
120	2.5 E	122.5
150	4.0 E	154
180	5.0 E	185
210	4.0 E	214
240	2.5 E	242.5
270	0.0	270
300	2.5 W	297.5
330	4.5 W	325.5
360	5.0 W	355

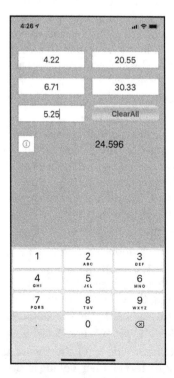

Figure 4-12. *A free mobile app called Interpolator that does double and triple interpolation. There are many options.*

Chapter 4 Glossary

compass deviation. The angular difference between compass north and magnetic north, labeled E if compass north is to the right of magnetic north, and west otherwise.

deviation table. A list of compass deviations as a function of either compass or magnetic headings, or both.

electronic compass. An electronic device that measures the direction of the horizontal component of the earth's magnetic field by direct measurement of the field strength. Although no magnetic needles are involved as with conventional compasses, it is still a magnetic compass and susceptible to magnetic interference just as a traditional compass is. Sometimes called a fluxgate compass.

heading sensor. An electronic compass used in radar, ECS, and autopilots.

interpolation. The process of finding an intermediate value using proportions of known values.

lubber line. The straight line between the compass card axis and the index line used to read the compass.

magnetic north. Direction of the horizontal component of the earth's magnetic field at any location.

natural range. The straight line between any two landmarks seen on the horizon.

navigational range. Two lights or signs at different elevations positioned to form a range when brought into alignment. The one nearest the observer is the front mark and the one farthest from the observer is the rear mark. The front mark is at a lower elevation than the rear mark. These ranges are usually established in areas where it is dangerous to be off of the range when entering or leaving a harbor or proceeding along a waterway.

range. (1) Another name for distance in various contexts. (2) The alignment of any two objects for the purpose of navigation. See navigational range and natural range. Also called a transit.

Small Angle Rule. The approximation that the ratio of the sides of a 6° right triangle is 10:1, along with the further approximation that this scales as 3° is 20:1 and 12° is 5:1.

steering compass. The main ship's compass, located at the helm, used to steer the vessel.

swinging ship. The process of driving a vessel slowly in a complete circle in order to check the compass on the cardinal and inter-cardinal headings.

CHAPTER 5
DEAD RECKONING

5.1 Speed, Time, and Distance

Navigation is called both art and science. To the extent that this is true, it applies more to typical small craft than to ships. Science is learned through principles; art is learned through practice. The art part of small craft navigation is knowing how your vessel will respond in various circumstances—knowing your limits and strengths.

The rest is, for the most part, science. Knowledge of your ultimate boat speed in various conditions is fundamental to safe and efficient navigation because it is required to predict the time it will take to cover a given distance (the passage time) or to predict how far you might go in a given time period (such as from now until sunset or high water). Predicting and then checking passage times along your route is the only way to monitor progress and learn about speed made good in various conditions.

Deciding whether to turn back or carry on along some particular route is a crucial decision that can arise in various circumstances of small craft navigation. Regardless of other factors (weather, fatigue, or the time of tides or sunset) that might determine the final decision, the predicted passage times in both directions remain essential to the choice. If the question of turning back came up at all—say if something went wrong—more wrong predictions at this point could make things worse.

Recall from Chapter 1 that dead reckoning means navigation without the aid of landmarks. You determine where you are or where you are going to be purely from a compass course and distance, using an anticipated speed and time underway. The basic problems in dead reckoning are to find speed when time and distance are known, to find time when speed and distance are known, or to find distance when speed and time are known. These problems can be solved with actual calculations or with tricks. The calculations are most easily done using formulas adapted for specific recurring questions. The adaptations mostly relate to keeping the hours, minutes, and seconds part of the time in order.

One of the first questions that arise when planning a trip is how long it will take. The distance of the trip is read from a chart, the anticipated speed of the boat can be estimated from the several factors discussed below, and from these two, the passage time can be calculated:

$$\text{Time (hours)} = \frac{\text{Distance (nautical miles)}}{\text{Speed (knots)}}$$

In marine navigation, speeds are always expressed in knots (1 kt equals 1 nmi per hour), and distances used in dead reckoning are always expressed in nautical miles. (The units are often abbreviated to "miles" in conversation and text. In this book, "miles" means nautical miles unless otherwise specified.) If you are sailing at 3 kts, a trip of 13 miles should take 13 divided by 3, or 4.3 hours. If doubts arise about the application of the formula or the results, they can be quickly checked by multiplication, usually without pencil and paper:

Distance (nautical miles) = Speed (knots) × Time (hours)

Checking the last example: 3 miles per hour times 4 hours is 12 miles, so 4.3 hours is probably right for 13 miles. Both formulas derive from the definition of speed:

$$\text{Speed (knots)} = \frac{\text{Distance (nautical miles)}}{\text{Time (hours)}}$$

If you traveled 8 miles in 2 hours, your average speed was 4 kts.

Actual speed along any route depends on how fast you are traveling through the water (boat speed), and how fast the water itself is moving (current speed). Boat speed depends on engine or wind power and "wave power"; current speed depends on the location and time of day. The simple question of how long it will take is not always so simple to answer. Many factors affect how fast you will proceed across the chart—called your *speed over ground (SOG)* at any one moment, or *speed made good (SMG)*, when averaged over some time period. When under sail, we must also account for tacking angles upwind and jibing angles downwind.

One approach to planning is to assume a boat speed typical of your vessel and use that for all cases. Six knots might be a typical speed for auxiliary sailing vessels and some trawlers. At 6 kts, each mile takes 10 minutes. A 5-mile run would take 50 minutes; a half mile run would take 5 minutes.

But any vessel that can average 6 kts also can likely make 7 kts for some period of time, or slow to 4 kts in some sea conditions. Boat speed can sometimes vary significantly over a single run, and it takes practice to estimate what your average speed might be in various conditions. Granted, it is not often that speed must be known precisely, but these are usually the same times that navigation itself is not a concern. When you must navigate, it is often important to know your speed. And in some circumstances, 6 kts, plus or minus 1 kt, is not adequate.

Knowing your potential speed is not merely an academic concern. One might get into trouble by overestimating progress against headwinds in a seaway. Arriving much later than planned at a coastal inlet anchorage, one might find breaking waves at the entrance since the favorable tide was missed.

But safety is not the only motivation for keeping track of speed. If navigation is to be a hobby—an attitude that ultimately does make boating safer—then knowing boat speed in various conditions is just part of the sport. Powerboaters who do predicted-log racing provide a good analogy. Log racing is pure navigation. The winner is the one who has done the best job of predicting the time required for each leg of the course, accounting for current, wind, and boat speed. They use compasses and knowledge of their boats, but no other navigation instruments. Predicted-log racers receive reduced insurance rates because they have fewer accidents than most boaters. Their hobby makes them safer boaters.

5.2 Finding Boat Speed

Well... the first solution might be to look at the knotmeter! *Knotmeter* is the name of the speedometer on a boat. Or, with no knotmeter, take a look at the GPS. It will tell you your speed over ground (SOG), which is often what you want to know because it accounts for current and leeway as well as knotmeter speed.

That is obvious, and indeed what we would normally do in most circumstances. The goal at hand, however, is to temporarily assume that these aids are not available. Or put another way, we go over now how we might check them with more fundamental measurements.

To learn your boat speed, begin by choosing a place out of the wind and current. From a chart, figure the length of a straight run between two landmarks, approximately one half mile apart or so, then use a stopwatch to measure the time it takes to travel the distance at a steady speed. Do this several times, in both directions, noting the wind direction, if any, then average the times.

Suppose the run was 0.45 mile long, and it took an average of 4 minutes and 20 seconds. Convert this time to decimal minutes by converting the seconds to minutes: 20 seconds = (20/60) minute = 0.33 minute. The average time was 4.33 minutes. Then calculate the boat speed from the following variation of the earlier speed formula, adapted to time in minutes:

$$\text{Speed (knots)} = \frac{\text{Distance (nautical miles)} \times 60}{\text{Time (minutes)}}$$

$$S = \frac{0.45 \times 60}{4.33} = 6.24 \text{ kts}$$

This speed is your benchmark to work from. Record it in a notebook with other details, such as the sails or rpm used, wind and water conditions, what the actual knotmeter read, etc. Then do this again, whenever the chance arises, to practice the procedure and get further information about your knotmeter.

To prepare for speed checks, measure the distances between prominent points along an intended route, figure the times each leg should take at various speeds (explained below), and note these times on the chart next to each course line. With this preparation, a common wristwatch or cell-phone timer is all it takes to monitor speed.

When traveling with the current, the current speed adds to your boat speed (see Figure 5-1). Traveling at 6 kts

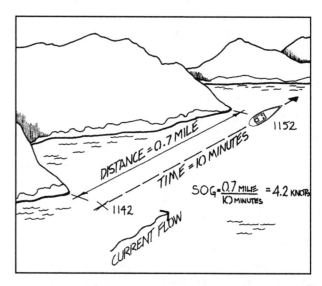

Figure 5-1. *Measuring speed over ground (SOG) by timing the run along a known distance. If the answer is faster than you know you are sailing, you are in favorable current, and vice versa.*

...In Depth

12.27 The Magic Circle

We do not need much math for typical small craft navigation, but speed, time, distance computation is one we do need. Some readers may find this mnemonic trick useful—as many seagoing captains have done so over the years...

with a favorable current of 1 kt, you will progress along the shoreline (speed over ground) at a rate of 7 kts. Sailing, for example, at a knotmeter speed of 4 kts against a current of 3 kts, you will be creeping along at 1 kt, while still heeled over a bit and the sails full. Current is clearly a major concern in a case like that. With a GPS, you can accurately determine the distance between any two points, which might serve as a convenient place to check knotmeter speed.

Another way to check speed without a chart or underway well off of landmarks is to use a long, light line with a float attached. Measure off at least 50 ft of line, tie one end to the boat and the other to a float (i.e., a small plastic bottle, partially filled with water). Without a tape measure, it is convenient to use the boat length on deck. Or learn the span of your outstretched arms, fingertip to fingertip. This is the original fathom measurement used by fishermen to measure line lengths, but individual spans will vary from exactly 6 ft (when I draw out 10 fathoms this way, I get 56 ft). Toss the faked-out line and marker forward of the boat, drive toward it, start timing when you pass the float, and stop timing when you first tow the float.

Boat speed in knots is then 0.6 times the line length (in feet) divided by the number of seconds it took to extend the line. The simple formula derives from the approximation that 1 kt is 100 ft per minute, which is equivalent to calling a nautical mile exactly 6,000 ft. If the line is 50 ft long and it takes 10 seconds to tow it, your boat speed is 0.6 times 50 divided by 10, or 3.0 kts. Individual short runs are not as accurate as those measured for longer runs, but the average of several provides a useful gauge of speed. This trick takes practice. The first attempt can put more knots into your line than you can get out of your boat.

A boat's log is the same as a car's odometer. It measures miles traveled through the water. It is usually the same instrument as the knotmeter. The spinning paddlewheel puts out a magnetic pulse at each turn. The rate of the pulses is converted to speed, and the sum of the pulses is converted to distance traveled. Usually, the difference between two log readings yields a more accurate measure of the distance run, compared with multiplying the time difference between the two points by an estimated average speed.

5.3 The Effect of Wind on Boat Speed

For power as well as sailing vessels, wind speed and direction sometimes affect boat speed—or at least progress in some desired direction—more than current does. Even modest winds of 15 kts or so can affect progress of low-powered vessels and have a significant effect on arrival time over a long run. Wind exerts force on all exposed areas of the boat, and this force increases as the square of the wind speed. Assuming a 10-kt wind exerts a force of approximately one pound on a two-square-foot area of the boat, this force would double to two pounds if the wind increased to just 14 kts (see Figure 5-2).

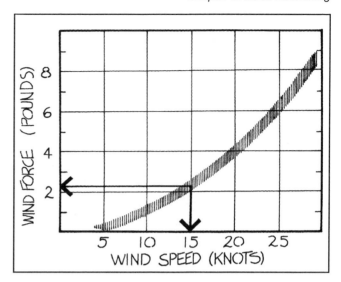

Figure 5-2. *The force of the wind on two square-feet of flat surface perpendicular to the wind.*

When moving at 6 kts into a 14-kt wind, the apparent wind on the boat increases to 20 kts. With 20 kts of wind on the boat, its force on this two-square-foot area increases to four pounds. In other words, with very little changing, the actual force on the boat has increased by a factor of four.

To make guidelines on expected effects of wind requires guidelines on judging wind speed, assuming wind speed instrumentation is not available for measuring it. Actual wave heights do not help with this, even if they could be estimated accurately, which is unlikely. It is better to use the general appearance of the water as described by the Beaufort Wind Force Scale in Figure 5-3. Wind speed can be read from the water this way to within a few knots, after practicing with an anemometer to check the guesses.

A wind speed of approximately 10 kts is the easiest to read from the water, which is fortunate because this is the wind speed at which low-powered craft must start considering the wind's effect on progress. With no current flowing, the appearance of the first few isolated whitecaps means the wind speed is approximately 10 kts. At this wind speed, search the surface to detect these few whitecaps that look like scattered bits of popcorn on the water. Current flowing into the wind steepens the waves, so they break

...In Depth

12.10 Log and knotmeter calibrations

Your DR is only as good as your speed reference. Here we learn how to determine and correct for any error in our knotmeter or log, using both conventional and electronic means...

Beau-fort number	Wind speed		Estimating wind speed	
	Knots	Seaman's term	Effects observed at sea	Effects observed on land
0	Under 1	Calm	Sea like a mirror.	Calm; smoke rises vertically.
1	1-3	Light air	Ripples with appearance of scales; no foam crests.	Smoke drift indicates wind direction; vanes do not move.
2	4-6	Light breeze	Small wavelets; crests of glassy appearance, not breaking.	Wind felt on face; leaves rustle; vanes do not move.
3	7-10	Gentle breeze	Large wavelets; crests begin to break; scattered whitecaps.	Leaves, small twigs in constant motion; light flags extended.
4	11-16	Moderate breeze	Small waves, becoming larger; numerous whitecaps.	Dust, leaves and loose paper raised up; small branches move.
5	17-21	Fresh breeze	Moderate waves, taking longer form; many whitecaps; some spray.	Small trees in leaf begin to sway.
6	22-27	Strong breeze	Larger waves forming; whitecaps everywhere; more spray.	Larger branches of trees in motion; whistling heard in wires.
7	28-33	Moderate gale	Sea heaps up; white foam from breaking waves begins to be blown in streaks.	Whole trees in motion; resistance felt in walking against wind.
8	34-40	Fresh gale	Moderately high waves of greater length; edges of crests begin to break into spindrift; foam is blown in well-marked streaks.	Twigs and small branches broken off trees; progress generally impeded.
9	41-47	Strong gale	High waves; sea begins to roll; dense streaks of foam; spray may reduce visibility.	Slight structural damage occurs; slate blown from roof.
10	48-55	Whole gale	Very high waves with overhanging crests; sea takes white appearance as foam is blown in very dense streaks; rolling is heavy and visibility reduced.	Seldom experienced on land; considerable structural damage occurs.

Figure 5-3. *The Beaufort Wind Scale, which relates sea state to wind speed.*

making whitecaps more easily. With a current of 1 or 2 kts flowing into the wind, the "popcorn" will appear sooner, at approximately 8 kts of wind. Current flowing with the wind stretches out the waves, so the wind speed must build to 12 kts or so before any specks of white are seen.

At an honest, sustained wind of 20 kts, the popcorn is the first thing that catches the eye. Individual whitecaps are bigger, and there are many more of them. During the first few hours of wind, before the seas build, the water looks like a speckled quilt of whitecaps, but there is little if any spray. Nearby wave surfaces, however, will show prominent streaks of cat's paws (ripples that look like fish scales), which show very clearly the instantaneous wind direction. Conspicuous spray blown off the crests of whitecaps and streaks of foam are the signs of 30 kts of wind. This, however, is very strong wind, indeed. There are not many places close to land where such winds last more than an hour, and even in these places, if this wind persists for over an hour it must be associated with a large weather system that would

have been well forecasted. A sustained wind of 30 kts will likely contain gusts to 40 kts or more.

To appreciate the forces involved, imagine holding a two-square-foot board (17 inches on a side) out of a car window when traveling at 40 miles per hour (35 kts).

Just for reference, at the low end of the spectrum, 4 kts of wind is the threshold for feeling the wind on your face or neck. This is not a particularly significant observation for powerboaters, but it is a fairly accurate measure that might be of interest to sailors. Weaker winds can be seen to move smoke but are not felt. If you can definitely feel the wind on your face, it is more than 4 kts.

For power-driven vessels, not directly propelled by the wind, one might make a rough estimate that the amount of speed to be gained when headed downwind is about the same as would be lost when headed upwind in the same wind. Headed into the wind, you have higher resistance due to increased apparent wind, but when going downwind, although your apparent wind is reduced, the extra speed you get from surfing down the waves usually more than compensates for the loss of push.

5.4 Figuring Passage Times

To figure the length of a trip, first estimate boat speed for each leg of the trip, taking into account wind and waves. Your average speed made good (SMG) in current can then be figured from the sum of your average boat speed and the current speed along each leg of the route that has different current.

Most tidal currents are changing with time, which complicates the reckoning. For realistic estimates of arrival times, this changing current must be accounted for.

For steady or insignificant current, progress is easier to determine. When the distances are known, but the use of a chart is not convenient, passage times are most easily determined by thinking of your average speed in minutes per mile. The conversion from knots to minutes per mile can be made by inverting the definition of speed, and replacing 1 hour with 60 minutes. This reduces to simply dividing 60 by your boat speed, as shown in Table 5-1.

...In Depth

12.6 Tacking DR and Progress to Weather

Making progress into the wind raises special concerns for both power and sailing vessels. Here we review guidelines and procedures that can help in strong wind...

| Table 5-1. Convert boat speed to minutes per mile ||
Speed in knots	Time/distance
1	1 min/100 ft
3	20 min/mi
5	12 min/mi
6	10 min/mi
7.5	8 min/mi
10	6 min/mi
12	5 min/mi
15	4 min/mi

Note that the easy ones to remember are those that divide into 60 exactly. If a speed of 7.5 kts is anticipated, then a 3-mile run should take 3 × 8, or 24 minutes.

Unless you are unusually adept at division in your head, problems such as figuring the time at 8.3 kts for a twenty-seven-mile run are much easier to solve with a chart. With a chart showing the full route in front of you, it is not even necessary to measure the distance first. Just set dividers (or fingers) to a separation in nautical miles equal to the boat speed in knots, using the chart's distance or latitude scale, and count the steps it takes to walk the route across the chart. With the dividers set this way, each step is 1 hour. Fractional steps at the end can be estimated.

The itinerary of a trip can be recorded on the chart by noting the times you expect to be at various waypoints along the route. Then a glance at a watch and a quick note on the chart of the actual time at the point is all that it takes to monitor progress. Average speeds can be figured later on to help plan the next day or the next trip.

Basic dead reckoning navigation from speed, time, distance, and compass course is fundamental to the navigation of all vessels, from kayaks to ships. And the reason is the same for kayaks and for ships: sooner or later, it may be all there is to go by. According to Murphy's law, this will happen just when good navigation is most important. Figure 5-4 shows a course line and the resulting position figured from dead reckoning as it might be recorded on a chart during a long run in the fog. Examples of applying and analyzing dead reckoning come up throughout the book.

5.5 Terminology and Logbook Procedures

Estimating speeds and arrival times is done before and during the voyage. Generally the term dead reckoning is reserved for the analysis done underway. The planning phase would simply be called route planning with associated ETAs (estimated times of arrival).

Once underway, some mariners make a distinction between a *dead reckoning position* (DR) and an *estimated position* (EP). To these navigators, the DR position should include just your log and compass data—assuming the log

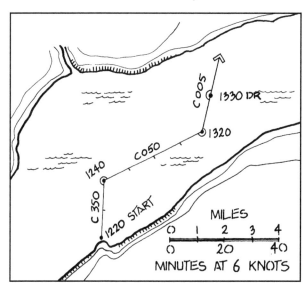

Figure 5-4. *A simple dead reckoning (DR) plot showing a DR position at 1330. Knowing your average speed in minutes per mile, your position can be estimated by tracing out your path on the chart as shown. This plot assumes there is no current present.*

and compass were corrected as needed before plotting the DR position. That is, from your last known true position, you draw a line on the chart in the direction sailed (recorded in the logbook) and mark off the distance sailed along that line (also from the logbook). Where you end up on the chart is your DR position, with no further corrections to be made.

In this line of thinking, you then take everything else into account that might have caused your actual position to be different from that of log and compass alone. The "everything else" would include, primarily, current, leeway and helm bias in a seaway. Once these are applied to the DR position, you end up with a new position called the estimated position.

In this parlance, we could ask for both the DR position and an EP, which would typically be somewhat different. The EP would then be your best estimate of where you are at the time, taking everything you know into account— short of an actual fix from piloting, because DR or EP is always based on information obtained from within your vessel only.

...In Depth

12.11 When Will We Get There?

The formulas for Time, Speed, and Distance are the foundation underlying all DR calculation, but there is often much more that must go into the reckoning of realistic arrival times...

#	Date	Time	Log	Course	Speed	Lat/Lon	AWA	AWS	Baro	Comments
1										
2										
3										
4										

Figure 5-5. *Sample logbook layout for sail or power. AWA and AWS are apparent wind angle and speed. The column size and selection will vary. This might fit on letter paper laid out in landscape, or spread over two facing pages on portrait orientation. It is the latter layout that calls for a row #; otherwise that is not needed. Log is either from the knotmeter log or from a GPS (these are not the same). Course is compass course; speed can be either knotmeter speed or SOG (again, not the same). Course is best kept as the one steered, and perhaps add another column for COG. Comments can include a description of your location, such as 1.5 mile west of Rocky Pt. The goal is to make a log entry anytime anything changes, and if nothing changes, make an entry every hour or so. Under sail, we have found that a column for the tack or jibe we are on is also helpful. Baro is barometer reading in millibars.*

I state this concept up front for the sake of completeness, because it is treated in many navigation texts as the standard to follow. However, my own experience in navigation and in teaching navigation shows that this concept of an EP as separate from a more generalized definition of DR is not a productive concept. We can, for example, simply define the DR position as our best estimate of where we are at any time, taking everything we know into account. In which case, the DR and the EP are the same.

It does not make much difference if we are just plotting a compass course, marking off a distance, and then correcting it for current and leeway. You can call the final point an EP or a DR. But once you start comparing your DR track on the chart with actual piloting measurements, the terminology starts to interfere, because these same standard references will now have new definitions of "estimated position," many of which originate with navy ship navigation that in this aspect is different from and not appropriate to small craft navigation.

Our recommendation is to not worry about this distinction, and when we think of, or record, or discuss our DR position, we mean by that our best estimate of where we are, taking everything we know into account. We will be able to get by quite nicely without ever using the term estimated position.

In this regard, it might be interesting to note that the term and concept of dead reckoning dates to the early 17th century (possibly earlier), and throughout the 17th, 18th, and 19th century the term was defined to include *all* information known to the navigator, specifically including current, leeway, and helmsmanship. It was only in the late 1930s that the term started to be used as compass and log only, and that was done to accommodate the then new navy innovation of a DR Machine, which could automatically compute a position based on log and compass alone. Since many of the standard navigation texts evolved from navy texts, that usage found its way off the ships and onto boats.

When plotting your DR track from logbook data, you have the choice of making any called for corrections before plotting, or plot log and compass directly and then correct the final position. The best choice depends on the circumstances. With just one straight leg to plot when steering 050, for example, knowing you have a leeway of 5°, you might as well plot the line at 055 and be done, rather than plot one line, then rotate it and plot another. You can indicate that you have made this correction by using a triangle or square in place of the normal half-circle for log and compass plot.

With multiple legs to plot and just current to correct for, it is easiest to just plot the uncorrected DR track and then move the final position by the amount your position was shifted by the current during that time, as shown in Figure 5-6. The US convention for that mark is a small square. In the UK, it is a triangle.

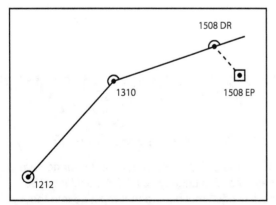

Figure 5-6. *Conventional notation for marking a corrected DR position. Alternatively, you could estimate the CMG for each leg and plot that using the square symbol rather than half-circle.*

...In Depth

12.3 Dead Reckoning Procedures and Uncertainties

It remains the most important goal of navigation—not just doing it, but knowing how well you are doing it...

All DR and EP navigation (however it is done) has no long-lasting value if we do not record it somewhere, and that somewhere is the logbook. As a rule, we should make a logbook entry every time anything significant has changed during the voyage. Even if nothing changes, we should make an entry every couple of hours. Logbook style will always remain a personal matter; no two navigators will want the same format or the same information. There are certain basics, however, that most would want to keep track of, which might be different for power and sailing vessels.

In our own navigation, local or ocean, we generally use a simple spreadsheet format, as shown in Figure 5-5. A printable pdf of this form can be downloaded from star-path.com/navbook for those who might like this style.

Chapter 5 Glossary

60 D Street. Another nickname for the "magic circle" way to remember speed, time, distance formulas.

apparent wind. The wind resulting from the vector addition of the true wind and the wind created by a vessel's motion.

Beaufort Wind Force Scale. A system for relating the appearance of the sea state with the speed of the wind creating it.

calibration. The process of comparing the result of one instrument with one that is known to be accurate or with more fundamental measurements of the same quantity.

cat's paws. Small scallop-shaped ripples on the surfaces of waves. These are capillary waves that build and fade instantly with changes in the wind.

downwind. From a line drawn perpendicular to the true wind direction, this is anywhere on the side toward which the wind is blowing.

estimated position (EP). Your best reckoning of your vessel's position without using any information from outside of the vessel. If plotted with corrections to log and compass, a square (US) or triangle (UK) is used, in place of the half-circle.

jibe. A vessel maneuver that brings the wind from one side of the boat to the other with the stern crossing the wind direction. See tack.

leeway. How much a vessel slips to leeward due to the force of the wind.

magic circle. The nickname for a mnemonic device for recalling the equations for speed, time, and distance computations.

Murphy's Law. The adage that "Anything that can go wrong, will go wrong."

popcorn. A nickname for small white caps.

predicted-log racing. The sport of predicting the ETAs at various check points along a specified race course route and then traveling the route without clock or electronic navigation aids to see who does the best job in making good their predictions. See predictedlog.org.

ripples. In sea state terminology, the same as cat's paws.

sea state. The combination of wind waves and swells.

speed made good (SMG). The average speed from start to finish between any two points on the chart found by dividing the direct distance between them by the time it took to get from one to the other, regardless of route followed.

speed over ground (SOG). An instantaneous SMG over a period of seconds derived by the GPS.

swells. Long, wide uniform waves created by distant storms.

tack. (1) A vessel maneuver that brings the wind from one side of the boat to the other with the bow crossing the wind direction. See jibe. (2) A point of sail, being either starboard tack, with wind on the starboard side of the boat, or port tack, having the wind on the port side.

true wind. The wind direction and speed relative to the fixed earth.

upwind. From a line drawn perpendicular to the true wind direction, this is anywhere on the side from which the wind is coming.

waves. Undulatory motion of the sea surface created by the wind and influenced by water depth and currents—best distinguished as wind waves, swells, or ripples.

wind waves. Waves created by the present wind. They have a statistical distribution of heights, lengths, and speeds depending on the wind speed, duration, and fetch

white caps. White foam seen at the top of breaking waves.

CHAPTER 6

PILOTING

6.1 Introduction

It is not often that a navigator must resort to pure dead reckoning for navigation, as it is not common to sail without landmarks in sight. But some degree of dead reckoning enters into all navigation, even with landmarks in sight. The simple act of figuring you should be halfway across a 5-mile-wide bay in 25 minutes when motoring at 6 kts is dead reckoning (recall 6 kts = 10 minutes per mile, times 2.5 nmi = 25 minutes). The navigation becomes piloting once you notice that after 25 minutes you are not halfway across, but closer to one side than the other.

It is also fortunate that pure dead reckoning is not often required, because it provides only a deduced position, not a true position fix as piloting does. Dead reckoning can be wrong. If you assume you are making good 6.5 kts but are in fact progressing at 7.0 kts, then the dead reckoning position goes wrong by 0.5 nmi each hour. In 2 hours, you would be 1 nmi farther along your route than figured from dead reckoning alone. This is where piloting comes in. To know where you truly are you must take a position fix using some piloting method. Most small craft navigation underway is done by frequent position checks from landmarks (or from the GPS!) with very little actual dead reckoning.

It is usually a surprise to all boaters when they first discover how rapidly surroundings become unfamiliar on the water. Just turning the first corner away from a bay you have sailed in for years is all it takes. Every corner you round provides new horizons. It is not like on land, where streets provide some continuity for orientation into strange surroundings. Looking back after sailing around a corner shows what to look for on the return, but the back view is just another new perspective on where you have been. It helps little to tell where you are at the time. Most shoreline terrain in a given area is similar. It is difficult to tell a bump in the shoreline from a major headland. You might think you are halfway across a bay, when only halfway to the bump.

Practice in chart reading helps with the identification of shoreline terrain, but even so, keeping track of position in unfamiliar waters is rarely a casual matter and certainly never becomes instinctive. Since a sailor cannot see around corners or bumps on the shoreline, the lay of the land must be judged from the perspective of a bug on an imaginary chart that has all the printed shoreside elevation contours raised to the proper scale as discussed under Terrain and Perspective in Chapter 2. But even this fails when the chart in use does not have adequate elevation contours to identify the curves and hills and headlands seen from the water. Furthermore, close to shore, the shape of nearby terrain is not apparent, and the shape that is seen farther off is often that of the treetops and not the land.

Things only get worse if you postpone the task and let your position become more uncertain. Without knowing where you are on the chart, it is often impossible to make useful judgments of what should be seen from an approximate position. Consequently, good navigation into unfamiliar waters, as when first rounding a corner, must be done with frequent reference to the chart—at least until you are quite convinced of what you see and where you are.

Identifying what you see does not tell where you are. Scenery must be viewed not with a sightseer's eye but with a navigator's eye. This type of looking—to see where you are—is called piloting. On clear days on inland waters there are many things to see, and piloting is easy. But when only one light shines through the fog or only one point or one peak can be identified on the horizon, piloting is more challenging, and only those who have practiced navigation will know where they are. A good navigator should be prepared to use whatever can be seen to find position. Piloting by natural ranges and compass bearings is fundamental to navigation and will be used many times on any trip. Other methods are crucial only in special circumstances; they can rest deeper in the navigator's bag of tricks.

Needless to say, we are talking here of position navigation without GPS. An obvious value of GPS is its ability to tell your position to within a few yards from a simple glance at the dial. A remarkable convenience, but also one that you could easily get used to and eventually take for granted. Once this happens, and then you lose power or it fails for some other reason, you will be glad to have learned these fundamentals of the traditional methods of piloting.

...In Depth

12.28 Limitations of GPS

It is certainly a valuable aid, but not one we want to depend upon entirely, for multiple reasons...

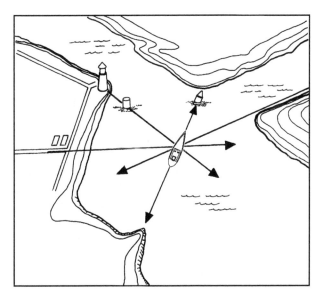

Figure 6-1. *Samples of natural ranges. Any two charted objects that appear in line from your perspective can be used to locate a line of position on the chart.*

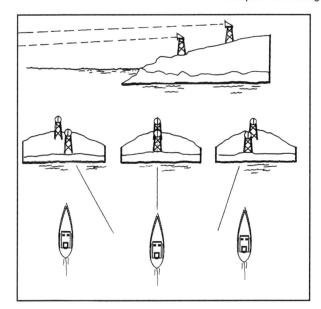

Figure 6-2. *A navigational range. Larger vessels will follow these ranges closely in confined waterways.*

6.2 Natural Ranges

If you are sailing along shore and notice that you happen to be directly in line with a long, straight street running down toward the shoreline, then you have done some very precise piloting as soon as you can identify that street on the chart. The street is a straight line on the land part of the chart that can be extended with a pencil onto the water part. If you are looking straight up the street, you must be located somewhere on that extended line. The extended line on the chart is called a *range*, and the fact that you know you are somewhere on that line makes that range a *line of position*, or LOP. It is called a line of position because you know you are on the line, but you do not know where you are on the line. A boat anywhere on that line would have the same perspective on the street, but only those who are on that line would get the runway view, straight up the street. Viewing in that direction from other locations, you might not see the street at all, or would see it partly obscured.

Range is a general term, meaning the alignment of any two objects, or the ends of one long feature such as a street or breakwater, used to find a LOP. In British usage, ranges are called *transits*, but this latter term is reserved for land navigation in American parlance. A range is only one example of a LOP; a compass-bearing line is another. But a range is an especially valuable LOP, because it is quick to take and easy to locate and plot on the chart, besides being more accurate than a typical compass-bearing line. A LOP from a range requires no instruments other than eyes, and eyes are very precise instruments for judging the alignment of two objects.

A range can be found from the alignment of two objects in front of the boat or in back of the boat, or from objects on opposite sides or opposite ends of the boat. (Examples are shown in Figure 6-1.) For objects on opposite sides of

the boat, it is best to use some guide for a sighting line to determine precisely when you cross the range. Just extending your arms out to either side pointing at each object will be better than just turning and looking at the objects. This is especially important when crossing a range diagonally, meaning the objects do not appear on the beam when crossing the range. Ranges of opportunity, drawn between various natural and man-made charted features, are called *natural ranges* to distinguish them from *navigational ranges*, which are those specifically set up by the USCG for navigation. Navigational ranges are two well-separated vertical markers (usually lighted), with the front mark (closest to the range line itself) set at a lower elevation than the back mark. These ranges guide vessels onto the preferred channel of a harbor or waterway. By noting whether the top mark is to the right or left of the bottom mark, navigators can tell at a glance if they are to the right or left of the range, as shown in Figure 6-2. Navigational ranges are important aids to larger vessels because the presence of such range markers means it is hazardous to be very far off the range they mark. If you see a large vessel approaching a harbor marked with an entrance range, you can count on it heading toward the buoy that is usually in place marking the outer end of the range, at which point it will turn onto the range itself. Knowing this you can plan your route through the area accordingly.

The white running lights of large vessels (over 50 meters long) are positioned on the deck like a navigational range: the forward one is lower than the aft one. These lights alone tell which way the vessel is moving and provide the first warning that it might be turning toward you. A ship's "range lights" are visible long before its red or green sidelights are. (Running lights and range lights are nicknames used only when the context is not in doubt. The proper term is *masthead lights*.)

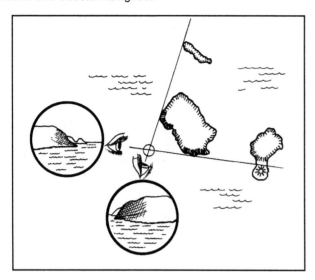

Figure 6-3. *Natural ranges along the tangents to islands. When one landmark first appears around the corner of another, their range line on the chart is your line of position.*

Figure 6-3 shows a special type of natural range that offers frequent opportunities for accurate LOPs in many areas. When the chart shows that an island, obscured behind a headland from your present perspective, will come into view shortly if you remain on your present course, prepare for a quick and accurate piece of navigation. The moment the island first peeks around the corner, you can draw an accurate LOP on the chart. The line of sight tangent to the headland must be drawn carefully, however, keeping in mind the elevation contours shown on the chart. The bluff that blocked the island could be well inland of the actual shoreline shown on the chart.

One range gives one LOP. A precise location on that line (a position fix) can be found from the point where a second range line, made from two other objects, crosses the first. This is the standard way that most piloting is done. A position fix is the intersection of two or more LOPs. To find position this way, the objects used for the ranges must be shown on the chart, or the lines cannot be drawn.

Another virtue of a range for navigation is that you can plot the LOP on the chart with a simple ruler. It is just a single, straight line, drawn right where it is observed. In contrast, you will see shortly that other types of LOPs require more complicated plotting, using special tools, or moving lines from one place to another on the chart. Piloting by ranges is accurate, versatile, and easy to plot.

Natural ranges made up from uncharted features also are still extremely valuable even though they do not provide a position fix or a LOP. A natural range can be made from any two things in sight that happen to line up, such as a treetop on the shore you steer toward and a distant mountain peak in its background. Neither of these will be on the chart, but the line is still there in front of the boat, and it can serve as a dependable guide.

You can, for example, use an uncharted range of this type to tell what the current is doing as you steer along the range. If the tree at the end of the range is more than a mile or so away, the compass heading to it is not a sensitive measure of where you are, which is what you need to know to judge the effect of current. Recalling the rule of thumb for small-angle triangles (see Figure 4-4), and keeping sight of a tree that is 1 nmi off, the current must push you 0.1 nmi off course to the side before the compass would

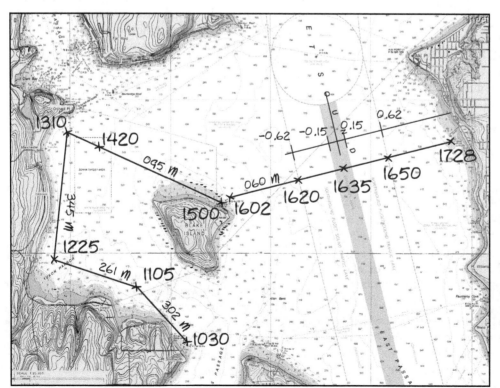

Figure 6-4. *Rule No. 1: Plot your position on the chart frequently, labeled with the time. Here we show a route planned out on the chart for cockpit navigation from a small sailing boat. Compass headings and tick marks every 0.5 nmi along the track are plotted on the chart, to be stored in a clear plastic chart pack. Once underway, we used a grease pencil (china marker) to write the time we passed various waypoints along the planned track. Also shown are the borders for a vessel traffic lane and the associated cross-track errors that we might read from a GPS using the trick covered in Chapter 10 (see Figure 10-4). In this passage, it took about thirty minutes to cross the lanes.*

show a 6° change in heading. In choppy waters with the compass card swinging around, this is approximately how large the shift must be to detect it.

Let's say you are sailing across a channel that has a current of 0.5 kts (water moves 1 nmi every 120 minutes). If you kept the boat pointed straight across the channel as you proceeded to cross, it would take twelve minutes for this current to drift you off course by the 0.1 nmi needed to cause a detectable bearing shift of about 6°. Depending on how fast you are going, however, you would be well underway in crossing the channel during these twelve minutes. The closer you get, the faster the bearing shift will occur, but in any event, noticing such a shift in an average-bearing angle will always be much slower than detecting the misalignment of a natural range.

The human eye can easily discern fractions of a degree in misalignment, which would translate in this example to seeing the effect of the current in a minute or two rather than twelve minutes. For example, note that a treetop and mountain peak dead ahead align exactly as you start across, and watch that they remain that way as you proceed—or conclude from which way they shift how you must adjust your course.

Natural ranges are a very good way to mark your position when anchoring or to monitor your position to see if you are dragging anchor.

During daylight hours on inland waters, look around long enough, and you can usually find two LOPs from natural ranges that will tell you where you are. Sometimes, the lines must be drawn on the chart to locate the intersection, other times an adequate position can be found by tracing the lines with a finger. But even if lines are not required, it is still good practice to make a note on the chart of the position found and label it with the time. It could turn out to be your last good fix from which subsequent positions must be found by dead reckoning. Put another way, it is poor practice to anticipate that conditions will remain favorable for good fixes, and therefore not bother writing anything on the chart. The farther back any dead reckoning must be carried to find present position, the more uncertain the results will be.

Indeed, this last point cannot be overemphasized. As noted earlier and probably later as well, this is the most important rule in navigation: mark your position on the chart, and label it with the time frequently, as shown in Figure 6-4. It does not matter how you arrived at the position; it could be from just passing close abeam of a buoy, or from a GPS reading, or from the intersection of two natural ranges. Regardless of how you get a position determination, find that position on the chart and label with the time, such as 0906, or 2106 for afternoon times.

What is meant by plotting frequently? That depends on the circumstances; it could be every hour or so, or even more frequently. In some cases it won't be needed so often, and every couple of hours might do—and in some cases,

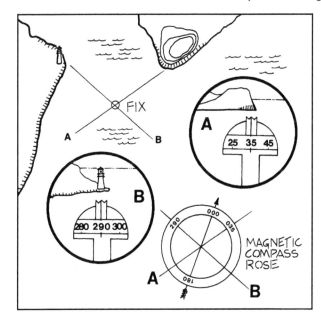

Figure 6-5. *A bearing fix from the intersection of two bearing lines.*

we do not need to navigate at all. But when we do navigate, this becomes Rule No. 1. This procedure alone tells most of what you need to know in a hurry, and it is the one procedure that will prevent most navigation problems underway. See notes in the caption for Figure 6-4.

6.3 Compass Bearing Fixes

Although in most daylight conditions on inland waters natural ranges are available for position fixing, it can sometimes take a while to find them. When ranges cannot be found in a reasonable time, compass bearings are the next best alternative. At night, natural ranges are rarely visible, so there is no alternative but compass bearings for finding position. The bearings can be taken with a hand-bearing compass or with a deck-mounted compass. In some cases, you can just sight over a binnacle mounted steering compass, or turn and point to the target for the bearings.

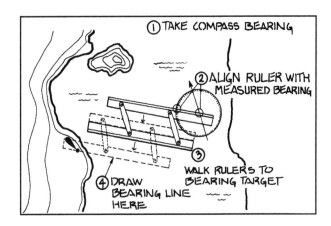

Figure 6-6. *Using parallel rulers to plot a bearing line to a light on shore. This job can also be done using a Weems roller plotter. See also Figure 2-20.*

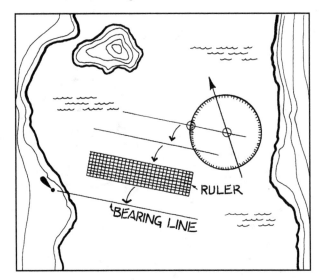

Figure 6-7. *Using a large flat ruler to draw a bearing line while underway. One option available is the "P-72 Protractor Plotter".*

Figure 6-8. *An improvised string plotter used to measure a course line. This model was made from a 5-inch square protractor. Read the true course from where the string crosses the protractor. Sometimes, using the protractor alone without the string is a more convenient way to measure course directions. It is very convenient for cockpit navigation.*

Good hand-bearing compasses give more precise bearings than just sighting over the steering compass. With either type of compass bearing, however, the procedure for obtaining bearing lines is the same (see Figure 6-5). The compass is aimed at the sighted object and then watched for a few seconds. The compass card will swing about, even in fairly calm conditions, so the observer must choose the best average reading. In less favorable conditions, this might take a minute or so. Once an average bearing is decided upon, the bearing line must be drawn on the chart—an imaginary line traced with a finger will not do for this application. The principle of the position line is easy: If a lighthouse is seen from the boat at bearing 290, the lighthouse attendant would see the boat in the opposite direction at a compass bearing of 290 minus 180, which equals a magnetic bearing of 110. The LOP on the chart is a line emanating from the lighthouse in direction 110, and this direction can be read from the magnetic scale of the chart's compass rose.

Bearing lines are drawn on the chart with the aid of parallel rulers. The rulers are first aligned in the proper magnetic orientation across the center of the compass rose nearest to the lighthouse symbol (magnetic directions are shown on the middle scale of the compass rose). The alignment of the rulers on the compass rose can be done using the observed bearing, without figuring its reciprocal (used above to explain the principle), because the line from the center to the observed bearing will automatically pass through its reciprocal. After alignment on the compass rose, the rulers are then stepped over to the lighthouse, and the line is drawn. This way the proper direction read from the compass rose is transferred to the lighthouse (see Figure 6-6).

Parallel rulers or a Weems roller plotter are the standard ways to draw the lines, but the lines can also be drawn with a wide ruler (sometimes called course plotter) that is moved to the lighthouse from the compass rose one ruler width at a time (see Figure 6-7). Navigation supply stores carry one popular ruler style that is 4 inches wide and 15 inches long with a grid of lines drawn across it parallel to the long edge. The grid facilitates the last step, which will be some fraction of a ruler width. The other extreme is a clear, grid template approximately 12 inches on a side. The wide ones will often span the distance from compass rose to sighted object without requiring steps. One edge of the template is kept on the object, as the template is rotated until a grid line crosses the center of the rose at the proper orientation. The grid is then held in place as the line is drawn along the edge of the template in line with the object.

A special chart tool developed for cockpit navigation is called a string plotter or Sutherland Plotter. It is a convenient way to measure bearings and course lines. It is a simple 360° protractor printed on a square grid with a string attached to the center. Align the base or one of the grid lines with the chart for proper orientation, and then pull the string out in the direction to be measured. Read the true bearing where the string crosses the protractor, as shown in Figure 6-8. The device is small, lightweight, inexpensive, and essentially indestructible. These are easy to make on your own using any large square protractor. Links at www.starpath.com/navbook include videos of using various plotting tools.

Bearing lines need not be penciled in all the way to the sighted object, but should just cross the water region of your approximate location. The more optimistic you are about knowing your position, the shorter the lines can be. A position fix will be found from the intersection of a second bearing line with this first one, and if the second bearing line does not cross the first because it is too short, it can

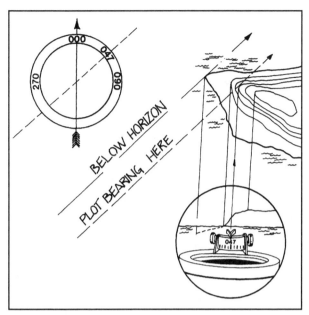

Figure 6-9. *In some cases, charted elevation contours must be considered carefully when drawing bearing lines.*

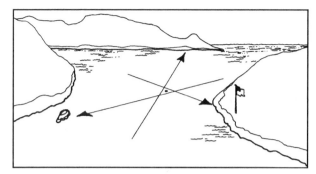

Figure 6-10. *A position from the intersection of three bearing lines. Because of unavoidable small errors in each individual measurement, the lines will not intersect in a single point. The size of the triangle is a rough measure of the uncertainty in your position fix. Taking multiple sights from a known position is a good way to practice the method. This is the only practical way to learn how the precision of the compass reading and plotting affects the final position location. Practice with different types of compasses will show why some cost much more than others.*

be extended as needed. A general goal of chart work is to make the minimum amount of marks on the chart required for neat, consistent, unambiguous notation.

When doing a position fix by compass bearings, there are several points to keep in mind that will optimize the accuracy of the fix. When using just two bearings, the two objects should be well separated on the horizon. Ideally, they would be 90° apart, but as long as they are more than 30° apart, the fix should be good. Sights of nearby objects (less than 10° apart, for example) give narrow intersection angles when the LOPs are plotted, and with narrow intersection angles, small errors in compass reading or in plotting the bearings result in a large error in the fix. This geometric enhancement of the errors diminishes rapidly for intersection angles over 30°. Likewise, fixes from intersection angles of 60° or so are essentially as good as those for perpendicular LOPs. With one arm pointed to one object and the other held at 90° to it, it is easy to judge where 45° would be, and from there to pick well-placed targets. A look at the chart from your approximate position helps identify good targets for bearing fixes. Reference to the chart before bearing fixes is often necessary anyway, since potential targets must be located on the chart if they are to be used.

It is also important to use the closest of two potential candidates for sights when you have a choice. Accuracy is again the reason. Small angular errors in compass reading or plotting cause large intersection errors when the object sighted is a long distance from your position on the chart. Think of the extreme cases: with an arm around a buoy, it does not matter if the bearing to it is completely wrong; you still know where you are, whereas the bearing to a distant mountain peak remains the same even after traveling several miles. Knowing the bearing to a very distant object does not help locate your position.

Permanent landmarks like lighthouses and peaks are better targets for bearing fixes than buoys. Although anchored, buoys have large scope, so their positions when used as close marks are not reliable or, worse still, they could have been moved from the charted location or dragged off station by currents. Tangents to bluffs and hills are frequently good for bearings, but as with their use in ranges, the lines must be drawn carefully by matching charted elevation contours with what was actually sighted (see Figure 6-9).

The uncertainty in a position found from compass bearings can be tested by taking bearings to more than two objects. Two bearing lines intersect at only one place, but three bearing lines will normally intersect each other at three places. Only if all three sights and lines are exactly right will the three intersect at a single point. Consequently, the spread of the three intersections is an approximate measure of the accuracy of the fix, as illustrated in Figure 6-10. This is not a rigorous test of accuracy when the lines do not agree, but it is certainly reassurance of the fix when they do nearly agree. After some practice, two lines taken carefully yield as good a fix as three lines do, provided you are certain of the location of the objects sighted. If the iden-

...In Depth

12.13 Running Fixes

When only one aid to navigation is visible, we can only get an LOP from a single observation. To use this object for a fix requires a *running fix*, which this note explains. It is a fundamental skill, and one that takes us beyond just careful, experienced boating and more into the realm of versatile navigation...

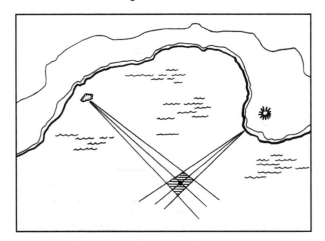

Figure 6-11. *The uncertainty of a position fix found from two lines. The width of the shaded area is approximately 200 yards per mile off the bearing target in typical measurements made underway, assuming bearing accuracy of ± 3° (Small-Angle Rule).*

tity of a peak or light is in doubt, then the three sights are necessary to remove the uncertainty.

Taking multiple sights from a known position is a good way to practice the method. This is the only practical way to learn how the precision of the compass reading and plotting affects the final position location. Practice is also required to develop your own preferred method of plotting the lines underway. Practice with different types of compasses also will show why some cost much more than others.

A graphic way to study the accuracy of bearing fixes at home with a chart and parallel rulers is simply to choose a location on the chart and two objects that might be used for sights from that position. Then measure the bearings from that location to the objects using parallel rulers, and assume these were the average readings obtained. The chart work is just the opposite of plotting bearing lines. Align the rulers with the lines from the chosen location to the chosen object, and then step them over to the compass rose to measure the bearing. Then, considering that each of these average values has an uncertainty of, say, ± 3°, plot the two extremes. If the average was 050, plot bearing lines at 047 and 053. This will yield a region of uncertainty, as illustrated in Figure 6-11, that shows how the fix depends on the precision of the measurement.

If you do the same with close objects and far objects, you quickly learn why close objects are better targets for bearing sights. With an uncertainty of ± 3°, the bearing-angle spread will be 6°, and the distance across the end of this triangle that represents your position uncertainty will be 10% of the distance to the sighted object (Small-Angle Rule). Using two objects, each approximately 0.5 nmi (1,000 yards) away, the full width of the uncertainty for sights accurate to within 3° would be 100 yards, so your position by bearing fix would be accurate to within ± 50 yards, in principle.

In the real world of small craft navigation, in less than ideal conditions, twice this uncertainty is closer to the

truth. To be safe, assume that bearing fixes made underway are only accurate to within ± 10% of the distance to the farthest object sighted, which translates into an uncertainty of 200 yards per mile off. With practice, a quality compass, and good conditions, you should, however, be able to reduce this uncertainty significantly.

Regardless of your type of vessel, it is still important to check that the place you are making the measurements from is not disturbed by local magnetic fields. Generally, the cockpit of a sailing vessel is safe for measurements from most locations, but it still should be tested. The simplest test is just to compare what you get for the vessel heading with what the steering compass reads, assuming it is correct. Better still, take bearings to some distant object from various places around the cockpit to see that they are all the same, and if not, use the GPS to plot your position and figure out from the chart which location yields correct bearings.

If you do not have that option, another (even better) way to test a hand-bearing compass location is to take a bearing to any distant object and then swing ship (turn 360°) and repeat the bearing measurement every 45° of heading change. Or just take the bearing when headed on each of the cardinal and inter-cardinal headings according to the compass. If the bearing remains the same all the way around the full 360° turn, you have found a good location for taking compass bearing sights.

We have found, for example, very strange magnetic behavior on the wooden vessel we use for our own training courses. In the pilothouse, bearings are just fine, but step out to the starboard side for a nice clear view and the bearings are off 10°. Walk around to the front of the pilot house and they are off 30°. But in the salon on the deck below, they are all just fine. An iron rail might be the culprit? On some steel vessels you may discover that handheld bearing compasses do not work at all. On most nonsteel boats, however, they will most often work just fine and be a most valuable aid to your piloting.

6.4 Finding Position from Water Depth

A good, well-calibrated depth sounder is invaluable to the navigation of all vessels, especially to small craft navigators. Unless the water is too deep or the bottom is too flat, the depth sounder provides valuable information about our position. We are not using it just to keep from running aground, but actually as a navigation tool.

When the slope of the bottom is gradual, these observations are not of much value, but in many waterways around the world, there are sudden drop-offs or shelves along the shoreline. These shelves are marked on charts by an abrupt change in depth contours, so whenever you notice you are crossing a shelf, you have found a crooked LOP—the charted contour of the shelf. A compass bearing to a landmark on shore then locates your position at the intersection of the bearing line and the shelf contour (see Figure 6-12).

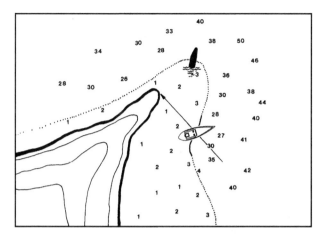

Figure 6-12. *A position fix from a bearing line and an underwater shelf visible from the boat. The shelf is effectively a crooked line of position on the chart.*

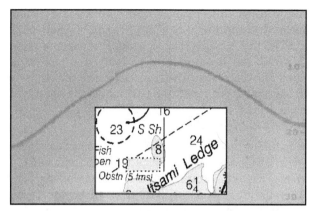

Figure 6-12a. *Actual depth sounder trace passing over the 8-fathom bump along the dotted line headed SW at 7 kts. There were 2 fathoms of tide at the time. Time on the trace is from left to right. The latest depth of the water was 18 fathoms; we approached the bump from about 24 fathoms of water. Such an observation is an accurate position fix since the width of the bump is only 200 yards. The chart describes the rectangular area to the SW as 5 fathoms, but we did not see that, being just north of it. For comparison, the GPS trail showed exactly where we crossed it.*

When such shelves exist, it is usually important to know where you are relative to them in order to find favorable current. Current speed and direction often change at the edge of a shelf. Riding with the current, you want to be in the deep water off the shelf; progressing against the current in a low-powered vessel usually calls for being in the shallow water on the shelf. Buoys often mark the corners of a shelf wherever waterways turn.

For more general position finding, remember that vast areas of shallow water might contain patches of deeper water. Detectable shoaling on banks can rise from very deep water indeed, as very shallow spits can extend a mile or more off the end of a headland. Shoaling that might be useful for navigation is usually shaded blue on charts. Often an extensive kelp bed signals the presence of a bank below it, even when the water is far too deep to see through. When such depth anomalies are shown on the chart, they should be anticipated for use with navigation (Figure 6-12a). And whenever you notice or suspect the depth has changed, check the chart to see if it might tell something about where you are. Marking such potential aids on the chart before the trip is part of navigation planning. In clear tropical waters, charted coral heads over 30 ft deep can still be seen when the sun is high and can be used for piloting offshore. Polarized sunglasses are a big help with these observations.

The sea state can also signal the presence of shallow water. Currents accelerate when flowing over banks, and when this current is against the wind, the waves steepen and break more frequently. Sometimes, the outline of a bank can be detected from the pattern of whitecaps on it—or along it, when strong current flows around it but not over it. Banks exposed to strong, deep current also can be detected by a fog boundary. The upwelling at the edge of the bank brings cold water to the surface, which cools the air to the dew point and forms fog. If a bank or other shoaling can be detected this way, it can help with orientation even though it is some distance off.

For more specific use of depth sounding navigation, we need to be more numeric. Consider this case. We have a bearing to a lighthouse on shore, which we have plotted on the chart, and we notice that along this bearing line, the depth changes significantly in the region we are located. Our job now is to use the depth sounder to find out where we are along that line.

First, we need to know how deep the depth sounder's transducer is below the surface. This is usually called its *draft*. Let us assume that the draft is 3 ft. Next we need to know the height of the tide at this time at our present location; let's call that the tide, and say it is 7 ft at the moment. (We look this up from a tide book or computer app.) Then we read the depth sounder, and let's say it reads 23 ft. So what do we look for on the chart to decide where we are?

There is a distance of 23 ft between sounder and bottom, and 3 ft between sounder and the water surface. So the water depth at the moment is 23+3 = 26 ft. Of this 26 ft, we know that 7 of it is tide, so the charted depth at our location should be 26-7 = 19 ft. We then go to the chart and look for a place where the charted depth on the plotted bearing line is about 19 ft, and we should be near that location.

This type of fix is not often as good as a crossed bearing fix, since the tide could be off some and the chart might not be right in that detail, but often, this type of observation is a good way to home in on our position.

A more sophisticated approach to depth sounding navigation can be applied when you notice definite structure to the bathymetry near you that is within range of your sounder. Holding a steady compass heading, start a log of depths at specific intervals of distance run read from the log, recording also the time of each depth measurement. Next, mark those distances and depths on the edge of a piece of paper or roller plotter, using the same distance scale as the chart to create a linear record of what you observed on that heading. Then keeping this paper or plotter oriented in the direction traveled, move it around on the chart until you match what you measured, and thus you will have found your track and positions at the times of the logged depths recorded. This type of piloting is referred to as using a *line of soundings*.

An interesting way to practice line of soundings navigation on land is to replace the depth sounder with a barometer and use the barometer to measure elevations. Then, after calibrating it at a known elevation in the present atmospheric pressure, walk off over the local terrain in a steady compass direction, periodically recording distance traveled and measured elevation. Then go to a topo map and determine your final position. Examples are given at starpath.com/navbook.

6.5 Visible Range of Land and Objects

Everyone is familiar with the image of a ship sailing over the horizon. As the ship sails away, less and less of it can be seen because the curvature of the earth limits the line of sight to the ship. The last thing you see with binoculars is the tip of the mast. The taller the ship, the farther off it can be seen; likewise, the higher you are when looking, the farther you can see. From the deck of a small vessel, you can easily see a freighter 10 nmi off, but you cannot see another small vessel traveling along beside it. Knowing how to estimate the actual visible range of other vessels, rocks, peaks and islands, and elevated lights is fundamental to marine navigation. It is important for navigation, and it is important for safety.

During daylight in clear weather and flat water, the visible range of an object is called its *geographic range*. It is determined by the curvature of the earth and the heights of the object and the observer. The proper mathematical solution to the geometry problem is presented in tabular form in the *Light List*. The table gives geographic ranges for various heights of objects and observers. These results, however, are needed more often than the *Light List* is, so it pays to know how to figure geographic range without a table. In clear weather and flat water, geographic range in miles can be estimated from:

Geographic range = $\sqrt{\text{Land height}}$ + $\sqrt{\text{Eye height}}$,

where both heights are in feet above the water (see Figure 6-13).

Eye height from a small vessel might be about 9 ft, so your own elevation would add approximately 3 nmi to the geographic range of landmarks.

If an islet is 49 ft tall, the top of it would be first discernible on the horizon at 7 plus 3, or about 10 nmi off. The square roots of less convenient heights should be computed with a calculator or can be approximated by squaring

a few guesses. High precision is not required because even the best theories of what this range should be are only accurate in practice to within 10% or so. Likewise, beyond 10 nmi off a 49-foot-high island could not be seen, even if it had a bright light on it (at ground level) and you looked with binoculars. The elevations of shoreline cliffs, peaks, and inshore rocks that are needed to figure their geographic ranges are charted or listed in *Coast Pilots*.

Results of the simple square root formula for geographic range are 17% smaller than the tabulated theoretical values in the *Light List* that apply to ideal conditions. The lower values of our approximation, however, are more dependable in practice. A slight chop on the water or haze in the air can reduce this range by more than this 17% when looking for low features. Even the simple square root predictions should be considered optimistic predictions that apply best when using binoculars in clear weather and flat water. These predictions are naturally limited by the prevailing atmospheric visibility. If the atmospheric visibility is 15 nmi—a relatively clear day—you could not see a peak 2,500 ft high until you were within about 15 nmi of it, even though the tip of it is over the horizon at 50 nmi off. This is, in effect, the definition of *atmospheric visibility*.

The formula can be used not only to predict when an island or peak should first be seen (depending on atmospheric visibility), but it can also be used to tell how close you must be to it if you do see it. If a bright navigational light, for example, is charted as 25 ft high, whenever you can see the light at all viewed from an eye height of 9 ft, you must be within 5 plus 3, or 8 nmi of the light, although you do not know the actual distance off by just seeing the light. On the other hand, when you *first see the light*, you can assume you are approximately 8 nmi off.

Predictions of the geographic-range formula are also of interest to safety. A ship that is about 81 ft high would be

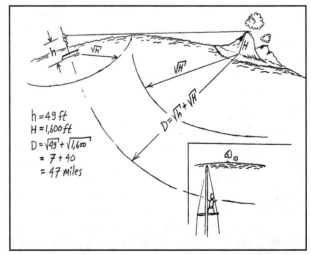

Figure 6-13. *A landmark will first appear above the horizon when you approach it to within the geographic range (D), provided the atmospheric visibility is at least as far as that geographic range. The sailor's eye height (h) and the height of the land (H) are in feet above the water.*

seen first (looking carefully in best conditions) at a distance of 9 plus 3, or about 12 nmi off. Two small vessels will lose complete sight of each other at a separation of about 6 nmi in flat water. In rough seas or swells, however, they would have only intermittent sights of each other at much closer distances, when one or both happen to be on a wave crest. In big waves, you can lose sight of each other when only a few boat lengths apart.

In the case of an emergency at night in rough water, it is clearly important to carry flares that can be shot into the air. For routine sailing in even moderate seas, there is virtue in each crew member carrying a steady light (like a chemical light) *in addition* to a personal strobe light. In some conditions, the steady light would be a better way to be spotted. Strobes can be seen from farther off and are definitely superior for attracting attention, but it is very difficult to judge distance off a bright flashing light. Consequently they are less valuable as aids for homing in on a rescue. They also have a probability of being out of phase with the waves, unlike a steady light.

In fog, rain, or snow, the visible range of unlighted land is more complicated to determine. First, you must be within the geographic range of the land or you will not see it; this limit does not depend on the atmosphere, but only on the curvature of the earth. When well within the geographic range, the visible range of unlighted land is simply called the *visibility* or atmospheric visibility. It is not something you can calculate; it must be measured by reading from a chart the distance to the farthest objects you can barely see.

One trick that helps estimate this range when no visible features are present is to note whether you can discern the sea horizon—a line between sky and water or distant land and water. From the geographic-range formula (at eye height 9 ft), you know that if you can see the horizon, the visibility must be at least 3 nmi—the answer corresponds to putting the height of your target equal to zero feet.

6.6 Finding Distance Off

In rough water, strong wind, or fast current, many a small craft operator must keep their hands on the wheel or tiller. Consequently, piloting in these conditions is at its best when it can be done without the use of hands, as when using natural ranges or noticing a sudden change in water depth. The next best methods are the ones that use the hands the least. (As throughout much of this book, we are referring to cases where there is no GPS available).

Finding position from intersecting compass bearings is accurate and versatile, but it occupies the hands for some time to plot the fix. A convenient compromise is a single compass bearing to an object that you can estimate the distance to. If you know you are 1 nmi away from a lighthouse in direction 215, then you can point to your position on the chart. Sighting over the steering compass for the bearing makes this a quick operation.

The other virtue of this approach is that it takes only one identified feature to find position. Natural ranges take four (two features per range, two ranges for a fix); bearing fixes take two. Whenever only one charted feature can be identified, estimates of distance off become essential to finding position. Furthermore, a position fix can be found from the distances to two separate features without the aid of a compass, which could prove useful if the compass was lost on an extended trip. There are several ways to find distance off—some take more hands than others, and some take more practice than others. These measurements are a challenging and rewarding part of the sport of navigation. They will be convenient more often than crucial, but are well worth the practice and could save your boat (so to speak) some day.

6.7 Guessing

Guessing distance is a cultivated skill. Some boaters do it well; others, like myself, might be fair at 25 yards (the length of a swimming pool) and 100 yards (the length of a football field), but must admit shaky results for unaided guesses of miles. But regardless of skill level, sea state and time of day also affect the result. This method is mentioned only for the sake of those who might potentially do it well—something that can be discovered only by practice from known positions in different conditions. Anchored or moored with a radar or electronic chart available is an ideal way to practice judging distance since you can check yourself instantly.

Many of those who get useful results from guessing use various tricks to get some modicum of measurement into the guess. "Don't shoot until you see the whites of their eyes" is such a rule for short distances. Obviously, distance judged this way depends on your eyes, as well as the eyes of the target. The same uncertainties inhibit the accuracy of the common guidelines listed in Table 6-1.

Table 6-1. Visibility of distant objects	
Approximate distance	*Typically visible to naked eye*
5 nmi	Large houses, towers, ships
2 nmi	Large trees, chimneys, can count windows
1 nmi	Large sea buoys, tree trunks, branches, can count trees
1/2 nmi	Small buoys, people appear as dots or posts
1/4 nmi	Hands, arms, kayak paddle blades, outboard motors
1/8 nmi	Faces, clothing, deck gear, buoy shapes, numbers, or letters

To be of value, these guidelines must be adjusted to individuals and to the scenery. You may find that a rule that works in one area will not work in another, or you may find other useful guidelines for specific places or scenery. It is something to try, and then decide how useful it is for you. It is possible, for example, to be in the middle of a bay, 3 nmi across, and be able to see individual trees on the west side but not on the east side. All such rules are approximate at best.

Commercially available range finders are not always much better than guessing. These are optical instruments that read distance off similar to the way the focus adjustment on a camera does. Large, expensive ones used on artillery do the job, but the small, expensive ones designed for marine navigation typically do not. Specific brands have limited ranges over which they work reasonably well, but they are generally not dependable. Furthermore, even if they did work, they are redundant, since accurate distances off can be measured with fingers. The same applies to the range finders built into some expensive binoculars—these can indeed work well, but we must study the manuals to learn the valid conditions. By understanding what we describe below under vertical sextant angles, it will be easier to take advantage of the range indicators showing in some binoculars.

Estimating distance off relative to the width of a channel or bay, such as one half or one third of the way across, can be a more quantitative form of guessing. With practice, this is a useful technique. A variation is to estimate that your distance off a point is about equal to the distance between two features on shore. You might, for example, estimate that your distance off a point to the south of you is about equal to the width of the cove that follows it around the point. You can then locate your approximate position on the chart without measuring any distances from the chart, as shown in Figure 6-14.

You can reverse this last generic process to make a very specific piloting procedure that is well suited to small craft

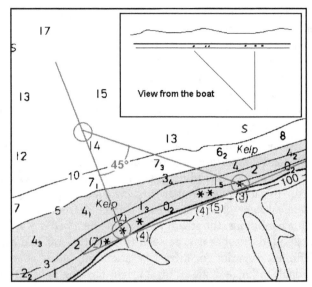

Figure 6-15. *Piloting trick for estimating position without the use of the hands. When looking straight onto a shoreline, notice what charted feature lies straight ahead and then what charted feature lies to the right or left by 45°. Your distance offshore is then equal to the distance between the two landmarks sighted. Diagonals drawn at 45° on the deck in front of you or on your transparent chart protector cover could be used to locate the relative bearing of 45°.*

navigation in many circumstances. To discover your distance off a given charted feature on a more-or-less straight shoreline, look straight toward the shoreline at that feature and then look 45° to the right or left. If you happen to see at one of those locations another identifiable charted feature, then you can immediately know that your distance offshore is equal to the distance between these two features on the chart. This is a very good trick that takes little practice to master. There will not always be some convenient reference feature right where you want it, but you can sometimes estimate what you want, such as "my 45° mark is halfway between that church and that road," etc. Notice that since you know you are a given distance straight off the shoreline from a particular point, you have here not just a distance off but an actual position fix. This method relies on the simple property that the sides of a 45° triangle are equal (see Figure 6-15).

6.8 Horizontal Angle

To get precise distance off, you must know the actual dimensions of what you are looking at. The width of a bay, the width of a big rock or island, or the distance between two rocks or two peaks are typical horizontal dimensions that can be read from a chart and used for figuring the distance to them. The procedure requires a measurement of the angle that this known distance subtends from your perspective. This measured angle emanating from your eye, along with the known base width of the charted feature, defines a unique triangle whose height is your distance off the base. For small triangles—meaning the distance off is

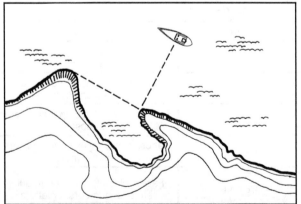

Figure 6-14. *A position fix from a relative bearing and distance off: This helmsman knows he is oriented parallel to the coast, with the headland near his beam, and at a distance off that is about equal to the width of the bay. With these observations, a position can be noted on the chart.*

much larger than the width of the target—this distance can be determined easily by scaling known triangle proportions.

The Small-Angle Rule is the simplest way to scale the result, since it states that the ratio of the sides of a 6° triangle is 1:10—for small angles, it is not important to distinguish between sides and heights. Suppose the chart shows that the entrance to a bay lying dead ahead is 0.3 nmi across, and an accurate compass shows that the bearing to one side of it is 050 and to the other side is 056. The bay subtends an angle of 6° from your perspective. The short side of the triangle is 0.3 nmi across, so the long side of the triangle (distance to the entrance) must be 10 times as long, or 3 nmi off.

That is the principle of how the method works, but not a practical way to do it. Only the best bearing compasses used in ideal conditions can provide bearings precise enough for this application. The more practical approach is to measure the subtended angle directly, without individual bearings to its edges. These angles can be measured with a sextant, and even the most inexpensive type (Davis Mark 3) will do the job nicely. Small angles, however, can be measured to a precision adequate for this application without a sextant.

The angle measurements are made by scaling a similar triangle whose base is held at arm's length, and whose height is the length of the arm. The proportions are shown in Figure 6-16, but each of the several ways to improvise the measurement must be calibrated to the individual. One method is to use finger widths for the base dimensions. The average finger width at the average arm's length subtends an angle of approximately 2°. The bay in the last example would have been three fingers across.

Accurate measurements, independent of arm and finger sizes, can be made with a simple instrument called a *kamal*. It is just a graduated base plate attached to a string that keeps the eye-to-plate distance constant. For a string 57 centimeters long, each centimeter along the edge of the plate subtends exactly 1°. This is a convenient length to hold forward in a comfortable position. A common 15-centimeter plastic ruler makes a convenient graduated plate. It can be attached to the string by a bridle to keep it from tilting, as shown in Figure 6-17. A knot at the end of the string is held in the teeth, which frees one hand and keeps the measurements consistent. Measured with a kamal, the bay in the last example would have been 6 centimeters across.

A kamal is easy to make and easy to use, costs and weighs nearly nothing, and is extremely valuable for the vertical-angle method discussed later in this section. It is named after an ancient Arabic device of similar design used to measure the height of the North Star for dhow navigation along the Arabian Gulf and east coast of Africa.

The Small-Angle Rule can be converted into a formula for distance off that can be used for this type of small-angle measurement (angles less than 30°).

$$\text{Distance off (in miles)} = 60 \times \frac{\text{Target width (in miles)}}{\text{Target angle (in degrees)}}$$

A bay 0.3 nmi across that appears 5° wide (or 5 centimeters on a kamal) must be 60 times 0.3 divided by 5, or 3.6 nmi off. This is the distance to the center of the bay at the point on the chart where its width was measured. If the two sides of the bay are not equally distant from you, the width of the bay must be estimated as it would be seen from your perspective. The direction of your perspective can be determined from a compass bearing. If two inland peaks are used for a target, the same consideration of perspective and measurement point applies (see Figure 6-18).

For narrow features viewed from closer distances, the distance formula can be modified to:

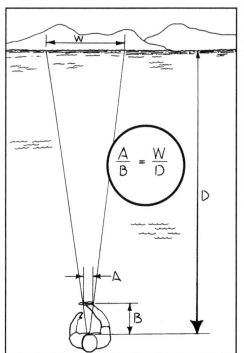

Figure 6-16. *Horizontal angle proportions that can be used to measure distance off a landmark. A hand width (A) at arm's length (B) covers a width (W) at the shoreline at a distance (D) away.*

$$\frac{A}{B} = \frac{W}{D}$$

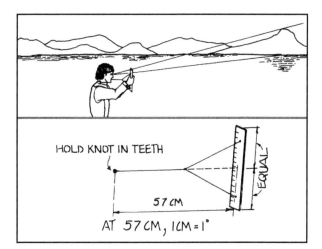

HOLD KNOT IN TEETH

57 CM

AT 57 CM, 1 CM = 1°

EQUAL

Figure 6-17. *The construction and use of a kamal for measuring vertical angles.*

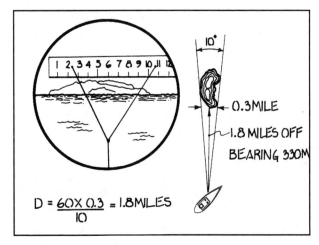

Figure 6-18. *Finding distance off by horizontal angle.*

$$\text{Distance off (in miles)} = \frac{\text{Target width (in feet)}}{100 \times \text{target angle (in degrees)}}$$

This formula is equivalent to dividing the target width, expressed in hundreds of feet, by the angle in degrees. Two prominent rocks separated by 300 ft that appear 2° apart must be 3 divided by 2, or 1.5 nmi off.

The calibration of a kamal can be tested by measuring the angles between stars. The Pointers on the cup end of the Big Dipper are 5.4° apart, and the equivalent two stars of the Little Dipper (called the Guards) are 3.2° apart. In southern latitudes, use the Southern Cross Pointers, which are 4.4° apart. The three stars of Orion's belt, visible from north or south latitudes in the winter, form a short line that is 2.7° across. When the stars are high, the head should be tilted back to keep the eye-to-kamal distance the same as it is when looking forward. Star pairs can also be used to estimate the angular widths of fingers, but this might be better done by just assuming a width of 2° and then adjusting this assumption until the formula reproduces the proper distance off a known position.

A convenient variation of this method that works well with practice is to put graduation marks for angle measurements directly onto the shaft of a dinghy paddle or boathook, as shown in Figure 6-19. Then only the paddle need be raised to make a distance measurement. The proper spacing for 1° intervals depends on arm length, but it should be within a few millimeters of 1 centimeter. One

way to test it is to tape a photocopy of a centimeter ruler on the shaft and then use it to measure the widths of several features at varying distances from a known position. If each of the distances figured from the formula (assuming 1 centimeter is right) turn out to be 20% too large, then reduce the factor of 60 in the formula by 20%, that is, use 48 instead of 60 for future measurements. Raised graduations work better than a taped-on scale, if some variety store product can be found that does the job.

6.9 Winking

A clever variation of the horizontal-angle method employs the distance between the eyes as the base reference for the angle measurement. The average ratio of eye separation to arm length is approximately 1:10, which means a finger held at arm's length will shift 6° across its background when viewed with alternate eyes. In the bay example used above, if the finger were aligned with one edge of the bay viewed with the right eye closed, it would align with the other edge of the bay with the left eye closed. By noticing that the finger shifted one bay width, you know the bay is 6° across, and therefore must be 10 times the width of the bay away from you.

With this method, it is not actually necessary to go through the intermediate step of figuring the angle. You can just figure distance off is 10 times the distance that your

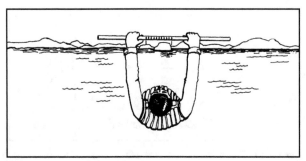

Figure 6-19. *A makeshift kamal on a boat hook or mop handle*

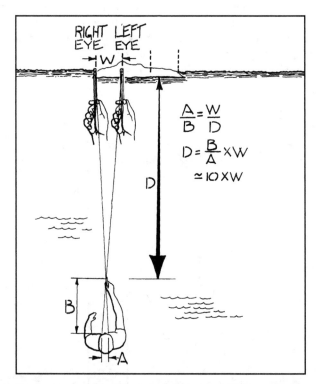

Figure 6-20. *Finding distance off by winking. The pencil mowed a distance (W) equal to one third of the width of the islet that is located a distance (D) away. For an islet that is 900 ft across, the pencil moved 300 ft, so your distant off is about 3,000 ft or 0.5 nmi. A is the distance between the eyes; B is an arm's length.*

finger shifted along the horizon (see Figure 6-20). If your finger had shifted only halfway across the bay when you winked (the finger moved 0.15 nmi), then your distance off would be 10 times 0.15, or 1.5 nmi. Had your finger shifted past the other edge of the bay by half again the width of the bay, the distance off would be 10 times 0.45, or 4.5 nmi.

This method is more approximate than the use of a sextant because you must judge by eye alone the fractional shift of the finger relative to the size of the target. But it is quick and much better than an unaided guess. It can be improved by fine-tuning the factor of 10. To do this, measure the distance from eye to finger, and then divide it by the distance between your eyes. Eye separation can be found by adjusting binoculars to fit and then measuring the separation of eye-pieces, center to center. The result will likely be somewhere between 8 and 12, and it is this ratio that should be used in place of 10 when figuring distance off by winking.

Or better still, use the method to measure a known distance to a known width, to learn what factor you need to multiply the shift by to get the right distance off. The self-calibration should be worth it as you then have this skill with you permanently, on or off the boat.

6.10 Vertical Angle

For navigation within a few miles of target landmarks, it is often more convenient to use the height of an object for distance off rather than its width. A peak location is better localized than horizontal features when viewed from nearby, and the same height can be used from various perspectives without having to re-measure the proper width as the perspective changes. Most peak heights and the elevations of lights are charted. *Coast Pilots* include the heights of some rocks and peaks not specified on charts, and they point out which peaks are conspicuous and thus candidates for this application.

Heights are used the same way as widths are to find distance off. The vertical angles that span the features can be measured with fingers—in practice, fingers are generally better for this than they are for horizontal angles. Nevertheless, measurements taken with a sextant are still more accurate and preferable. The angle to measure is from the top of the peak to the shoreline directly below the peak, as shown in Figure 6-21. It does not matter that the shoreline is closer to you; the answer obtained is the distance to the charted peak location. The distance formula is the same as used earlier:

$$\text{Distance off (nmi)} = \frac{\text{Target height (in feet)}}{100 \times \text{target angle (in degrees)}}$$

Again, the distance off is just the charted elevation of the peak expressed in hundreds of feet divided by the kamal angle in centimeters. A 240 foot-high peak that spans 2 centimeters on the kamal must be 2.4 divided by 2, or 1.2 nmi off. Usually, this calculation can be done adequately without resorting to notes on the chart.

The formula is not so nice when the elevations are given in meters, since the factor of 100 in the formula must be changed to 30. A peak 200 meters high that spans 4 centimeters on the kamal must be 200 divided by 30 times 4, which equals 50 divided by 30, or 1.7 nmi. In feet or meters, however, even if the division must be approximated, the answer will be more accurate than an unaided guess.

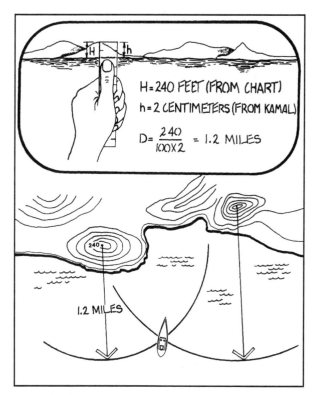

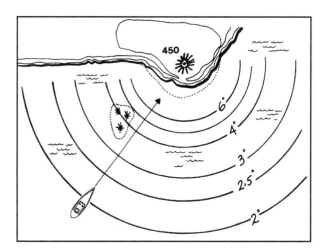

Figure 6-22. *Preparing a chart with danger circles of equal distance off to keep track of position. You will be approaching the rocky shoaling when the peak appears 3° high on a sextant or kamal.*

Figure 6-21. *Finding distance off by vertical angle using a kamal. A position can be found from the distances off two landmarks. H is the height of the land; h is an angle or distance on the kamal. A Davis Mk3 sextant will also do this job very nicely.*

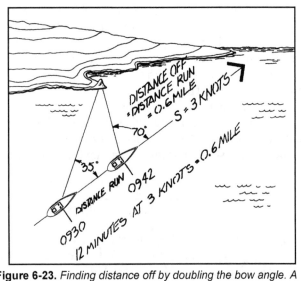

Figure 6-23. *Finding distance off by doubling the bow angle. A distance off a charted landmark and a bearing to it is a fix. This method can be applied to uncharted landmarks as well.*

If it is known ahead of time that a particular peak will be useful for keeping track of position, the chart can be prepared with circles of equal distance from the peak that correspond to specific heights on a kamal. This way no calculations at all are required to use the peak for a reference. With a few bearing lines also drawn on the chart, as shown in Figure 6-22, accurate position can be maintained with a few quick observations and a glance at the chart. This can be an easy and accurate way to navigate along an exposed coastline toward one large rock, offshore island, or peak on a headland.

Unlike the horizontal-angle methods, this method is restricted to distances fewer than 2 nmi or so. If the answer is 2 or more miles, then it must be considered approximate until you get closer to the target. The restriction occurs because the mathematical approximations used in this application of the formula required that the true shoreline below the object be in view. From the cockpit of a small vessel, the earth's curvature blocks the shoreline view at about 2 or 3 nmi off, which begins to interfere with the results.

6.11 Doubling the Bow Angle

The methods covered so far require information from a chart. Distance off an uncharted feature also can be figured from its change in bearing as you sail by it. The accuracy of the result depends on the accuracy of your estimated boat speed, which means the method is less reliable in strong wind or uncertain current. A related condition is that the reference landmark must be within a mile or two, so that its bearing changes significantly in a reasonable time. In these somewhat special circumstances, the method works when called for. A common application is to find distance off a shoreline when there is no urgency for the answer and no identifiable charted landmarks along the shore—to find, for example, where you are relative to an underwater shelf or shipping lane.

Any landmark, charted or uncharted, that lies within 20° to 50° (one to two outstretched hand widths) off the bow can be used (see Figure 6-23). Start by reading the compass heading of your course, and then use a bearing compass to take a bearing to the landmark, a prominent tree on the shoreline, for example. Figure the bow angle of the tree by subtracting the two compass readings. If the course is 100 and the bearing was 140, the bow angle was 40°. Start a stopwatch, and maintain the original course at a constant speed until the bow angle to the tree has doubled. When the bow angle has doubled, the distance off the mark is equal to the distance you had to travel to double it. In this example, the bow angle would have doubled when the bearing to the tree reached 180. If this took 5 minutes traveling at 6 kts (10 minutes per mile), the tree is 0.5 nmi off at the time of the second bearing. If the mark was a charted rock instead of a tree, you could get a fix from the distance off and bearing. Figure 6-23 includes another numerical example of this technique.

Sailing along a straight shoreline, this can be done without altering course to measure bearings by doubling 45° to 90°, using nothing more than a diagonal line across the chart mark. Just take for a mark whatever happens to line up with the 45° line, and then time how long it takes for this mark to reach the beam. Distance off the shoreline is then the distance you had to travel to move the mark from 45° on the bow to 90° on the bow, which is on the beam.

As another example, suppose you are sailing along a floating bridge and notice a sign on the bridge that says, "All boats stay 200 yards off the bridge." Start a stopwatch, note which mark on the bridge is 45° off the bow, and keep sailing at 3.5 kts. The mark passes the beam in fifty seconds. How far off the bridge are you? A speed of 3.5 kts is 350 ft per minute (since 1 kt is 100 ft per minute), so without further figuring, you know you are too close. The actual answer would be 50 divided by 60 times 350, which is just under 100 yards.

If you have access to special tables from the *The American Practical Navigator* (usually just called *Bowditch* after its original author), or access to navigation calculators like those at www.starpath.com/calc, then you are not restricted to doubling the bow angle for a fix; you can use any two angles. Measure the run between, say 30° off to 84° or even 156°; then just look up in the tables the distance off in terms of the distance run between sightings. The *Bowditch* Tables also allow for more versatile vertical sextant angle measurements.

6.12 Radar Navigation

In marine navigation, radar is one of the most important electronic aids. We do not cover radar specifically in this book, but will outline here what it does for you. Marine radar has several, more or less independent, applications to safe, efficient navigation. One is collision avoidance, for which it is the undisputed king of the electronics dashboard. Another is actual position fixing, for which it competes with GPS (favorably in many cases) and in any event is always a very convenient way to verify a GPS position. Finally radar offers a unique and powerful aid to what might be called general vessel piloting. Specific procedures within each of these applications are listed below.

Position fixing or verification

• The electronic bearing line (EBL) and variable range marker (VRM) allow quick measurements of range and bearing to vessels and landmasses within radar range. Ranges to radar targets are very accurate; bearings are less accurate and require more care because they are dependent upon knowledge of your vessel's heading.

• Radar range and bearing to a charted landmark offers a quick position fix providing a convenient verification of the GPS position. The fix is quick to plot on paper or echart. See Figure 6-24.

• An accurate position fix can be obtained by radar alone using the intersection of circles of position measured from several radar ranges to charted features (Figure 6-25). With an echart program on a computer or mobile device, the range fixes are especially quick to plot by assigning range rings to marks placed on each of the targets.

• Approximate positions often can be made by just looking at the radar screen: "I am in the middle of the channel, just off this point", or use the EBL to identify natural ranges you are on that lay out an accurate LOPs on the chart. Once we enter confined waterways, it is the radar position that we rely on most often. A glance at the radar and a glance at the electronic trail on an echart is a modern means of efficient navigation.

Radar piloting

• The ship's heading line (SHL) on the radar screen projects forward showing where you are headed relative to the land images seen on the radar. You may think you are running parallel to the coast, but the radar tells in an instant if you are angled slightly in or out. Or knowing what island pass you wish to make or headland you need to round, you can read the proper heading off the radar once the SHL crosses your destination as you turn, which is an excellent corroboration of your chart work. There are numerous applications.

• The VRM can be used in countless ways to guide your course. If your goal is to stay 0.2 nmi off the shore, for example, set the VRM to 0.2, and then don't let that circle touch the shore as you proceed. This is a very useful technique for rounding hazardous points, or transiting narrow channels with hazardous sides.

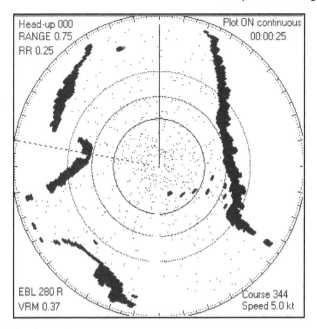

Figure 6-24. *Radar screen showing the measurement of the range and bearing to a headland using the VRM and the EBL. The radar is in head-up display mode on course 344 M. The headland is 0.37 nmi off in direction 344 + 280 = 624 - 360 = 264 M. In head-up mode, the EBL output is always in relative bearings. Since a range and bearing is a fix, the radar provides a quick way to locate your position or to confirm what you learn from the GPS. Screen capture from the Starpath Radar Trainer software.*

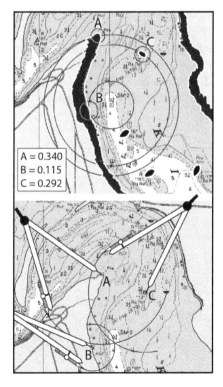

Figure 6-25. *Three-range fix. The top view shows three ranges measured from the radar, with the radar image overlaid on the chart. A is to a point of land, B is to the nearest shore on the port quarter, and C is to a prominent radar reflector on a daymark. This harbor is lined with these radar reflectors, which are labeled "Ra Ref" on charts. They are excellent nav aids. The fix is established by plotting circles of positions from the reference points as shown on the bottom view. This can be done by hand on paper charts, or can be accomplished quickly on echarts by placing a mark on each of the reference points and then setting a range ring on each mark corresponding to its distance off. Adapted from* Radar for Mariners, *Starpath Publications, 2013.*

• For more security, set a guard ring sector on top of the VRM, from dead ahead to abeam on the landward side. Then if you get too close, an alarm will go off. The sector option on guard rings lets vessels pass you on the other side without setting off the alarm.

• With a GPS input to the radar (usually a very simple connection), modern radars will mark the active waypoint on the radar screen in a *lollipop display*—a dotted line extending out from the center of the screen terminated with a circle at the Lat-Lon of the active waypoint. If that waypoint happened to be a buoy, you want to see a nice little radar target inside the lollipop for confirmation of your navigation. If there is no target there, something is wrong that needs to be sorted out—assuming you are close enough to see the buoy on radar.

• The lollipop feature is also valuable when the waypoint is on or just off any prominent radar target. Consequently, even if your radar does not have lollipops, it is best to place waypoints near what you might guess will be prominent radar targets. The interplay between GPS and radar is the key to safe efficient navigation. GPS offers continuous readout of range and bearing to the active waypoint, and with radar these are very easy to monitor. A thoughtful selection of waypoints in light of radar applications will be most rewarding.

• Many radars allow the reference point of the EBL and VRM to be offset from your own position at the center of the radar screen. This powerful feature allows you to measure the distance and bearing between any two points on the radar screen. There are unlimited applications in identifying radar targets among a complex display, as well as applications in collision avoidance. This type of floating or offset EBL can also be used to estimate how close you will pass a headland far ahead if you proceed on the same course made good. The official name of this option is *Electronic Range and Bearing Line* (ERBL). It is sometimes called a *floating EBL*.

Collision avoidance

• The EBL is a basic tool for collision avoidance. Place it on a suspected vessel target when it first appears. If the target moves forward of the EBL, it will pass in front of you; if the target moves aft of the EBL it will pass behind you. If the target tracks straight toward you along the EBL, you are on a collision course with that target. See Figure 6-26.

• The radar's *wake* or *trail* function, however, tells much more about the approaching target. With a 3-minute trail engaged, you have a complete picture of how every target on the screen has moved during the past 3 minutes. It is the key feature of radar when it comes to evaluating risk of collision. The length of the trail tells the speed of the target relative to you. If you are moving at 7 kts, an anchored buoy will move 0.35 nmi on your radar screen in 3 minutes, because that is how fast you are moving. Likewise, all land will have 3-minute trails that long. Any target with a trail longer than that is moving faster than you; any one with a shorter trail is moving slower than you. This is the way you tell if the target coming straight toward you is traveling at 20 kts, or if it is something dead in the water you are about to run into—both are closing in on you, so you have to evaluate the length of the trail to figure out what is what.

• To measure the closest point of approach (CPA) for targets approaching diagonally on the screen, use the floating EBL to project its trail past your vessel (center of the screen), then use a centered VRM to measure the CPA.

• To estimate the time of CPA, measure or estimate how many trail lengths fit between where the target is now and the CPA, and multiply by 3 minutes.

• Using the trail display and the floating EBL, you can figure the true course and speed of any approaching target. The procedure is straight forward and mastered with little practice. Once you know the target's true course, you can, for example, determine what lights you should look for at night. You might guess red and green from the radar screen alone, when the real answer is red only, or even white only. It all depends on relative motion.

6.13 Three-body Sextant Piloting

Many of the old techniques of piloting have long been left out of modern textbooks, but there is at least one that deserves reconsideration, even in modern times of GPS. That one is the onetime famous procedure of finding an accurate position from the horizontal sextant between three landmarks on the horizon. It is similar to the makeshift methods discussed earlier using a kamal, but optimized with higher accuracy measurements possible with a sextant.

The three-body fix (as it is called) is the most accurate piloting technique, and it is also one that is very easy to do and to resolve on the chart. There are several solutions.

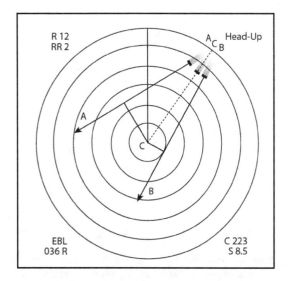

Figure 6-26. *Using the EBL as a guide to collision avoidance and closest point of approach. Adapted from* Radar for Mariners, *Starpath Publications, 2013*

The technique is often considered marine surveying rather than piloting because of its high accuracy.

A new interest in this method might come about once it is recognized that we do not need an expensive sextant to do the measurements. The simple Davis Mark 3 plastic sextant (under $50) will do the job very nicely, and indeed in many applications the inexpensive model is preferred to sextants that cost $2,000. We do not need the precision of a high-quality metal sextant in order to obtain high precision in this sextant piloting procedure. A few tenths of a degree is plenty of accuracy, and this is easily achieved with the Davis Mk 3 unit.

The procedure is to identify three well-defined charted landmarks on the horizon that are less than some 90° apart in bearing. Then use the sextant, held horizontally, to precisely measure the angles between the center one and the left one, and then the center one and the right one. Calling the points A, B, and C, as shown in Figure 6-27, we end up with two angles AB and BC.

You could take compass bearings to A, B, and C, and then subtract them to get the angles AB and BC, but this will not be nearly as accurate, although it might be a way to practice the plotting technique on a chart without a sextant.

Figures 6-28 and 6-29 show how to get a fix from the two angles. The first method requires a special tool called three-arm protractor. These days, inexpensive plastic ones are available. In the old days, the instrument was made with extreme precision and was called a station pointer. The second method is done with a simple protractor and ruler, or parallel rulers and a compass rose on the chart.

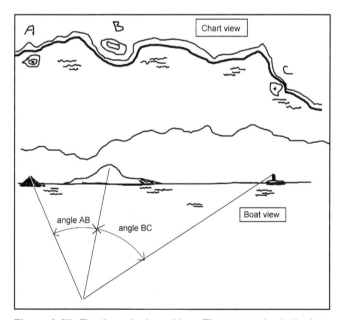

Figure 6-27. *The three-body problem. The top section is the lay of the land as seen on a chart. Below it is what the navigator might see. The sextant is held horizontally to measure the angles indicated. The fix is highly accurate, but there are limits on what targets qualify for a strong fix.*

The virtue of this sextant fix, besides its precision result, is that it is not affected by compass errors and is actually faster than taking compass bearings in many situations. Generally, it is best to take the sights as rapidly as possible when you are moving, because correcting for vessel motion is more complicated for these sights. The fix is especially well suited for checking a GPS position from a stationary location, or to check to see if you have dragged your anchor.

The disadvantage of the method is that not all landmarks that meet the angle requirement will yield a good fix. The principle of the method is based on the geometric fact that any three non-collinear points in a plane define a unique circle, and if you measure the angle between two of these points from the third one, you can compute or construct the circle that passes through all three. We measure the angle between A and B, and from that we can construct the circle that passes through points A, B, and our location. We then do this with B and C, and our fix is the intersection of the two circles of position. Generally, you can assume that if the circles intersect at an angle of greater than 20° or so, you have a good fix, if you plot carefully.

If your position, however, is near the circle defined by the points A, B, and C that you selected, then no fix can be achieved. With little practice, it is easy to see how this works, and if you have chosen poor targets, you can see how to make better choices. Three objects more or less in a line will always work well.

Note that if you get stuck with wanting to plot one of these solutions and do not have a draftsman's compass to draw the circle, you can tape or tie a pencil to one leg of your dividers, or just punch two holes in a piece of cardboard with the divider tips and then use a pencil point in one and the divider point in the other for a convenient draftsman's compass. A pencil and a piece of string can also work if used carefully.

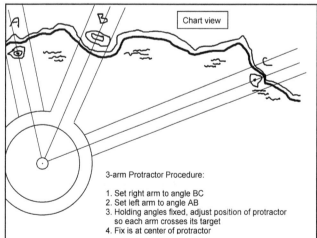

Figure 6-28. *Three-body fix solved with a three-arm protractor. Inexpensive plastic models are available. Alternatively, the problem can be solved by direct plotting with a protractor and draftsman's compass, as shown in Figure 6-29.*

If you try this under varying circumstances, you will run across nuances in the plotting procedures, depending on where you are located relative to the bodies, but for objects more or less in line that are less than 90° apart, the results shown in 6-29 are typical. A good reference for this and related measurements is *How to Use Plastic Sextants: With Applications to Metal Sextants and a Review of Sextant Piloting* (Starpath Publications, 2009).

6.14 Danger Bearings

The compass bearing to a landmark can provide a safety check to a safe route past a hazard, as shown in Figure 6-30. After identifying the full extent of the underwater hazard, measure on the chart the compass bearing along a line that conservatively marks the extent of the hazard, 055M in the example. Then as you sail pass this hazard you monitor the compass bearing to that light to be sure it does not become larger than 055 M. The standard notation for danger bearing lines is NMT (not more than) or NLT (not less than) the danger bearing. In other words, the bearing to this target should not read above 055 M. If it read 040, then a while later 045, and then 050, you have clear warning that you are getting pushed into danger and need to turn away more.

This simple method has many applications; it is especially valuable when you suspect you might be set by wind or current down onto the hazard. Buoys marking a hazard can be a tempting target for danger bearings, but should be used with caution, because their precise position can be uncertain.

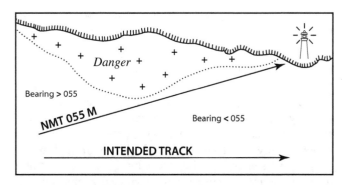

Figure 6-30. *Sample danger bearing. Sailing passed a point of land in an onshore breeze or current, you can use a bearing to a landmark to insure you are not in danger. Anywhere above this line the bearing to light would be larger than 055M; below it the bearing is less than 055M. Thus watching that the bearing is not more than (NMT) 055M insures you are in safe water.*

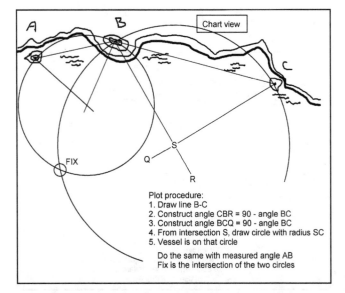

Figure 6-29. *Graphic solution to the three-body problem. There are numerous solutions. This one was the most popular in the old days and remains the easiest if we do not include numeric computations in the process.*

Chapter 6 Glossary

bearing compass. A handheld compass used for piloting or collision avoidance.

bearing fix. A piloting fix made from two or more compass bearing lines.

bow angle. The angle to a target measured relative to the bow (0° to 180°, port or starboard). Not the same as relative bearing, which is 0° to 360°.

Bowditch. Nickname for the The American Practical Navigator, NGA Pub. 9, originally by Nathaniel Bowditch.

closest point of approach (CPA). Used in radar and other navigation settings to refer to the minimum passing distance between two vessels.

danger bearing. A compass bearing to a landmark used to mark the safe water side of an underwater hazard.

depth sounder. Electronic device that measures the depth of the water.

distance off. The distance from a vessel to a charted landmark or other object or vessel.

draft. A dimension on a vessel relative to the water level. Depth sounder draft is the transducer depth below the water. Vessel draft refers to the depth of the keel below the water. Air draft refers to the highest point on the vessel above the water.

electronic bearing line (EBL). A user-controlled line on a radar screen or ECS display used to measure the bearing to a target from the vessel location.

electronic range and bearing line (ERBL). A user-controlled line on a radar screen or ECS display used to measure the range and bearing between any two points on the screen. Pronounced "urble."

geographic range. The straight-line distance from an observer's eye height to an object on the horizon.

horizontal angle. Effectively, the difference in the bearings between two objects on the horizon, usually assuming this difference is measured directly with an instrument such as a kamal or a sextant.

kamal. A calibrated stick or plate used to measure angular dimensions of objects seen on the horizon. The concept dates from early Arab sailors trading along the east coast of Africa when it was used to find latitude from the height of Polaris.

line of position (LOP). A line on the chart upon which the vessel must be located based on piloting measurements. Related concepts are circle of position and depth contour of position.

line of soundings. A list of measured depths and the corresponding distances run between them used in piloting by depth sounder.

lollipop display. A circle-and-handle type icon used to mark an active waypoint on a radar screen.

P-72 plotter. A 4" × 15" ruler with a protractor, scales, and parallel lines used in chart plotting. This now common name for this tool from any source stems from a part number of a particular manufacturer.

radar reflector. A metal device hung in the rigging to enhance radar reflections from the vessel.

radar wake. An optional radar display that displays the track of past positions on the screen, usually for a specified time period such as 6 minutes. Also called trails.

relative bearings. Bearings referenced to the bow at 000 R. Starboard beam is 090 R, stern is 180 R, port beam is 270 R.

Rule No. 1. As used in this book: "Plot your position on the chart labeled with the time as often as possible."

running lights. A common nickname for the sidelights, masthead lights, and sternlight required for all vessels underway.

sextant. A handheld instrument used to measure angles accurately. Originally developed for celestial navigation but also used for piloting since the 1700s.

ship's heading line (SHL). The line emanating from the center of a radar display in the direction the vessel is headed.

string plotter. A round or square protractor with a string secured to its center that can be used to measure bearings or course lines on a chart.

three-arm protractor. A chart plotting device that allows two angles to be set accurately so the place on the chart that would give rise to those observed horizontal angles or bearings can be located.

three-body fix. The historically common name for the piloting technique of finding an accurate position fix by measuring the two horizontal angles between three objects seen on the horizon.

variable range marker (VRM). A user-controlled range ring on a radar screen used to measure the distance to radar targets.

vertical angle. The angle measured at the vessel between the top of an object on the horizon and the waterline directly below it.

visible range. The distance an object can be seen from the height of eye of the observer in the present atmospheric conditions. This is a very generic term that has more specific meaning in specific contexts. See luminous range, nominal range, geographic range, and atmospheric visibility.

Weems parallel plotter. A plotting tool that rolls without sliding used for similar tasks as parallel rulers. Invented by PVH Weems, who invented or improved numerous navigation aids. He originally called this one the "Weems paraline plotter," but that name is not used these days.

Winking. As used in this book, the method of estimating distance off by noting the relative horizontal shift of an object on the horizon viewed from either eye alone.

CHAPTER 7
ELECTRONIC NAVIGATION

7.1 Introduction

This chapter outlines the practical use of electronic aids, primarily GPS. At one time a luxury, it is now essentially required equipment, although there are some mariners who still consider it a backup to traditional log, compass, and radar navigation.

"Electronic navigation" primarily means using some form of *electronic chart system* (ECS), which is a computer program that displays electronic charts as well as our current GPS position overlaid on the chart and moving across it at the speed and in the direction we are traveling. There are free computer versions of ECS such as OpenCPN and qtVlm, and popular commercial computer versions such as Expedition, Coastal Explorer, and Time Zero. There are also many brands of console mounted units usually called "chartplotters."

Practice with an ECS helps us better understand how to combine this powerful technology with the traditional methods we learn in this book, if they know ahead of time what the ECS can do. The remaining chapters of this book, however, are still written as if high-tech tools did not exist—which remains, in fact, a prudent approach to navigation.

The Global Positioning System, known universally as GPS, is an extensive satellite-based navigation system developed through Department of Defense contracts during the late 1970s and early 1980s. It was conceived as a military system and remains under military control. The loss of the Korean airliner that was destroyed when it wandered into Soviet air space in 1983 was influential in making the system accessible to civilian use to prevent similar disasters. As of about 1989, it was available for public use on a limited basis; today it is the primary electronic navigation system for essentially all vessels, commercial and recreational—not to mention, vehicles, aircraft, and pedestrians! GPS is now officially under the control of the US Space Force.

A similar satellite system from Russia called GLONASS is available to commercial receivers. The Galileo system from the European Union is also available, designed to be interoperable with the US and Russian systems. "GPS units" can now offer the ability to receive GLONASS and US GPS with an integrated solution that should yield higher accuracy and redundancy. All such systems are often referred to as "GPS," but the proper generic term is GNSS (global navigation satellite system), of which the US GPS system is the leading example. India and China also have GNSS systems, but they are not often incorporated into US commercial instruments.

GPS can tell you where you are (in terms of latitude and longitude) almost anywhere on earth with a good view of the sky and in any weather with astonishing precision—along with the direction you are moving and the speed of your motion, accurate to a tenth of a knot. The ECS that is reading the GPS signals, can also tell us the course and distance to any other location, but this is a geometric computation, not dependent on satellite connections.

Anyone can use an ECS for any application. GPS receivers are readily available online from sophisticated console units to handheld units. These days, essentially any smartphone or smartwatch has a GPS in it and some form of electronic charting app can be added. There are also GPS sensors without their own display intended to be connected to a computer via USB cable, Bluetooth, or local wifi.

Before getting to the practical use of this tool, I will share the personal conviction that GPS is one of the most dramatic technological developments in history. It was the first example of space-science technology that has significantly influenced multiple aspects of modern life. Its application to guiding boats around the world is now a rather peripheral application. It has, for example, revolutionized the fields of surveying, mapping, and exploration. GPS instrumentation mounted near geological faults and volcanoes is being used to measure otherwise imperceptible motions of the earth's surface to forecast earthquakes and eruptions. It is standard equipment in cars, linked to miniature on-board computers. Such equipment can produce electronic maps with encyclopedic indexes to services and addresses. With a few keystrokes, for example, you can call up a map of the shortest route through one-way streets to the nearest Italian restaurant in a town you have never visited. Ambulances or other emergency vehicles can travel directly to any address in the most efficient manner. Combined with automated position broadcasts from moving GPS-equipped vehicles (AIS), tracking systems could be developed to warn of collision courses between cars, planes, or boats. There are GPS units available that have stored in their memories the precise location of most navigational lights and buoys in the United States and Canada. New applications are being developed daily.

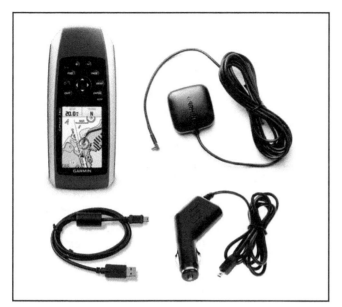

Figure 7-1. *A Garmin GPSMAP 78s (garmin.com) handheld receiver and accessories. The receiver is 6 inches tall. To the right is an external antenna; below it is a USB connector to a computer, and bottom right is a 12V DC adapter. This unit shows Garmin charts, as well as tide tables, a barometer, and an electronic compass. You can also use it to navigate on georeferenced satellite photos. Newer models replace this one.*

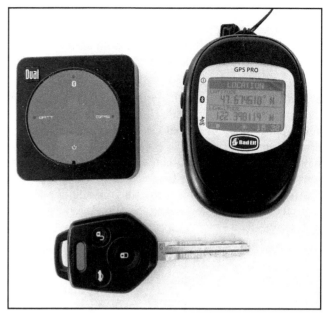

Figure 7-2. *Two popular Bluetooth GPS units: a Dual XG-PS150A (dualav.com) and a Bad Elf GPS Pro (bad-elf.com). Both will also pair with iOS and Android apps. The Bad Elf Pro is also a data logger that records location, course and speed, even when not connected to an app.*

On the downside, the more efficient any tracking capability becomes, the more the question of privacy arises, not to mention hostile or terrorist use of automated precision navigation. Also, who is liable when a freighter owned by one country and chartered by another country collides with a tanker from another country causing damage to yet another country, when both were navigated by American satellites that temporarily failed? Anyone can use the equipment, and no licenses or permits are required. Political, social, and legal issues develop in parallel with this, as with all high-impact technologies.

7.2 Use of GPS Underway

As noted GPS comes in several generic categories. A hybrid that meets the needs of many small craft operators, is a handheld unit in a bracket at the nav station with an external antenna and maybe another bracket at the helm. There are models, even with charting, built into a device that is similar to a large watch. These might be the good solution for small boats or kayaks. The console models are larger with better displays, always with external antenna,

---

...In Depth

12.12 Wrinkles in Practical ECS

Procedures for optimizing navigation with electronic chart systems...

---

and often with built-in echart displays in some format. A tablet version of the ECS is a popular compromise.

Physically, handheld GPS receivers look a bit like a cellular phone with its keypad and display screen. They easily fit in a shirt pocket. A small integral antenna communicates with satellites, so the unit must be placed on deck when in use, with as much view of the sky as possible. Use in an open cockpit often calls for waterproof operation, which many include now as standard. Figure 7-1 shows one model and its accessories; Figure 7-2 shows two Bluetooth GPS receivers.

Modern GPS units are quicker to initialize (locate themselves) than older ones. If you have an older GPS, when first turned on, the unit should be programmed with an approximate position, the time and date, and height above the water along with choices such as preferred units for distances and true or magnetic headings. You also must specify two-dimensional (latitude and longitude) or three-dimensional (includes elevation) position fixes. The obvious choice on the water is two dimensions; this mode requires communications with just three satellites. Measuring elevation requires seeing four satellites, which is sometimes difficult near steep shores that limit the view of the horizon, not to mention that elevation data from a GPS is not often very accurate without WAAS connections (Section 12.29).

Once programmed, the unit must accumulate basic almanac data from the satellites. This takes a few minutes extra on the first run of a new or older unit. After that, simply turn it on, and in a minute or so, it starts functioning; from then on, all navigational data are available in seconds.

If you transport the unit a long distance or do not use it for a long time, it might be necessary to repeat some of the above. For daily use, it can be turned on and off with no delay in operation.

The units often run on several AA batteries or rechargeable internal batteries. Either will last up to 10 hours depending on the brand. Since the units need to be run continuously only in special circumstances, this working lifetime could cover many days of typical cruising. Some have a battery saver mode that shuts the unit off in a minute or so if no key is pressed. Care must be taken, of course, if this mode is selected to ensure that the unit doesn't unexpectedly shut off when longer operation is required, such as for crossing currents or for crossing a complicated bar. For expedition sailing away from civilization, rechargeable batteries and a solar-powered battery charger are options. For use as a console substitute, a DC adapter is valuable to save batteries. For power-driven vessels that distribute AC throughout the vessel, an AC-to-DC adapter facilitates use of the DC adapter—on the boat or at home. Don't be surprised if an external antenna plus a DC adapter might together cost as much as the unit itself.

ECS on mobile devices

An ECS app running on a large cell phone will often meet navigation needs, especially if it is compatible with output from a computer version so routes and tracks can be transferred between them. A tablet version is even more likely to meet more general needs because of the larger screens, but there is a nuance to use of the popular iPad tablet.

Essentially all phones include a GPS receiver, but on iPads only the cellular models include a GPS, which cost 25 to 30 percent more than wifi alone. Note, however, that you do not need to actually use the cellular features of the iPad. The extra monthly cost of a new phone line is the usual large expense of the cellular connections, but you do not need to activate that service to access the GPS. You just need that model of iPad.

Alternatively, you can use an external Bluetooth GPS to send signals to the iPad. Another solution, good to know even if just used as a backup, is there are ECS apps like qtVlm for the phone that will in turn broadcast all of the sensor data from the phone via a wifi to your tablet, so that the phone serves as a GPS receiver—as well as a heading sensor, heel sensor, and barometer; all internal phone sensors useful for navigation can be sent to the tablet via wifi.

...In Depth

12.29 WAAS-Enhanced GPS

The key to optimum GPS accuracy and its derived functions is to be in view of a WAAS satellite, but there is more to the story...

Regardless of connections, however, use of the locations services (GPS) on a phone or tablet is a large battery drain. External connection to a power supply or battery pack is required for extended use, as is some form of waterproof covering.

7.3 Position Navigation

Your position is indicated on the display screen in latitude and longitude, specified to the nearest one-thousandth of a minute, such as 47° 38.532' N, 122° 24.791' W. Recall from Chapter 2 that 1' of latitude is about 6,000 ft, so a precision of 0.001' corresponds to about 6 ft, but for several reasons, a GPS signal is not this accurate on any dependable basis. A typical accuracy might be ±33 ft (10 meters), but it could be half that or twice that at times. The remarkable thing here is that the numbers you see on the screen are usually correct within these uncertainties, if you are stationary long enough. The small handheld gadget can tell you where you are on the 200 million square miles of the earth's surface to within a boat length or two!

The usual difference between the best accuracy and typical accuracy is whether or not you are using the corrections from a WAAS (Wide Area Augmentation System) satellite. Most modern units will acquire and use this data automatically. See Section 12.29.

An interesting way to evaluate position uncertainty or jitter is to use an ECS with the GPS input to it. Then with the GPS unit kept stationary, with a good view of the sky in a window or back porch, select the option that leaves a trail behind the boat, and zoom in to within 100 ft or so and let the program run overnight. In the morning, you will see how the stationary GPS position wandered around the room. If the option is given, choose high precision track.

If the unit suspects that the data may not be good when you are underway, it will provide various warning signals or icons on the screen with codes that tell of the problem, such as missing satellites, weak signals, and the like. Although most interactions with the satellites are done automatically, you do have the option in some cases to adjust satellite choices or erase calculations and start the position determination all over. These user interactions, however, are very rarely called for. This is truly a black box. You turn it on; it tells you where you are; and you hope it is right.

With the use of GPS, position navigation reduces to plotting your known latitude and longitude on the chart—to find out where you really are! This is not a trivial task in a vessel underway, especially if you wish to retain anywhere near the actual accuracy you know. In fact, in most cases, you cannot plot the accuracy you know, no matter how or where you do it, because of the limitations of the chart scales. On a large scale chart such as 1:25,000, a pencil dot one sixteenth of an inch across spans 130 ft on the chart. If you can get that dot on the chart in the right place, you know you are in the middle of it. Plot the position wrong by one dot width, and you have thrown away accuracy. On a 1:40,000 chart, that dot is 208 ft across.

One quick plotting approach underway is to have latitude and longitude lines already drawn on the chart at convenient intervals and then to locate your position relative to them, either by simply estimating the place or using a special tool. Some lines are, of course, printed on the chart to begin with, but they are too far apart to be convenient. On a 1:40,000 chart, the parallel lines of latitude are typically printed only every 5', which spaces them about 9 inches apart. If you draw the lines by hand every 1' of latitude and longitude, it is much easier to estimate where your position lies by interpolation.

The procedure can be improved by constructing a special plotting tool using waterproof cardboard or plastic and

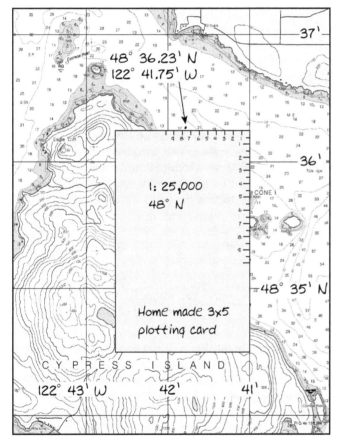

Figure 7-3. *Homemade tool for quick plotting of GPS positions. The chart must be prepared with Lat-Lon lines at each 1' interval. To use the card: (1) align the right edge of the card with the minutes part of your longitude on the chart; (2) adjust the vertical position of the card to align the tenths part of your latitude minutes (read on the card) with the whole-minutes line of your latitude on the chart; and (3) mark the chart at the minutes part of your longitude read from the card. At this scale, the hundredths of minutes parts of latitude and longitude must be interpolated by eye. Separate plotting cards (or separate sides or corners of the same card) are needed for each chart scale and latitude region. These cards are especially valuable for plotting on small craft folio charts. For these, the Lat-Lon spacing marks are at 1' intervals and the reference lines on the charts (meridians and parallels) are marked every 5'.*

waterproof ink. The plotter is illustrated in Figure 7-3. It must be customized for each chart in use, and it requires that the chart be prepared with latitude and longitude lines. The tool can be tied to a chart case along with a china marker or other waterproof pen for cockpit navigation. I have used this plotting technique extensively in sailboat racing whenever quick plotting was essential and echarts were not in use. It is much faster than conventional methods, regardless of the tools or space available.

On the other hand, the conventional use of dividers and parallel rulers or a plain ruler will likely be the most common method used at the nav station, except possibly when using folio charts. There are videos at starpath.com/navbook that illustrate the use of several tools.

A reminder, though, that no matter how you plot it, or even how you obtained the position fix in the first place, recording that position on a paper chart and labeling it with the corresponding time remains the key to good navigation. The more often you do it, the more you will learn from it, and the better off you will be when you need it. This remains Rule No. 1 in navigation.

7.4 SOG and COG

A GPS receiver includes a computer and a clock. The clock is updated continually from the satellites and displays the precise UTC—same as GMT, or Zulu time (i.e., 12z).

With computer memory and a clock, the unit knows not only where you are, but where you were. From this, it can figure your true course and speed at any time. It is important to understand that the speed and course it tells you are your true speed and true course, called *speed over the ground* (SOG) and *course over the ground* (COG). This is not the same speed that a knotmeter would read and not the course that your compass would read. SOG and COG are measures of your true motion that take into account your boat speed, the speed and direction of the current, and any leeway you might have if the wind is blowing. In most navigation COG and SOG are what you care about.

If you were sailing at 6 kts through a tidal stream moving at 2 kts, the GPS would show a SOG of 8 kts, assuming the current was flowing in the same direction you were sailing. In this case, your COG would be the same as your compass course.

...In Depth

12.14 Meaning of Terms COG, SOG, and So On

Exploring the meanings and uses of COG, SOG, and VMC, which are the most important information available from GPS...

If, on the other hand, you were sailing at 6 kts due north magnetic (000 on the compass), across a current flowing toward the northeast (magnetic) at 2 kts, the GPS would show a SOG of 7.55 kts and a COG of 010.8 M. It has told you very plainly you are not going in the direction you are pointed, which is what the compass reads.

On a long passage or in dangerous waters, it is the COG and, to a lesser extent, the SOG, that you really care about, not so much your actual position at any one time. COG and SOG are the data that warn you immediately that you may be getting into trouble, or that you are at least not doing what you think you are. It is, nevertheless, the high accuracy of the position data that allows the instrument to figure the course and speed accurately and quickly.

Since the COG and SOG are so crucial to navigation, it is important that they be displayed in the most useful manner. The high accuracy of the instrument can work against you in some cases. When sailing in gusty winds or bigger seas, your actual course and speed change every few minutes or even every 5 or 10 seconds as you adjust or respond to the seas or gusts. But since the instrument is so accurate, it measures each of these intermittent changes. Each time you look at the screen, you see a new course, which means you are back to not knowing which way you are going. To correct this, reprogram the GPS to display the *average* value of the COG and SOG over the past 30 seconds or few minutes.

7.5 Waypoints and Routes

Navigation with GPS, or by any means for that matter, is facilitated by setting up specific locations called waypoints and sequences of these called routes. A planned trip would begin at your departure point by selecting from the chart various points (usually turning points) along the intended route, and then entering the latitude and longitude of these points into the GPS unit. Most models will accept several hundred such points, which can be numbered and given text names. The sequence itself can then be named and stored as a specific route. Waypoints also can be copied from a previously stored route and built into a new one. Or you could define, say, Waypoint 22 as 2.4 nmi NE of Waypoint 57. The format is versatile. It is also possible at any time when you are underway to store your present position as a numbered waypoint. With this option, you could travel a route you have not programmed and store key points along the way to use for a programmed return trip.

Once a route is entered, you can review it (still sitting at home), asking for the course and distance between each waypoint to sum up the trip or for other planning. And this is exactly what you would do underway as you proceed from point to point. From your starting position, you call up the route of interest and the first waypoint on it. Then from your present position, the unit tells you the course and distance to that waypoint. As you proceed in that direction, it will figure your speed and tell how long it will take to get there at that average speed. If you wander off the direct line route to the waypoint, it will tell you so, but regardless of where you are, it continually tells you the course and distance to the assigned waypoint. When you arrive at the waypoint, select the next one and carry on; or use the automatic mode, which will switch to the next waypoint when you pass within a certain distance to the first one.

7.6 Currents, XTE, and Plotters

There are two basic ways to navigate with GPS using waypoints. The first is to call up the desired destination waypoint, read the course to it, and head in that direction, or set the GPS to navigate to that waypoint. The second is to navigate by a route, in which case you show on the screen the line between the last waypoint and the next, and you navigate relative to that line, still with the next waypoint as your near-term destination. In either case, as you proceed, set up the display screen to show your track of past positions, then watch how your course made good (CMG) compares to the desired course to the next waypoint. If you are in current, if your compass is wrong, or you are simply not steering the course you intended, the CMG will show that you are not making the desired course, and you must alter course until these two agree.

Notice we are making a distinction in terminology between COG and CMG, as discussed in the In Depth link to Section 12.14. COG is an instantaneous live value; CMG is from our past track.

For example, suppose the computed course to the waypoint is 050, and holding that course for a few minutes, you notice the COG is 070, although the compass still reads 050 and you have held this fairly well (CMG also 070). You

...In Depth

12.15 Racing with GPS

The main difference between racing and cruising navigation is the speed at which things must be done and how close the corners might be cut. There is a higher emphasis on performance evaluation from the GPS data. This note discusses these factors...

...In Depth

12.16 Marine Radios

A look at ship-to-ship and ship-to-shore communications via VHF and single-sideband radio, and also the maritime uses of cellular and satellite telephones...

are getting set to the south, most likely by a southerly current. In this case, you will have to point north of the desired course, into the current in order to track straight to the waypoint.

For a simple attempt at correction, since you are getting set 20° south, you could just steer 20° north of 050, toward 030, and then watch how that develops. If you are then tracking to the mark, you are done—assuming you remain at the same speed. If you speed up or slow down, the numbers will change, but in any event, the unit will tell you immediately what course to steer to achieve your desired course. Or take all way off completely and let the COG and SOG be a measure of the current speed and direction—provided there is no significant wind pushing you across the water.

When crossing currents in this manner, using just one waypoint and the COG, it is important that you monitor both courses (desired course to the next waypoint and COG) simultaneously during the process. This is important for fairly close destinations, since the desired course will change as you get set off the original track line.

The way around this problem, which is most important in crossing strong currents or when setting off on a long passage with hazards to either side, is to navigate by routes and not just waypoints. Choose not only a destination waypoint, but also a departure point, from which the computer will establish the straight line track between them. With this method, you can guide the boat along that track through all sorts of hazards, in strong current, or in thick fog. It is the mariner's version of flying by the instruments.

Using this option, you can steer by what is called *cross track error* (XTE). This display shows how far you are off to the right or left of the intended track. In some circumstances, this is a convenient way to navigate. Typical displays that you could select underway might read:

TO SMITH ROCK		ROUTE 10 LEG 3
050° M 2.48 NM	or	47°38.41'N 124°35.03'W
XTE 0.03 NM RIGHT		COG 057° M SOG 3.9

The first shows that you have called your immediate destination "Smith Rock" and that it is located 2.48 nmi away in magnetic direction 050, and at the moment you are 0.03 nmi to the right of the track you planned to travel.

...In Depth

12.28 Limitations of GPS

It is only prudent to use GPS, but it is also prudent to recognize its limits and know how to navigate without it...

As is often the case, it pays to recall that 1 nmi is about 6,000 ft, so this means you are 180 ft (0.03 × 6,000) off course to the right. It remains impressive: you can draw a precise line mathematically between two points that are, say, 10 nmi apart, and at any position along that route know immediately whenever you wander more than 60 ft off that line.

The alternative display shows that Smith Rock is the destination of the third leg of what you have numbered the tenth route of your travels. Your present position is shown, along with the fact that at the moment your course over ground is 057 M at a speed over ground of 3.9 kts. If you want to get back on track (050 M), you will have to point more to the left.

Note that in this case if you happened to be steering 050, and then used the previous reasoning, you would alter course to steer about 7° high to correct for the set. What would likely happen, though, is when you steadied out headed toward 043, you would indeed start making good the course you wanted of 050, but you would not be back on the track you wanted. You just straightened out your COG to be parallel to your desired track. You will have to overcorrect for a while to get back on to the actual track, and then fall back to 043.

Remember that these are all *average* courses. You cannot, usually, steer a course of, say, 043 precisely; in all circumstances, your compass course swings around as you proceed. But you can get fairly close, especially when you have such a powerful tool as GPS to help. Just do whatever you are doing, and watch the average course on the GPS; if it is not quite right, do a little more or little less of it.

In the terminology suggested, if at some point, you notice that the COG is staying rather different from the past CMG read from the track, then you have detected that something has changed.

Circumstances and personal preferences will decide whether the tracks or XTE presentation is best at the moment. Actual tracks on an echart display seem the most fundamental for telling what is taking place and what might have changed. Also, the past tracks can usually be saved or converted to routes, which can then be used to backtrack to where you started.

Despite the potential conveniences of these features, it remains prudent and still of utmost importance to record your position on a paper chart with the corresponding time as frequently as possible (Rule No. 1). If you put all your eggs in one little plastic box, you might get caught up the creek with your batteries down.

7.7 How GPS Works

GPS finds position from the intersection of circles of position that indicate ranges to satellites whose locations are known precisely. The procedure is analogous to that shown back in Figure 6-21, which uses an ancient kamal to measure the ranges. High technology enters in the way the satellite ranges are determined: measuring the time it takes the radio signals to travel from the satellites to the receiver. Time measurements accurate to nanoseconds (billionths of a second) are used, with timing errors removed using a third satellite for the fix. This is the reason three satellites are required for a two-dimensional fix that could otherwise be done with just two, as shown in Figure 6-21.

The US GPS system consists of a constellation of twenty-four active satellites with several operational spares, of which five to eight are visible from any place on earth at any time, assuming a clear view of the horizon. Accuracy and other performance specs define a "clear view of the horizon" as seeing above 5° elevation in all directions. The Coast Guard coordinates civilian use of GPS. Latest information is available from the USCG Navigation Center website (google "uscg navcen"). Policies and goals are officially presented in the Federal Radionavigation Plan, which is updated every 2 years. This publication is available from the NavCen website. More discussion of principles and use of GPS are included at starpath.com/navbook.

7.8 Sensor inputs to ECS

A typical ECS does not just accept your GPS signals for accurate position, COG, and SOG, but we can also input our knotmeter reading so we have speed through the water (STW), also called "knotmeter speed" or just "boat speed." Also very common and important is the input of a heading sensor so we can record and use our course through the water (CTW), often called just "heading." For small craft this is typically a magnetic heading, but the ECS can convert this to a true heading either by reading a variation we input manually or by a direct computation of the variation for any time and place using the World Magnetic Model app called GeoMag. There is also a mobile app version called

CrowdMag, which includes a compass read out and other functionality. A sample of a heading sensor is shown in Figure 7-4.

Chapter 8 covers the important role of tide and current apps in ECS, as well as the use of mobile device apps that also provide tide and current data, and that functionality is indeed one of the key aspects of electronic navigation. Besides their use within an ECS, an unused phone can run one of the apps for a stand alone data source. These do not need internet access to compute tides and currents.

Wind instruments, barometer, and seawater temperature can also be input to the ECS to use for weather analysis, especially in those ECS that import wind, wave, and current forecasts. Usually plots of the observed data as a function of time are extremely valuable for monitoring changes in your environment. High accuracy and high functionality barometers are also available as mobile device apps. A sample is shown in Figure 7-5.

7.9 Trends in Electronic Publications

Historically, marine navigation resources and equipment manuals have all been books or other printed publications, but this has changed in navigation, just as it has in all walks of life. The internet provides resources and communications on a previously unimaginable level. Information is more timely, more compact, and better indexed, and much more extensive. Even very specialized publications are now accessible from remote locations. Essentially all the documents we might need are available for download from the internet, mostly as PDF files.

Figure 7-4. *A combined electronic inclinometer (heel angle) and compass heading sensor. It uses a fluxgate sensor, with the ferrite core floating in liquid. This sample is from Autonnic Research Ltd, posted on Wikipedia. Newer models are available.*

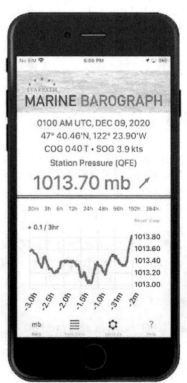

Figure 7-5. *An example of the many apps developed for mariners. See starpath.com/marinebarometer. There is a free version as well as this one that also records nav data such as COG. SOG, position, time, and barometer, which can then be exported as a GPX file to import into navigation apps.*

Even nautical charts are available as PDF files, but the actual echarts are likely more useful. See starpath.com/getcharts to access all NOAA chart products. In modern times, there is no reason we cannot have all the charts we might ever need downloaded and ready to go. Even if we do not routinely use ECS, we can have one loaded on a computer or mobile device to use as backup with every chart along our route loaded and ready to use.

Our getcharts link above as well as starpath.com/navbook includes notes on the new generation of NOAA printed charts called NOAA Custom Charts (NCC) as well as a link to our summary of free apps that display ENC. See also Section 12.17 on POD and NCC charts.

You can now download for reference all crucial navigation publications such as: *Coast Pilots*; *Sailing Directions*; *Light Lists*; tide and current predictions; *Navigation Rules*; Notices to Mariners; massive nautical glossaries; boating magazine articles; and so on; plus all the manuals and user guides to all equipment on the boat. These documents are PDF files that can be read on any computer or mobile device.

Convenient document storage

Load the documents into your device and then open them in an ebook reader such as Kindle or Apple Books. Then you can create a special "collection" of documents called, say, Nav Docs, and then move all your nav docs to that collection, or bookshelf. There the pubs can be sorted or searched for when you have a lot.

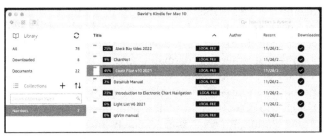

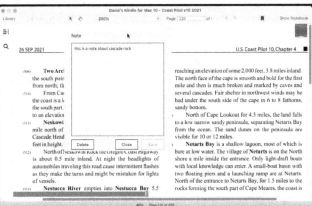

Figure 7-6. *Top. Storing multiple navigation PDF documents in a sub folder (collection) of a Kindle library, which can then be shared to all of your devices. Bottom. A book-marked document page with a highlight and note added.*

Once opened in the app, you can search the document, make highlights, and add bookmarks and notes. This is a good way to keep a large number of documents organized. Unless another reader is preferred, the Kindle has an app for all devices and computers. The pubs will then be automatically shared over all of your devices, which is a good back up. A sample is shown in Figure 7-6

Chapter 7 Glossary

Bluetooth. A short-range wireless technology used to communicate between two electronic devices.

cross track error (XTE). The perpendicular distance between the vessel location and the line between the last and next waypoint. It is computed by most ECS.

Federal Radionavigation Plan. The official US document that outlines present and future policies in electronic navigation and communications. It is updated not less than every 2 years.

fluxgate compass. An electromagnetic device that measures the horizontal component of the earth's magnetic field using electronic circuits and gimballed coils that sense the field components.

jitter. Random fluctuations in the output of an electronic device due to electronic noise or other small, natural or artificial influences.

quick plotting card. A Starpath procedure for labeling a card and chart for quick manual position plotting.

radio direction finding (RDF). The process of finding an approximate LOP oriented toward a radio antenna. Although not much used in aviation or marine navigation today, it can still be called upon in an emergency.

route. A sequence of waypoints, between departure point and destination.

USCG Navigation Center. The primary resource for all matters of marine navigation. See navcen.uscg.gov.

UTC (Universal Coordinated Time). The international time system used in navigation, previously called Greenwich Mean Time. Also called Zulu time in many weather applications, i.e., 1800z = 1800UTC.

velocity made course (VMC). The SMG in the direction of the next waypoint.

WAAS (Wide Area Augmentation System). A system for improving GPS accuracy by comparing signals at specific known locations and then broadcasting back the corrections needed from one of several dedicated stationary satellites located over the equator.

CHAPTER 8
TIDES AND CURRENTS

8.1 Introduction

All waters that lead to the ocean are subject to the rise and fall of the tides. In many waters, tides and tidal currents have dramatic impact on many aspects of inland navigation. In other parts of the world, this is not a factor at all. If you are from an area like that—with no significant tides or currents—then you can skim through this section to see how lucky you are!

Please keep in mind that this book is also used by those who travel the beautiful waters of the Pacific Northwest, where we are indeed challenged by large tides and very strong currents. Tidal currents of 10 to 15 kts occur routinely in a few places, and currents of 3 to 6 kts are quite common at many places in WA, BC, and AK, as are tide ranges of 10 to 15 ft.

Tide height must be known when planning routes through shallow waters or when planning an anchorage. Changes in tide height overnight will determine anchor scope, for example, and tides must also be known when we are to navigate by the depth of the water. The reference water depth, called chart datum, which is used to define tide heights and soundings was discussed in Chapter 2.

In contrast to tide height, which must be known only in special circumstances and is usually easy to predict, some knowledge of tidal current is needed at all times, and it is usually not so easy to predict. If you plan to go through a pass or across a channel that has strong currents, you need to know when the current will be the weakest at the crossing site and also the state of the current along the route to the crossing site from your present position, because that determines how long it will take to get there and whether you will make it there by slack-water time.

Furthermore, current flowing against the wind in any waterway causes a dramatic increase in the steepness of the waves, often causing breaking seas that make progress downwind a much bigger challenge to boat handling. When traveling upwind in strong favorable current, the short steep seas caused by the opposing wind, along with the adverse force of the wind itself, often hinder progress more than the favorable current aids it. Changes in tidal current in just a few hours can turn an easy sail at 5 or 6 kts made good into an endless struggle to make good just a knot or two, and when crossing a river bar, a time miscalculation of less than an hour can change the crossing from pleasant to hazardous.

Only when sailing in landlocked lakes or reservoirs (where there are no tides) or in specific areas where it has been confirmed that tides have minimal influence can a mariner get by without an ongoing awareness of the state of the tidal cycle. Although tidal current has more significant influence on navigation than tide height does, the tides drive the currents so they are the starting point to understanding navigational implications of both.

8.2 Tide Height vs. Tidal Current

The gravitational force of the moon pulls the oceans up into a bulge on the moon side of the earth as shown schematically in Figure 8-1. This leaves the ocean surface slightly depressed on the sides of the earth and (relative to the sides) another bulge is created on the backside of the earth opposite the moon due to centrifugal force. As the earth rotates daily beneath the moon, the two bulges and the two hollows between them tend to hold their position relative to the moon. This causes the tidal wave envelope made up of the bulges and hollows to circle the earth as long waves causing the tides to rise and fall twice a day. Under the influence of these moving tidal bulges, water depths at specific locations oscillate between deeper than average and shallower than average approximately every 6 hours. The range of water depths on inland waters can be quite dramatic in special locations—40 ft or more in extreme cases—even though the actual height of the tidal bulge in mid-ocean is only about 18 inches: the extremely long wavelength of the tidal bulge causes the height of the wave to build as it enters the shallower water of the continental shelf. It then builds even more in funnel-shaped tidal channels inland, just as small ocean swells build in height before breaking as they run up a beach. In special cases, the size of coastal embayments match their tidal periods, which also causes large tides by resonance, just as there is an optimum speed to slide back and forth in a bathtub to create large waves.

Peak water elevations in the tidal oscillation are called *high waters*; minimum water elevations are called *low waters*. The terms, however, are relative to successive water levels in the tide cycle; it is possible for the actual water depth to be greater at low water on one day than it was at high water on another day. The heights and times of high and low waters vary slowly on successive cycles at specific locations, and they can vary considerably from place to place around the world. The height difference between high and low waters is called the *range* of the tide.

As the earth rotates daily, the moon rises in the east and sets in the west. At its peak height in the sky, it bears either due south or due north depending on your latitude. This moment is called the meridian passage of the moon, because the moon crosses your longitude at this time. The time period between successive meridian passages is called the lunar or tidal day; it is about 24 hours and 50 minutes long. A high water typically occurs 1 or 2 hours after the moon's meridian passage. The precise time lag depends on location, but it remains fairly constant from day to day at specific places. The time lag occurs because friction slows down the tidal bulge, so it does not follow directly under the moon, but some distance behind it. The sun also influences the tides (its gravitational pull on the water is about one-half as strong as that of the moon); so the relative orbital positions of the sun and moon (the moon's phase) also affect the tide height. In broad terms, the location of the more important moon determines the time of the tides, and the phase of the moon determines the range of the tides.

If the water goes up and down at the coast, it must at some time go in and out of coastal embayments. The up-and-down motion causes the *tide height* to change; the in-and-out motion causes the tidal current to change. It is important, however, to distinguish in language and thinking between tides (vertical motion) and the resulting tidal currents (horizontal motion). These two motions are not as simply related as might be guessed, because the size and shape of a tidal basin affect the flow of water within it. The common practice of referring to tidal currents as "the tides" is misleading and should be avoided.

Tidal current flowing into an estuary is called a *flood* current; when it flows out it is called an *ebb* current. The direction into or out of an estuary is not always clear from charts; so the direction as well as speeds are always specified in current predictions for each referenced location.

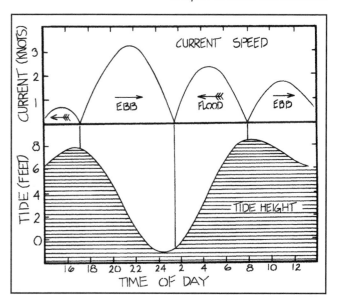

Figure 8-2. *Tides and currents off Bush Point, in Admiralty Inlet, between Puget Sound and the Strait of Juan de Fuca, Washington, on October 20 and 21, 1986. This is predominantly a standing wave tide with slack waters near high and low waters and peak flow about halfway between slack waters. Compare this behavior with Figure 8-3 from the same period in the Strait of Juan de Fuca.*

The brief time between flood and ebb currents when no current flows (or current speed is minimum) is called *slack water*. Most tidal currents of inland waters are *reversing currents*, which means the flood current at a particular location flows in one specific direction, and the ebb current flows in the opposite or near-opposite direction. Starting from slack water, the current speed increases to a maximum value, called *maximum ebb* or *maximum flood*, and then diminishes as the next slack approaches. Maximum flow in each cycle often (not always) occurs approximately halfway between successive slack-water times. The phrase "a 2-kt flood" usually refers to the entire flood cycle that peaks at 2 kts.

When considering the relationship between tide height and the associated tidal current, it is tempting to guess that slack water occurs at high water and at a low water—based on the reasoning that when the water stops going up, it stops coming in; and when it stops going down, it stops going out. This oversimplified common guess of the general behavior of tidal current is usually wrong, and it has gotten numerous boaters into trouble. This type of current behavior is actually characteristic of the fairly specialized circumstance of a *standing wave* in the local tidal basin. In a standing wave pattern, the water responds to tidal forces by sloshing up and down in the local tidal basin as it might in a large bathtub. When one end of the basin is high and slack, the other is low and slack. Some location near the center of the basin behaves as a pivot point (called the *nodal point*) in that it has a near-zero tide range even though current flows through it. In a standing wave tide, peak flow at any location along the bathtub occurs halfway between high water and low water. Standing wave patterns

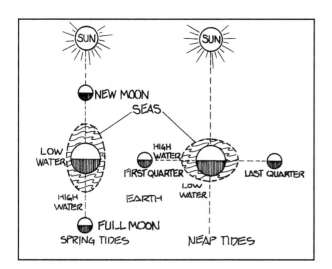

Figure 8-1. *Tidal bulges on the oceans are caused by the gravitational attraction of the moon and sun.*

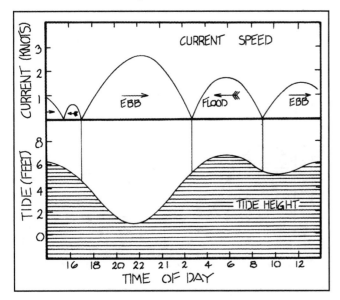

Figure 8-3. *Tides and currents off Angeles Point, WA in the Strait of Juan de Fuca, on October 20 and 21, 1986. This is predominantly a progressive wave tide with peak flows near high and low waters, and slack waters closer to the time of mid-tide. Compare with Figure 8-2. This is typical behavior; the date is not significant.*

"being full" at high water, and continues to run in for some time after the water depth begins to fall. Although several factors contribute to this behavior, the basic causes are momentum of the flowing water and differences in tide ranges and times at the two ends of the waterway-differences that are often amplified over long obstructed waterways.

Looking at this behavior in more detail, as the progressive wave of the tidal bulge enters the waterway, it raises the water level at the entrance sooner than it does the more inland end. This puts a slope on the surface of the waterway that causes the current to flood inward as gravity pulls the water level to equilibrium. (The opposite slope is created in basins where all the water rises at about the same time, but the inland end rises much higher.) The momentum of the flowing water then keeps it flooding inward, even after the slope on the surface of the waterway reverses—which it does as soon as the trough following the tidal wave crest enters, lowering the level of the entrance end. Slack water occurs only when the driving force of the new slope can overcome the momentum of the flowing water. Because the shape of a waterway affects the progress of the tide wave and water flow through it, it also affects the specific relationship between tide times and current times. In some

are established whenever two identical waves are running in opposite directions, which occurs in long dead-end tidal basins that reflect the incoming tidal bulge from the inland end of the basin. Consequently, in some large, partly enclosed waterways this common guess of tidal behavior is, indeed, a fairly close description of the relationship between tides and currents (an example is shown in Figure 8-2). In many other places, however, this guess could be seriously wrong and lead to danger, particularly where currents are strong.

Instead of a standing wave, an inland tide can behave more like the *progressive wave* of the oceanic tidal bulge that brings the tides to the estuary. In a progressive wave, there are no nodal points; the wave shape moves forward just as wind waves and swells do, and the associated current flow reflects the normal horizontal flow associated with the circulation of water particles in waves. In an undisturbed progressive tide wave, the peak forward flow (flood) occurs at the crest of the wave (high water), and the peak backward flow (ebb) occurs at the trough of the wave (low water). Large, open waterways exposed to the ocean often show tidal behavior strongly influenced by this pattern, as shown in Figure 8-3.

Tides in most areas, however, are to some extent a mixture of both standing waves and progressive waves and consequently behave in an intermediate manner, with no simple relationship between tides and currents. In some inland waterways with strong currents, the water continues to run out in the ebb direction long past the time of low water. Toward the end of the ebb cycle in these cases, the water level is actually rising while still running out. The same occurs on the flood cycle—the water runs in long past

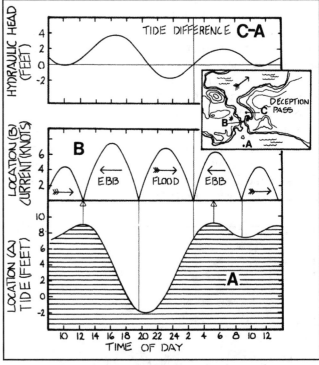

Figure 8-4. *Tides and currents at Deception Pass, WA, on May 21, 1986. This current is driven predominantly by the difference in tide height (hydraulic head) across the pass (location A to location C), which also is shown in the figure. Notice that at the first high water (location A) the pass is near slack, but at the second high water of the same height, the pass is near-peak flow at 6 kts (location B). It is not possible to judge the timing of current flow from the timing of the tides in many places. In most cases, the shape of the current rise at this pass is probably closer to that of the dashed lines in Figure 8-5.*

channels, the flood can continue for 3 hours past high water (mostly progressive wave); in others, it persists for only a few minutes (mostly standing wave). The same is true with the ebb at low water. It is impossible to simply look at a chart of a complex waterway and guess this behavior.

A third type of tidal behavior—distinct from standing waves and progressive waves—occurs at narrow passes leading into large confined bodies of water. In these cases, guessing that slack water at the pass occurs at high or low water at the pass could be as wrong as possible because these could be the times of maximum flow, not minimum flow. The constricted channel keeps the inside water level more or less constant as the seaward side rises and falls with the tides. Low water on the seaward side then corresponds to the maximum water slope across the length of the pass and consequently the peak current strength out of the pass. The same happens at high water with peak flow inward through the pass. On the other hand, in open water just a few miles from this type of pass, the timing of the tides and currents could be completely different. An example of tidal behavior at a pass showing these effects is illustrated in Figure 8-4.

The difference in tide height that drives a current through a channel in this manner is called a *hydraulic head*. Hydraulic currents do not vary with time in a smooth

sine function shape as wave-driven currents do, but instead they increase more rapidly after slack water (proportional to the square root of the developing hydraulic head) and remain at maximum flow for longer periods as shown in Figure 8-5.

Besides the separate mechanisms that drive tidal currents, other geographic details of the tidal basin can cause prominent anomalies in current behavior. One example is the persistent absence of one half of the current cycle in some places. In some specific locations within complex waterways, the tidal current can ebb continuously or flood continuously regardless of the state of the tide or of other tidal flow in adjacent waters. In such cases, flow only weakens during the time it should have reversed. These conditions can usually be traced to a unique flow of strong current into the region—a small-scale analogy would be the unidirectional current adjacent to a narrow point; because of back eddies that develop during both floods and ebbs, the net flow at the point is straight off the point most of the time, regardless of whether the mid-channel current is flooding or ebbing (see Figure 8-6). Another anomaly in flow pattern can occur on a temporary basis (for different reasons) in areas where flood and ebb strengths are significantly different. In these locations, the weaker cycle can periodically diminish to zero, leaving the current either ebbing all day (as occasionally happens in Puget Sound, Washington) or flooding all day (as occasionally happens in the Aleutian Islands, Alaska).

With these various examples in mind, it should be clear that guessing the time of slack water or peak flow, or even the direction of the flow, from the time of the tides is risky business without precise local knowledge. The relationship between tides and currents can change from day to day as the range of the tide changes, and it can change from place to place along the same waterway. The common terms "ebb tide" and "flood tide" are ambiguous when considering the relationship between tides and currents. Even the relationship between tide range and current speed must be considered carefully. The only safe rule is that the maximum speed of a current *at a particular place* is proportional to the range of the tide at that place: If the range of the tide today is 10 ft and last week the corresponding range was 5 ft, expect the associated current to be roughly twice as large today as it was last week. It is not possible, however, to estimate the relative current strengths between *two separate places* by comparing their tidal ranges. Contrary to expectations, a location with a small tide range could have much stronger currents than another place with large tide range.

There are separate predictions for tide heights and for tidal current flow. When tides are needed, check the tide predictions; when currents are needed, check the current predictions. Remember, also, that predicted tides and currents may not yield the actual values encountered. Winds, river flow, and atmospheric pressure also may affect the tides and currents, and unforeseen variability in these factors cannot be included in the tabulated predictions.

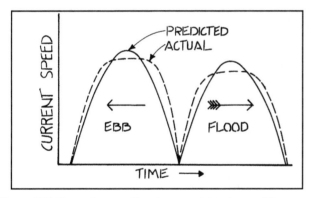

Figure 8-5. *Current versus time in a constricted pass. The solid curve is the shape shown in many current plots, but the dashed curve is likely to be closer to the actual currents. The difference is due to the different driving force of a hydraulic head, further influenced by friction and momentum.*

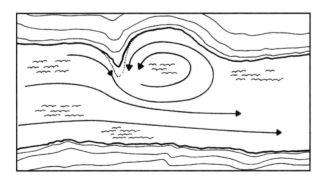

Figure 8-6. *Current flow near a point or spit. Sand shoals off the point are often a result of this flow pattern.*

8.3 Tide Patterns

The shape of the curve of tide heights throughout the day depends on location, time of the month, and time of the year. On the Atlantic coast of North America the tides are predominantly *semidiurnal*, which means there are two high waters and two low waters of approximately the same heights each day. This is the most common type of tide throughout the world. Along the northern shore of the Gulf of Mexico, and in several individual locations such as Victoria, British Columbia, the tides are predominantly *diurnal*, with just one high and one low water each day. This is a much less common tide pattern. Tides along the Pacific coast of North America are called *mixed* because they include both semidiurnal and diurnal wave forms; the typical one having two high waters (called the *lower high* and *higher high*) and two low waters (called *lower low* and *higher low*) each day, with significant inequalities in the two high-water heights and two low-water heights. The shape of the pattern at various places around the world is determined by the shape of the entire ocean basin exposed to the tidal waters, as well as that of the local water basin. In the Pacific Northwest, the pattern changes significantly in the 70 miles between Victoria, British Columbia (often diurnal), and Seattle, Washington (mostly mixed), as shown in Figure 8-7 along with the data from an intermediate station at Port Townsend, Washington.

The *mean range* of the tide at any location is the difference between the average high-water height and the average low-water height at that location. Mean ranges vary with latitude, being generally larger for inland waters at higher latitudes. Places in the Magellan Strait in southern Chile and Alaskan waters near Anchorage have mean ranges of more than 30 ft, whereas coastal waters around Hawaii and Florida have mean ranges of only 1 foot. Another tidal range called the *diurnal* range is useful in describing mixed tides. It is the average difference between the higher high and the lower low each day. Diurnal range is always larger than mean range. Some references list alternative tidal ranges called *spring* range and *neap* range. Spring ranges are average values of the large tides that occur near new moon and full moon, when the tidal wave forms of the sun and moon are aligned crest-with-crest. Neap ranges are the average values of the weak tides that occur when the sun and moon produce tide wave forms that are at right angles to each other, near the times of quarter moons (which appear in the sky as half-moons). Tidal currents are weakest during neap tides and strongest during spring tides. *Spring* in this usage is not related to the season, though they both come from the Saxon word *springan*, meaning to swell. *Neap* is from the Saxon word *neafle*, meaning scarcity.

8.4 Important Changes at NOAA

Prior to 2021, NOAA provided daily tide and tidal current predictions at specific *reference stations* across the country, and then provided an extensive list of detailed corrections (called *Table 2*) that was used to compute tides and currents at the vast number of other stations subordinate to each of the reference stations. NOAA then sanctioned several publishers to print the reference station daily data and the Tables 2 for tides and currents, along with several ancillary tables, in four volumes: East and West Coasts, Tides and Currents. At that time, these same books included international data spanning several continents.

That system and its terminology were discontinued in 2021. There is no longer an official list of Table 2 corrections, and the last versions from 2020 are now outdated for many stations, only to become increasingly so as time passes. NOAA no longer sanctions the publication of that data. Reference stations are now called *harmonic stations*, and NOAA no longer provides any international tidal data.

The new official source of tide and current data is the NOAA website tidesandcurrents.noaa.gov. Examples of its output are in sections 8.5 and 8.7. Extended discussion of the NOAA site with latest step by step procedures are linked at starpath.com/navbook.

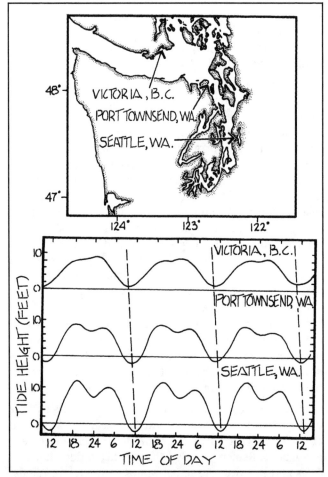

Figure 8-7. *Tide patterns in the Pacific Northwest on July 12-14, 1984. Victoria, BC, tides are often diurnal, similar to those in Louisiana and Texas; Seattle, WA, tides are mixed with large inequalities, which is more characteristic of West Coast tides.*

Prior to 2021, a notable challenge to many navigators was the struggle through the sometimes complex application of Table 2 corrections. That is all history now! There are no Tables 2. There is an online presentation of the data for every individual station, both for tides and for currents. Also for each station there is the option to download a PDF of the full annual predictions for each station. There are four letter size pages per year, per station. You can also now print out a graph (tide or current vs time) for one or more days. Thus going forward, we can make our own book of the tides and currents we care about.

In modern practical navigation, tides and currents can also be obtained for any location and time directly from within most navigation programs. It is important, however, at some point to check these computed predictions with the official data from NOAA. Chances are that a station checked at one time, will be valid at other times, but one station right, does not mean a different station is right. The few minutes it takes to check the ones you rely on is worth it. There are popular apps in use at the moment that have outdated tide and current data. Also, as of 2023, the outdated 2020 Table 2 corrections are still in print in some books without any warning that many of the stations have been discontinued due to inaccuracy.

8.5 Tide Height Predictions

Tides are uniform over large areas, so the nearest station not totally blocked by land should be good for you. If you are a long way from the nearest station, then look for a station in the other direction to see if an interpolation might be called for. An accurate tides and currents app in a nav program is usually the easiest way to find the nearest station, but the NOAA site itself makes this easy. Without dependable internet underway, these predictions should be compiled before departure.

Referring to starpath.com/navbook for details, we can obtain the types of tide data shown in Figure 8-8 from tidesandcurrents.noaa.gov.

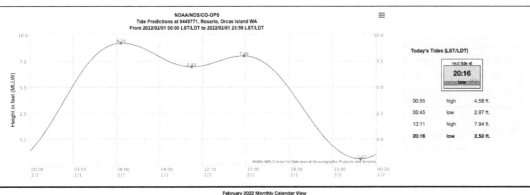

Figure 8-8. *Formats of tide height data available.*

Top is a graph of one or more days along with simple one day list of peaks.

Middle shows a one month calendar view of mini plots of the tide throughout the day.

Bottom is a section of the 4-page annual printout for this station. This would be the minimum we might want for important stations to have onboard. Without a graph, the Rule of Twelfths can be used to figure intermediate values.

StationId: 9449771
Source: NOAA/NOS/CO-OPS
Station Type: Primary
Time Zone: LST_LDT
Datum: MLLW

NOAA Tide Predictions

Rosario, Orcas Island, WA, 2022
(48 38.8N / 122 52.2W)
Times and Heights of High and Low Waters

	January					February					March				
	Time	Height		Time	Height	Time	Height		Time	Height	Time	Height		Time	Height
	h m	ft cm		h m	ft cm	h m	ft cm		h m	ft cm	h m	ft cm		h m	ft cm
1 05:22	8.8 268	**16** 05:58	8.4 256	**1** 06:20	9.2 280	**16** 06:11	8.3 253	**1** 05:03	8.4 256	**16** 05:43	7.6 232
08:57	7.8 238	10:13	7.5 229	11:14	6.9 210	11:13	6.0 183	10:12	5.8 177	11:05	4.9 149
Sa 13:05	8.9 271	Su 13:14	7.9 241	Tu 14:52	8.0 244	W 14:57	7.0 213	Tu 14:17	7.2 219	W 15:28	6.4 195
21:36	-2.9 -88	22:00	-1.1 -34	● 22:56	-1.9 -58	○ 22:43	-0.4 -12	21:54	-0.9 -27	22:37	0.4 12
2 06:08	9.4 287	**17** 06:29	8.6 262	**2** 06:53	9.1 277	**17** 06:33	8.2 250	**2** 05:32	8.4 256	**17** 06:03	7.6 232
10:14	8.0 244	11:05	7.4 226	12:04	6.2 189	11:45	5.5 168	10:54	5.0 152	11:33	4.1 125
Su 13:50	8.9 271	M 13:54	7.8 238	W 15:59	7.5 229	Th 15:55	6.8 207	W 15:32	7.0 213	Th 16:33	6.4 195
● 22:23	-3.1 -94	○ 22:33	-1.2 -37	23:37	-1.1 -34	23:15	0.0 0	● 22:37	-0.3 -9	23:14	0.9 27

Tides at intermediate times

Annual NOAA Tide Predictions give data only at the predicted extremes of high and low water. Without a tide app to do this for us, it is our job to interpolate the tide height at intermediate times. It is best to do this before departing, so that at any time you can glance at your own table or graph of tide height versus time to learn the state of the tide. Tide variation between high and low water is not a straight line decreasing in proportion to time, but instead it takes the form of a bell-shaped curve with the tide height lingering at the high and low depths. There are tables that do this interpolation, but many navigators prefer to make their own corrections using the *Rule of Twelfths*, which is illustrated in Figure 8-9.

To use this rule, divide the range of the tide by 12 to get the size of the range step and divide the duration of the rise or fall by 6 to get the size of the time step. The rule gives the tide height at 5 time steps across the duration. During the first time step, the tide changes 1 range step; during the second tide step, the tide changes 2 range steps; and during the third time step, the tide changes 3 range steps. After 3 time steps out of 6, you are halfway through the duration, and the tide has changed by half the range (6 steps out of 12). The second half is symmetric to the first half. Most tide changes are similar to this pattern.

This rule is usually presented with the assumption that the duration is exactly 6 hours, which makes the time steps exactly 1 hour. Very often this is an adequate approximation, but for large tides with durations longer than 7 hours or so, it is necessary to use the proper time step in order to get the tides right to within 1 foot.

Tide and current prediction apps

The official source of tidal data remains the NOAA website, but we can usually get the data we need much more efficiently using a tide app within the electronic chart system (ECS) we use. These apps use a set of harmonic constants to compute the tide at any time and place. In principle these constants—some 20 or more unique numbers for each station—should be the same values used by NOAA to compute their predictions. Then for all US waters, the app can show the locations of all stations, which can in turn be clicked to get contemporary data, usually with a graph of tide height vs time.

There are many stand alone tide apps for mobile devices, but seeing the stations plotted on the ECS we use is a big advantage. The most important concern, however, for any app, stand alone or part of an ECS, is are they giving us the right data! Accurate results depend on accurate harmonic constants, and it is the navigator's responsibility to check that these are up to date. NOAA continually improves and extends their measurements, which leads to new values, leaving older values out of date with inaccurate predictions. These constants are updated by NOAA quarterly; the convenient free set (called XTides) used by many apps is updated annually at flaterco.com.

Tide apps are very convenient, but it is always best to check the predictions for the stations you care about with the official data from tidesandcurrents.noaa.gov. This only has to be done once. It takes just minutes. A sample tide app display is shown in Figure 8-10. At the time of this writing we found several popular apps with outdated harmonics. Check with the program provider if the data are in question. A similar tidal current app is shown in Section 8.7.

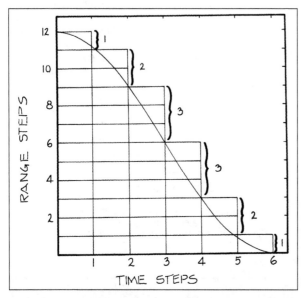

Figure 8-9. *The Rule of Twelfths method of determining tide height between high and low waters. The time steps are each one-sixth of the time between high and low waters (which can often be approximated as one whole hour). The range steps are each one twelfth of the difference between the high-water height and the low-water height.*

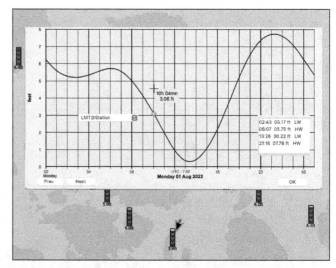

Figure 8-10. *Tide prediction app in the free nav program OpenCPN. It plots the station locations, then click one to see details as shown above. Move the cursor along curve to read values at specific times.*

8.6 Guidelines for Guessing the Tides

There is no substitute for doing your homework on tide prediction; but if you should end up navigating by the seat of your pants and get caught without your resource, the following guidelines might help with a guess.

• Know the local pattern (semidiurnal, diurnal, or mixed). With a mixed tide, a large range will be followed by a smaller range; in the others, successive ranges are similar.

• Look around (at shoreline, pilings, breakwaters) for signs (barnacles, seaweed, beach rubble) that mark the high-water line.

• The typical duration between high and low water is 6 hours and 15 minutes (mixed, semidiurnal) or 12 hours and 30 minutes (diurnal).

• High and low waters on successive days are 50 minutes later each day, and the next day's ranges will not be much different from the previous day's—ranges change only slowly from day to day. If high water is 10 ft at 0800 today, expect a high of about 10 ft tomorrow at about 0850.

• Spring ranges (new and full moon) are about 20% larger than average; neap ranges (half-moons) are about 20% smaller than average.

• The largest spring ranges (higher highs and lower lows) occur near the solstices (June 21 and December 21); the weakest neap tides (smallest diurnal inequalities) occur near the equinoxes (March 21 and September 23).

• In many places along a coast or not far from it, high tides occur within 2 hours of the moon's meridian passage. For spring tides this will be near midnight and midday; for neap tides, it will be near 6 AM and 6 PM local time.

• In many places, the compass bearing to the moon (when visible) will be nearly the same for that location on alternate high waters, regardless of the moon's phase. The intermediate high waters will be about 12 hours and 30 minutes later, but the moon will not be visible.

• Over a long enclosed waterway, tide range on the inland end is usually larger, and the tide times later than at the seaward end. On the Washington State coast, for example, the mean tide range is 6 ft and high water closely follows the meridian passage of the moon; whereas in Olympia, Washington, at the base of Puget Sound (168 miles inland) the mean range is 11 ft and high tide trails the moon by an average of about 5 hours.

• Final rule: any of the above could be wrong! A good navigator is not the one who can guess the tides, but one who has looked them up ahead of time and has proper information at hand at all times.

8.7 Tidal Current Predictions

The changes at NOAA described in Sec. 8.4 apply to their tidal current predictions as well. There is no longer any official Table 2 of corrections to be applied to "reference sta-

tions" to get values at subordinate stations; the hourly data for every valid station is presented at tidesandcurrents. noaa.gov, where we create our own tables for stations of interest. Current data provided are the times and speeds of maximum flow (flood and ebb) and the times of slack water. Ebb speeds are traditionally labeled negative, but this has no practical significance.

The big difference between tide predictions and current predictions is the location of the stations. Tides are uniform over large areas, whereas current predictions are for the precise location of the station. Tide heights predicted several miles from us are likely good where we are, but that is not at all guaranteed with current predictions. We have to look carefully at the lay of the waterway to judge this; current speed, direction, and timing could be significantly different just a few hundred yards away from the station location.

Furthermore, most of the current stations are located in mid-channel, which do not necessarily represent current flow along the edges of a waterway where much small craft navigation is carried out. Consequently, these on-station predictions are often just the starting point to current predictions in the waters you plan to traverse.

The closest station to your location can be found from the NOAA webpage (Figure 8-11), or from a tidal current app. There are data for different water depths. For small craft navigation we want the shallowest depth, near the surface.

Although it is difficult to speculate on how well you might estimate the current locations away from these stations, it is fair to assume that the tabulated predictions at

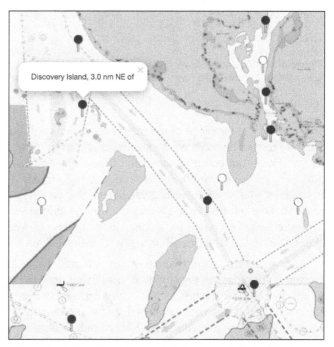

Figure 8-11. *NOAA tidal current stations as plotted on their webpage, tidesandcurrents.noaa.gov, with the nautical chart background option on. A cursor over the station shows its name; click it to go to that data page.*

Discovery Island, 3.0 nm NE of

Discovery Island, 3.0 nm NE of (PUG1744) Depth: 41 feet
LAT/LON: 48.4521° N 123.1554° W

Note: Depth is measured below chart datum.

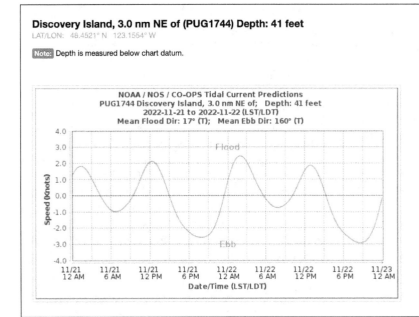

DOWNLOAD: TEXT | CSV | XML

Time (LST/LDT)	Event	Speed (knots)
2022-11-21 01:18 AM	flood	1.81
2022-11-21 04:24 AM	slack	-
2022-11-21 06:48 AM	ebb	-0.99
2022-11-21 09:24 AM	slack	-
2022-11-21 12:18 PM	flood	2.11
2022-11-21 03:00 PM	slack	-
2022-11-21 07:48 PM	ebb	-2.59
2022-11-21 11:24 PM	slack	-
2022-11-22 02:00 AM	flood	2.45
2022-11-22 05:42 AM	slack	-
2022-11-22 07:48 AM	ebb	-0.75
2022-11-22 10:06 AM	slack	-
2022-11-22 12:54 PM	flood	1.85

Station ID: PUG1744 Depth: 41 feet
Source: NOAA/NOS/CO-OPS
Station Type: Harmonic
Time Zone: LST/LDT

NOAA Tidal Current Predictions

Discovery Island, 3.0 nm NE of, 2022
Latitude: 48.4521° N Longitude: 123.1554° W
Mean Flood Dir. 17° (T) Mean Ebb Dir. 160° (T)
Times and speeds of maximum and minimum current, in knots

	October				October				November				November				December				December		
	Slack	Maximum			Slack	Maximum			Slack	Maximum			Slack	Maximum			Slack	Maximum			Slack	Maximum	
	h m	h m	knots		h m	h m	knots		h m	h m	knots		h m	h m	knots		h m	h m	knots		h m	h m	knots
6 Th	02:42 10:30 16:12	00:24 07:30 12:54 18:00 19:36	0.8F -2.3E 2.3F -0.5E -0.4E	**21** F	03:12 10:18 16:30	01:42 07:00 13:00 18:48 21:54	0.4F -1.8E 2.2F -0.7E -1.0E	**6** Su	03:54 10:24 15:36 23:24	01:06 07:42 12:48 21:00	1.9F -1.7E 2.3F -2.2E	**21** M	04:24 09:24 15:00 23:24	01:18 06:42 12:18 19:54	1.8F -1.0E 2.1F -2.6E	**6** Tu	06:24 11:06 14:48 23:48	01:48 09:24 13:00 21:00	3.1F -0.7E 0.9F -3.0E	**21** W	06:30 09:12 14:18 23:30	01:36 07:36 12:18 20:12	3.0F -0.1E 1.1F -3.1E
7 F	03:48 11:18 16:48 23:48	01:18 08:24 13:36 21:54	1.2F -2.4E 2.5F -1.0E	**22** Sa	00:06 04:06 10:54 16:48	02:06 07:42 13:36 21:54	0.8F -1.8E 2.5F -1.3E	**7** M	05:12 11:12 16:00	01:54 08:42 13:30 21:30	2.4F -1.4E 1.9F -2.5E	**22** Tu	05:36 10:06 15:18	02:00 07:48 12:54 20:30	2.4F -0.7E 1.9F -2.9E	**7** W	08:12 12:24 14:48	02:36 10:36 13:36 21:36	3.5F -0.7E 0.4F -3.0E	**22** Th	07:36 10:30 14:48	02:12 08:54 13:06 21:00	3.4F -0.1E 1.0F -3.1E

Figure 8-12. *NOAA tidal current predictions output options. The data can be printed as text or CSV (comma separated values) spreadsheet format for any date range. Bottom is a section of the annual predictions for this station.*

or very near the locations of the reference stations will be accurate to roughly 20% on the strengths and 20 minutes on the times—not counting abnormal winds, atmospheric pressure, and river runoff, as discussed later. Samples of the current prediction formats available are shown in Figure 8-12. One solution would be to print out the annual set of predictions (four pages per station) for stations you care about, thus creating your custom set of "Current Tables."

And we stress again, that there are outdated Table 2 current station data in print. Use of any of that data must be checked against the official NOAA predictions. In 2020 the last official tables were published, and marked as such. Now the same Table 2 data are published but without any NOAA sanction legally indicated.

Tidal currents at intermediate times

Unlike NOAA tides, which are given only at highs and lows, NOAA currents do have an option for an hourly print out of current speeds. The annual predictions that we are more likely to have onboard (Figure 8-12 bottom), however, just give the values at peak ebb and flood and the times of slack water, so we need a way to find the intermediate values. The easiest way is to use a tidal current app, as shown in Figure 8-13, and discussed in Section 8.5.

Without that convenience, you can use a simple rule we devised to make these estimates, illustrated in Figure 8-14. Separate the duration between slack water and peak flow into three steps. During the first time step after slack, the current speed increases to 50% of its peak value; during the next time step the current increases to 90% of its peak value; and during the last time step the current in-

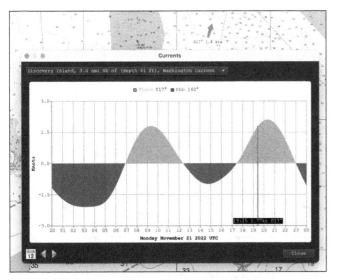

Figure 8-13. *Tidal current app from the free nav program qtVlm, which is unique in offering a convenient way to see data for any date, as well as giving results for all depths available. Usually we want the data closest to the surface. Slide the cursor along the curve to read specific values.*

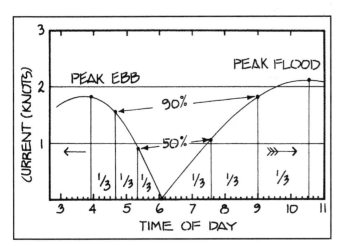

Figure 8-14. *The Starpath 50-90 Rule for figuring current speeds between slack and peak flow. Divide the time between slack water and peak flow into three steps. In many cases, each step will be approximately 1 hour long. During the first step, the current increases to 50% of its maximum value, and during the next step it increases to 90% of its maximum value. The same procedure will reproduce the fall in current speed after maximum flow.*

Table 8-1 Interpolating Currents with the 50-90 Rule				
	Adjustment			*Adjustment*
1230			Slack	
1330	1230 + 1h 0m		2.0 kt Ebb	0.5 x 4.0
1430	1230 + 2h 0m		3.6 kt Ebb	0.9 x 4.0
1530			4.0 kt Ebb	
1650	1530 + 1h 20m		3.6 kt Ebb	0.9 x 4.0
1810	1530 + 2h 40m		2.0 kt Ebb	0.5 x 4.0
1930			Slack	

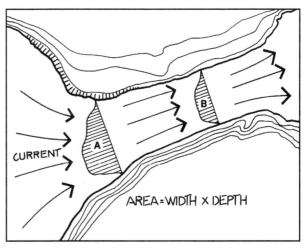

Figure 8-15. *Current speed is often inversely proportional to the cross-sectional area of the waterway, which depends on its depth profile as well as its width. In this example, area A is twice as large as area B; so the current at B would be expected to be twice as fast as it is at A. Whenever the location of an official current station is not at the most constricted point of a channel, peak currents in the channel can be significantly larger than predicted.*

creases to its peak value. Following peak flow, the current decreases in a similar pattern: during the first time step it drops to 90% of what it was, and during the next time step it drops to 50% of what it was. The only thing that might change is the size of the time step. Although most currents rise in about 3 hours and decrease in about 3 hours, there are exceptions. If the time between slack and peak flow is 3 hours and the time between peak flow and the next slack is 4 hours, the time step going up is 1 hour and the time step going down is 1 hour and 20 minutes (4 times 60 divided by 3). An example is shown in Table 8-1 for a 3-hour rise followed by a 4-hour fall.

It is important to check the *Coast Pilot* or *Sailing Directions* for notes on local current behavior. These publications often add information that cannot be discerned from the current predictions themselves. When you find such notes, write them on the chart at the proper places as reminders.

Some charts show current flow with arrows pointing in the flow direction and labeled with the average values of the maximum currents. The points on the chart where the arrows are located mark locations of NOAA current stations, and in this sense these charts are convenient guides to telling where the currents are predicted. When these symbols appear, the flood arrows have feathers, the ebbs do not. Unfortunately, not all stations are included on the charts; so it is still necessary to check the NOAA website or a tested app to see whether uncharted stations might be more appropriate and then mark their locations on the chart to save doing this again.

For a few areas around the country, there are commercial current guides or atlases that show strength and direction of current flow plotted on charts of the regions. These often include additional notes on current flow from the *Coast Pilot* and *Sailing Directions* along with very convenient tables that show what chart applies to any hour and day of the year. When such aids are available, they greatly reduce the problem of figuring currents and planning around them. A sample for the Pacific Northwest is the popular *Tidal Currents of Puget Sound* (Starpath Publications). As noted above, tide and current apps inside electronic charting programs are especially convenient in this regard, because they show all the stations plotted out at their right locations.

The first practical step toward current prediction in areas without these guides available is to plot these data in a similar fashion on your own chart. With this overview of the distribution of stations, use the guidelines in the following section to help you interpret and extrapolate these predictions into the actual areas you plan to sail through.

8.8 Guidelines for Judging Current Flow

• If a confined waterway narrows, horizontally or vertically, its current speed increases. This happens because the current tends to pile up at the constriction, and the developing hydraulic head adds a new driving force that pushes the water through faster. The speed increase in many areas is proportional to the reduction in cross-sectional area of the water, which often can be estimated fairly accurately from the average cross-channel depth and the width of the channel read from a chart. An example is shown in Figure 8-15. Because the current accelerates in narrow channels, the easiest route across current in a narrowing channel is usually not the shortest route.

• Current in shallow water along a shoreline is slower than current in deep water farther offshore, because a larger proportion of it is slowed down by the frictional resistance of the bottom. (To appreciate the illusive effect of surface drag on a fluid, consider how fast a cup of water might run down a sheet of glass compared to a sheet of sandpaper.) Because of this effect, traveling *against* the current is best done when possible in shallow water along the shore. The best ride *with* the current is in deep water away from the shore.

• Current along the outside edge (concave shore) of a smooth turn in a uniform waterway is faster than it is along the inside edge (convex shore), because the path around the corner is longer along the outside shore. If the water did not move faster, the water would pile up along the inside shore.

In principle, when traveling with the current in no wind through such an idealized turn (like a meander in a river), it does not matter which side of the turn you take, because the increase in current speed along the outer edge is proportional to the extra length of the route; so the transit times are the same. When progressing against the wind, however, the inside of this ideal turn is favored because the seas will be less enhanced due to the weaker contrary current. Traveling against the current, on the other hand,

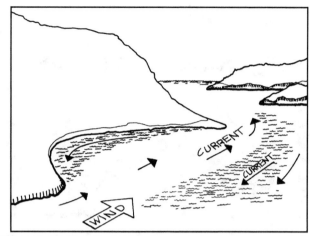

Figure 8-16. *The effect on surface texture of opposing wind and current. The direction of current flow can sometimes be determined this way even in light winds. In strong winds and fast currents, this texture turns into terrible water, with steep breaking waves.*

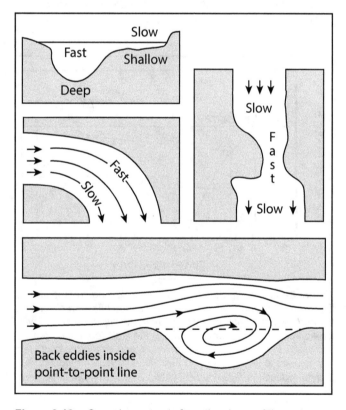

Figure 8-16a. *Guessing currents from the shape of the waterway.*

the outside edge is doubly bad; the route is longer and the current is stronger. Bear in mind, however, that this is an idealized waterway. Usually, the depth and shorelines are not the same on either side, and these differences can dominate the current flow around the corner and the best choice of routes. The inside or middle could be deeper, which would make it faster water, or, as is more likely, the inside could be shallower, which would cause steeper waves even though the current was weaker. In short, there are not many turns in open tidal waterways that fit this idealized description. Turns in meandering rivers or narrow channels provide more pertinent examples.

• Back eddies (circulating toward the shore) develop in bays downstream of points protruding into the waterway. At maximum flow in the main channel, a reverse current can be expected inside the point-to-point line across the bay. A sandspit at a point is usually a good sign that back eddies are common and well developed on either side of it, because sand deposits from the eddy circulation are what the spits are built from. If the eddy current is significant, however, there likely will be tide rips at the points; so getting into favorable back eddies when trying to progress against the mainstream flow must be done with caution. On the other hand, when riding with mainstream flow, it is best to stay offshore enough to avoid the bays and inlets that might have contrary current. The sizes of shoreline back eddies are proportional to the perturbations in shoreline contour that created them. They can be several boat lengths across or several miles across. Small ones are more often found along steep shorelines. Current eddies of all sizes also are found well offshore, formed when opposing currents collide or when slack water allows the nearshore eddies to wander out of their bays into the mainstream. It is usually difficult, however, to predict the locations of offshore eddies, and consequently, their effect on navigation cannot be anticipated.

• When a waterway changes from flood to ebb or vice versa, it does not often do so uniformly across its width. Current usually changes directions first in the shallow waters along its edge, because the water in the deeper mid-channel region has more momentum to be overcome by the new tidal forces. This process often leaves a current shear line on the surface (parallel to the shore) that separates currents flowing in opposite directions. As the main flow proceeds to reverse, this current line moves out toward mid-channel. In this manner, currents often change directions from the edges in, as much as they do from one end to the other. Spotting this line when present and getting onto the proper side of it can make a difference of 2 or 3 kts in your speed made good.

• In shallow water, the directional trend of anchored seaweed shows the current direction as does the wake behind buoys or rocks in deep water. In light winds, the set of an anchored boat or crab pot marker shows the current flow. Full sails and wake but not moving relative to the shoreline is an obvious sign of an opposing current direction, as is a fast passing shoreline at very low RPMs—although it is usually simpler to tell that you are not moving than to tell you are moving too fast. When sailing farther offshore, current lines can be detected from a change in the texture of the water surface (see Figure 8-16). Water on the rough side of the line is flowing into the wind; the smooth side flows with the wind. In winds of about 10 kts, you might see occasional whitecaps in water flowing into

the wind and none in water flowing with the wind. In winds of more than 15 kts and currents of more than 2 kts, there is a dramatic distinction in sea state between current flowing with or against the wind. Some surface effect, however, is noticeable in nearly all conditions because current flowing against waves always steepens them and current flowing with the waves always smooths them out, regardless of whether the waves are 6-foot ocean waves, 3-foot swells from a passing freighter, or 1-inch ripples from a 3-kt wind.

Current lines are also present along the edges of back eddies (called *eddy lines* in this case) as they migrate toward mid-channel during slack water when the main flow reverses. Even before the current starts to change directions, these eddies have current along their shoreward side flowing opposite to that in midstream; so when the current starts to change directions, which it does first along the shore, the increasing speed of the new current does not counteract the eddy circulation; it just pushes the eddy offshore. Large eddies that have drifted offshore often trap floating debris in their centers, which is a good sign of their presence. On the other hand, debris is also often seen lined up along a current line. If the opposing currents are strong enough, small particles or patches of foam along this line spin in circles, showing the flow directions clearly. As you sail across a prominent line, the torque of the opposing currents will tend to turn the boat toward the flow direction you are entering. Judging flow direction this way, however, is like noting that a storm is coming when the wind picks up and it starts raining.

Nevertheless, if the new current is not favorable, you can turn and get back out of it. Current flow often follows the paths of deep underwater trenches, which are only discernible from depth contours on a chart. If a prominent shelf, for example, extends well off the end of a point, expect the main current flow to follow the contour of the shelf around the corner as opposed to the contour of the shoreline. Current in such areas is usually strongest just at the edge of the shelf. Traveling with the current, stay just off the shelf; traveling against it, stay well onto the shelf if you have enough water depth. Similarly, current that flows around and over shallow underwater banks is often significantly accelerated over the mainstream flow. If published current predictions show irregular behavior in open water, check the shape of the bottom for a possible clue to understanding it.

• Current flowing out of a pass acts much like water from a hose. If unobstructed, it fans out and weakens; but if it is directed toward a shoreline, it will pile up against it creating larger-than-average downstream currents along that shore or in the deeper water just off that shore.

• To guess current behavior at points intermediate to those where published predictions are given, sketch flow lines parallel to the predicted directions at the nearest stations, then interpolate the current strengths between the published points. In open areas where nearby predictions differ significantly (speeds differ by 1 kt or more; times by 30 minutes or more; or directions by 45° or more), the current flow is clearly complex and probably sensitive to the range of the tide. Check the tide range at the time of your current prediction and compare it with the mean tide range for the place. If these ranges differ by about 30% or more, it is likely that the current predictions will be off in some details. Read the *Coast Pilot* and study the timing and directions of the predictions to look for any indication of eddies in the area that could be potentially dangerous. Charted notes of tide rips are further warnings of questionable predictions for the area. Areas with charted tide rips will likely not go slack at all, but remain erratic ("weak and variable") throughout the slack period.

• If published current predictions for a particular place or time seem unusual, plot the tide height versus time for the period in question to see if some clue is to be had. If the water is brown or gray instead of its usual blue or green, it has probably changed colors because of the silt from excessive river runoff. Normal runoff is included in the

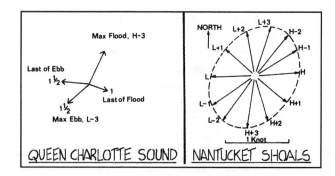

Figure 8-18. *Actual current diagrams for coastal waters of Queen Charlotte Sound, British Columbia (51°N, 129°W) from the Canadian Sailing Directions and from Nantucket Shoals, Massachusetts (41°N, 70°W), from the historical NOAA Tidal Current Tables (see starpath.com/navbook). The styles of the two diagrams are different, but they convey similar information. The currents in Queen Charlotte Sound are much larger. In areas with mixed tides, the corresponding diagrams have two loops, reflecting the inequality of the highs and lows.*

published current predictions; excessive runoff (after long rains or unusual snowmelts) is not. When present, this extra fresh water adds to the ebb strength and reduces the flood strength of tidal currents. It also extends the duration of the ebb cycle (it starts earlier and ends later, leaving maximum flow at about the predicted time) and reduces the duration of the flood cycle. In extreme cases, or at particular points near the source of the river water, weak flood cycles might be completely masked by runoff, leaving the water ebbing all day. During periods of drought, ebb currents will be weaker than predicted.

• If a steady wind blows over any body of water for half a day or longer, it starts a surface current flowing at a speed of approximately 3% of the wind speed. A 20 kt wind for half a day creates a wind-driven current of about 0.6 kts. In confined waters, this current flows with the run of the waterway; in open waters of the Northern Hemisphere, the wind-driven current is deflected about 45° to the right of the wind direction by the Coriolis force. Along a coast or on inland waters, the deflected current may meet a shore and elevate the water level. Once this occurs, the wind-driven flow follows the wind direction more closely. Local winds can create wind-driven current in lakes that have no tidal flow, and in tidal waters the wind-driven current must be added to the normal tidal flow. When the wind flows in the flood direction, for example, it lengthens and strengthens the flood cycle and shortens and weakens the ebb cycle. A crude estimate of the increase or decrease in tidal current speed could be 3% of the wind speed. The change in slack-water times depends on the current strengths. As a rough rule of thumb, a steady 15 kts of wind will shift the slack-water times by 60 minutes divided by the peak current strength in knots. A 2-kt current cycle flowing with the wind would start roughly 30 minutes earlier than predicted and end 30 minutes later than predicted.

At one time, NOAA published special current charts for nine large waterways around the country (including

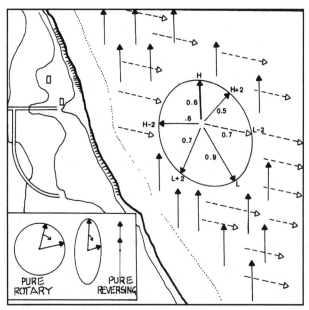

Figure 8-17. *A rotating current diagram that describes coastal currents. As opposed to pure reversing currents found inland, which alternate their direction, coastal currents tend to rotate their direction with little or no change in speed. At the time of high water, this coastal region has a north current of 0.6 kts; at 2 hours before low water, the current flows east-southeast at 0.7 kts. Note that the coastline shown could be 50 miles long or more. The arrows on these diagrams are usually scaled to the current speeds, but the location and overall size of the diagram has no significance. The current is not in any way emanating from the location of the diagram on the chart, nor is the behavior it describes limited to that region. The diagram describes currents throughout that region of the coast. Also, the timing of the currents is not necessarily associated with the local tides. The tide stations used to reference the currents could be far from the current site. If a particular tide cycle near the current site is much different from its mean value, the rotation diagram could be wrong in both current speed and rotation rate.*

Long Island Sound, Tampa Bay, and Puget Sound). These showed pictorially the speed and direction of current flow throughout the waterway for each hour of the flood and ebb cycles. Some of these charts are still available from commercial sources. They can be used on any day of any year; the time and speed scales that apply to each page for a specific day were determined from tidal current data available at that time. Some of those data are now out dated, but the general flow patterns presented are still useful. The Canadian government also publishes current charts for specific regions. Current charts and diagrams for specific areas also are included in many *Coast Pilot* and *Sailing Directions*. Whenever they are available, current charts are a convenient way to get an overview of the flow pattern for large areas and long periods of time, which is useful for planning long trips through variable currents.

8.9 Coastal Currents

Current flow within a mile or so of a coastline is typically the result of a complex set of forces. Contributing factors include tidal current, wind-driven current, prevailing offshore ocean circulation, and local currents running parallel and perpendicular to the shoreline, which are caused by the surf. Unusual hydraulic currents also might flow along a coastline following long storms. These hydraulic currents can occur with no wind, no waves, nor any tidal changes as the sea-surface slope readjusts to calm conditions. Near headlands, bays, or entrances to inland waters, the coastal flow also is strongly affected by the shape of the coastline.

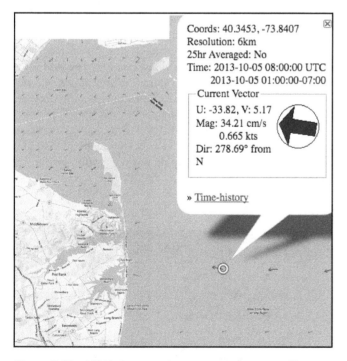

Figure 8-18a. *HF Radar current measurements approaching New York. Similar data are available along much of the US coastline. This is now the main resource for near-coastal currents. See latest links at starpath.com/currents. With the data in view online, you can click any arrow for specifics, as shown in the insert.*

Because so many forces influence the flow, it is difficult to predict coastal currents of interest to small craft navigators without local knowledge. Nevertheless, these currents are important to navigation because they can severely hinder progress along routes that are exposed to sudden weather changes. The height and direction of swells also can change in a few hours with no change in local weather, as wave remnants of distant storms first reach the coast. Coastal currents can vary significantly in speed and direction at any one location and vary rapidly and irregularly from point to point along a coast. Although in many areas the currents farther offshore (off the continental shelf) are fairly well understood and documented in *Sailing Directions*, it is questionable whether much of the knowledge gained from extensive traffic of larger vessels farther offshore can be extrapolated shoreward into regions of sounding well onto the continental shelf (depths less than 100 fathoms).

An exciting new development in coastal currents are the HF Radar measurements that are in place along much of the US coastal waters. The data are available online. Depending on the station, they include hourly as well as daily averages, extending out to as much as 60 nmi or so. A sample is shown in Figure 8-18a. A time history is included that can help with making predictions of your own. We try to keep related current links updated at starpath.com/currents.

Because there are few predictions and sources underway for the region that lies between the surf zone and the shelf, it is important to measure the current yourself (as explained in Chapter 9) as often as possible when traveling along close-in coastal routes. It might then be possible to correlate this information with the state of the tide, wind speed and direction, lay of the land, and state of the surf, and gain some insight into the local current behavior that might help plan the rest of the trip. Nearshore current is a difficult subject in oceanography. When dealing with currents in these waters, your surprise threshold must be fairly high.

The tidal part of coastal current is typically rotary as opposed to the reversing currents found inland (see Figure 8-17). A pure rotary current changes directions without changing speed; so there are no slack waters. Historical *Tidal Current Tables* (see Glossary), *Sailing Directions*, and some nautical charts provide diagrams that can be used to predict the speed and direction of rotating tidal currents based on the times of high and low tides at coastal reference stations. Examples are shown in Figure 8-18. Tidal currents in coastal waters rarely exceed 1 or 2 kts, and well away from the entrances to inland waters, the average values are much smaller—although as with all currents, coastal currents accelerate near headlands and diminish at the mouths of bays.

The rotations are also not purely circular near long open coastlines. The current direction does rotate (clockwise in the Northern Hemisphere) through 360° every 12 hours or so, but the rate of rotation is not uniform and the speeds are not exactly the same in all directions. Most tidal streams well removed from inlets into inland waters flow faster and longer parallel to the coastline than perpendicular to it. Their rotation diagrams are not circles, but ellipses with the long axes lying parallel to the coastline. Near entrances to inland waters, on the other hand, the ellipses are more aligned with the inlet because of the flow in and out of the waterway.

In many areas, however, the rotary tidal flow is completely masked by wind-driven current whenever the wind blows steadily for half a day or longer. Expect this contribution to be approximately 3% of the wind strength, directed about 45° to the right of the wind direction in the Northern Hemisphere. Wind-driven currents tend to be stronger in heavy rains, because brackish water slips more easily over the denser salt water below it. If *Sailing Directions* predict north-flowing currents of 1 or 2 kts, for example, expect the stronger end of the prediction when the wind blows toward the north and the weaker end of the prediction when the wind blows toward the south.

When waves strike the shore diagonally, they set up a current along the shore, inside the surf zone, flowing in the general direction of the wave motion. These currents in-

Table 8-2. Average Values of Fully Developed Deep-Water Waves.					
Wind speed (kts)	10	15	20	25	30
Period (seconds)	3	4	6	7	9
Length (ft)	28	62	111	173	249
Speed (kts)	7	11	14	18	21
Height (ft)	1	2	5	9	14
Required Duration (hr)	2	6	10	16	23
Required fetch (miles)	10	34	75	150	280

side the surf zone are not strong—0.5 kt might be typical for large waves—so these currents would rarely have direct influence on navigation. Nevertheless, water accumulated shoreward of the surf zone has to periodically escape seaward forming large rip current cells that can contribute to the prevailing flow outside of the surf. See Current Hazards in the following section for further discussion of this topic.

Although nearshore coastal currents are difficult to predict with much dependability, every effort should still be made to establish the range of potential currents when planning coastal routes, which now includes the HF Radar data. Check out the Time History plots they offer to see the patterns.

NOAA current predictions help in some locations, but *Coast Pilots* and *Sailing Directions* are the primary printed references in many areas. Whenever possible, also check with local fishermen who work both on and below the surface. In some areas, for example, commercial divers (who gather sea urchins, abalone, geoduck, kelp, herring roe, or sea cucumbers) are an excellent resource because they work daily in precisely the waters you might cruise, and they are aware of the current under many circumstances. Sport divers contacted through local diving shops also might be a source of local knowledge. Sailing or navigation schools that do regular tours in an area you might visit are also an excellent way to supplement what you learn from other sources.

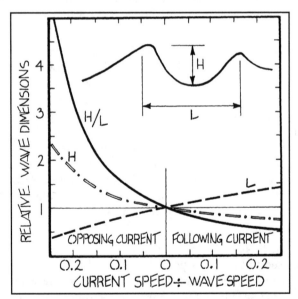

Figure 8-19. *Wave steepness as a function of current speed. Developed wind waves move in the direction of the wind at about 0.7 times the wind speed (average properties of the waves are given in Table 8-2). When they meet opposing current, they steepen according to the graph, where H is the height of the wave and L is the length of the wave. A wave in 10 kts of wind would be moving at about 7 kts with a length of about 25 times its height. If this wave traveled against 1.5 kts of current (0.2 times the wave speed), it would steepen by a factor of 3.5, according to the graph, making a wave whose length is only 7 times its height. Waves break at this steepness; so the gentle waves of a 10-kt wind in still water would be breaking in 1.5 kts of current. The graph also applies to swells from ships. These are already steep when produced and moving at the relatively slow speeds of the vessel. Those that are not breaking already will certainly break in opposing current.*

...In Depth

12.18 Accuracy of Current Predictions

Tidal current predictions give us data to within 1 minute of time and 0.1 kts of current speed, but how does that relate to the real world? Here we take a look at what are realistic expectations on these predictions...

8.10 Current Hazards

The most common and illusive current hazard to all small craft is fast water flowing into strong wind. This is an ever-present concern to mariners in tidal waters. The rapid increase in wave steepness that accompanies these conditions can, quite literally, stop you cold. In a low-powered craft, you might be surfing downwind, for example, with a 15-kt southerly at your back in 2 kts of favorable current, and get lured offshore with waves that tended outward. The apparent wind might be a comfortable 7 kts or less, depending on how fast you were going. In some areas, however, atmospheric convergence zones can reverse the wind direction in a matter of minutes. If this happened in this example, a brief lull would be followed by a sudden, cold northerly of 15 kts full on your face, which would feel even colder due to the enhanced spray and wind chill factor. In 15 minutes or so, the water would change from gentle rollers with occasional surfers going your way, to short, steep waves coming straight at you and breaking over the bow every few minutes. Your fun ride would suddenly change to an unpleasant and potentially dangerous struggle just to get to shore.

Always keep in mind the relative wind and current directions that lie ahead. These conditions can change suddenly where a waterway turns, and they always change when the tidal current reverses. Do not let yourself get caught in a low-powered vessel far from the shoreline when the current reverses. Current flowing with the wind actually smooths out the seas, so the potential sea state is deceptive before the current turns. The effect of current on wave steepness is shown in Figure 8-19; average values of deep-water waves are given in Table 8-2.

The second most common hazard is simply fast water that occurs in narrow passes. For navigable passes used by larger vessels *Coast Pilots* and *Sailing Directions* provide

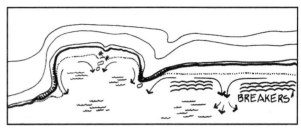

Figure 8-21. *Typical locations of rip currents on close-in coastal routes. This current is from water trapped against the shoreline from onshore waves and swells. With no waves or swells, there will be no rip currents. When approaching a calm beach, look for sandbars offshore. This is where the breakers will develop if swells roll in; rip currents run out in the deep water between the sandbars.*

ample warnings and speed predictions. Shoal draft vessels, however, can go through narrow openings between rocks or islets that will not be covered in these publications. So it is important to remember that whenever current is flowing and the waterway narrows significantly, the current speed will increase proportionally (see Figure 8-15). Furthermore, in most cases of accelerated current, there are associated fast back eddies and whirlpools that can be sudden hazards to safe navigation. These usually occur downstream of the constriction; so they might be detected only after you have committed yourself to going through. Even worse, you might find hydraulic jumps or standing overfalls at the constriction. If you are not prepared for this type of water, it is best to avoid fast currents in narrow openings or passes, even when the current is flowing in the direction you want to go.

Tide rips are another source of potential danger. They are always associated with fast water, but they are not restricted to narrow passages. A tide rip is a localized region (typically an acre or so in extent) of fast, turbulent water with steep waves that occurs whenever the smooth flow of strong current is abruptly altered. Rips occur over isolated shoals well offshore and at points of land along the shore; consequently, both of these areas are always potential danger points to low-powered craft during strong currents—in fact, prominent points and spits are potentially dangerous to small craft even in slack water if any waves are present, because wave and swell energy is concentrated at the points by reflection and refraction. Rips also can occur in deep offshore water wherever opposing currents meet, either head-on or in passing as along a current line. Channels with irregular bottom topography also will have tide rips in strong current. Tide rips are always most prominent when the current flows against the wind, because the rips effectively trap the approaching waves, and as they slow down they increase in height, just as swells steepen and break on beaches when the shallower depth of the shore slows them down. A relatively mild rip can become more exciting when a freighter passes by, and the swell from its wake is trapped and amplified in the rip zone. (All waves steepen when they slow down—by dragging on the bottom in shallow water or when they meet opposing current—because the kinetic

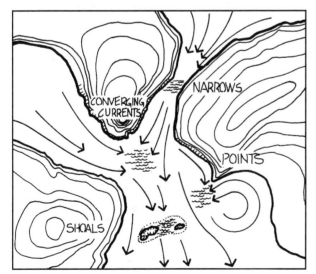

Figure 8-20. *Locations of tide rips where the water converges or slows. Rips are biggest when flowing against strong wind or swells. Remember current flows through the rips; so in a low-powered vessel you will punch out of the other side eventually.*

energy they lose with their speed must be converted to the potential energy of height.)

Areas of prominent tide rips are shown on charts with symbols or words (see Figure 8-20). These warnings should definitely be heeded as they imply potential hazard for even some large vessels. In some cases, tide rips are not shown on all charts of the same area; these are charting errors that should be corrected on your chart. Small craft operators, on the other hand, will frequently find areas of rips significant to them that are not shown on charts. These also should be marked on your chart, along with a note of the current speed and direction at the time. Severe rip zones near points or rocks are also often left uncharted, because they are too close inshore to be of concern to larger boats. When approaching any point or shoaling, look ahead for signs of whitecaps.

Overfalls are related current hazards that occur along the interface of two colliding current streams. Sometimes a standing wave is formed when one current "falls over" the other, which can be quite impressive in sight and sound. The range of severity of charted overfalls is as large as that of tide rips; so it is especially important to check *Coast Pilots* or seek out local knowledge when they are marked on a chart. The same chart notation ("overfalls") is used for the mild and the mighty. Overfalls can also be formed when strong currents first meet strong headwinds at the mouth of an outlet or when a waterway turns.

Inshore coastal routes, and especially river bar and inlet crossings, present current hazards that can be more severe than those found inland because the waves are bigger—at major headlands and some inlets the currents might be quite large as well. For inshore coastal routes, charts may not warn of even very severe conditions close to points and near rock groups because they do not expect vessels to be there, and it could well be that we should not be there.

Coastal routes also have certain unique current concerns, which may or may not present an actual hazard if anticipated. *Rip currents* (to be distinguished from tide rips) are one example to keep in mind when traveling just offshore along beaches with surf. The water that piles up along shore inside the surf zone with each breaking wave must run back out. Part of it usually does so in fast narrow streams at specific places where the surf is weakest, such as points of land, localized rock formations, or where a trough cuts through the offshore bar (see Figure 8-21). Rip currents, however, also are present at regular intervals along straight, uninterrupted beaches. Along such beaches, the surf usually alternates between regions of high surf and regions of low surf. Expect an outward flowing current in narrow regions offshore of where the surf remains consistently weaker. Rip currents can reach speeds of 2 or 3 kts and typically increase with a falling tide to peak values just before low water. Outside of the surf zone, this current weakens and turns parallel to the beach as it flows back to the regions of larger surf on either side.

A special type of rip current occurs periodically in waters around tropical islands enclosed by reefs. On windy days, the waves continually break over the windward side of the reef depositing water into the lagoon. The water trapped inside must flow out of the passes, which are typically narrow breaks in the coral sometimes caused by freshwater runoff from a river. In these circumstances, the flow is nearly always directed out of the pass regardless of the state of the tide cycle. Similar effects are occasionally found in higher latitudes where a reef or other natural breakwater has waves breaking over it into a confined area. Water that gets into it must come back out.

The interaction of current and waves is a much more important concern in places where a river enters the sea. Notorious breakers can occur at the bar (just off the mouth of the river) whenever the tidal current is ebbing at the river entrance. Conditions are even worse with any swell running offshore. The swell steepens as it enters the current and breaks at the bar. River bars that look timid during the flood can have huge breaking waves during the ebb. These conditions are deceptive when viewed from seaward, because beaches to either side of the river might be calm, and viewed from the back breakers at the bar might be difficult to detect. A popular maritime poster on the West Coast shows an 82-foot yacht standing on its stern totally engulfed in a breaking wave about to capsize it. The vessel attempted to head out across the bar at Moro Bay, California, in defiance of Coast Guard warnings not to. Similar incidents occur yearly at several dangerous bars along the West Coast.

Naturally, a small craft navigator would not plan to enter or exit a river over the bar and against the ebb. It may not be possible in some cases and could be very dangerous in others; even close shoreline routes into a river must be planned carefully for small craft. A more realistic problem is the route *across* the mouth of a river that might take you near the bar in transit. Such a crossing should always be considered potentially dangerous due to the drastic change in sea state that can accompany the change from flood to ebb. When crossing river entrances, be certain you can make it across during the slack before the flood and not get caught near the bar during the ebb, especially when there is any swell running. Similar cautions must be taken at the mouths of inlets through the barrier islands that separate the ocean from the inside waters along the East Coast.

In any fast current flow, the upstream side of any obstruction in the waterway also presents a potential hazard to small craft if it is approached too closely. The water is fast and turbulent where it abruptly changes directions to go around the obstruction. Examples include rocks in midstream, buoys, wing dams, or bridge pillars.

Tidal rapids are another phenomena that might be considered current hazards in some areas. These are found in steep, narrow embayments that fill at high water. They are easy to enter at high water, but when they ebb the water flows back out to sea as fast rivers. There can even be rapids and overfalls along them that are impassable at certain times. Side trips along such waterways should be done with local knowledge or at least the awareness that you might see an entirely different waterway on the way out.

And then there are places like Devil's Hole and Dent Rapids in British Columbia, where violent tidal whirlpools develop as large as 100 ft across and 12 ft deep. Navigation, however, is not an issue in waters like these; seamanship, boat-handling skills, and common sense, along with Edgar Allan Poe's *Descent into the Maelstrom*, would be more to the point.

Chapter 8 Glossary

50-90 Rule. A guideline developed at Starpath for estimating the speed of the current at any time between peak flow and slack.

back eddy. An eddy circulating in a bay whose flow direction at its outer edge is contrary to the main flow outside of the bay.

current charts. Diagrams that depict the current flow across the charted region.

diurnal. Occurring once a day, or equivalently, having a period of one day, as a tide pattern with one high and one low each day.

ebb. The flow of tidal current away from shore on the coast or out of a tidal estuary inland. The ebb direction at any specific place in a complex estuary may not be apparent from the lay of the land.

eddy. A circulating current pattern within or adjacent to a main flow of current, usually created by currents interacting with land or contrary current patterns. Dimensions vary from feet to many miles.

eddy line. The common name for the boundary between two contrary currents or a mainstream current and an isolated eddy.

flood. The flow of tidal current toward the shore on a coast or into a tidal estuary inland. The flood direction at any specific place in a complex estuary may not be apparent from the lay of the land.

high water (HW). The peak height of a rising tide. Mathematically this occurs for just an instant, but in practice there is no perceptible change in tide height for some period of time called the stand of the tide, or high-water stand.

HF Radar. A new technology used in many US coastal areas to provide accurate live and archived current data out to 60 nmi in some cases. See starpath.com/currents.

low water (LW). The minimum height of a falling tide. Mathematically, this occurs for just an instant, but in practice there is no perceptible change in tide height for some period of time called the stand of the tide, or low-water stand.

mean high water (MHW). The average of all HW values at a particular location over the NTDE.

mean higher high (MHHW). The average of all HHW values at a particular location over the NTDE.

mean low water (MLW). The average of all LW values at a particular location over the NTDE.

mean lower low (MLLW). The average of all LLW values at a particular location over the NTDE.

mixed semi-diurnal. A semi-diurnal tide pattern where the two highs and two lows are typically at different values.

National Tidal Datum Epoch (NTDE). The specific 19-year period adopted by the NOS over which tide observations are taken and reduced to obtain mean values for tidal datums. The present NTDE is 1960 through 1978. It is reviewed annually for possible revision and must be actively considered for revision every 25 years.

neap tide. A diminished tidal range that occurs near a quarter moon (seen as half-moon in the sky), at which time the sun has the least contribution to the tidal pull. Neap ranges are about 20% smaller than mean ranges.

nodal point. In a standing wave tide pattern, it is the point in the estuary that has no or little tide height change, even though the current can flow rapidly though the point.

progressive wave tide. A tidal wave pattern similar to ocean waves, wherein the wave peak progresses across the water but the water itself is just rising and falling as it passes. This pattern is reflected in tidal behavior in some large estuaries open to the ocean. In a progressive wave tide, the slack occurs about half way between HW and LW, with peak speeds at the stands of the tide, just the opposite of the more common standing wave tide.

range of the tide. (1) The difference between successive values of HW and LW. (2) Mean range is the difference between MHW and MLW. (3) Diurnal range is the difference between MHHW and MLLW.

reference station. Terminology used prior to 2021 for the chart locations where daily data are provided for tides or currents. These are now called harmonic stations. Harmonic tide stations are typically not located at the same place as harmonic current stations.

reversing current. A current that floods and ebbs in nearly the opposite directions.

rip current. A narrow strong current setting seaward through the surf zone that removes excess water brought into the zone by waves and longshore currents.

rotating current. A current that changes from ebb to flood by rotating direction with little or no change in speed.

Rule of Twelfths. The prescription for figuring the height of the tide at times between HW and LW by dividing the range into 12ths and assuming that the time between HW and LW is 6 hours.

semi-diurnal. Occurring twice a day, or equivalently, having a period of half a day, as a tide pattern with two highs and two lows each day.

slack. The time at which a flood current turns to an ebb or vice versa. The drift is minimum at this time, but rarely zero except in a pure reversing current. See progressive wave tide and standing wave tide.

spring tide. Refers to an enhanced tidal range near full moon or new moon, especially when these occur near a solstice.

stand of the tide. The period of time around HW and LW when there is no perceptible change in tide height, called HW stand and LW stand. The length of the stand depends on the range of the tide, being longer for smaller ranges.

standing wave tide. A tidal wave in a constrained estuary that oscillates up and down without progressing down the estuary. In these patterns, slack water occurs near the times of HW and LW, but still may differ by an hour or so. This pattern is equivalent to two progressive waves of the same amplitude and speed moving in opposite directions.

subordinate station. A secondary tide or current station (a specific location on a chart) whose data are scaled from that at the nearest harmonic station.

tidal current. The horizontal flow of the water in response to the change in tide height.

Tidal Current Tables. Prior to 2021, NOAA published two books of annual tidal current predictions, one for the Atlantic Coast of North America and one for the Pacific Coast of North America and Asia. These included daily data from numerous reference stations (now called harmonic stations) along with an extensive table (called Table 2) of time and speed corrections for 1,816 (Atlantic Coast) and 1,308 (Pacific Coast) subordinate stations. The 2020 Table 2 current corrections are still (as of 2023) in print from third party printers, despite the fact that much of the data are no longer valid, and none is certified by NOAA. Other data historically included in these tables, however, can still be useful such as rotary current forecasts for coastal waters, and tables for interpolating the predictions. Links to the last official printings that include these extra data are at starpath.com/navbook.

tide pattern. A description of the relative highs and lows throughout the day. The US East Coast is typically semi-diurnal; the West Coast mixed semi-diurnal, and the Gulf coast is mostly diurnal.

Tide Tables. Prior to 2021, NOAA published four books of annual tide predictions, one for the East Coast of North and South America including Greenland and one for the West Coast of North and South America including the Hawaiian Islands. These included daily data from numerous reference stations (now called harmonic stations) along with an extensive table (called Table 2) of time and height corrections for 2,613 (East Coast) and 1,305 (West Coast) subordinate stations. Prior to 2021, NOAA also published two other books of annual international tides covering 3,452 stations around the world, but these books and all international predictions ended in 2020. The 2020 Table 2 tide corrections are still (as of 2023) in print from third party printers, despite the fact that much of the data are no longer valid, and none is certified by NOAA. Other data historically included in these tables, however, can still be useful such as the Table 9 summary of average tides across all US waters and tables for interpolating the predictions. Links to the last official printings that include these extra data are at starpath.com/navbook.

tide rip. Turbulent water formed when two tidal currents meet or a fast current crosses over an irregular bottom.

tide. The daily cyclic variation of the water depth in response to the gravitational pull of the sun and moon.

wave steepness. The ratio of wavelength to wave height (sometimes reversed). Waves become dangerous at steepness greater than about 10:1, and they break at about 7:1.

CHAPTER 9
NAVIGATION IN CURRENT

9.1 Introduction

Navigating in currents using GPS electronic equipment was covered in Chapter 7 and in Chapter 12 sections. Here we return to the fundamentals of traditional navigation using compasses, natural ranges, and so forth.

Currents usually flow parallel to shorelines. Consequently, when sailing along shore, you are usually moving directly with or against the flow of the current; so progress along the shore is figured simply from boat speed plus or minus current speed. Your direction of motion is not changed by current flowing parallel to the boat. Navigation while *crossing* strong current, on the other hand, is not as easy. Diagonal current affects both your direction and speed, and the resulting speed cannot be figured from simple addition or subtraction. The solution begins with determining the strength of the current that must be crossed.

Resources listed in Chapter 8 provide current predictions for many places, but when at a specific place at a specific time it is seldom possible to tell at a glance whether these predictions were right, or even close enough to be valuable. Your motion when riding along with the current flow of deep, offshore water is rarely detectable. Only in fast current close to a steep shore or close to something attached to the bottom (like rocks, seaweed, or buoys) can you actually see the water move, or watch the shoreline fly by with no way on at all. Even these observations are qualitative. It might be obvious that the current is strong, but you cannot tell just by looking whether it is 2 kts or 4 kts, unless you are actually traveling against it nearshore.

Floating objects (other boats, birds, parts of trees, loose seaweed) tell nothing about the current when you are all floating in it together. Objects might drift toward or away from you, but this is due to differences in leeway (windage) between you and them, and not the current. Everything floating in the water moves with the water at the same speed—assuming the current is the same everywhere you are looking. When the current is not the same everywhere in sight, its presence might be detectable, even in open water without fixed references. Floating objects would then move at different speeds, depending on the currents they were in, or they might even spin when trapped near the boundary of two adjacent currents flowing in opposite directions. In extreme cases, colliding currents form overfalls that you can hear, as well as see. But it is especially difficult to judge strengths of colliding currents from the churning water around them.

In most circumstances, precise current speeds are not needed. Just knowing whether the current is strong (over 1.5 kts), moderate (0.5 to 1.5 kts), or weak (less than 0.5 knot) is usually enough to navigate safely and efficiently. When you are in continuous sight of landmarks, even strong currents can be crossed on a desired track without knowing current speed. But navigation of large open waters where there are few useful landmarks, or navigation through currents at night or in the fog, relies on tabulated predictions, educated guesses, or actual measurements of current strengths. All tricks for crossing currents without knowing current strength require visible reference points on shore. Without these reference points, the accuracy of the crossing depends on knowledge of the currents.

If you anticipate losing landmarks during a crossing, it is best to learn as much about the current as possible before leaving. Because currents flow parallel to the shoreline, this can be done riding the current along the shoreline you plan to leave, using for references whatever charted landmarks are visible at the time. The same measurements would be needed to plan progress along the shoreline, if that were the route.

9.2 Measuring Current Strength

To measure current speed (without a GPS), you need to know where you are now and where you were some time ago. In piloting terms, you need two position fixes and two times. One approach is to measure the time it takes to drift a determined distance. You might, for example, drift along the edge of a channel—being certain that you are in the faster deep water you care about—past an islet that is 0.2

...In Depth

12.20 Currents from GPS

With a knotmeter speed and a compass heading we can figure precise values of the set and drift of the current using the COG and SOG from the GPS. Here we review this procedure, which is a good way to check our predictions once underway...

nmi long. If it takes 5 minutes to go from one end of the islet to the other, the current speed is 0.2 nmi per 5 minutes. To convert this speed to knots, multiply the drift rate in miles per minute by 60:

$$\text{Current (kts)} = 60 \times [\text{ Distance (nmi)/Time (min) }]$$
$$= 60 \times [\ 0.20/5.0\ ] = 2.4 \text{ kts}$$

This formula is a convenient way to find current speed when headed downstream. It is not as handy otherwise, but learning the current strength could well be worth a short drift in the wrong direction. The method, however, requires fairly calm wind or some extra measurements. If a tailwind pushed you along this run at 0.4 knot even without the current, your net speed during the run would be 2.8 kts (0.4 knot from the wind plus 2.4 kts from the current). The measured time would be proportionally shorter, and you would wrongly conclude that the current was 2.8 kts.

The trick would be to simply look at the knotmeter. The 0.4 kts of leeway will show up on the knotmeter. The wind is pushing you through the water. With wind in the problem you are in effect sailing, not drifting, which is equivalent to slowly sailing the route. We should check this whenever the wind is strong enough to move the boat (winds greater than 10 kts or so). The combined effect of wind and current might still help planning in some circumstances.

Current strength can be measured when underway, and the accuracy of the answer depends on your knotmeter accuracy during the measurement. As discussed in Chapter 5, boat speed is not just propelled speed, but boat speed plus the effect of wind and waves. The procedure is to measure your actual progress along the shoreline (called SOG or *speed over ground*) and compare it with your knotmeter speed through the water. The difference is the current speed. If you are progressing faster than you are sailing, the current is with you, flowing in the same direction you are steering. Otherwise it is against you. When traveling at a speed of 6.5 kts but progressing at a speed of only 5 kts, the current is flowing against you at a speed of 1.5 kts.

For example, while motoring at 5.5 kts in calm wind, you time a run past a cove that is 0.5 nmi wide. You do this far enough offshore that the current is not influenced by eddies around the headlands. It takes 7.5 minutes to pass the cove. Figure the current as follows:

$$\text{Boat speed } = 5.5 \text{ kts.}$$
$$\text{Speed made good } = 60 \times [\ 0.5 \text{ nmi}/7.5 \text{ minutes}]$$
$$= 4.0 \text{ kts}$$

so

$$\text{Current} = \text{Boat speed - Speed over ground}$$
$$= 5.5 - 4.0$$
$$= 1.5 \text{ kts (against you).}$$

Whenever the measured speed over ground equals your estimated boat speed through the water, there is no current—or at least the current is small compared to the uncertainty in boat speed.

This measurement has taught two things: the speed over ground along this route in the prevailing current is only 4 kts when motoring at 5.5 kts, and the current speed at this specific time and place is 1.5 kts.

The first result shows that a planned 8-nmi run along this shore will take 2 hours in this current when sailing at a steady pace of 5.5 kts. Tidal current flow on inland waters, however, usually changes direction every 6 hours or so, with speed increasing during the initial 6 hours and decreasing during the final 6 hours. Even if the current does not change directions, its speed is likely to vary along an 8-nmi run over a 2 hour period.

The second result, a measured current speed at a specific time and place, may be equally valuable. Comparing this measurement to the predictions for the area can help you plan the next leg of the trip. If the measured current is close to the prediction, you might have more confidence in believing predictions for later times in neighboring waters. On the other hand, if it is significantly different than predicted, you must be more careful and carry out similar measurements as you proceed.

Often a quick check of the current just to get its direction and approximate speed is valuable near slack-water time when you are not sure if the current has turned or not. When near a stationary mark within the main current flow (such as a buoy, the edge of a rock, or the end of a piece of attached kelp), you can make a quick check of the current by timing your drift past the mark. With no way on, start timing when the bow goes by and stop timing when the stern goes by. With a boat length of 30 ft and a drift time of 9 seconds, the current speed is 30 ft per 9 seconds. This speed can be converted to knots using the approximation that speed in knots equals 0.6 times the speed in feet per second:

$$\text{Current (knots) } = 0.6 \times \text{Drift (feet/second)}$$
$$= 0.6 \times 30/9$$
$$= 2.0 \text{ kts.}$$

In other words, in 2 kts of current it would take a 30-foot boat 9 seconds to pass a mark; in 1 knot of current it would take 18 seconds. When thinking of currents and when approaching a mooring, it is often helpful to remember that 1 kt = 100 ft/minute.

When anchored, you can, even more easily, reverse the process and time the passage of anything that happens to float by the boat, even a patch of foam. From shore you can get some idea of the current this way by throwing a stick into the water and estimating how far it drifts in 10 or 20 seconds —if you can throw it out far enough to be in the main current. A stick that drifts 30 ft in 10 seconds must be in a current of 1.8 kts (0.6 times 30 divided by 10). To get a more accurate result from any of these quick methods, however, they should be repeated several times, and the results averaged.

Current speed also can be judged by how much it pushes you downstream as you start to sail across it. Imagine a line drawn across the current from your starting point to your destination. With no current, you would sail straight along that line, with the bow continuously pointed to your destination, and the stern continuously pointed to your departure point. This will not be the case, however, with current flowing against the side of the boat; it will push you downstream of that line as you sail across. The angle between the way you go and the way you are pointed is informally called your *set*, or the *set of the boat*. This use of the word "set" must be distinguished from its formal definition as the direction toward which a current flows.

When sailing straight across a current, a set of 6° means the current speed is 0.1 times your boat speed (Small-Triangle Rule). A set of 12° implies a current of 0.2 times your boat speed, and so on, up to a set of about 30° corresponding to a current of 3.0 divided by 6, or 0.5 times your boat speed (see Figure 9-1). This convenient mathematical approximation takes part of the guesswork out of sailing in currents. The trick does not work for larger sets, but for those you might want to reconsider the crossing at the present time, anyway.

Whenever current speed, boat heading, and boat speed remain constant, the set angle also remains constant. With a known boat speed and an estimate of the set angle, you can get a good estimate of the current speed. The set angle at the start of a long crossing, however, must be judged by looking back over the stern, toward the closest landmarks. As soon as you enter the current and begin to get set downstream, your departure point (viewed over the stern) will shift upstream by the set angle, and remain stationary at that bearing. Looking over the stern, the set angle should be obvious after just a few minutes of sailing in the current (see Figure 9-2).

Distant landmarks viewed over the bow are not nearly as useful for warning of current set. Because they are far-

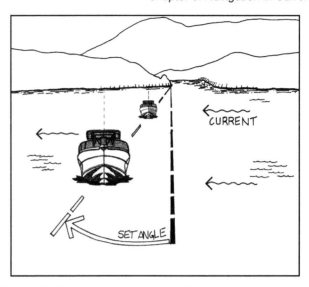

Figure 9-2. *Detecting a current and estimating the set angle by taking back bearings over the stern. With no current, the departure point stays on the stern; with current it moves upstream. Sailing at the same speed, it will stay at the same relative angle off your stern, but if you slow down or the current increases, it will move farther upstream of the stern.*

ther away, they will not shift suddenly and remain at constant bearings, but they will only slowly move upstream of the bow as you proceed across on a constant heading. You will not detect your full set looking forward until you are halfway across, which is perhaps the worst time to discover you might be in trouble.

For example, after 5 minutes into a crossing, you notice your departure point is no longer on the stern, but 24° (a hand width) upstream of the stern, where it appears to remain stationary. From this you can conclude that you must be crossing a current that has a speed of 0.4 times your boat speed. If the current remains constant, after 10 or 20 minutes the same observation would lead to the same conclusion—but looking back you did not have to wait that long. What you would see looking forward, on the other hand, depends on how far across you were. At the start of a crossing, bow bearings shift with current set in direct proportion to your progress across. Sailing at 3 kts on a 2-nmi crossing, you will be one-eighth of the way across in 5 minutes; so bow bearings to the shoreline ahead would have shifted only one-eighth of the set, or 3° in this example. Such a small shift in compass bearings is imperceptible; you would not even know you were in a current. Lesson: To check for current set, look back.

One convenient way to judge your set looking back is to use the angular span of your hand. A typical outstretched hand at arm's length is approximately 24°, although it is useful to check your own with compass bearings. After entering the current, and on steady course across it, check the landmarks directly astern. Sail for a few minutes on a constant heading by keeping an eye on the compass or distant landmarks on the bow. Then, keeping the boat on the same heading, turn around in the upstream direction and

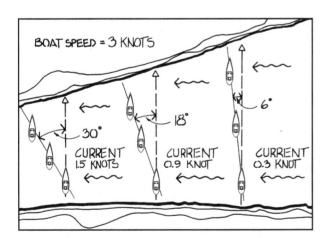

Figure 9-1. *When crossing current, the set angle can be approximated from the* Small-Triangle Rule *presented in Figure 4-4. Each 6° of set corresponds to a current of one-tenth of your boat speed.*

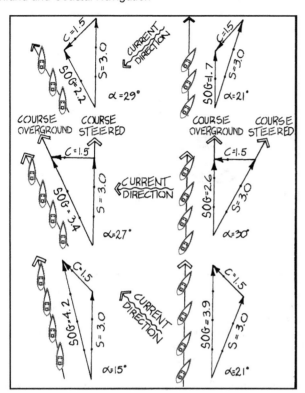

Figure 9-3. *Proper vector solutions to current problems for bow, beam, and quarter currents. Boats to the left are reaching across (in light air at 3 kts), allowing themselves to be set; boats to the right are ferrying straight across heading the proper angle into the current. This much set at 6 kts boat speed would require a current speed of 3 kts.*

point your arm back toward the stern. Extend your hand with the little finger aligned over the stern and see where your thumb falls on the shoreline relative to your departure point. If the departure point is one hand width upstream of the stern, you are being set 24°, which means you are sailing across a current of approximately 0.4 times your boat speed. If the current is not expected to weaken or change directions during the crossing, something must be done about this set now, or you will end up well downstream of your destination when you reach the other side.

9.3 Crossing Currents

When you know you are being set 24° downstream, the way to correct it is to alter the compass course 24° upstream. If the set is known in handspans, without a compass available, then alter the course upstream of the original target by the same number of units. This should take you straight across the rest of the way, assuming still that current and wind do not change much as you cross. This is not mathematically exact—the proper correction is not exactly equal to the set itself (see Figure 9-3)—but it is close enough for many practical purposes. What you are doing is called *ferrying* or *crabbing*—sailing a course upstream of your destination that will result in a straight tack across the current. As you sail upstream, the current continually sets you downstream; so you end up going straight across.

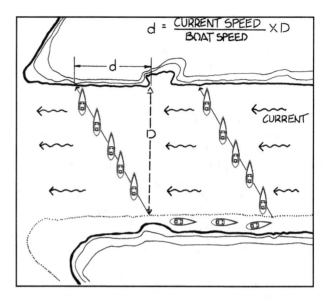

Figure 9-4. *The distance d that a boat is set downstream when crossing a current for a distance of D can be figured accurately from the equation shown in the figure, provided the boat and current speeds are constant. The "up-and-over" method of current crossing also is shown, wherein a boater makes his way upstream in the slower shallow water along shore.*

But keeping track of where you are as you cross this way can be tricky without natural ranges available, because when ferrying you are not moving in the direction you are pointed, and you are not progressing at the speed you are sailing. Furthermore, ferrying may not be the best way to cross the current in the first place. Deciding how to cross a current requires a closer look at how current moves the boat. (Again, we are considering low-powered boats in relatively strong currents. With a lot of power, we just head across and check our course periodically.)

First consider what happens if you ignore the current, point the boat to the other side, and start sailing (see Figure 9-4). You know you will be set downstream, but where will you end up? The answer is easy to figure. If you sail at constant speed and heading, straight across a current of constant speed, you will be set downstream during the crossing by a distance that can be found from:

$$\text{Distance set} = \frac{\text{Current speed}}{\text{Boat speed}} \times \text{Crossing distance.}$$

By sailing at 5.0 kts across 1.2 nmi of current flowing at 2.5 kts—keeping the bow pointed toward the opposite shore, not the destination, which will appear to move upstream as you proceed across—you will land downstream of your target by 2.5 divided by 5 times 1.2, or 0.6 nmi.

This is a big, and in many cases, intolerable error. It could, for example, put you into still stronger currents leading out into open water. But you learn a lot from this simple calculation. If you could sail at 10 kts, for example, you would still be set downstream by just less than 0.3 nmi, which may or may not be an issue. If 0.3 nmi downstream

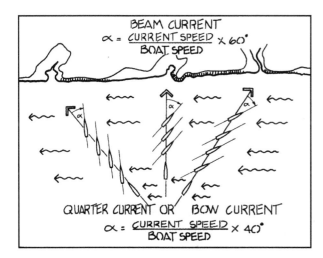

Figure 9-5. *Approximate formula for figuring ferry angles. The rule works adequately well for ferry angles up to 42° or so, which is equivalent to limiting its use to currents that are less than some three quarters of your boat speed. In most cases, knowledge of current speed and direction is not accurate enough to justify precise vector solutions. This formula is useful and easy to remember. Bow and quarter currents take less of a correction, but they are the same in each case. The only difference is the resulting speed over ground. Bow currents slow you down, quarter currents speed you up. Bow, beam, and quarter current directions are defined for this application with the boat pointed toward the destination, as in the starting position shown on each route.*

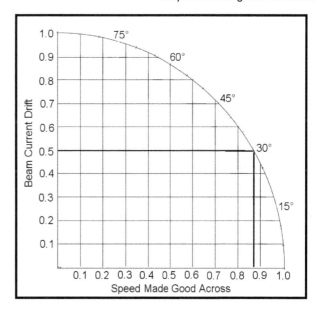

Figure 9-5a. *Crossing speeds as a function of ferry angle. If the current you must cross, for example, is 0.5 of your boat speed, then the ferry angle it will take is 30° and your speed made good across will be just under 0.9 of your boat speed. Note that even at ferry angles as large as 45°, one is still making good some three-quarters of your boat speed going across.*

$$\text{Ferry angle} = \frac{\text{Current speed}}{\text{Boat speed}} \times 60°$$

The formula applies to sailing straight across, with current on the beam. Sailing at 3 kts across 1.5 kts of current, the set would be 1.5 divided by 3.0, times 60°, which equals 30°. When starting across, point the boat toward your destination (assumed here to be straight across the current), read the compass, and then head 30° upstream from that course. If you cannot see your target, read the compass course that leads across from a chart and apply the correction to it. By steering the corrected compass heading all the way across, you should track straight toward the target, even though you are not pointing at it (see Figure 9-5).

When the current you cross is not on the beam, but closer to "on the bow" or "on the quarter" (45° forward or aft of the beam), then the same ferry-angle formula will work with the factor of 60° replaced with 40°. The proper ferry angle is the same for bow and quarter currents, although bow currents slow you down, whereas quarter currents speed you up.

The ferry-angle formula is an approximation to an exact vector solution (see Figure 9-3), but for currents less than about three-quarters of your boat speed, it is good enough for all practical purposes. Current strength (or direction) cannot be known precisely; so there is no need for precise solutions. The formula, however, does not warn of the natural limits to the method. You cannot ferry straight across a current that is faster than your maximum boat speed—even though the formula claims that a ferry angle of 60°

still puts you too close to danger on the other side, another approach should be considered. It might be possible to sail upstream for half a mile on this side of the channel and then head straight across. The current in shallow water near shore would likely be much weaker or even flowing in the opposite direction from the deep water in the channel. Starting from upstream, the downstream set during the crossing would put you on target.

This "up-and-over" method may not be the best choice or even a possible choice, but it is an alternative to crabbing that might be considered for low-powered craft in some circumstances. The time it takes to get across open water this way, for example, is also easy to figure. Do it just as if no current were present: 5 kts is 12 minutes per mile, so 1.2 nmi would take about 14 minutes. When the boat is kept perpendicular to the current (current on the beam), as when sailing straight across a channel, the time it takes to cross is figured using the distance straight across. It does not matter that the boat, in fact, travels farther during this time, ending up downstream. Current on the beam pushes the boat downstream but does not alter its forward speed.

If you choose to ferry across, the task reduces to measuring the ferry angle as explained earlier. When this is not possible, but you do have a reasonable estimate of current speed, the ferry angle can be estimated from the following approximation:

would do it. This formula simply cannot be used for current speeds approaching three-quarters of your maximum boat speed. In practice, this is not a serious restriction on the value of the formula.

Ferrying lets you cross in the direction you choose, but you sacrifice open water crossing time. Ferrying speed across the channel will be slower than your boat speed; so the actual exposure to the channel is longer than when going straight across while getting set. Generally, the best way to cross depends on what is going on around you. If the goal is just to get across the channel as quickly as possible, and it does not matter if you get set downstream, then let the current carry you downstream as you cross. This would be the case when going that way to begin with, and when there were no downstream hazards on the other side—but you still wanted to get across fast open water (of windy shipping lanes, for example) as quickly as possible.

On the other hand, to go straight across to a specific place on the other side, ferrying is usually the fastest way to get there, even though crossing speed is reduced. Not much speed is lost when ferrying, unless the current is strong enough to require a large ferry angle. The largest ferry angle that might be used is approximately 60°, corresponding—in real terms, not the approximations of the formula—to a current of just under 0.9 times your boat speed. In this case, speed over ground would be about one-half of the knotmeter speed (Figure 9-5a).

The alternative method of letting yourself be set downstream and then sailing back up the other side to your destination, or sailing up this side and then riding down as you sail across, is usually slower in total time underway than a direct ferry across—especially if the current is not slack along the shoreline and you have to sail against a weak current as you make up for the midstream set. Nevertheless, the time difference between these two methods is rarely the critical factor in choosing how to cross. The mid-channel wind also can have a strong influence on the crossing, but it is difficult to predict its effect on the time it takes to cross. Wind with the current smooths the seas you meet while crossing, but its added leeway is equivalent to increasing the current speed that must be compensated for. Wind against the current pushes you in the right direction, which effectively reduces the current, but it steepens the seas you must cross, which slows you down.

It is interesting to note that for crossing very fast or very slow currents, ferrying is not any quicker in total crossing time than going up and over the current. To go up and over a weak current requires only a short run upstream to compensate for the set; so net crossing time is just slightly longer than a straight slack-water crossing. Likewise, to ferry across a weak current requires only a small ferry angle, which only slightly reduces speed over ground; so this crossing time also would be just slightly longer than a slack-water crossing.

In the other extreme, currents approaching boat speed require ferry angles of approximately 60°, which reduces crossing speed to one-half of boat speed; so it would take twice as long to ferry across as it would to sail straight across in slack water. Going up and over this current, on the other hand, requires sailing upstream a distance equal to the width of the crossing, because this is how large the set would be when current equals boat speed. The total trip would be twice the crossing width; so the net time to cross also would be twice the slack-water crossing time—the same as when ferrying—provided the shoreline was indeed near slack.

Only when crossing currents of intermediate strength (1 to 2 kts) is there any significant time difference between the two methods. Even in these cases, ferrying is only faster by approximately 30%, on the average. When planning to cross a current of 1 or 2 kts, first figure how long it would take in slack water, and then figure that it will take approximately 20 minutes longer per hour of slack-water crossing time to go up and over than it would to ferry across. Then judge whether the time factor has any bearing on your choice. Related factors that influence the choice include prevailing wind, crossing distance, shape of the waterway, and state of the tidal cycle.

When planning to cross strong currents, it should not matter, as far as crossing time is concerned, which method is used. But for strong currents that lead past a headland into open water, it is clearly prudent to use the belt-and-suspenders approach: sail upstream for some way, and then still ferry as you cross, making every possible use of natural ranges to monitor progress along the way.

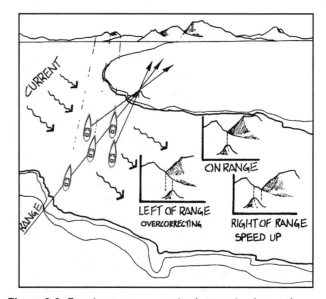

Figure 9-6. *Ferrying across current using a natural range in front of the boat. Once the proper ferry angle has been found, distant landmarks can be used for a steering guide, as shown. With waves or swells running, your course also can be maintained by the relative angle at which you meet the waves. This can help in the fog when no landmarks are in sight.*

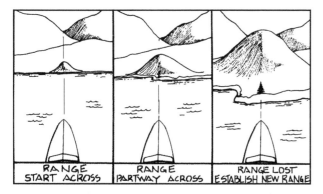

Figure 9-7. *Losing a front range. Keep this common problem in mind when relying on front ranges alone. When you lose a front range, choose another guide range or look for other ranges to the side to check your progress across.*

9.4 Using Natural Ranges

When sailing within continuous view of landmarks, it is often possible to cross currents in a controlled manner without knowing precise current strengths or boat speeds—although it always helps to have estimates of both—and without having to rely on calculated ferry angles. The best way to do this is to use natural ranges to mark the route and to monitor progress as you cross. The two range marks can be on either side or on opposite sides of the waterway.

Figure 9-6 shows a *front range* made from a nob near shore and a distant mountain valley. This type of range would not be found from the chart but by simply looking toward where you want to go and seeing what lines up. To progress straight along the range, you must point the boat upstream of your destination by an amount (the ferry angle) that depends on boat speed and current speed. Accurate knowledge of these is not needed with a range for a guide, but it still pays to use what is known to decide if it is closer to 5° or to 25°. For quick guesses, just use the previous formulas for ferry angle, (current/boat speed) × 60°.

It will not matter if these guesses are wrong. The range will tell. As you start across keep an eye on the alignment of the nob and valley. If your ferry angle and speed are not adequate to hold the range against the current, you will notice it immediately as you slip downstream of the range. The nob will shift left of the valley. This calls for higher speeds or pointing more into the current. If neither one of these corrections gets you back onto the range, then turn around and head back or choose another acceptable destination downstream, and range on that one. You are not making it as planned.

On the other hand, if you start creeping significantly upstream of the range as you proceed, then you are over-correcting and could, in principle, reduce the ferry angle and head more toward your destination. It is always prudent, however, to put a little in the bank by making way upstream of the range on the over-corrected course—especially if you are not yet to mid-channel where the current is likely to be the strongest. What was an overcorrection at

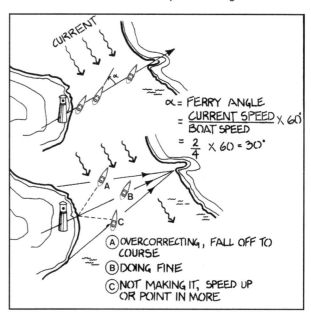

Figure 9-8. *Use of a crossing range with marks on each side of the waterway. Sighting along a boat hook or along the edge of a cabin top are accurate ways to check back-bearings to judge your progress.*

the start might barely hold the range at midstream. More generally, if you can barely hold the range at the start, assume you will not be able to hold it at midstream and turn back. Also keep the wind in mind. Wind behind you can aggravate the problem. It gets you out there faster but makes going back against it harder.

Once it is clear that the crossing is under control and you have settled in on a good course that holds the range, check your compass or look for distant landmarks on the bow for steering guides, such as saddleback peaks shown in the figure. These then mark the heading that will keep you on range. Such marks must be at least 10 or 20 times farther away than the length of the crossing; otherwise their bearings will change as you proceed across. A steering compass is clearly an asset when no distant landmarks are in sight. Without landmarks or a steering compass, it takes continual course adjustment using close landmarks to hold the range.

Front ranges are the easiest to follow, but they may not last all the way across because your perspective on the shoreline changes as you get closer. Figure 9-7 shows how a front range might be lost as you get closer. Keep this potential problem in mind when picking front ranges, and also remember that the range marks need not be prominent things like peaks and nobs; they could be a bush and a gray spot on a bluff behind it, or an inshore rock and a log on the beach. A *back range* on the shore you leave also would do the job if it could be seen all the way across, but it is less convenient for small ferry angles.

On longer crossings toward a shore that is barely discernible, you might find only one mark on the far side. In this case, pick the second mark on the shore you leave and

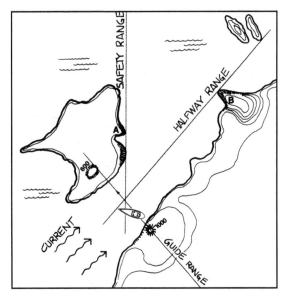

Figure 9-9. *Use of several ranges for crossing current. When the Twin Islands align with point B, you are half way across. At this point, the bay at point A should be obscured by the cliff*

use the range that lies between them, as illustrated in Figure 9-8. Again, estimate the ferry angle, set off, and check the range as you proceed. As mentioned in other applications of ranges earlier, it is always best to use some guide to check the range rather than just looking. Outstretched arms will do, or a boat hook will do an excellent job. Point the pole at one of the marks—whichever is the most convenient—and see where the other mark is relative to the other end of the pole, as shown in the figure. With either kind of range, however, it pays to have some backup means of checking progress. Always ask yourself what you would do if the range you plan to follow somehow disappears. You cannot use a rock on one side, for example, that you could not see from the other side. A general rule of navigation is never to rely on any single aid to navigation. In other words, do not put all your boat in one basket. This means choosing more than one potential range for any crossing, using what you can see by looking around, and noting what the chart shows that might be seen when partway across. Checking the chart before crossing is important in any event, because it helps a lot with interpreting what you do see by just looking around.

For this type of planning, you can consider various kinds of ranges: guide ranges to mark the route, checkpoint or cross ranges to monitor progress across, and safety or danger ranges that warn of hazards. Examples are shown in Figure 9-9. Here the guide range is from the 1,000-foot nob to the 600-foot ridge. As you start across, you can see the bay at point A behind the bluff in front of it. If you hold the range, you expect the bay to gradually fall behind the bluff and disappear. If you continue to see the bay as you cross, you know you are not making it, even if you lose your guide range. The cross range from spit B to the Twin Islands marks the halfway point on the crossing. With a good crossing on range, when you see daylight between

spit B and Twin Islands, point A should be gone. This type of planning makes the crossing safe. It is good training in chart reading and an enjoyable part of the sport of navigation. Each crossing presents new challenges to your ingenuity in choosing these ranges from the chart.

9.5 Time and Place to Cross

Time and energy can be saved by crossing currents at the right time and place. In some circumstances the right choices are obvious; in others they must be found from quick calculations. Fast currents generally go slack for only a short period every 6 hours; so without careful planning and some luck, it is not likely that a channel will be slack when you want to cross it. Furthermore, on a downstream route you might not want to be crossing in slack water; with no current hazards in the area, you might want to spend as much time as possible in the faster water. To optimize both getting across and getting downstream, you could cross headed slightly downstream (the opposite of ferrying), with the start timed to put you in mid-channel at maximum flow—a maneuver that might require sailing along shore at first, to wait for the current to develop fully in the favorable direction.

Currents that threaten progress, however, take more consideration than those that aid it. Slack water is usually the best time to cross dangerous or adverse current, but even this choice depends on the nature of the tidal cycle. In areas where flood and ebb strengths are much different, the slack before a strong adverse current might not be the safest time to cross. Strong currents accelerate after slack water more rapidly than weaker currents do, which makes getting caught in fast water more likely if the slack-water timing is off. Starting the crossing well into the preceding cycle of slower current might be more prudent.

The best time to start this type of crossing depends on the maximum current strengths on either side of the slack and the length of the crossing. Current predictions list the times of slack water and the times and strengths of maximum flow, but this alone does not tell whether the water will be slack enough for long enough to get across without ferrying. The tabulated slack-water time is the *moment* the water is predicted to change directions. Technically, it never stops flowing; it just slows down in one direction then speeds up in the other. Even this is an idealized picture, because large eddies can persist throughout the slack-water period. In areas known for strong current, slack water is rarely still water. To plan crossings in such areas, it is not so much the actual direction of the weak current near slack that matters, but rather how long it remains weaker than some specified speed.

This can be determined from Table 4 (Duration of Slack) in the historical NOAA *Tidal Current Tables* (see Section 8.4), and when traversing or crossing dangerous channels this table should be consulted for specific predic-

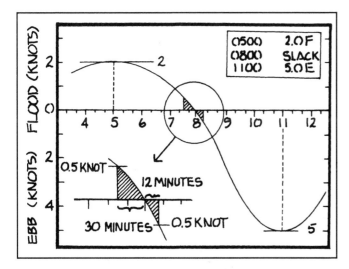

Figure 9-10. *The Slow-water Rule for estimating the duration of slack water: Current will typically stay below 0.5 knot on either side of slack water for the length of time it takes the water to move 1 nmi at peak flow (60 minutes divided by the peak current speed in knots). 5 kts is equivalent to 12 minutes per mile, and 2 kts is equivalent to 30 minutes per mile, so in this example you have 30 minutes before slack and 12 minutes after slack (from 0730 to 0812) to cross the channel in less than 0.5 knot of current.*

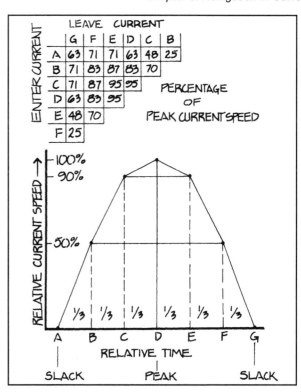

Figure 9-11. *Use of the 50-90 Rule to estimate the effect of a changing tidal current on net progress. Divide the duration of the cycle into six parts, then use data from the inset to find the constant current speed that is equivalent to the changing current of the cycle. Sailing in a current with a peak speed of 3 kts from relative point B to point E, the current would be increasing from 1.5 kts to 3 kts and then decreasing to 2.7 kts during this time. From the inset, you can assume that this will move the boat as if in a constant current of 0.87 times 3, or 2.6 kts. Note that staying in a current from slack to peak (A to D) or slack to slack (A to G) is equivalent to sailing in a constant current of 0.63 times the peak current speed.*

tions. For more general planning, a rule of thumb should suffice. The Slow-water Rule tells how long the current speed will remain less than 0.5 knot as it approaches slack or as it builds in the new direction following slack. The answer is 60 minutes divided by the peak current speed in knots, which quite accidentally is the number of minutes it takes the water to move 1 nmi at its peak speed. An easy way to remember the rule is to think of the slow-water time in terms of the peak current speed in minutes per mile. The current of an ebb cycle that peaks at 3 kts will spend 20 minutes (60 divided by 3) less than 0.5 knot at the start and end of the cycle. A current cycle that peaks at 10 kts will take 6 minutes (60 minutes divided by 10) to build to 0.5 knot just following slack, and will decrease to 0.5 knot at 6 minutes before the next slack.

As an example of the use of the Slow-water Rule, consider the question of how long the current will remain less than 0.5 knot during the transition from a 2-knot flood to a 5-knot ebb, although it does not matter which is flood or ebb in this question (see Figure 9-10). There will be 60 divided by 2, or 30 minutes of slow water before slack as the flood diminishes; and 60 divided by 5, or 12 minutes of slow water following slack as the ebb builds. In this case, you have a 42-minute window of slow water to cross in, but most of it is at the end of the flood cycle. If the crossing is less than 2 or 3 nmi long, it could be done in less than 0.5 knot of current by starting 30 minutes before slack water. Remember, though, that the tabulated slack-water time could be off by as much as 30 minutes; so you would want to start sampling the water about an hour before slack to be sure that you do not miss it.

For longer crossings or to plan progress in current on long passages, it helps to know the average effect of a full current cycle or some part of the current cycle. If you stay in a current from slack to slack, the net effect of the first increasing, then decreasing current is the same as that of a constant current of 63% of the peak current strength. This result is independent of the length of the cycle or its peak strength. The same result applies to staying in the current for exactly one-half of a cycle from slack to peak or peak to slack, but these time periods are more difficult to judge accurately. If the peak flow is 2 kts throughout the region you plan to traverse, and you stay within this region from slack to slack, you will be moved by the water as if the current speed were constant at 0.63 times 2, or 1.3 kts.

If you plan to make good 6 kts during this time, you should figure your net progress over the 6-hour period of the current as 7.3 kts. This is a convenient way to plan progress in favorable current; so you might arrive at the next leg of your route at the best time. It does not help with long-term planning in adverse current, because it is natural to avoid the main flow of adverse current whenever possible, which prevents determining a proper average. Figure 9-11 shows how to estimate the net effect of a changing current for arbitrary time periods spent in the current.

It is important to remember that traversing a long pass with strong current is similar to crossing a channel when it comes to timing the currents. In some long passes, there is no shelter from current in shallow water along the edges— or worse, the edges might be rocky with dangerous eddies. Such passes might even be dangerous in midstream at full speed, even when the current is flowing in the right direction. If you wait until after maximum flow to traverse the pass, consider the Slow-water Rule as a guide to how fast the adverse current might build against you, and be certain you can get through in the time allotted. If the current builds to 0.5 knot in 10 minutes, it will build to 1.5 kts in approximately 30 minutes. In some passes, however, the current might build even faster than this rule suggests; so it is best to check Table 4 in the historical NOAA *Tidal Current Tables* to be safe. Passes with anomalous current behavior are often footnoted in the tables or given separate data in Table 4.

When crossing channels, remember that current accelerates as the cross-sectional area of the waterway diminishes (see Chapter 8), and this is not always apparent from looking at the surface shape of the waterway alone—the area reduction might be all underwater. It is best to survey the chart to choose the best place to cross whenever you have an option. A longer crossing in slower water can be more efficient and safer than a short one in fast water. Always look downstream of your route across to see what would happen if the current anywhere on the crossing is much larger than predicted. Specific examples of navigation in current are given in Chapter 11. An example of a current corrected DR plot is shown in Figure 9-12.

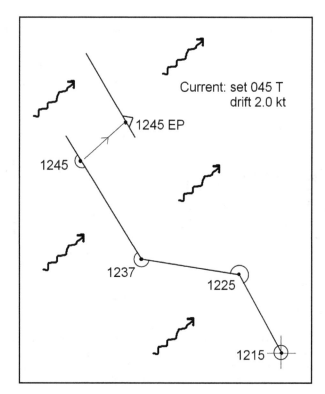

Figure 9-12. *A current-corrected DR plot. From the fix at 1215, there were two course changes, which led to a DR position at 1245. The current during this time was assumed to be constant at 2.0 kts flowing toward 045 T. The boat was in this current for a total of 30 minutes since the last fix, which means the DR position must be offset in the direction of the current by 1.0 nmi. That is, the water we were moving through moved 1 nmi to the NW during this period of time. Often a corrected DR position is referred to as an Estimated Position (EP), and is plotted as a triangle. DR positions are always half circles, fixes are full circles.*

Note that to make this correction you only need to know the current set and drift and how long you were in it since the last fix. None of the details of maneuvers up till then matter so long as they were all plotted out properly on the chart.

Chapter 9 Glossary

back range. A range used for navigation viewed aft over the stern.

crabbing. Steering a heading into the wind or current to make good a desired course.

drift. (1) The speed of a current. (2) The motion of an unpowered vessel in wind or current.

ferrying. Another name for crabbing.

ferry angle. The offset needed from the desired course to correct for current or leeway.

front range. A range used for navigation viewed forward over the bow.

on the bow. Bearing approximately 045 R or 315 R.

on the beam. Bearing approximately 090 R or 270 R.

on the quarter. Bearing approximately 135 R or 225 R.

set. (1) The true direction toward which a current flows. (2) The course offset caused by current.

Slow-Water Rule. A guideline developed at Starpath for estimating the time a current remains below 0.5 kts at the time of slack.

CHAPTER 10
RULES OF THE ROAD

10.1 Introduction

Regardless of your sailing preferences, encounters with other marine traffic cannot always be avoided. A long trip in a boat will likely bring you into close proximity with other vessels—ships, ferries, fishing boats, tugs and barges, or recreational powerboats and sailboats. In some areas, seaplanes, jet skis, sailboards, and paddle boards might be additional concerns. Encounters with other traffic always must be considered a potential hazard. As it is for air traffic and for other marine traffic as well, the biggest danger occurs in clear weather. In fog, everyone tends to be more careful; there are fewer collisions and near-collisions in reduced visibility than there are in clear weather.

In this chapter we go over key rules and concepts behind them, but we do not mean this as a complete presentation. We concentrate on those aspects of the rules that apply to any vessel, regardless of size or means of propulsion. A list of selected references for more details is presented at the end of this chapter in Section 10.9, along with printed and digital sources of the Rules. You may find it helpful to have a full set of the Rules at hand for this Chapter.

10.2 Legal Matters

The laws that govern the interactions of all vessels on all waters are collectively called the "Rules of the Road" or just the "Rules." The main body of the Rules appears in the Coast Guard publication called *Navigation Rules,* although further regulations are listed in the *Code of Federal Regulations* (Titles 33 and 46), parts of which appear in each *Coast Pilot.* Additional local and state laws occasionally apply to inland waters (defined later), and these supersede federal laws in most cases. Important interpretations of the rules are only available in the records of various admiralty court cases compiled by the International Maritime Organization, Sub-Committee on Safety on Navigation, a body of the United Nations, with headquarters in London. *Farwell's Rules of the Nautical Road* is one of several excellent advanced texts on the legal interpretation of the rules.

As with all laws, ignorance is no excuse. When sailing in traffic, your finances as well as your safety are at stake. Small sailboats have been heavily fined for violating the Rules, just as large ships have been. Negligent operation of any vessel that endangers life or property (including your own) costs $1,000; gross negligence costs $5,000. Attempting to sprint between a tug and its tow would be a clear example of the latter.

Some rules on right of way refer to specific kinds of vessels: power-driven vessels, sailing vessels, and vessels doing specific kinds of work such as fishing or towing. Muscle-powered craft such as kayaks, canoes, and rowboats are not specifically mentioned in the sections on right of way. Many of the fundamental rules, however, refer only to "vessels," and muscle-powered craft are definitely vessels, which are clearly defined in the Rules as "every description of watercraft used for transportation on water".

When reading through the official rules, bear in mind that although it would seem true, a rowboat is not a "vessel restricted in her ability to maneuver" nor is a boat with several people fishing over the side equal to a "fishing vessel." These are special terms, with special meanings. A rowboat or skiff is just a "vessel," or, as distinguished in some rules, a "vessel of less than 12 meters in length." If you have a sail up on your dinghy, however, you become a *sailing vessel,* even if you are not moving. Terms like these are defined in the Rules; we explain other special terms in Section 10.8.

Before discussing the important practical aspects of sailing in traffic, it is useful to review the formal rules that apply—bearing in mind, of course, that these are legal aspects of navigation that are not always pertinent to actual encounters on the water. If you were run over by a Mack truck or a drunk driver on the highway, you might not care much whether he or you or both of you were technically or even flagrantly in violation of the law. But somebody will care, and somebody will pay the bills. In this sense, some Rules of the Road might be of more interest to your heirs than to you. In any event, when you navigate in traffic, you should know the Rules. You will be safer.

But before getting directly into a subject that might seem dull, or bothersome, or irrelevant to some boaters, I would like to share a personal attitude about the Rules of the Road. If you choose to sail, row, or paddle in traffic, you are truly entering into the world of maritime affairs. You immediately become the master of a vessel, regardless of its size, interacting with other vessels and their masters, regardless of their size. You begin to share the broad concepts of good seamanship with other seamen. And a key point to good seamanship is your mutual understanding that each knows and obeys the Rules. I want to imply that it is more than just law; it is part of nautical tradition—a tradition that you are choosing to take part in. And I want to suggest that the Rules of the Road, as a body of knowledge, is a fundamental and fascinating part of that tradition.

Studying the Rules can be a very rewarding pastime, both practical and captivating. They constitute a remarkable document with an immense assigned task—the prevention of collisions between a vast array of vessels in a vast array of circumstances: vessels barely visible at 100 yards to vessels the size of horizontal skyscrapers; vessels drifting along without power or traveling at 30 kts or more; vessels following unmarked lanes or crisscrossing open waters offering nothing more than an educated guess as to their intended course in all conditions of weather, clear or fog, calm or storm, and often with no common language among their drivers.

But despite this enormous assignment, they do the job. Collisions can always be traced to at least one violation of the Rules by *each* of the vessels involved. The key to avoiding further proof of this is a thorough understanding of the Rules and how to apply them, including what to do if an approaching vessel does not obey the Rules. In the following, we cover the basics of right of way, distilled down to the parts relevant to all vessels—as distinguished from specific rules for powerboats or for sailboats. I hope the discussion encourages you to think through the Rules and be able to apply them. Sometimes, just staying out of the way of everybody might not be in your best interest. In these cases, it is valuable to know what your rights and obligations are. Remember, too, these are international rules; they apply everywhere in the world.

We first consider the law when you are in open water, outside of traffic lanes, narrow channels, or fairways. Maritime traffic lanes are *vessel traffic separation schemes* set up by governments in the waters approaching major ports around the world. They are discussed later in the text. *Narrow channels* are just that: any place the width of the waterway limits the course of vessels. They can be man-made in the middle of a city or natural passes between two islands in the middle of nowhere. *Fairway* is a more subtle concept in the Rules and calls for more careful attention by small craft. Fairways are simply direct routes from one waterway to another, usually marked by buoys. They are often dredged channels through an otherwise open uniform waterway, but they could be simply a direct route across open unobstructed water between one point and another. Within fairways, the Rules are the same as if the route were a narrow channel. As masters of vessels upon navigable waters, we are obligated to know this distinction and recognize this feature from a chart, from the layout of the buoys, or from simply looking at some ship or boat and asking ourselves "where is he going and why is he going that way?"

10.3 Your Rights as a Vessel

The following applies when you are outside of traffic lanes, fairways, and narrow channels. *The wording of the Rules presented here has been abbreviated and paraphrased.*

Rule 2 (b). Responsibility. All vessels approaching you should take into account the limitation of your vessel, which might require a departure from the Rules on their part if necessary to avoid immediate danger.

Rule 6 (a). Safe Speed. All vessels approaching you should travel at a safe speed, meaning slow enough that they maintain full control and could avoid a collision in the prevailing conditions of weather and traffic. Outside of traffic lanes, fairways, and channels, "I couldn't stop" is not a valid defense in a collision.

Rule 7 (a). Risk of Collision. All vessels approaching you should continually assess whether there is a risk of collision. If doubt exists, they must assume that there is a risk of collision and act accordingly.

Rule 8 (a) to (e). Action to Avoid Collision. A vessel approaching you with a risk of collision should maneuver early enough to stay at a "safe distance" when passing by using whenever possible a prominent course alteration that you can readily detect, as opposed to a series of small course and speed changes.

Notice that none of these rules gives you "right of way" over another vessel; they just prohibit other vessels from running into you, just as they prohibit you from running into the way of some other vessel and then claiming categorical innocence of any damages done. *These rules apply to you as well as to the vessels that approach you.* In any small craft, common sense and courtesy are usually reliable guides to what should be done when the proper rule doesn't come to mind immediately. The only time any vessel automatically assumes actual right of way over another vessel is when the other vessel is passing (overtaking) you in clear weather, as stated in Rules 13 and 16. Again, we are not covering the specific right of way rules, just the general rules that apply to all vessels.

Rule 13 (a) to (c). Overtaking. Any vessel approaching you from behind (on a compass course that lies within 67.5° of your own) must stay well clear of you as it passes. From your perspective, that is any boat approaching from an outstretched hand width aft of your beam: If you hold your arm straight out to the side, with your hand outstretched and your thumb on the beam, overtaking vessels are those that approach from aft of your little finger. Vessels approaching forward of your little finger are called

---

...In Depth

12.21 Traffic in the Fog

Picture this. You are cruising through a thick fog, 100 nmi from land, and out of the gray silence you suddenly hear a loud prolonged blast of a fog horn. It is obviously close, and it seems to be from somewhere on the port bow. What do you do?

crossing vessels, and only the fundamental rules listed earlier apply.

Rule 16. Action by Give-way Vessel. When a vessel is overtaking you, it should take early and prominent action to keep well clear of you when passing. For what it is worth, it is against the law for them to just miss you as they go by. When you are being overtaken, however, *you* become a vessel *with* right of way (the *stand-on* vessel) and as such have certain obligations included in the following section.

10.4 Your Obligations as a Vessel

The wording of the Rules presented here has been abbreviated and paraphrased.

Rule 2 (a). Responsibility. You (and the boat's owner, if different) are responsible for anything that occurs as a result of a violation of the rules or a neglect of any precaution, which may be required by the "ordinary practice of seamen." The good seamanship clause of this rule has been cited in cases where weather reports were not checked ahead of time (so inevitable bad weather could not be used as a defense), and in cases where equipment failures could not be used as defense in a collision because it was known to the skipper that the equipment was faulty before departing. This rule also has been applied to cases in which the skippers were not familiar with the handling characteristics of their vessels. Part (b) of this rule requires that you be aware of the limitations of your own vessel as well as those of the other vessel when interpreting and complying with the rules. Parts (a) and (b) of Rule 2 are interrelated. Often cited in poor seamanship arguments is the failure to plan ahead. In any vessel, planning ahead must take into account the vessel's limitations. It can be useful to consider an analogy of driving a car on a busy freeway. If you know you have to get off up ahead, you must get in the proper lane now, while you have a chance to.

Rule 7 (d). Risk of Collision. You must continually assess the risk of collision by every possible means, but among these *must* be included the angle on the bow (compass bearing) method discussed in the section on Practical Matters. Every boater is required by law to know and use this piloting technique.

Rule 5. Lookout. In all conditions of traffic, visibility, wind, and sea state, you are required to keep a *proper watch* for other traffic in all directions. This apparently simple rule is actually quite complex, and it is often critical in legal arguments about collisions. Proper watch is not defined in the rules, but it has been established in various court cases. Among the many fine points, the one of interest to small craft is: The person on watch must have no other duties that distract from his watching for traffic. Courts, however, have ruled that a solo sailor standing at the wheel can constitute a proper watch. This nevertheless raises the question of whether rough seas (in open water or narrow channels), which must be continually watched

and carefully negotiated to keep on course, constitute such a distraction. Again, common sense is a reasonable guide. When conditions are so bad that you are continually distracted from watching for traffic, you should not be alone in traffic. This rule simply makes this obvious choice a legal requirement.

Rule 17. Action by Stand-on Vessel. When you do have right of way (as a result of being overtaken or due to other Rules we have not covered yet) you should maintain course and speed until the other vessel has passed you. This requirement can create tense moments in some cases, but it is a well-motivated law, and it should be adhered to as long as you feel safe in doing so.

If you tried, for example, to get out of a passing vessel's way by altering course or speed, regardless of good intentions, you might in actuality increase the risk of collision rather than reduce it. When an overtaking vessel is first detected at some distance off, it is difficult to judge which side it plans to pass on (the Rules do not specify this choice). If you happen to turn toward its intended course, it would not know what to expect from you next, and from then on things only get worse. Have you ever, for example, bumped into someone face-to-face on the sidewalk as you jogged back and forth trying to guess which way the other was going?

On the other hand, if you believe that the vessel is not keeping clear as it passes, you have the right and obligation according to rule 17 (a) and (b) to take whatever action you can to avoid a collision. We must always be especially careful when we have the right of way. You are the privileged vessel, but your burden is high.

Rule 9 (a), (b), (d). Narrow Channels. Whenever it is safe to do so, you should transit narrow channels as close to the right-hand side as possible. In any event, however, you are not allowed to impede vessels that can only navigate safely in certain parts of a channel or approaches to the channel (fairways). "Not impede" could be interpreted as meaning not cause them to alter course or speed in order to keep well clear of you. In 1989, however, a new part was added to Rule 8. Rule 8 (f) (i) states that "not to impede" means to take early action to allow sufficient sea room for a safe passage. This restriction applies when you are crossing channels or fairways as well as when following them.

...In Depth

12.22 More on Navigation in Traffic

Another look at various encounters at night and in the fog...

This rule might require charts to identify fairways, even though the use of charts is not required for finding or keeping track of position in the case at hand. Larger vessels, for example, might be following buoys or range marks along a dredged channel through wide open but shallow water. The fairways are not always apparent from a casual look over the waterway. Nevertheless, as mentioned earlier, it is your obligation to know about them from the lay of the buoys, range markers, or daymarks (as you see them from the boat or on the chart), and treat these fairways just as you would treat narrow channels with steep walls on either side.

Strictly speaking, however, these rules do not apply when your vessel (not under sail) meets sailboats *under sail* in narrow channels. If you are obeying the channel rules—meaning staying to the right and out of the way of power-driven vessels that must follow the channel—the sailing vessel should stay clear of you; they have no rights over you or anyone else when sailing within narrow channels.

Likewise, other small craft that can maneuver safely within the confines of the channel also do not have categorical right of way over you. "Small" in this case formally means less than 66 ft long (20 meters), but it is important to remember that some boats in the 30- to 66-ft range can navigate safely only near mid-channel in some cases and therefore should not be impeded. Some sailboats, for example, have deep keels that restrict them to deep water. This gives them right of way in a channel with shallow sides (as a matter of good seamanship), even though they are officially small craft powerboats when using their engines and as such would not otherwise have categorical right of way over you. If it happens to be you that wants this right of way in a channel because of your deep draft, then it can be useful to use your VHF to explain that to any approaching vessel.

Note that Rule 9 does give you (in a small, low-powered craft) the right to travel down the middle of a narrow channel whenever the sides are unsafe because of large waves (clapotis from wakes), but the remainder of the Rule still has priority—you must not impede large vessels restricted to the channel. From a practical as well as legal point of view, with other traffic around, you should simply wait, looking forward and backward, for a clear time to go through or across, and then do so rapidly.

If you do illegally impede a large restricted vessel in a channel, it is nevertheless still bound by the fundamental Rules. This point has been further emphasized in the new Rule 8 (f) (iii). It cannot run you over if it has the ability to stop (which a tug and tow, for example, might not have), but it certainly can report you to the local police or Coast Guard and have you fined for impeding it.

Rule 10 (j). Traffic Lanes. You must not impede any vessel following a designated traffic lane, which means ships and other large vessels. These lanes are established to facilitate safe traffic in busy shipping areas. Just as any

small craft operator does not want ships running around on random courses, the safe navigation of large commercial traffic cannot accommodate "every description of watercraft," sometimes barely detectable on radar screens and barely detectable by sight, randomly traversing these designated lanes. It would be difficult to defend in court any of your generic rights as a vessel, if a collision with a ship should occur inside traffic lanes. Think of it as jaywalking across a busy street. Organized sailboat races and other events that take place in or across traffic lanes are always prearranged with the Coast Guard and published in the Local Notice to Mariners.

Specifics of the *Navigation Rules* may seem far removed from the sailing experiences of many, nevertheless, when sailing in traffic they remain the law for "every description of watercraft used for transportation on water," from a dinghy with an outboard to a 130-ft yacht. In maritime court cases, liability and fines are often distributed among the participants. Even if a larger vessel violated one or more rules in an encounter with you that ultimately led to a collision and injury, your behavior, down to the last detail, would still be analyzed strictly according to the *Navigation Rules*. Any violation that could be remotely interpreted as contributing to the collision could be influential, regardless of how impractical the Rule might have seemed at the time.

On the other hand, not having proper lights at night, impeding traffic in narrow channels or shipping lanes, approaching too close to fast vessels, and other such things are clear violations of the Rules that could earn a sizable share of liability in any case.

To illustrate the rigidity of the Rules and their application, consider the unusual case of *Rumpelheimer v. Haddock* in the British Admiralty court of 1935 (described in an appendix to *Collision Cases,* by F.J. Buzek and H.M.C. Holdert, Lloyd's of London Press, 1990). Damages were sought in an encounter between a rowboat and a motor car being driven on a flooded road (legally a power-driven vessel upon navigable waters, since the flood was from a river that led seagoing vessels to the ocean). The rowboat, with legal right of way according to the Rules of the day, refused to yield this right, and the car was damaged expensively when attempting to go around it in deeper water. The court held that the *Navigation Rules* did indeed apply and ruled in favor of the rowboat.

10.5 Procedures Near Traffic Lanes

In most of the waters of the world, traffic lanes do not exist; so they are not a concern. But many miles of wonderful waterways leading to major ports of the world are crisscrossed with a maze of these invisible maritime streets. In these areas, the lanes cannot be completely avoided; so it is important to know the rules for sailing in or across them. Also, the general discussion of interactions with large vessels covered here would apply, even outside of regions where traffic lanes exist. In the middle of the backwaters of the Inside Passage to Alaska, where no other vessels might be seen for days, you might suddenly be confronted with a giant cruise liner hauling down on you in some relatively narrow waterway.

Each regional traffic system is controlled by the local Coast Guard district, which usually publishes a pamphlet that describes its traffic system and its rules. Addresses and telephones numbers for all Coast Guard district offices are listed in the appendix to each *Coast Pilot*. The fundamental rules and procedures are common to all systems and serve as a guide for foreign systems as well.

It is your obligation to know if lanes exist in a particular area and precisely where they are. When in effect, traffic lanes are shown clearly on all nautical charts. Looking seaward, the outbound lane is on the right side of the waterway; the inbound lane is on the left side, separated by a *separation zone* that runs down the middle of the waterway in most areas. The waterways on the shoreward side of each lane are called the *inshore zones.*

Whenever possible, sail in the inshore zones and stay well clear of the traffic lanes and separation zone. Although no ship traffic is supposed to be in the separation zone, it is still a part of the lane system that should be avoided; it is a particularly dangerous place to travel.

When you must cross the lanes, do so at a right angle to the lanes so as to cross them as promptly as possible.

As a small craft operator, you do not have any right of way in the lanes; when you see approaching ships, you must stay clear of them. If you were 0.5 nmi in front of a ship traveling at 15 kts, for example, that ship would be where you are in 2 minutes. Sailing at 4 kts perpendicular to its course, it would pass 800 ft behind you (a distance of about two ship lengths for *smaller* ships). You would be illegally close to the ship, and its bow wave and the turbulence in its wake would create potentially dangerous seas in the area. Ship waves are especially hazardous (often steep and breaking) when running against strong current or across

prevailing waves. A typical ship speed for traffic lanes is 15 kts, but some travel as fast as 20 kts. If you passed half a mile in front of a vessel making 20 kts through rough seas and winds that limited your escape speed to 2 kts, the ship would pass much less than a ship's length behind you, and its bow wave and wake would present a definite hazard to your safety. In short, half a mile is much too close to be in front of a ship.

Even 1 nmi is marginal for safe navigation. Court cases, for example, have established that when a vessel is directed by the rules to stay clear of another (as small craft are in traffic lanes), it should do so in such a manner that not only avoids risk of collision, but also avoids any potential *development* of risk. When considering a crossing distance, ask yourself if you could get out of the ship's path if the wind slackened off some, when under sail, or if the current was 50% bigger in front of the ship, etc. Neither of these would be much of a leg to stand on in a court case.

Remember also that from the bridge of a ship a small vessel might not be seen from much farther than 2 nmi or so in clear weather and flat water (imagine how close you would have to be to see your vessel riding on the bow of the ship), and that some ships cannot see anything in the water that is closer than half a mile off due to the obstruction of its own bow and cargo. There are also large blind spots on some ships with aft bridges and congested foredecks. A large, fast ship might have the opportunity to see you for a period of only 3 or 4 minutes (in swells or waves, the time window could be even shorter). With nearby traffic or other navigational matters on the mind of the skipper and pilot during this critical period, they might not see you at all, even in the clearest weather and best of conditions.

When an approaching ship sees you in a potentially hazardous location, it will likely sound its horn but maintain course and speed. In an emergency, it will naturally maneuver as best it can to increase the safety margin, but a ship's maneuverability is very limited. The usual sound signal for such a warning is one very long blast if a developing risk is detected, or five rapid short blasts for imminent risk of danger. When you suspect that you are in a dangerous place and an approaching ship does not sound its horn,

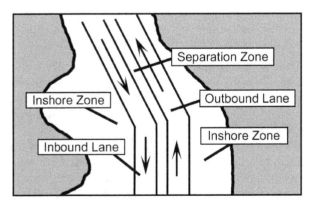

Figure 10-1. *The regions defined in a Traffic Separation Scheme. Small craft are directed to use the inshore zones whenever possible and to cross the main lanes at right angles when possible. All vessels should avoid using the separation zones. Typical zones are about 1 nmi wide.*

...In Depth

12.23 Sound Signals

Sound signals are used to identify vessels in the fog and to clarify maneuvers, signal intent, or issue a warning when two vessels are in sight of one another. The Rules on the latter are the main thing that changes between the International Rules and the US Inland Rules. This note goes over these issues...

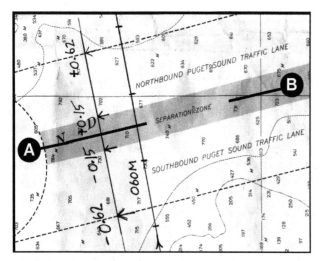

Figure 10-2. *Section of a traffic separation scheme (TSS) on a chart that is set up to sail across using GPS. Waypoints A and B define the "centerline route." Cross track errors relative to this route show at a glance whether or not we are in the lanes. See application of this planning in Figure 6-4.*

then chances are very good that it does not see you or you have misjudged the risk of a close passing. In any event, do not count on the ship going around you. Modern cargo ships are lumbering giants; they maneuver about as well as a 50-story office building would when making 20 kts through the water. They turn very slowly and take a mile or more to stop, even when the stop is planned ahead. An unplanned emergency stop poses a threat to the safety of the ship itself. They can go out of control or lose an extremely expensive engine when attempting an emergency stop.

Needless to say, GPS is a wonderful aid to navigation when you must sail in the vicinity of shipping lanes, as it is to just about every other application of actual navigation. There are numerous ways to apply it in this case, but one slick trick stands out as particularly handy for boaters who must use this device with the minimum of interaction. This method lets you know if you are in the lanes or not from a simple glance at the screen. Select two waypoints (A and B) that are located in the center of the separation zone between the inbound and outbound lanes, as shown in Figure 10-2. Sometimes you can use the buoy locations that mark the centerline of the lane system, but these need not be the choices. The main requirement is that there is one waypoint at one end of the region you sail, and one at the other end, and that they mark the precise centerline between inbound and outbound lanes. Then define a fictitious route between these two waypoints. Next, go to the chart and measure the width of the shipping lanes relative to this centerline route. For example, you might find that each lane starts at 0.15 nmi from the centerline and ends at 0.62 nmi from the centerline. Shipping lanes are usually symmetric in width and spacing. Here we have two lanes that are 0.47 nmi wide (0.15 to 0.62) that are separated by a zone that is 0.30 nmi wide (2 × 0.15).

Now to use this trick when sailing in the region of these lanes, just take out your GPS, select the fictitious route, and tell it that you are sailing to waypoint A of this route (or waypoint B, it doesn't matter). You won't actually be sailing to waypoint A or B at all, but the GPS will think you are and when you ask it to display the cross track error (XTE) it will tell you how far you are off of that route, which happens to be the centerline of the shipping lanes. Hence, if the XTE is greater than 0.62, you know you are not yet in the lanes. If it is less than 0.62 but greater than 0.15, you are in the lanes, and when less than 0.15 you are in the separation zone. In this application, you will not be using the GPS to tell you your precise position. You could, of course, get that by asking for latitude and longitude, but instead you are getting what you usually care more about, which is where you are relative to the lanes.

10.6 Practical Matters

From a practical point of view, the main concern in traffic is judging, as soon as possible, whether you are on a collision course with approaching traffic. The standard way of deciding this is to watch the vessel's angle on your bow (see Figure 10-3). To do this, first check your compass course, a distant landmark, or a natural range in front of you so that you can hold a steady course; then check the bearing of the vessel relative to your bow. The vessel's bearing can be noted several ways, depending on the circumstances: by just looking, by using hand-widths off the bow, by noting the vessel's location in your rigging, by noting where the vessel lies relative to distant landmarks in its background, or by taking an actual bearing with a precision hand compass, which is often the best. With radar, we would be also marking the target on the radar screen.

Then, carefully watch how this angle on your bow changes with time. If the vessel moves forward on your bow from this point, it will pass in front of you; if it moves aft with time, you will pass in front of it. If the vessel does not move on your bow, you are on a collision course. To judge collision risk this way, it is important to be on the same heading (by compass course, natural range, or distant landmark) each time you check the bow angle, although you could sail on different headings between the checks.

The method of noting angle on the bow while holding a constant heading is just a simplified practical way of taking compass bearings to the traffic. It fulfills the requirement of Rule 7(b) that you must take compass bearings to approaching traffic if there is any doubt about collision risk. This measurement is required because a constant compass bearing to a target approaching from a distance means it is closing in on a collision course (regardless of the actual heading of the ship as you look at it). If its bearing changes as it approaches, it will pass you.

The direct compass bearing or bearing relative to your own bow are methods most suitable when the traffic is fairly far off. For very close traffic, on the other hand, it is

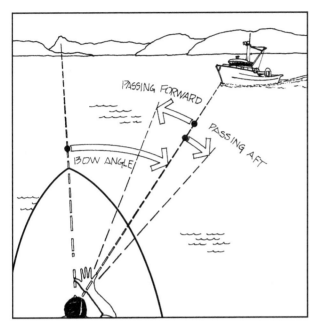

Figure 10-3. *Judging a collision course from the relative angle on the bow. If the vessel does not move on your bow, you are on a collision course. An actual compass bearing is even better for this evaluation.*

best to watch the bow of the approaching vessel relative to its own superstructure or cabin top as illustrated in Figure 10-4. This is an accurate and easy way to judge relative course lines and course changes at close range, although it is obviously prudent to avoid getting so close that you need to use it.

Either of these checks, however, only tells of the risk of collision; they do not tell how close you will pass if both of you maintain course and speed. The guidelines for judging distance off given in Chapter 6 can help with this. A large ship that appears one finger width high will be somewhere between 0.4 and 0.8 nmi off, depending on the sizes of the ship and your finger (practice with docked or anchored vessels to calibrate your fingers this way). You are likely to be dangerously close to any ship that appears two or three finger widths tall. Another guideline is the appearance of people on board. At about half a mile off, they appear as dots or posts; when you can see heads, arms, or clothes, the vessel is within a quarter of a mile or so. Any people you see clearly should be going by you, not toward you.

Although vessels following traffic lanes will not often alter course to accommodate isolated small craft (they would sound their horns instead), you can be fairly confident that they will follow the lanes. Since the lanes are straight lines between specific turning points, *it is very important to know where the turning points are.* A ship that appears to be safely crossing ahead of you might be approaching a turning point where it will turn to head straight for you. Any time you are in or near the lanes it is valuable to pick out natural ranges or use dead reckoning to keep track of where you are relative to the lane boundaries.

Large car ferries are the same as ships as far as the Rules are concerned and as far as sailing around them is concerned. They do differ, however, in that they have better visibility, and they are much more maneuverable. Their skippers also have more experience in traveling through small craft traffic. If they see you cannot get out of the way, they will go around you if they can; but if they see you headed into their path, they will sound a warning blast. Ferries cross traffic lanes more often than they follow them, but nevertheless they are participating in the traffic lane system, often following specific fairways, and as such must not be impeded. When sailing in areas of ferry traffic, it is your responsibility to know the ferry routes and anticipate their presence. Be especially cautious when crossing harbors with ferry terminals. Look ahead to see what the cars are doing, and listen for the ferry's horn. It will often sound one long blast or some other prominent signal before departing. As you approach the harbor, watch the horizon for ferries that also are headed that way.

The most common concern in traffic, however, is not necessarily with ships or other commercial traffic but with smaller powerboats traveling at high speed. Some boats in the 14- to 40-foot range can travel at 30 kts or more. When traveling that fast, they fly off the tops of even the smallest waves with their raised bows blocking their view more often than not. When all you can see approaching is the bottom of a hull and a bow spray thrown off to each side, the driver most likely will not see you as soon as you see him.

Many drivers of these speedboats are not familiar with the pertinent details of the *Navigation Rules;* so you cannot anticipate that they will pass you at a safe distance. During these encounters, survival is the main concern, not the rules. Nevertheless, it is still much easier and more accurate to judge relative course lines if you hold a steady course yourself as you watch them approach; at the same time, be ready for quick action at the last moment. Waters used for waterskiing or waters that lie between popular sport-fishing grounds and public boat ramps are often riddled with this type of traffic at certain times. In any event, it is good policy to carry flares or smoke signals readily at hand when sailing in any area of potential traffic, day or night.

...In Depth

12.25 How Close is "Too Close"?

The issues of "do not impede," "stay clear," "keep out of the way of," "sufficient sea room," etc are all terms we might consider when interacting with traffic in the traffic lanes. The terms are not defined, but we have guidelines to help us make the decision...

But we should also not lose sight of the fact that an actual collision course is very rare. Close passings are far more likely than an actual collision. That is why stopping and being ready to maneuver as needed is always good advice.

Encounters with traffic always should be considered when planning times and routes of boat trips. Dangerous encounters between ships and boats are more often the fault of the boater than the ship, because the routes and behavior of large vessels are usually predictable, and their skippers (in vast majority) know and obey the rules. Dangerous encounters among small craft, on the other hand, are more often simply incidents of poor seamanship that result from an ignorance of the Rules. Sailing small craft in congested waters must be like defensive driving: Do not watch the street light, watch the cars that are supposed to stop at the street light. In any kind of vessel traffic, remember to look back. Also remember that both hearing and vision are impaired when you are looking downwind with the sun in your eyes.

Figure 10-4. *Judging relative course lines at close quarters by watching the ship's bow relative to its superstructure. This observation is clearly made from within an extreme situation that we would want to avoid getting into.*

10.7 Sailboat Right of Way (Rule 12)

This rule governs the conduct of sailing vessels when in sight of each other. It is the same in International and Inland waters. There are two main aspects to the rule, equally important; one is usually referred to as "port-starboard," the other as "windward-leeward." Then there is a special clause that covers possibly ambiguous cases when the tack of a vessel cannot be determined.

When two sailing vessels on opposite tacks are approaching each other so as to involve risk of collision, the sailing vessel on the port tack must stay clear. In sailboat racing, the hail often used by the starboard vessel to attract attention to its right of way is simply a loud "STARBOARD." This is supposed to remind the other vessel that you are approaching on a starboard tack and he is supposed to stay clear of you. *This hail is in no way part of the Navigation Rules*, nor is it recognized by the racing rules, but it is common practice between two approaching sailing vessels, even off of the race course. According to the Rules, the proper signal would be five short blasts if you are in doubt of the other vessel's intentions and want to warn them of that.

The *Navigation Rules* specify this rule in a manner that incorporates the definition of tack in that it reads: "when each has the wind on a different side, the one with the wind on the port side shall keep out of the way of the other." Since a port tack boat is a boat with the wind on the port side, the port tack boat must keep clear.

The Rules further define a tack with reference to the side the mainsail is carried on; however, this is not a good definition for modern sailing vessels sailing into the wind. It relies on the fact that in most cases, the main is set on the side opposite to the side the wind comes across. So a

starboard tack vessel would usually carry the main boom to leeward of the centerline, on the port side of the boat. On most points of sail, this is indeed an obvious guideline to the tack of the vessel, but when close-hauled (sailing into the wind as close as possible), this guideline could be misleading. One can, indeed, see close-hauled sailing vessels sailing with the mainsail boom exactly amidships, or even to weather a bit. Nevertheless, one would not want to claim starboard tack rights on a port tack with the mainsail boom pulled up onto the port side—this would be stretching the literal wording of the rules beyond reason. Generally one can tell which side of a vessel the wind is on from the boat's heel angle or the shape of the mainsail, regardless of precisely where the boom is aligned.

The windward-leeward part of the rule requires that we understand these terms and not confuse them with upwind-downwind. Upwind and downwind refer to a line drawn through your vessel perpendicular to the wind direction, whereas windward-leeward refers to sides of your vessel. Imagine a line running through your centerline that extends out in front of you, over your bow, and out behind

...In Depth

12.24 Sailboat Lights

The Rules on running lights for sailboats involve more complexities than their counterparts for power-driven vessels. For safety as well as legality, it is important to understand the requirements.

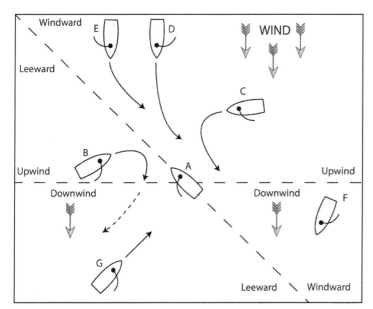

Figure 10-5. *Sailing vessel right of way. See discussion in the text for the various cases*

you over the center of the stern. On a starboard tack, everywhere on the right side of that line is to windward of you, everywhere to the left of that line is leeward.

When two sailing vessels approach each other with risk of collision and they are on the same tack, the boat to leeward of the other has the right of way. Here the hail one might hear is "LEEWARD." Another way to put it is the windward boat must stay clear.

Neither of these rules depend at all on the point of sail, but only on the relative windward-leeward, port-starboard configurations. One could be going upwind and the other downwind, or both upwind, etc.

The terms and rules are illustrated in Figure 10-5. Consider vessel A, which is on starboard tack, as the reference boat.

B must give way to A, because B is on a port tack.

C must give way to A, because it is also a starboard tack but it is to windward of A.

Likewise vessel D is a starboard boat "to weather" (to windward), and so D must give way to A,

and E is a port boat, which must give way to A on starboard.

When B turns right and "falls off the wind," then it must keep clear of G, because it will be a port boat to windward of another port boat G.

When E, which is on a port tack—in this case usually called a port jibe—turns left and "comes up on the wind," then it must stay clear of D, because D is on a starboard tack (jibe). The Rules do not distinguish between tacks and jibes, but sailors generally refer to the tack they are on as the jibe they are on when sailing downwind.

D must also stay clear of C so long as C remains on a starboard tack, but the maneuver illustrated involves a jibe onto the port tack.

This sort of traffic nightmare is characteristic of sailboat racing but should not occur in normal sailboat interactions according to the *Navigation Rules*. A prudent sailor not racing would not sail into a group of boats like this, and indeed should not according to Rule 8a and Rule 16. The vast majority of sailboat interactions will be between just two boats, and the rules are straight forward once the terms are understood. Port gives way to starboard, and windward gives way to leeward on the same tack.

Tacking to keep clear does not change your status in the interaction. When obeying the *Navigation Rules*, you cannot, for example, come in on port, then tack in front of a starboard boat, and then claim he is overtaking you or that you are now the leeward boat. The pertinent rules here would be 8a and 8d, among others. In some cases, one can get away with such things in the sailboat racing rules, but when not racing, or even when racing if you are interacting with a nonracing vessel, then the *Navigation Rules* take complete precedence over any racing rules, and there are no questions of how long on a tack counts as a new situation, etc. If you are required to maneuver to stay clear, you maneuver and monitor that you have indeed stayed clear until all risk of collision has gone. This is, of course, the same when power-driven vessels are maneuvering to stay clear. You do not change the status of your original situation because of a new aspect of your vessel after maneuvering to stay clear. See also discussion of Navigation Rule 1, with regard to the racing rules. Sources for full copies of the Rules are in Section 10.9

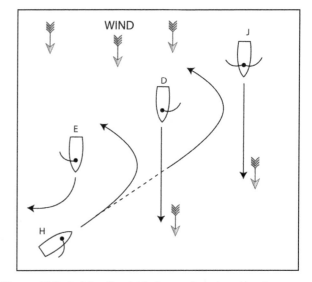

Figure 10-6. *Judging the right of way of windward boats. Vessel H has right of way over E, because E is windward boat on the same tack. But D has rights over H because it is a starboard boat. H cannot tell what tack J is on, so must assume it is starboard and stay clear (although it is not often that we cannot tell what tack a boat is on these days).*

Figure 10-6 shows an important variation of what is shown in Figure 10-5. Port boat H is approaching two boats to windward. E is also on port tack; so E must stay clear of the leeward H. But D is on starboard tack; so it has the right of way over port boat H.

If D were not there, and H noted another boat approaching from windward, but H could not tell the tack of boat J, then H must also stay clear of that boat. This comes from part a (iii) of Rule 12. Note that if you are a starboard boat and detect a sailboat approaching from windward, you know you have right of way over it regardless of its tack.

There is a not-so-hidden message in this Rule 12 for sailors tinkering around in the presence of a lot of sailboats on, for example, a crowded lake on a sunny day: stay on a starboard tack as much as possible!

Remember too, that Rule 13 on overtaking, has precedence over Rule 12. If a sailing vessel is overtaking any other vessel (sail, power, or paddle), it must stay clear. When a sailing vessel is overtaking another sailing vessel, it does not matter what the tack of either boat is; the overtaking vessel must stay clear.

Note the situations with regard to wind terminology of vessels B and F relative to A. B is upwind yet to leeward of A, whereas F is downwind and to windward of A. The Coast Guard exams do not have tricky questions in this area, but you can see the potential for making them if one wanted to. From the boat itself, it is usually not so tricky at all, because you are judging the rights of a vessel based on which side of the boat it is on relative to which side the wind is on.

10.8 Special Terms

Most terms used in the Rules are specifically defined within the Rules, but there are some very important exceptions. Indeed, the ultimate decision on how to respond in some circumstances depends explicitly on your understanding these special terms. The following are a few examples.

close quarters

Generally "close quarters" refers to that space about you that you require in order to maneuver on your own to prevent collision regardless of what the other vessel might do, suddenly and unexpectedly. If you let a vessel get that close, you have given up control of your fate.

The shape and extent of this space depends on the circumstances. Passing slowly in a narrow channel, it might be yards. Passing at high speeds in the open ocean, it is more likely a mile or more. It also depends on the weather, sea state, and visibility.

day versus night

"Night," as regards showing nav lights is concerned, is defined as sunset to sunrise (See Rule 20b). Official sunrise and set times are listed at the NOAA and USNO websites or in the *Nautical Almanac*. Day shapes must be shown *by day* (see Rule 20d). This phrase "by day" is most likely

(most safely) to mean from morning nautical twilight until evening nautical twilight. Note by contrast, automobile lights are required to be on from evening civil twilight until morning civil twilight.

At civil twilight, the center of the sun is 6° below the horizon, and at nautical twilight the sun is 12° below the horizon. In normal atmospheric conditions, at civil twilight it is dark enough to see the brightest stars, and at nautical twilight it is too dark to see the horizon. Precise times of twilight are also listed in the *Nautical Almanac*.

narrow fairway

This important term is used in Rule 9 (a to f), Rule 30e, Rule 34c, Rule 34e, and in the Radiotelephone Act, Section 26.03 (a)(4) and (e)(1) and (e)(2).

This is a term that always appears with Rules related to narrow channels. A fairway can be a buoyed channel through otherwise open water, not necessarily constricted by any other boundaries. They are often marked by buoys, but they need not be prominently marked by buoys or dayshapes. A fairway route could be marked on a chart with no other signs on the water. In some areas, a fairway crosses busy waters or runs along the edge of one. It takes special care to remember that the narrow-channel rules apply in narrow fairways as well, even though the water may not look like a narrow channel at all.

head-on

Meeting "head to head" is defined in Rule 14 in general terms. It implies both sidelights are in view at night. The horizontal range of sidelights is specified in Annex I, Part 9a. They are purposefully screened to be seen at least 1° across the bow, but must not show more than 3° across the bow. Courts have ruled that vessels whose courses lie within 6° of opposites are considered on "nearly reciprocal" courses. Eight-degree encounters in the open ocean, on the other hand, have been considered crossing courses. Courts have also extended this interpretation significantly in narrow channels. See good discussion of head-on situation in *Farwell's Rules of the Nautical Road*. Note that the wording of Rule 14b implies it is the relative heading of the vessels that matters here, not their courses over ground, even when these latter directions might be significantly different from the headings due to current or leeway.

impede

The phrase "do not impede" is used in Rule 9, Rule 10, and Rule 18. The simplest interpretation of not impede is to maneuver so as to prevent the development of risk of collision.

For example, a smaller power-driven vessel crossing a channel (headed, say, eastbound) is instructed not to impede a vessel (ship) following the channel (headed, for example, southbound). In open water, this small vessel would be the stand-on vessel in this encounter, and would have right of way over the ship that would have to maneuver to stay clear, but in this channel the small vessel does not have right of way. In fact, it has less than no right of way! It is more burdened than a normal give-way vessel. If it were simply a give-way vessel (i.e. westbound across the channel), it would have to maneuver to stay clear once within risk of collision. Here in the channel, this vessel must maneuver even before risk of collision exists, that is it must maneuver early enough that no risk develops.

In short, "do not impede" is a stronger obligation than "keep out of the way of," and it develops before risk of collision exists.

inshore traffic zone

Vessel Traffic Systems divide waterways into several zones. There are the two main traffic lanes, outbound and inbound, a separation zone between them, and the two so-called inshore zones, which are the waterways between the main traffic lanes and the shorelines. See Figure 10-1. Rule 10 discusses the use of VTS lanes. See also Tables in the appendix to the *Navigation Rules* on VHF channel assignments for traffic systems.

making way

"Making way through the water" or "not making way" is referred to several times, mainly with regard to proper lights and sounds. See Rules 26, 27, and 35. Each time the phrase is "making way *through the water*." Drifting at 3 kts in a current not moving relative to the water is not making way in this interpretation. This motion would not be detected by other vessels watching visually, if they were drifting in the same current, but their Automated Identification System (AIS) units would report the vessel moving at 3 kts. Furthermore, the observer could be in different current. So this is a subtlety to look out for when interacting with the vessels involved in the presence of strong currents. See related discussion of the special term head-on

proper lookout

Proper lookout is not defined in the Rules but has been elaborated upon extensively in court cases. Elements of "proper" include: good two-way communication with helm, no other distracting duties, still required when radar is in use, helmsman might qualify as proper watch in some circumstances, use of binoculars could be crucial, hearing could be as important as seeing, proper combination of instrumental and human watch keeping, etc. There is extended discussion of this important concept in the References.

risk of collision

Collision risk is addressed in Rule 7. The unstated implication is that collision risk exists if two approaching vessels would arrive at the same place at the same time if they continue on with their present speeds and courses. The Rule requires evaluation of this situation using compass bearings. This situation could exist, however, when the vessels are still separated by a great distance, large enough that in a practical sense there is no risk of collision yet.

Hence when does the risk begin which triggers the actions required by the Rules?

This is not explicitly answered in the Rules, and even court cases involving collisions are reluctant to assign a numerical distance to this separation. There are too many variable factors involved. Rather vague generalities have been proposed by several authors (based on court statements), the most common one repeated is that risk begins when the vessels are so close that a collision can indeed occur if either does not obey the Rules.

Certainly, the separation calling for action is farther off than the realm of close-quarters. In other words, on deciding when to maneuver to keep clear of a crossing vessel on your starboard side, one should do so well before being exposed to risk from a sudden (illegal) turn to the left on their part—or the sudden (again illegal) tack of a sailing vessel you are passing.

Rule 17 requires the stand-on vessel to hold course and speed when risk exists, but the stand-on vessel is also given the right and even obligation to maneuver themselves to avoid collision if they deem the give-way vessel is not maneuvering in time. Clearly their own perception of close quarters enters their decision here. Consequently, the interpretation of "take early action" in Rule 16 must mean we should certainly maneuver well before the other vessel perceives we are entering their close quarters.

Keep in mind at all times, however, the catch-all Saving Grace of Rule 7a: If there is any doubt, the answer is yes. And if there is any further doubt about what to do, the answer is stop (Rule 8e).

separation zone

The narrow waterway between the outbound and inbound traffic lanes in a Traffic Separation Scheme (TSS). See Figure 10-1 and 10-2. Rules related to it are in Rule 10.

special circumstances

That is, those that might require a departure from the Rules as stated in Rule 2b. These include the meeting of more than two vessels, interactions involving underway vessels and anchored vessels, some unusual sudden weather phenomenon, the clear indication that following the Rules is going to lead to a collision, etc. Note, however, that these will always be *very special* circumstances, because one of the normal rules (Rule 8e) states that if you don't know what's going on, you should stop!

tack

The *Navigation Rules* do not use the term "tack" specifically to describe right of way, but do refer in Rule 12 to the side that the wind is on. Hence, a sailing vessel with the wind on the port side would be a port tack vessel, etc. This is independent of point of sail; so a port jibe would be the same as a port tack with regard to right of way. In Rule 12b, the windward side is determined by the location of the mainsail boom.

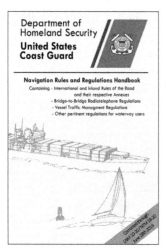

Figure 10-7. *Cover of the official USCG printing of the Navigation Rules. It is a 6" x 9" paperback, available at the US Government Bookstore or third party outlets. One side of each facing page is International Rules, the other side is the corresponding US Inland Rule. Every mariner should have a copy of this book. PDF copies from the USCG are no longer available, but complete, fully illustrated color copies of the Rules appear in each US Coast Pilot, which are available as PDFs.*

10.9 References on the *Navigation Rules*

There are many good books on the *Navigation Rules*. The following are ones we are familiar with and refer to often.

Farwell's Rules of the Nautical Road, Ninth Edition by Craig H. Allen, Jr & Sr (Naval Institute Press, 2020).

Collisions and their Causes by Richard A. Cahill (Fairplay Publications, 1983).

Collision Cases Judgments and Diagrams by F.J. Buzek and H.M.C. Holdert (Lloyd's of London Press, 1990).

The Collision Regulations by Richard B. Sturt (Lloyd's of London Press, 1991).

A Guide to the Collision Avoidance Rules by A.N. Cockcroft and J.N.F. Lameijer (7th edition, Butterworth-Heinemann, 2012).

Canadian Modifications to the Navigation Rules. A copy of the COLREGS with each Canadian modification marked in red and inserted in the proper location. www.starpath.com/downloads.

trawling, trolling, etc.

The *Navigation Rules* distinguish very clearly between vessels fishing by "trawling" compared to other methods of fishing. Trawling is briefly defined in Rule 26b with further instructions given in Annex II.

Trolling usually means pulling baited lines through the water, as opposed to trawling that involves dragging large, heavy nets through the water or across the bottom. Vessels trolling are not classified as fishing vessels but are considered simply as power-driven vessels. See definition of fishing vessel.

When underway, you can always tell if you are interacting with a fishing vessel, because it must show the proper lights or day shapes (Rule 26). If no such signs are shown, then the vessel is a power-driven vessel, regardless of what apparent fishing gear is in sight. Likewise, every real fishing vessel is just a power-driven vessel on the way to and from the fishing grounds. The fishing vessel status applies only when the gear is hampering its maneuverability, and they can only show these day shapes and lights at that time.

Figure 10-8, Right. *Starpath Pocket Navigation Rules Handbook. Section of the top of this super convenient online resource on the Nav Rules. Distinguishes US Inland from International Rules, and cross references cited rules and definitions. Also all related documents (Annexes, CFRs, etc) are all presented on the same web page, so you can search all at once—use Crtl+F for PC or Cmd+F for Mac. You can open this page in your phone or other mobile device and then save it to the home screen for use offline. See www.starpath.com/navrules/NavigationRulesHandbook.html*

STARPATH POCKET NAVIGATION RULES HANDBOOK
Compliments of starpath.com.

Latest USCG PDF copy includes pictures of vessel lights. A printed copy is available.

Rules 1-38 below are an amalgamation of the International Regulations for Preventing Collisions at Sea (COLREGS) and the US Inland Navigation Rules. Text unique to the Inland Navigation Rules is *italicized*, sometimes with brackets with a vertical bar separator [International wording | *Inland wording*]. Larger differences are presented in side-by-side columns.

Click Blue-text to jump to a specific Rule or to open a new window of an associated Rule or of information not contained in the Rules.
Click Back to return to the top of the page.

PART A - GENERAL

    Rule 1 - Application
    Rule 2 - Responsibility
    Rule 3 - General Definitions

PART B - STEERING AND SAILING RULES

I - Conduct of Vessels in Any Condition of Visibility

    Rule 4 - Application
    Rule 5 - Look-Out
    Rule 6 - Safe Speed
    Rule 7 - Risk of Collision
    Rule 8 - Action to Avoid Collision
    Rule 9 - Narrow Channels
    Rule 10 - Traffic Separation Schemes | *Vessel Traffic Services*

II - Conduct of Vessels in Sight of One Another

    Rule 11 - Application

Chapter 10 Glossary

Admiralty Law. A distinct body of law governing navigation and shipping. In the UK there is a separate Admiralty Court, but in the US admiralty cases are under the jurisdiction of the federal district courts. It shares much with the civil law, but it is separate from it. Also called Maritime Law.

close quarters. A minimum clear zone around your vessel that you must maintain in order to avoid a collision with your maneuver alone regardless of the motion of the approaching vessel.

Code of Federal Regulations (CFR). The documents published in the Federal Register that implement laws passed by Congress, which are themselves recorded in the United States Code (USC). Thus we see many maritime regulations cited with both a CFR reference as well as the USC reference for the statutory authority. The CFR is the main reference. Most aspects of maritime affairs are addressed 33 CFR Navigation and Navigable Waters and 46 CFR Shipping. All CFRs are online and easily searchable

do not impede. Means do not put yourself into a position that could cause the approaching vessel to change course or speed regardless of what might take place on your vessel.

fairway. A direct route followed by draft-limited vessels in their normal course of travel from one waterway to another. It may or may not be marked with buoys, but will be obvious from a chart. All narrow-channel rules apply to narrow fairways as well.

Farwell's. A nickname for Farwell's Rules of the Nautical Road, now in its 8th edition by Craig H. Allen. It is the definitive US text on understanding the *Navigation Rules*. The original author Captain Raymond F. Farwell was, and the present author is, a Professor at the University of Washington in Seattle.

fishing vessel. A vessel engaged in fishing (other than trolling) such that its gear restricts is maneuverability, which is signified with the appropriate lights and shapes.

give-way vessel. The vessel that is required to maneuver to avoid a collision when interacting with another closing vessel.

inshore zone. The waterway between the shoreside boundary of a traffic lane and the shoreline.

International Maritime Organization (IMO). A United Nations-sanctioned organization based in Switzerland that coordinates international maritime laws related to the safety and security of shipping, and the prevention of maritime pollution. COLREGS, SOLAS, STCW, INMARSAT, and more recently the ISPS Code (International Ship and Port Facility Security Code) are a few among many well-known programs they administer on behalf of participating (treaty) nations.

leeward. The downwind side of a line running through the centerline of your vessel.

making way. Underway and moving through the water, but in a current with a measurable SOG, you are also in a sense making way even if your knotmeter reads zero.

not under command. Means by some extraordinary circumstance you cannot maneuver your vessel. This is beyond restricted maneuverability, this is no maneuverability. This status is not limited to power-driven vessels, but we must have the lights or shapes to indicate it if we choose to declare it.

overtaking. Approaching another vessel from more than two points aft of its beam.

port tack vessel. A vessel with wind coming from the port side of the boat. In the Rules, they assume this means the main is on the starboard side of the centerline.

restricted ability to maneuver. Means because of the nature of your normal work, your gear is restricting your ability to maneuver, which is indicated by the appropriate lights and shapes.

restricted visibility. In the Rules, this means visibility limited by fog, rain, snow, sand, smoke, etc. It does not include nighttime limitations or obstructions from land.

right of way. An unofficial term that is used to describe the stand-on vessel in an encounter when one must maneuver (the give-way vessel.) In actual practice, the burden of the vessel with "right of way" is often higher than that of the give-way vessel.

sailing vessel. A vessel without an engine running that is under sail. There is some gray area here with the engine. The rule says engine is "not being used." But when on and ready to go into gear, you do have the maneuverability of a powerboat if needed, and thus you could lose some of your rights as a sailing vessel in a collision court case.

separation zone. The zone between the incoming and outgoing vessel traffic lanes.

stand-on vessel. The vessel instructed to hold course and speed in an encounter with another vessel (the give-way vessel) when risk of collision exists.

starboard tack vessel. A vessel with wind coming from the starboard side of the boat. In the Rules they assume this means the main is on the port side of the centerline.

Traffic Separation Scheme (TSS). USCG-monitored vessel traffic lanes, usually an inbound and outbound, separated by a separation zone. Sometimes called shipping lanes.

trawling. Fishing with large nets that drag along the bottom, often in deep water.

trolling. Fishing with lines, sometimes many, over the side. Considered a power-driven vessel in the Rules, and not a vessel engaged in fishing.

underway. Not anchored, moored, or aground.

vessel. Any description of watercraft used for transportation on the water.

Vessel Traffic Service (VTS). The division of a local USCG district office that monitors ship traffic. They describe their instructions as advisory, but they have the authority to change them to commands.

windward. The upwind side of a line running through the centerline of your vessel.

CHAPTER 11
NAVIGATION PLANNING & PRACTICE

11.1 Preparation

The amount of preparation needed always depends on the vessel and the voyage in mind. Here we take the extreme case of a small boat, perhaps single handed, where much of the navigation must be done from the cockpit. Nevertheless, even a short voyage in a large vessel is more relaxed and more efficient when some level of navigation preparation is made. In any vessel we must always plan for tides and currents, be sure we have the right charts, etc. Here we go even farther into considering all we might do to make things easier underway, anticipating as many situations as we can. (Needless to say, we would have all of our waypoints entered into the GPS ahead of time; even though we are here, we are preparing for a non-electronics mode.)

The resources listed in Chapter 3 will help you choose the best time and place for a trip. Start with short trips in sheltered waters to test gear and to practice navigation and boat handling, and then work toward more challenging trips. It is especially valuable training to practice in strong winds and waves in protected waters rather than meet these for the first time in open or isolated waters. In larger bodies of water, it may help to keep in mind that the waves will be larger on a downwind shoreline (where wind is blowing toward the shore). So if you are looking for bigger waves, that would be the place to go; but if you are trying to avoid them, practice on an upwind shore. Waves near a windward shore (where wind is blowing off the shore) are small, because the fetch necessary to build the waves starts at the shoreline.

For all boating in any waters, however, leave word of your intentions with someone ashore. The Coast Guard calls this *filing a float plan;* this precaution is fundamental to all boating. This plan, however, cannot be filed with the Coast Guard; this is not one of their services. Tell a friend or family member where you plan to go, when you plan to be back, the number of people in the party, and a description of the boat. Include contingency plans, and be sure to let them know when you have returned. Also, in some circumstances it might be appropriate to tell them where you will be parking your car along with the make, model, and license number. On coastal routes, remember that it might be easier for you to contact the Coast Guard by marine radio than to reach your interested parties on shore directly in the case of a delay. Therefore, when planning exposed routes, be sure your contact person knows how to reach the Coast Guard.

Once you have a proposed route in mind, even on short trips, check your exposure along it. For each leg of the route, consider the potential for wind, waves, swells, current, and traffic; then note where shelter from any of these might lie. That is, look for escape routes along any exposed section. To plan each day's sail, look up the time of sunrise and sunset, estimate your average speed along each leg, taking into account the current as explained in Chapter 6, and then figure the time each leg will take. When strong currents are present at some point along the route, estimate passage times carefully, trying to spend as much time as possible in favorable current.

Chart preparation before departing can be a key to good navigation underway. Most of what you might want to know underway can be figured ahead of time and noted on the chart. When short-handed sailing or racing, for example, you may not have the time or conditions that allow much chart navigation underway. Chart plotting is awkward from the cockpit. To prepare a chart, draw in course lines along each leg and label them with the compass headings. Make mile markers along each leg as shown in Figure 11-1, and note the times you expect to be at various points along the route. Then when you pass these points, note the time on the chart to monitor your progress and schedule.

When water depth is a factor in navigation, highlight the shelves and spits that might affect current flow, cause tide rips, or go dry at low water. Make a list or graph of

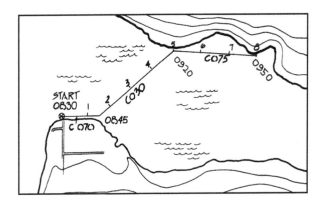

Figure 11-1. *The planned route for an 8-nmi sail at an average speed of 6 kts. Compass courses, mile markers, and estimated times can be charted before departing.*

the tides and currents for each day of the trip, and note the key data on the chart. In areas with extensive foreshore, remember that the land can appear quite different with changes in tide height. Compare the anticipated range of the tides with the local mean high water (listed on the chart) that defines the land side of the green foreshore on the chart in order to anticipate what you will see.

Highlight potentially dangerous rocks or other landmarks that are expected to be conspicuous along the route. For longer crossings, draw in a few compass bearing lines emanating from these landmarks to monitor progress. Look for ranges along the route that will mark your position, and draw these on the chart as well. Figures 11-2 and 11-3 show several examples. For prominent peaks or other features with charted elevations, draw in a few circles of equal distance off, using whatever units are convenient (degrees, centimeters along a kamal, or finger widths). With this chart preparation, it is a simple matter to keep track of where you are by just glancing at the chart and the horizon around you.

Charts must be protected from water and abrasion underway. This can be done by keeping them in waterproof clear plastic bags if they are going to be used from the cockpit, soaking them in various plastic solutions (available at marine and outdoor supply stores), or by actually laminating them in plastic or transparent contact paper. For most of these options, a grease pencil (china marker) is the best way to make notes on the chart covering. As with all boating gear, the chosen system must be tested to meet your needs. In some climates, condensation can occur in chart bags, although many boaters have used this method extensively without this trouble. Clear contact paper is convenient, but the charts do not fold well.

Although damp charts cannot be written on with a pencil, wetness alone will not destroy a chart. Wet charts dry quickly in a warm cabin. Abrasion when wet is the bigger concern; this will destroy the chart or make parts of it illegible. Chart bags are a popular solution for both problems. Big ones are better than small ones. They allow you to expose a full day's sail (using both sides of the bag if necessary) and leave enough chart showing that you can identify more distant landmarks. Another option is to carry a large-scale chart on one side of the bag and a smaller-scale chart on the other. It can be difficult to unpack and refold a chart underway in wind, waves, and rain. Having a full day's sail laid out in front of you also makes it easier to gauge your progress at a glance, if you fall off the estimated schedule marked on the chart.

Also practice reading the chart from the cockpit or wheelhouse while at the helm. In complex waterways or island groups, it is often necessary to keep the chart in continuous readable range in order to keep track of where you are without interrupting your driving. When wind and waves are not too severe, a self-fastening fabric such as Velcro might be used to attach the chart bag to a cockpit seat.

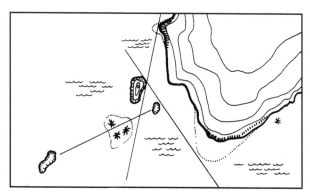

Figure 11-2. *Natural ranges plotted to locate potential underwater hazards such as the rock group and spit shown.*

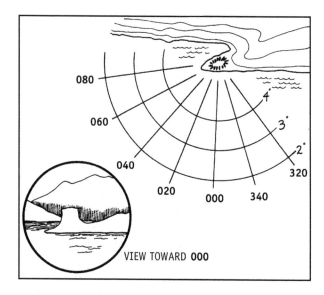

Figure 11-3. *Charted bearing lines and circles of equal distance off are a convenient way to keep track of position in special circumstances. The circles correspond to angular heights of a sextant.*

When you fold a chart, you might not be able to expose a miles scale and compass rose where you want them. The miles scale (or latitude scale) might not be critical if the planned route has miles marked off on it, as discussed earlier, and you are using a log to measure miles covered. If need be, a compass rose can be added to any part of the chart using transparent adhesive compass roses available from navigation supply stores. There is a free download option at starpath.com/navbook to print on clear label stock as well. Even with several bearing lines drawn to key features, a chart rose might be required for bearings to other objects. For longer trips, photocopies of the relevant sections of the *Coast Pilot* and *Light List* should be carried, if there is not room for the full publications. It also helps to carry a notebook for navigation notes along the route. Generally, there is more information to keep track of than can be noted on the chart. This book also can serve as a log or diary of the trip to record navigational information

Table 11-1. Navigation Checklist

- Nautical charts
- Chart catalog
- Handheld GPS + manual
- Bearing compass
- Mk 3 sextant
- 3-arm protractor
- Watch (waterproof with stopwatch)
- Kamal (homemade instrument)
- Pencils and eraser
- Plotting tools*
- Logbook
- Navigation notebook
- Eyeglasses (plus spare)
- Sunglasses
- Tide predictions
- Tidal current predictions
- *Coast Pilot* or *Sailing Directions*
- *Light List*
- *Chart No. 1*
- *Navigation Rules*
- Special current references
- Marine Weather Services notes
- Cell phone (check coverage)
- Portable VHF radio + manual
- List of VHF channels
- SW / AM radio receiver
- EPIRB (boat and personal)
- Binoculars
- Light for chart reading
- Compass lighting
- Spare bulbs and batteries
- Heavy-duty rubber bands
- Waterproof bag to hold this gear

* itemized in Table 12.5-1

accumulated underway. Table 11-1 is a checklist of navigational gear.

In many parts of the world, there are seasons when it is essential to listen to marine weather broadcasts before setting out on any trip. Even in clear weather or in areas not known for foul weather, it is still best to check the marine weather before heading out onto the water. It is the responsibility of every mariner to take advantage of the information available. Sources are listed at the Ocean Prediction Center (opc.ncep.noaa.gov). On long trips, weather broadcasts should be monitored frequently.

A waterproof wristwatch with a stopwatch option is a valuable asset to all navigation.

11.2 Shoreline Routes

Most small craft navigation is done along the shoreline, within half a mile or so of land, and there is good reason for this. It usually keeps you out of the traffic and close enough to have a good view of what you are passing. Along shore there is much more to see than there is in the middle of a large waterway, and if the wind should suddenly build or the current reverse, you are not far from shelter. The navigation is also generally easier with closer references. Nevertheless, there are still several navigational matters to consider when planning shoreline routes.

First to consider is the nature of the shore itself. If the shore is extremely steep, as along cliffs or large rocks, then it may not be the best place to travel, after all. Such a shore offers no shelter, and in fact it can be a hazard because it reflects incident waves, creating steep confused seas. Strong winds can also get focused along a cliff and become accelerated. Even without wind waves, wakes from ship traffic can create choppy water near steep shorelines. Furthermore, currents and back eddies can be quite strong along a steep shoreline. Also, close in along the shore would not be good if the water depth is changing, and you have to continually look out for shoaling.

To avoid these potential issues, study the proposed shoreline route carefully on the chart before departing. Shoreline and depth contours on the chart should reveal these features. If either feature is in the way, determine from the chart where along the shore you should angle out to go around it and note ranges or bearings that will tell when you are at that point.

Inshore rocks are another concern. Along rocky shorelines it takes a good large-scale chart to pick them out. Pay special attention to rocks that might be just under the surface (see Chapter 2 on rock symbols). It pays to use a colored marker to highlight hazardous rocks on the chart when planning the route. Look for signs of barely submerged rocks as waves pass over them. If you know from the chart where to look for them, you can often spot them by the irregularities in wave patterns or slight ripples in otherwise smooth water. On coastal routes, big swells over such rocks can be quite dramatic and proportionally more dangerous. These are sometimes detectable from residual foam streaks on the surface, even if the breaking boomer was not seen.

To identify rocks, and sometimes the lay of the shoreline itself, it is necessary to know the tide height when sailing even the simplest shoreline routes. In areas with a wide foreshore (shown green on the chart), remember that the water extends to the inshore side of the green at mean high water and to the offshore side of the green at zero tide level. Determine the tide height as a function of time, and note it on the chart before departing.

Navigators must always consider the wind direction, especially along a close inshore route. If the wind has any onshore component, the seas will be quite choppy near shore. If you have the option, take the side with the offshore wind component, such as the east side of a north-south channel in a northeast wind. It will have the smoothest seas because the wind has no fetch on that side. In contrast, the lee side will have the full width of the channel to build waves on.

A frequent decision a sailor confronts along a shoreline route occurs at each bay or inlet along the shore: follow the shoreline along the inside edge of the bay or steer straight across to the next point? Straight across is the shortest route, but it might not be the fastest. In adverse current, ducking into the bay is probably best as there may be a favorable back eddy inside. On the other hand, when riding favorable current along the approaching shoreline, you might lose this advantage by ducking into the bay and even run into the adverse flow of a back eddy.

At the mouths of large bays, there is usually a shift in wind direction that also might enter into the decision. Any wind over the offshore waters tends to funnel into or pour out of the bay, which causes the offshore wind to shift to some extent toward the orientation of the bay. Wind from any direction will usually shift (to some extent) toward the beam as you cross the mouth of a bay. Headwinds shift to bow winds, bow and quarter winds shift to beam winds, and tailwinds shift to quarter winds. The same effect occurs at the mouth of a valley leading down to the shoreline, even without a prominent bay at its base.

In many cases, the wind also will be stronger near the center of a bay or valley than it is along the shoreline approaching it, because the wind is channeled along the bay and because you lose the shelter of the shoreline as you start to cross the bay. A steep shoreline shelters the near-shore waters from wind blowing both offshore and onshore. The shoreline is in the shadow of offshore winds, and onshore winds tend to rise to go over steep shores before reaching the actual shoreline.

A principal element in deciding to go in or across a bay is the nature of the point or headland that marks the far side of the bay. If you conclude from the chart and what you can see ahead that this is an area with dangerous rips that must be circumvented from outside of the rip zone, then it might be best to go part way across and angle out around the rip from somewhere along the mouth of the bay. Following the shoreline around might take you directly into the rip at the next point. For large bays, a compromise might be called for, such as heading in somewhat to keep from getting too far offshore, and from somewhere inside the bay start angling back out to miss the point. This is not necessarily the fastest route, but it may be the one that feels best under the circumstances, depending on the wind and current in the bay and the potential traffic in the bay. If the large bay has much ship or ferry traffic, any route through the bay should take into account the routes of other traffic out of the bay. Check the chart for buoys or daymarks that show their route and try to cross it as promptly as possible.

When passing headlands, also keep in mind that ships or tugs passing well away from you can still influence your conditions. The long, slow swells that they generate will shorten and steepen or even break as they reach shallow waters on the point. A tide rip at the point that is questionable becomes even more of a challenge as a ship or ferry passes by.

As mentioned at the beginning, however, these concerns are all relative to your vessel and the conditions. A light-weight vessel that is low powered (i.e. a 23-ft sailing vessel with an outboard) will have more of these concerns than a heavy 35-ft powerboat that can make good 8 kts or more.

Also keep in mind that not all tide rips are a threat to your safety. Generally, there is current flowing through them; so you do get pushed out of the rip in some direction. When charted, however, it is a flag up to pay attention to.

11.3 In and Around Islands

Sailing through island groups in tidal waters is a fine test of navigation skill. Island sailing is different from shoreline or coastal sailing in that you usually have more options when choosing routes and more factors to consider when making the choice. To go around an island usually requires going two ways relative to wind and current, which might not be the case following straight routes along a coast. As always, wind and current are the primary uncharted concerns, but particularly near islands there might be sparse data for the precise places you want to go—winds and currents are difficult to predict throughout the small and complex waterways through a group of islands. The task is to combine what is known with what you think will happen from your knowledge of general principles and the pieces of local knowledge you have gathered.

When circumnavigating an island, you must first decide which way to go around. The right choice can make the difference between an efficient and enjoyable trip and just the opposite of these. Tidal currents, for example, change directions about every 6 hours. In idealized circumstances, it might be possible to sail up one side of an island riding a flood current and then sail back down the other side riding

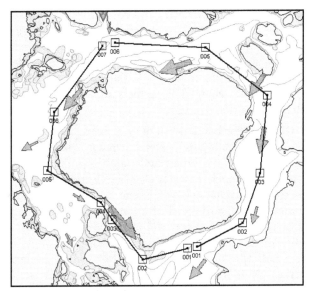

Figure 11-4. *Current flow around an island in Alaska. This screen capture from Nobeltec's Visual Navigation Suite echart program illustrates how they show all the current stations with currents at any given moment. Also shown are two proposed routes around the island. The large arrow represents a current of about 6 kts. A cursor on the arrow shows precise values and the option to open a display of current vs. time for that location. See Figure 11-5 for other features of that program.*

an ebb current. Going the right way could be fast and easy; going the wrong way might not even be possible. Currents, however, are rarely of the same speed or duration on opposite sides of an island—see Figures 11-4 and 11-5. Furthermore, wind speed and direction might be more important to progress than currents are, or it could be that the relative

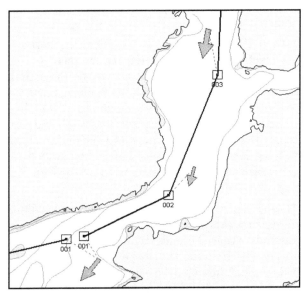

Figure 11-5. *Current stations linked to waypoints. The Nobeltec program allows users to assign a current station to each waypoint of a route. Then when an ETA or route transit time is computed, the times are corrected for current speed. This convenient feature offers a quick way to check the computations done by hand using data from Figure 9-11.*

direction of wind and current is the main concern. Current flowing against wind must always be noted with caution, because it enhances the steepness of the waves.

Sometimes the choice of rounding direction is obvious; other times it takes careful planning in anticipation of conditions you cannot see or of conditions that have not yet developed. Local knowledge can be crucial. Check with someone who has done it, or read all you can find about the area first. These days, it is remarkable how much we can learn about very specific places by just searching the internet. In some cases, it has paid to find a shop of some sort near the area of interest and just call them with questions. They will likely know someone who fishes or sails in the area who can help.

The adventure of spontaneous exploration is an attractive lure of the cruising mariner; but it is not wholly consistent with good navigation. Rounding a large exposed island or rounding individual islands of a group that are each surrounded with fast channels and many points of tide rips requires more planning than a simple look at the chart might imply. Without doing your homework, it is possible to get stuck halfway around looking for an anchorage where none is to be found, as you wait out the current or adverse winds. Good navigation planning should minimize surprises that threaten your convenience as well as your safety.

Ideally, the wind would be either calm or behind you throughout the rounding. But winds change as the weather changes or as the local terrain changes, and even without changes in weather or terrain, winds often change with the time of day. In many areas, the wind is calm in the morning and builds as the day heats up. The general direction of the building wind called a sea breeze even on island waters is usually known locally and is often given in *Coast Pilots*. In very broad terms, these winds blow from the area of most water toward the area of most land. (Remember: a north wind is from the north; a sea breeze is from the sea.) Sea breezes increase in strength fairly rapidly starting about midmorning, peak about 2 hours after midday, and die off completely at sunset. Sea breezes can build routinely to more than 20 kts in some areas. On a smaller scale, winds through channels and islands tend to follow the curves of the waterways, because channeled waterways usually have elevated shorelines that channel the wind as well as the water. Exceptions occur only near large bays or valleys along the channel as discussed in the section on shoreline routes.

Planning must include current and wind, although wind is just as likely to be the factor that must be considered first. You can get out of adverse current more frequently than adverse wind, and over a long run adverse wind can do more damage to your time schedule. Currents are eventually going to change; winds might not. It is valuable to know if the source of wind is a weather pattern or a sea breeze. Weather pattern winds can last anywhere from a few minutes to a few days. Wind in the morning or at night is not from a sea breeze. If it was calm in the morning and

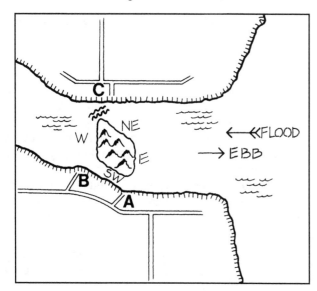

Figure 11-6. *A hypothetical island exposed to both wind and current.*

blowing from the seaward direction in the afternoon, it is probably a sea breeze that will go away at night.

Sometimes, choosing a route calls for a choice between adverse winds versus adverse current (two evils) or between favorable wind versus favorable current (two blessings). For sailing vessels, the wind is usually the dominating factor, but strong currents can easily change that.

When winds are not a critical factor, choose the route and schedule that will put you in the best current for the most time. If the currents are bad at some point in both directions, check the chart carefully to see which route might offer the most opportunities for getting out of the current—bays and coves with back eddies or routes with shallow shorelines. In some cases, however, an isolated area of strong current can completely determine the route and timing of the entire trip.

Consider the circumnavigation in a low-powered trailerable boat of the hypothetical island shown in Figure 11-6 during times of strong currents and strong afternoon sea breezes. You have a trailerable boat and three options for launching it. From various resources, it is known that the winds are calm all around the island in the mornings, but in the afternoon the east side is exposed to strong easterlies, and the northeast side has strong southeasterlies along the shore. The east and west sides have weak currents at all times; the northeast side has weak ebbs but strong floods, and the channel along the southwest side has very strong floods and ebbs with no shelter from the current. Assume it takes a day to sail around the island, and you can start in the early morning from any of the points A, B, or C. What would be the best choice for this trip?

A peak flood during midmorning that turned to ebb at midday would be ideal for rounding the island to port (counterclockwise) starting from point A. The eastern side would have no wind or current at the start; sailing along

the northeast side, the wind and current would build behind you; and you would round the potentially hazardous north point near slack water as you turned into shelter from the strong east wind. The west side would be slack and calm as the ebb increased in the channel ahead. You would meet the channel along the southwest side at peak ebb for a nice ride home.

On the other hand, if you did not figure the sea breeze into the route, but simply stood at point A in the morning looking at the calm air and water flowing northward along the channel—or even checked *Current Tables* for the southwest channel—you might be tempted to head around to starboard (clockwise) on a rocket ship ride up the southwest side. You would feel good about the choice until well around the north point because you would get there early with the fast current. But somewhere along the northeast side things would start to get bad, and get bad fast. The building ebb would be straight into the building headwinds, and the rest of the trip would be a lot wetter, if not dangerous. For many vessels, maintaining course and speed with strong wind on the beam (the east side of this trip) is as much or more trouble than strong headwind is once the waves build.

Point B is not even an option for starting a circumnavigation in a low-powered vessel with the midmorning flood. You could not head off on a port rounding with the channel flood building against you, and if you started off to the north, the channel would be ebbing by the time you got around to it—after fighting the easterlies along the east side. You would be stuck at point A. Point C is a possible starting point, but not a good choice because you could not escape strong east wind along the east side. On the other hand, a midafternoon flood would make point C the best choice (to starboard) and point A the worst choice (in either direction).

When circumnavigating a lake along its perimeter, wind direction is the only concern because there is no current in landlocked lakes. A lake running north-south that takes about a day to sail around, for example, might have a persistent northerly sea breeze building over it in the afternoon. In this case, starting from the south end in the morning would put the afternoon wind behind you for the return leg. A phone call to local sailing organizations that use the lake could provide such wind information if not known ahead of time.

Islands along exposed coastal waters present additional hazards of the seas along their seaward sides. Fast channels at the ends of coastal islands might even generate breaking waves on the ebb cycle. The steepest waves occur when an ebb flow out of the channel meets the onshore ocean swell. A coastal channel between islands might not be passable even when the current direction is favorable.

Keeping track of position as you go around an island takes extra care whenever there is little to be seen in the background away from the island. The view from close in-

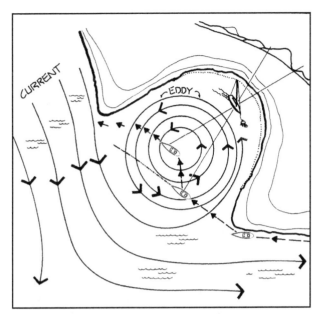

Figure 11-7. *The use of natural range to monitor progress across a bay. A course jog into the eddy center gets this boater out of adverse current, which was detected from the range.*

shore along bays and coves is often restricted to the island itself. Although there is obviously no doubt you are on the edge of the island, after some sailing along a round island it is easy to lose track of the side you are on. A close watch on the compass and a few notes on the charts as you go around will solve the problem and avoid throwing off your schedule.

We should point out that even though the last example would be more of interest to low-powered boats, here is something else to consider: There are several places in Pacific Northwest waters of Canada and Alaska where, as one transits a narrow channel of potentially very strong currents (7 or 8 kts, for example), one cannot help but notice that all along the sloping beaches are acres of giant logs washed up onto the beach at high water—about 4 ft in diameter and 30 ft long. Here would be a wrong time to go through that pass: high water after a long period of rain (that refloats all of these logs), at a time near peak current flow (when they are all out there spinning around in the eddies). This would be a monster of a hazard to any vessel in any condition of visibility, not to mention that fog and heavy mist is very common in these areas.

These floating logs, even in not so dramatic a situation, are common occurrences in these waters, which make travel at night risky most of the time. This is just another reason to read books like the *Coast Pilot* and *Sailing Directions,* which will tell about such things. The worst kind of floating logs are called deadheads. They are completely water logged and float vertically, with just a foot or less showing above the surface.

11.4 Open-Water Crossings

With moderate wind and no current, long crossings of open water (ending up well offshore in the process) are mostly a matter of watching out for traffic and steering a compass course (or with GPS, watching your track across the plotter relative to the line to your next waypoint). Examples are sailing across a large sound, strait, or lake or sailing from one point to another across a large bay. To optimize the chances of light to moderate wind, it is usually best to plan long crossings for early morning, before sea breezes build. On crossings that take a several hours or more, any current present is likely to change with both time and place. With little to see in the background, it is often difficult to monitor the effect of the current (without electronics, which is our premise here). In some cases, it might be necessary to just make your best estimate of the current and how it is going to change en route and crab across it accordingly. When your target is not in sight as you depart, back bearings to the shore or point you leave from will help you gauge the current during the start of the crossing.

When crossing large bays within fairly clear sight of land at all times, progress across can often be checked with ranges. Even when details of the horizon are difficult to discern, it might be possible, for example, to watch an anchored boat off your beam relative to the terrain behind it. If the boat does not move relative to the background, you are not making progress (see Figure 11-7); you might as well head into the bay and take the longer route, closer to shore, where the adverse current is less or is even favorable. You may not have to go all the way into shore; your lack of progress farther out might have been due to adverse current that extends only a short way into the bay. With such a convenient natural range to watch (the anchored boat with a peak behind it), you could tell how far into the bay you must go to get out of the current. When you start making progress on the anchored boat, you know you are getting out of the bad current.

In a case like this, if you run into much flotsam as you head into the bay, it is further confirmation that you might have been sailing in an eddy current. Often there are bits of bark, branches, seaweed, or various kinds of rubble trapped in the centers of large eddies. The outer edge of a prominent eddy—farther offshore in the last example— also is marked by flotsam in many cases, trapped in a line along the edge. This outer edge is also often marked by a conspicuous change in the texture of the water whenever the wind is blowing roughly parallel to the current flow (see Figure 8-16). Water flowing into the wind is rougher than that flowing with the wind. This is just a microscopic example of how opposing wind and current enhance waves, even when the waves are just ripples.

Oftentimes the issue of open-water crossing has more to do with boat handling than with navigation. Some vessels are not as well suited to handle the larger waves one might be exposed to in open waters, or the overall comfort of the crew or passengers might be the main concern. In these cases, it is generally the planning around the weather, which is the main factor. For weather planning and analysis, see *Modern Marine Weather*, Starpath Publications, 2013.

11.5 Coastal Routes and Weather

Coastal cruising exposed to the open sea is definitely an advanced part of the sport. Many mariners find adequate enjoyment and challenge in waters well sheltered from the open sea. Trips into coastal waters should be planned carefully and usually done first in the company of experienced sailors.

Coastal sailing can call upon all the mariner's skills in seamanship and navigation. Although the sea can be and often is as calm as an inland lake, it can change rapidly into hazardous waters of strong winds and big waves. Strong winds can develop quickly from offshore or onshore—afternoon sea breezes are quite strong along some coasts, especially near the openings to bays and canyons. Either wind direction could pose a problem. A strong offshore wind could force you into open water or a strong onshore wind could blow you into a dangerous surf or a rocky coastline. Even in calm air and flat water, large swells from distant storms can arrive, turning a gentle beach into a hazardous surf zone within a matter of hours. Frequent monitoring of marine weather broadcasts is essential in coastal waters. The sea state as well as the weather is forecasted for coastal waters every 6 hours. Reports of actual conditions are often given every hour and sometimes checked on a real-time basis.

Escape routes are often the primary concern along coastal routes—places where you can get out of the ocean if you need to. These might be inlets or bays, or river bars. Sailing the West Coast (WA to CA) is an example we cover in detail in Section 12.7. Seasonal weather as well as present sea state and weather forecasts are crucial. That area, like others around the world, does not have many all-weather inlets. That is, ocean swells can actually close down the entrances to the bars along the way before the storms even get there and you are then stuck in the ocean—which means that every coastal passage in that region has to be prepared for as an ocean passage.

When planning an extended run along a coast, choose several landmarks to use for navigation along the way, and prepare the charts accordingly. Carefully monitor progress to avoid getting stuck halfway between two protected escape points. Piloting is especially important along a coast, because coastal currents are difficult to predict—although you may benefit from HF radar predictions discussed in Section 8.8. It is also difficult to predict progress against wind and waves if they should develop. Needless to say, a GPS and radar are fundamental aids to coastal navigation.

Even sailing downwind, it is difficult to know ahead of time what your ultimate course made good will be in big

seas. The seas are made up of irregular wind waves built upon smooth rolling swells. Wind waves grow and subside with the wind, and they move in the direction the wind is blowing. The height and direction that swells move, however, are not related to local winds; swells are the wave remnants of distant storms. When swells and waves run in different directions, the seas are confused and difficult to predict. It is not easy to know ahead of time what course through them will be the safest to sail, even when you are headed generally downwind. It might be that the course that is easiest to sail is angled in toward a dangerous coastline.

Always keep in mind that escape routes might close with the onset of bigger swells or swells from a new direction. A rock passage or river bar that was smooth in one sea state could have large breaking waves in another. An escape route also can close with a change in wind speed or wind direction or with a change in tidal current flow. An ocean entrance in calm water across a bar near slack water can be blocked in less than an hour by breaking waves on a building ebb flow out of the river. Changes in tidal current

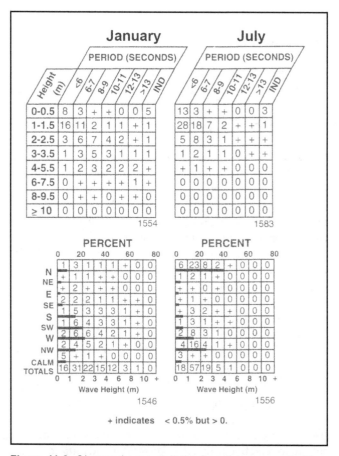

Figure 11-8. *Observed wave statistics from the area west of the WA and OR coasts for January and July from the* Canadian Sailing Directions, Vol. 1, 16th Ed. *Values in the boxes are percentages. For January, waves 3 to 3.5 meters high with periods of 8 to 9 seconds occurred 5% of the time, and waves from the South with heights 2 to 3 meters occurred 3% of the time. The PERCENT label on the bottom pictures applies to the bar graph. 20% of all waves in January were from the SW, with just slightly more from the W.*

flow or tide height also can block exits through rock passes or remove the shelter of a tombolo.

A storm predicted to arrive late in the evening might have associated swells that arrive many hours or even a day earlier. The advancement speed of swells is derived from their parent wave speed in the distant storm. Within a storm, wave speeds build toward the wind speed as the storm develops, but the storms themselves move across the ocean at much slower speeds. Consequently, swells outrun the storm that produced them, arriving well before the storm itself—the storm might not even come to your area, or it might be dissipated by the time it does arrive. Even without an increase in wind, when new swells are first detected consider what is happening along shore where you plan to cross a bar or enter an inlet, even though these new swells pose no present threat to sailing offshore. Large swells will break in any confined or shallow water and might close down your entrance. Such areas often have a USCG base nearby, which can be called on the VHF to check entrance conditions.

Navigation procedures in coastal waters are otherwise no different than in sheltered waters; each of the points listed in the earlier examples applies to coastal waters. There is just more at stake along the coast, in more frequent instances. Skills in piloting, dead reckoning, and chart reading are required, but these are not the only prerequisites. Practical knowledge of weather and oceanography is more critical in the ocean, and sailing in or through large waves requires more skill in boat handling. In short, the decision to sail coastal waters has as much to do with the preparation of the boat and crew as it does with specialized navigation skills.

It is important to know your resources, and to use them. The *Coast Pilot* includes extensive information on coastal weather. In coastal waters, strong winds do not require a storm. Thirty-knot northerlies lasting for days off the California coast are common in the summertime, and they occur without storms or frontal systems, under clear skies or in dense fog. Strong sea breezes are another example of potentially dangerous winds that do not require bad weather systems. Local weather occurrences such as these are discussed in the *Coast Pilot*. Figure 11-8 shows an example of sea-state statistics from the *Canadian Sailing Directions*.

Listen to the weather broadcasts, and watch the sky and wind direction. When bad weather is forecasted, it is usually out there. It is dangerous to assume the forecasts are wrong simply because reports of present weather are wrong. The occasionally uncertain aspect of a forecast is not the existence of bad weather—this is clearly seen in satellite photos and verified by ship or other weather station reports—but the precise arrival time of the weather system. Because of the potential uncertainty in the arrival time, successful planning around the weather can depend on your ability to judge this timing on your own. This is less of a problem on the East Coast than on the West Coast, because weather systems move from west to east, and they are monitored by many more weather stations on land getting to the East Coast than they are over water getting to the West Coast.

Throughout most of the northern temperate latitudes, fair wind is from the northwesterly quadrant and foul wind is from the southerly quadrant. To go from fair to foul, the wind must go from northwest to south, and it does so in most cases by shifting to the left (a backing shift), i.e., from northwest to west, to southwest, to south. Consequently, the approach of foul weather is often first detected by a backing shift in the wind direction, accompanied by lowering clouds. As you start a coastal passage, watch carefully for this shift by noting in your logbook precise wind directions—as opposed to the simple awareness that the wind is, say, westerly. If you notice, for example, that the wind has shifted in the last few hours from 270° to 255° on the compass, be aware that this is one of the first things you might expect to see if you were going to lose good weather in the next half a day or so.

A wind shift alone, however, is not a completely reliable indicator along a coastline. Along a coast, the wind direction often shifts seaward (blowing more toward the land) as a sea breeze builds on a clear day. This effect can confuse the interpretation of a wind shift. Sea breezes, however, usually occur in clear skies or under fair-weather cumulus clouds; so watch the clouds as well as the wind direction. Cloud caps building on coastal peaks near midmorning means that air is rising up the peaks, and this air often comes from sea breezes. A backing shift is a stronger sign of an approaching weather system when there is not a building sea breeze.

In areas of prominent sea breezes, an approaching weather system might be detected by the *absence* of a sea breeze on a clear day or a gradual dying off of the winds in the afternoon when they should be building. Sea breezes occur because the rising air over the warmer land creates a local low pressure region that pulls in air from the higher pressure over the water. As the low pressure of a bad weather system approaches the coast from offshore, the pressure difference driving the sea breeze disappears and the wind dies. Even in the absence of this particular process, fair winds often die off from the northwest and then fill in from the south some time later, rather than smoothly backing around as they build. In general, a dying fair-weather breeze in the afternoon when it should be building, accompanied by lowering clouds or new kinds of clouds, also could be a sign of approaching bad weather. The lowering clouds inhibit the heating of the land that drives a sea breeze. This calm period before the new winds fill in is often described as muggy or unusually still. (When sailing in a long waterway with steep hills on either side, be prepared for the wind to fill in from the opposite direction after going calm in this manner.)

Because storm winds predicted for the evening or next day might arrive earlier when these signs are present, when conditions create doubt about making it to the next escape

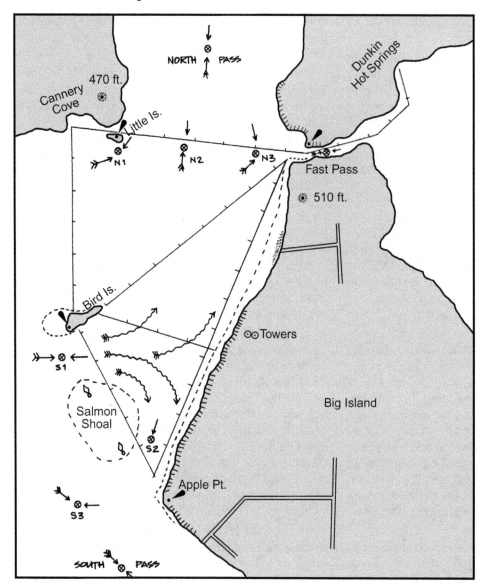

Figure 11-9. *Chart sketch of a hypothetical cruise in exposed waters. Circled "X"s mark the location of tidal current reference stations. Potential track lines are marked in 2-nmi intervals. Tide and current data needed to work through this exercise are in Figure 11-11. The region is constructed for learning purposes, but the conditions and data of the exercise are realistic.*

Feathered arrows at the current stations mark the flood direction. Curved arrows mark typical current flow as one might learn or discern from reading the Coast Pilot *and current table notes for the region.*

point, it could be better to head back or make alternative plans. Also, any prominent fog bank seen approaching from the sea is most likely moving in because the wind is blowing it in that direction, even if the wind is calm where you happen to be at the time. Consider the potential for strong wind *and* fog when making plans in this situation. In any waters, it is always better to wait out bad weather on shore than to tough it out on the water.

This section has been just a brief overview of some of the weather factors that should be taken into account in route planning. For those interested in pursuing this important knowledge, please refer to *Modern Marine Weather*, mentioned earlier.

11.6 Planning around Wind and Currents

Here we consider a more detailed example with built-in hazards to illustrate their analysis in a typical situation affected by wind and current. Consider the area shown in

Figure 11-9, which we will assume to be inland waters but not sheltered from the westerly direction, where there are about 50 nmi of open water leading to the ocean. It is also an area with strong tidal currents. When we check the current predictions, we find that there are stations providing current information at each of the positions marked by a circled "x." The only chart available for the entire region is at a scale of 1:80,000 (about 8 nmi per hand span); but more detailed charts (1:25,000 or about 2.5 nmi per hand span) are available for the Cannery Cove and Fast Pass areas. Both of these areas require these detailed charts for safe navigation. The place is hypothetical, but numerical values (distances, winds, currents, etc.) and available descriptions of the place are realistic.

Our round-trip must start Friday A.M. and finish Sunday P.M. at Apple Point; we would like to visit Bird Island, Cannery Cove, and Dunkin Hot Springs, spending at least 4 hours at each place; we do not mind sailing at night if we have to, but would prefer not to. We could anchor, if neces-

| Duration of Bright Twilight (Sunset to Civil Twilight = Civil Twilight to Sunrise) | | | | |
| | (evening) | | (morning) | |

Latitude	0° N	20° N	40° N	50°N	60°N
June 21	22 min	25 min	33 min	45 min	107 min
Sept 23	20 min	22 min	27 min	32 min	41 min
Dec 21	23 min	24 min	31 min	38 min	58 min

| Duration of Dimmer Twilight (Civil to Nautical Twilight = Nautical to Civil Twilight) | | | | |
| | (evening) | | (morning) | |

Latitude	0° N	20° N	40° N	50°N	60°N
June 21	26 min	29 min	42 min	66 min	all night
Sept 23	24 min	26 min	32 min	39 min	50 min
Dec 21	26 min	28 min	34 min	42 min	57 min

Figure 11-10. *The length of twilight. At civil twilight it is typically dark enough to see the brightest of stars, and at nautical twilight it is too dark to see the horizon. During mid-June, the total twilight period is 75 minutes long (33+42) at latitude 40° N. Most observers would agree that in clear weather it is still daylight at 33 minutes past sunset, but sometime near 42 minutes past sunset, everyone would agree it is dark.*

sary, at just about any place we could get inshore in this region, with the exception of the beach along the south part of Big Island, beneath the bluff, indicated by hatch marks.

Question: Is this a reasonable trip plan, and if so, what would be the best route? We like to cruise along at about 6 kts average in flat water, but we can go a knot or so faster in some conditions. It is usually valuable to clarify your goals as a regular part of the planning. Indeed, the goal of the trip is to cover some ground and get time on the water; we are not necessarily looking for a guaranteed completely leisurely trip, but we also don't want to tackle more than we can handle.

In planning any trip, a first consideration is its total length. In the process of measuring this, it is easy to draw individual legs of the route and mark them off in miles right on the chart. I find this very helpful for keeping track of position underway. Compass courses also can be marked on each leg for further convenience, as well as pre-drawn bearing lines to prominent features to be used for piloting. The point to point round-trip distance in this case is about 88 nmi. At just 4 kts, it would take 22 hours to cover the distance in still water. With around 60 hours allotted for the trip, of which 16 or so should be spent sleeping and at least 12 spent sightseeing, we still have 10 hours to spare for eating and other necessities. This might appear ample margin, but with strong currents involved and the usual preference for sleeping at night, we are not at all finished with even the feasibility study. The trip could still be anywhere from not possible to a cake walk.

A check of the *Nautical Almanac* (or a smartphone app!) tells us that sunrise will occur at 6 A.M. and sunset at 7:45 P.M., where these times have been adjusted to account for daylight saving time and for our longitude. (Sunrise and

sunset times are tabulated for specific latitudes in terms of the times at the local standard time meridian. Time zones are an hour wide; so the longitude correction fine tunes this with a ±30 minute correction. Instructions are usually in the tables.)

Equally important are the twilight times, which usually must be obtained from the *Nautical Almanac*, or estimated from the table shown in Figure 11-10. For our example, we will assume that nautical twilights occur at 5 A.M. and 8:45 P.M. As a rule in normal atmospheric conditions, it is totally dark only from evening nautical twilight to morning nautical twilight. In our case, we can expect fairly good light from about 5:30 A.M. till about 8:15 P.M.

A key point to our timing is the location of Dunkin Hot Springs inside of Fast Pass. The *Coast Pilot* warns all small craft to check the current predictions, because currents in the narrowed part of Fast Pass can reach speeds of 8 kts. Without skillful eddy-hopping along the edges, which we are not interested in doing, we cannot enter this pass against an ebb. Furthermore, because the currents are so strong at peak flow, we can expect turbulent water even in midstream; so we don't even want a rocket ship ride through the pass on a flood. We want to traverse this pass at slack water and even then we want to do it carefully and expeditiously. But we do want to do it; Dunkin Hot Springs is a don't miss place in this part of the world. We must simply plan around getting in and out of there.

Tidal currents for Fast Pass and other points in the region for the allotted days are shown in Figure 11-11. The current pattern is complex; so it will take a couple of hours to prepare a table like this one using standard current tables, maybe 1 hour if we don't make mistakes. Reference points N1, N2, and N3 are secondary stations, meaning the Current Tables provide only corrections at these points. We must correct both the times and the speeds at each point, and the corrections at each point are different. The primary hourly data are given at the center of the North Pass. The same is true for points S1, S2, and S3, relative to hourly data at South Pass.

Before looking into this current pattern, note that many places around the world that have complex currents where there is much commercial boat traffic will have available government or commercial current references (beyond the standard NOAA predictions) that show hourly current arrows and speeds throughout the region. These aids greatly alleviate the detective work that we will have to do here. They are called by various names: current charts, diagrams, atlases, or guides. Sometimes, however, these aids do not provide all the details boaters might care about in this particular region; for example, they do not show several important points that we can glean from using the actual government station reports.

Once the data are accumulated (as shown in Figure 11-11), we can sit back and think about it. Station S2, for example, is a strange one. We learn from the NOAA predic-

FRIDAY MAY 22

N1		N2		N3		Fast Pass	
0402	S	0415	S	----		0624	7.5 E
0854	3.6 E	0831	2.3 E	0701	1.7 E	0941	S
1302	S	1350	S	----		1303	71. F
1600	3.0 F	1630	2.0 F	1640	2.3 F	1645	S
2013	S	2026	S	----		1924	7.1 E

S1		S2		S3	
		0222	0.9 E		
0432	S	----		0909	3.2 E
0852	1.6 E	----		0909	3.2 E
1203	S	1342	1.6 E	1336	S
1527	1.4 F	----		1541	0.7 F

SATURDAY MAY 23

N1		N2		N3		Fast Pass	
0506	S	0519	S	----		0404	S
0942	3.4 E	0919	2.2 E	0749	1.6 E	0716	7.6 E
1344	S	1432	S	----		1032	S
1640	3.0 F	1710	2.0 F	1720	2.3 F	1350	7.1 F
2040	S	2053	S	----		1728	S

S1		S2		S3	
		0309	1.0 E		
0532	S	----		0439	S
0945	1.5 E	----		1002	3.0 E
1249	S	1435	1.5 E	1422	S

SUNDAY MAY 24

N1		N2		N3		Fast Pass	
0629	S	0642	S	----		0501	S
1002	3.6 E	0939	2.3 E	0809	1.7 E	0807	7.5 E
1400	S	1448	S	----		1121	S
1709	3.5 F	1739	2.3 F	1749	2.6 F	1437	6.9 F

S1		S2		S3	
		0352	1.0 E		
0633	S	----		0540	S
1034	1.3 E	----		1051	2.6 E
1334	S	----		1507	S
1652	1.2 F	1524	1.3 E	1706	0.6 F
2031	S	----		2133	S

Figure 11-11. *Tidal current times and speeds in the vicinity shown in Figure 11-9. At station location N1, the water is slack at 04:02, at which time it starts to ebb. The ebb increases to a peak speed of 3.6 kts at 08:54, and then begins to decrease. At 13:02, slack again as it turns to a flood. Slack times at N3, just outside of Fast Pass, cannot be predicted because of the influence of the pass. S2 also has unusual behavior explained in the text. We expect daylight during this period to extend from 05:30 to 20:15.*

tions that the current always ebbs here, meaning always flows south, regardless of what nearby currents are doing. They also say the maximum speed of the ebb at this point occurs 5 hours and 15 minutes later than at South Pass, and its average speed is about 0.4 times the peak ebb at South Pass. The key to understanding this is the location of Salmon Shoal. We must conclude that the flood enters from the west and diverges when it hits Big Island, as shown by the wavy arrows we have drawn in ourselves—these were not on any chart. Thus, the "flood" through the underwater channel at S2 flows in the same direction as the ebb does. This shoaling is all underwater; so standing at Apple Point looking west over the water, you would have no way at all to guess this current behavior. We learn it (guess it?) from doing our homework.

When we look at the currents between Little Island and Fast Pass (N1 to N3), we notice another important point. The current differs significantly as you head west across the mouth of North Pass, especially on the ebb. Or more to the point, the current is very strong around Little Island.

We should even anticipate that it might be stronger still in that part that gets compressed behind Little Island. Here is an example where neither the chart nor the *Coast Pilot* warns of tide rips in the vicinity, but we should nevertheless expect rips of fast turbulent water in this region. There simply cannot be almost 4 kts of current turning a corner around a small island without causing a hazard to small craft. We must treat this as a dangerous area at maximum current flow. With just 10 or 12 kts of wind blowing against this current, the area will be covered with whitecaps.

Another feature to note is the lack of correlation between currents in Fast Pass and those just outside of the pass. There is some agreement with the time of maximum ebb on Saturday and Sunday, but even this does not hold on Friday. There is particularly no correlation between slack in the pass and slack in the channel, just a mile or two outside of it; it is, in fact, just the opposite. The pass is nearly at peak flood when the approach to it is slack. This, however, should not be a surprise. In most narrow passes with strong currents and large bodies of water on either side, there is not, in general, any correlation between current speeds or times in the pass with individual currents or tide heights on either side of the pass. Without specific current predictions for a narrow pass, one must always approach it very cautiously, knowing only that you will not know what is going on in the pass till you get there. Fast Pass is a major waterway, however, as are many such passes around the continent; so specific predictions are available.

There are no predictions in between the north stations and the south stations; so we must interpolate these currents, assuming a more or less smooth, continuous flow. For example, at about 0900 there is 3.6 kts of ebb at N1 flowing southwest and at the same time 1.6 kts of ebb at S1 flowing west. We are reasonably safe, then, to assume that there will be about 2.6 kts of ebb flowing about southwest at the point halfway between N1 and S1 at 9 o'clock on Friday. We also can assume that the flood will be fairly weak along the Big Island shore, where it fans out to the north and south.

We also must remember that these currents are only the best predictions possible without our knowing ahead of time what effects wind, atmospheric pressure, and unseasonable river runoff might cause. As a rule, we might guess that very near the actual station locations, these predictions will likely be accurate to within some 20% in the speeds and some 20 minutes in the predicted times. In rare cases, they could be off by 50% in speed and over an hour in time. The effect of the wind is the easiest to put numerical guesses on. If the wind blows in a steady direction for half a day or longer, it will add an additional current to the tidal flow of some 2% to 3% of the wind speed, flowing in the direction of the wind. A day-long 20-kt northerly in this region, for example, would add about 0.6 kts to the ebb and take away about 0.6 kts from the flood. The ebb cycle would be longer and the flood cycle shorter than predicted in this case, but they would still peak at about the same times.

Excessive river runoff is signaled by a brown or gray color to water that should be blue or green. River runoff always adds to the ebbs and reduces the floods.

The chart shows a shallow shelf along the west side of Big Island extending out about 0.4 to 1.0 nmi. If we must proceed against current, we can travel on this shelf for some relief; when sailing with the current along this shore, we may well want to stay off this shelf for a better ride. As a rule, currents are weaker in shallow water. They also change directions earlier in the shallow water of a shelf than they do in the deeper water just off the shelf that carries much more momentum with it. Our small scale chart (1:80,000) does not tell much about Bird Island, other than its shape and its navigation light and the presence of a shoal to the west of it. The *Coast Pilot,* on the other hand, tells us that the island is very low on the east side, with the wide western part rising steeply to an elevation of 75 ft. It also warns that the shoal to the west of the island has dangerous tide rips on a strong flood. To determine what they mean by a *strong* flood we must go back to the *Current Tables* and check the primary station at South Pass. Checking the tabulated average value of the flood at South Pass (which covers an 18-year period), we find it is 2.0 kts, whereas the South Pass floods on our weekend will be about 3.0 kts. We have a strong flood, indeed, and should keep these flood rips in mind when we sail around Bird Island looking for its namesakes.

The *Coast Pilot* is also the best readily available source of climatic weather data. It obviously can't promise what will actually happen, but it does summarize what typically happens at this time of the year. If there is a local marine weather forecast for the region, it would be the obvious supplement to the *Coast Pilot.* But official predictions will only be good for 3 days or so, (at most 5)—especially in places like this one, where on one weekend the sky can be clear, the water flat, the air calm, and the fish a-jumpin—with the next weekend bringing pea-soup fog, 30 kts of wind, and seas considered big to 80-ft boats.

Weather information is spread throughout the *Coast Pilot*—statistics in the appendix, overviews in the introductions, and local effects in the individual sections for specific places. For our region, we learn that fair wind here is from the north or west, with storms typically bringing easterlies or southerlies. On clear days, we can expect a building westerly sea breeze that might reach 20 kts or so by late afternoon at this time of the year; but if this is the only wind, it will be calm in the mornings. These waters are known for early morning radiation fog on calm, clear, spring days (the kind of fog that burns off by midmorning); but because the area is exposed to the cold ocean, we also should be prepared for sea fog blowing in from the west, and this type of fog will not burn off. If fog is present or forecast, it will be important to monitor the weather broadcasts. They are generally accurate about fog conditions, even if they might be off in the wind forecasts in this area of complex terrain.

The steep cliff right along the southern beach of Big Island will offer good shelter from easterlies and even some from westerlies as the wind rises to go over the cliff. A strong westerly with 50 nmi of fetch, however, will certainly bring big seas onto the shore in the late afternoon, which would put surf all along that beach and make progress difficult. As nearly always, we must think about the wind as well as the current in planning this route. We must think about the wind's effect on us and its effect on the sea. We know we have strong currents to reckon with and could have strong winds as well. When strong winds oppose strong currents, we have the additional, even bigger concern of steep seas.

Referring to Figure 11-11, we can enter Fast Pass on Friday, if we choose to go there first, at about 0941 in the morning or 1645 in the afternoon—the times are mentioned to the minute to identify them in the table, but they are certainly not that precise. In fact, we want to be there at least 30 minutes early to cover cases where the Pass goes slack earlier than predicted. Narrow channels with strong peak currents do not stay slow very long at slack; if we were late for slack in the afternoon with the Pass turning to an ebb, things could get bad very fast. We could get stuck camping outside the pass and have to wait until 1032 on Saturday to get through in daylight all that time wondering what was going on at Dunkin Hot Springs, just around the corner. It is about 24 nmi from Apple Point to Fast Pass, so leaving at first light (0530) only gives us about 4 hours to make it up there for the first slack, or early part of the flood. With the current along the beach ebbing against us at a knot or so, we can't safely make this without leaving well before daylight. We should go someplace else first. We could go to Bird Island first; it is 12 nmi off as the crow flies (about 2 hours in slack water), but we would have to plan around a building ebb setting to the south as we proceed across. We could then hang around Bird Island to as late as 1400 or so and set off for the 1645 slack at Fast Pass riding a building flood to the north. This also fits into the anticipated winds: light in the morning and an afternoon westerly to help push us to the northeast.

I wouldn't head straight from Apple Point to Bird Island, however. There will be about 1.6 kts of ebb setting to the west as we approach the island at 0830, and nothing but open water and stronger current to the west of it. The safest bet would probably be to steer north along the beach, staying on the shelf to avoid the building southerly ebb, and then ride the ebb back down and across to the island. We could carry on the beach leg clear north of Bird Island and not lose much time, because we will be going across to it at about 4 kts once we get into the ebb. In this case, it is much better to sail a few extra miles than risk being set off into nowhere—all the time wondering what was going on back at Dunkin Hot Springs.

The planning so far looks good. We leave at first light, make it to Bird at 0930 to 1000 at the latest; look around there until about 1400; and set off for Fast Pass in favorable current and likely good wind. A strong westerly or southerly would only help us; a strong easterly would probably call for heading more directly back to Big Island and then north in its lee. It would be more work, but still doable. A strong afternoon northerly against the strong flood would be the major threat to our getting north from the open waters of Bird Island. In this case, we would have to head straight back to Big Island—not much danger if we are blown to the south on this route—and then claw our way north, not counting on making the 1645 slack, but anchoring as far north as we feel like going—a manageable setback in our plans.

With anything but a strong northerly, the trip north would be a good ride. The current starts flooding at 1203 at Bird Island but does not peak out at the north until 1640. We will have almost 2 kts of flood behind us as we approach the Pass. We will be in the flood for almost a complete half cycle, which means our net current boost will be approximately 0.6 times the average peak current along the route (see Figure 9-11 and related discussion). The average peak is about 2 kts in this case; so we will effectively sail north with an extra 1.2 kts or so throughout the leg. The 16-nmi run should not take much longer than 2 hours, even with little help from the wind. Nevertheless, with possibly weaker-than-predicted currents and a safety margin of 30 minutes at the pass—this slack is turning against us, so we don't want to be late—if there is no favorable wind, we probably should not leave later than about 1330.

Assuming we get in on Friday, there is only one daylight slack on Saturday (1032) and then only one again on Sunday (1121). If we do not get out on Saturday, we will have to skip Cannery Cove, which we would not want to do if we were that close to meeting our goals—unless, as Fletcher Christian decided, we just don't want to leave Dunkin Hot Springs at all. To get out, though, we must be waiting and watching the water just inside Fast Pass by about 1000 Saturday (this slack is also turning against us if we are late), which means getting out of Dunkin by at least 0830 for the 8-nmi run to the pass—even though we will have an ebb pushing us toward the Pass from Dunkin.

The crossing to Cannery Cove also works out well with the currents. We anticipate exiting the Pass at about 1100, which puts us about halfway through the decreasing side of the ebb cycle in the channel. It is about 16 nmi or some 3 hours in still water over to Cannery Cove, which would mean arriving there at about slack, just as we would like because of the anticipated rips at Little Island if we were to arrive there in strong current. Looking ahead, however, we must now check the Sunday weather forecasts carefully. Because of the strong afternoon floods, once we get to Cannery, we will have to stay there till Sunday. At Cannery Cove, we are the farthest from our final destination, and it is mostly an exposed route on the way back. We should only proceed on if the weather forecast for the following day is a good one. We could probably handle northerlies or westerlies, but southerlies or easterlies would be bad news.

Assume that the next day's forecast is for light air, so we head on over. This calls for a somewhat more realistic evaluation of the trip across the channel. We will be setting off in a fairly strong ebb (probably averaging about 1 kt to the south). If we sail due west at 6 kts, we will get set about 2 nmi to the south by the time we reach the vicinity of Little Island. We should either crank in some ferry angle on departing (about 10°) or just not worry about it, knowing we will eventually get set back to the north as the flood starts to build. In any event, it pays to know what is likely to happen and then watch it develop. In these waters, a surprise should be a nice orca whale visit, not an unplanned trip into the ocean due west of here. If we choose to look around Little Island today, we should do it as soon as we get there, because it could be dangerous after about 1500 (3-kt flood at 1640). Alternately, we could check it out about 0630 Sunday morning.

Since the current floods strongly to the north all afternoon Saturday, the best bet is to spend the night in the Cannery area and ride the morning ebb (1002) back to the south on Sunday morning. This will be a 4- or 5-hour open-water crossing, and with all going well we will be right on schedule. We must bear in mind that the ebb sets more to the southwest than to the south through most of this passage. We could even get tricky and ride the ebb down to Bird Island, leaving about 0800, heading about 8° to the east of the island to compensate for the southwesterly set, arriving about lunch time at Bird; picnic and play around there till about 1600 and ride the unusual flood around Salmon Shoal straight to Apple Point, arriving well before dark for a perfect textbook ETA.

We have concentrated on currents and winds, as they usually require the most creative planning in waters like these. Other matters, however, are also important in the end. These include a careful study of the detailed charts for the Fast Pass, Dunkin, and Cannery Cove areas (checking for anchorage sites, shelves, etc.); checking *Coast Pilot* and local tour guides for services such as food or fuel or potential repairs; checking land maps or internet for access to civilization in case of emergency, such as the road to the beach on Big Island; checking with the local USCG office to learn the VHF channel for the local marine operator, if any—you might get stuck and want to call home to report a delay; again, it is always better to wait out bad weather in a sheltered anchorage than to tough it out on the water.

And check for cellphone coverage. Some coastal ports only have roaming service and others might not have service at all. In contrast to the past when it was a routine procedure, these days it is difficult to find a marine operator that will place a phone patch to a land line over the VHF radio; so the cellphone coverage becomes more an issue. For remote locations, you might even consider renting a satellite phone, then you would have coverage worldwide for both communications and weather data.

As we have stressed throughout the book and experienced in this planning example, there is much more to navigation than simply locating your position on the chart. The distinction between good navigation and good seamanship is a fuzzy one. There is obviously a need for a close relationship between skipper and navigator, when there is more than one person involved. It is usually the navigator who has the responsibility for choosing the best route and all of these factors contribute to that.

11.7 Navigation at Night

Good navigation planning through hazardous waters calls for leaving plenty of time to get to your destination before nightfall. Narrow entrances, rocky shorelines in strong current, and tide rips in even relatively sheltered waters are especially hazardous at night when you cannot see what is going on around you. In some circumstances, plans must be changed and a new anchorage found when darkness sets in. In coastal waters it might even be necessary to stay offshore overnight (hanging out at the entrance buoy) and wait for an entrance opportunity during daylight the next morning.

Nevertheless, when planning any trip in a boat, it is best to be prepared for sailing and navigation at night. Even on local waters, equipment failure or sightseeing distractions might call for sailing home after sunset.

This means carrying the proper lights and knowing how to interpret the lights we will see when underway. In protected waters, comfort with night sailing extends the potential range of a trip; it could also get you back on schedule after an unexpected delay. As a side benefit, sailing at night sharpens your sense of feel for a boat, because you must rely less on visual aids and more on feel and instrumentation.

On the aesthetic side, nighttime sailing is also a good way to experience the beauty of marine phosphorescence. The illuminated trails of fish, seaweed, marine mammals or any other form of turbulence are a wonderful part of the marine environment. Besides its eerie beauty, it provides a unique navigation aid in some cases. The flow of phosphorescent kelp, for example, can show the current direction even on a dark and foggy night.

Nighttime navigation involves three broad categories of lights, which we might call *working lights,* that we carry on the vessel or personally for safety and operations; *vessel lights,* required by the Nav Rules (sidelights, stern lights, etc.); and *navigation lights* (lighthouses, lighted buoys, etc.).

Working Lights

A separate light for attracting attention and sending distress signals is required on all vessels according to federal boating safety regulations. The onetime-traditional two D-cell flashlights should not be relied upon for either of these purposes, because they are typically not bright enough to attract the attention of distant vessels. Furthermore, these conventional flashlights are not bright enough to illumi-

nate shoreline features, aid a search for another vessel, or to read the numbers on a buoy. Spotlights or 6-volt hand-held lights can help with these tasks; they also can be used to check the surface for kelp, crab pot buoys, etc. But things are changing rapidly in the world of lights. Modern technology in batteries and LED lamps have produced remarkably bright lights in very small units. Read and compare the specifications of lights before choosing one. Naturally, all lights used underway should be waterproof.

Practice with the use of a warning light is essential for singlehanders, because without practice it can be awkward to show it quickly and maintain the helm, especially in rough water. Spotlights from larger vessels attempting to identify your light are especially hazardous to night vision. If a spotlight is shined on you, turn your head immediately or night vision will be lost for some minutes. According to the *Navigation Rules*, vessels are not supposed to shine spotlights on you in this manner, but they do, so you must be prepared.

Also test your compass light at night. If you must steer a compass course on a dark featureless night, you might

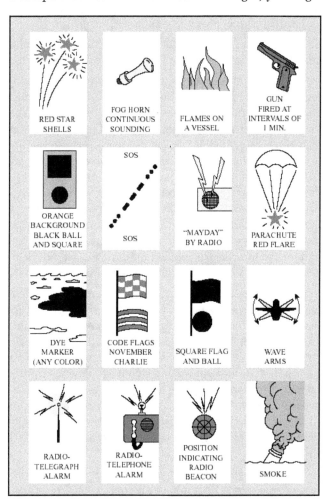

Figure 11-12. *Official distress signals on any waters. Other distress signals include a strobe light (on inland waters only); a US flag flown upside down; a square shape over or under a round shape. Note the special arm wave that should be reserved for distress situations.*

discover that your compass light is too bright, meaning it deteriorates your night vision if you look at it. Fortunately, most nighttime horizons are not featureless; so an occasional compass check to a star, cloud, hill, or light on the horizon is adequate. As in daytime compass steering, take a bearing to the reference mark, and then steer relative to it. Most mariners are surprised to learn how much they can see at night once their eyes adapt to the dark. On clear nights, you can see quite well, except that there is no color perception, and depth perception is very poor. At night it is important to frequently evaluate the distance to shore, ships, or navigation lights. On the other hand, peripheral vision is enhanced at night, which is an asset in some cases.

Nighttime sailing calls for full safety gear on each crew member. This should include wearing a PFD with a personal strobe light as well as a personal low-intensity steady light. LED life preserver lights are long-lasting and provide many hours of low-intensity light in all directions, which is often the preferred way to home in on an overboard person, once they are located by the strobe. It is difficult to judge distance off a strobe light.

For coastal routes, I would also strongly recommend each crew member have on their life jacket a personal EPIRB, such as the ResQLink (acrartex.com) or a similar device. These have saved the lives of many mariners.

Another light is needed at the chart table for chart reading and general navigation. Some navigators prefer a small flashlight for this, which is stored with the pencils. You know it is there when you need it, even if the ship's power has failed. As with all lights you carry or use, practice first to see how well they work; many low-intensity lights are not adequate for detailed chart reading. The value of red lights for chart reading while protecting night vision is overrated. Charts are difficult to read in red light, and red is not a magic color for saving night vision. Brightness is more important to night vision than color is. It is inefficient battery use to make a brighter light dim with red filters instead of using a dim white light in the first place.

As mentioned earlier, in addition to running lights, federal law requires mariners in most waters of the type we are discussing in this book to carry a minimum of 3 daytime and 3 nighttime USCG-approved visual distress signals. Official distress signals are shown in Figure 11-12. Note especially the side arm waving signal as this one requires no aids. This type of waving should be reserved for emergencies. Nighttime visual signals are flares, strobe lights (in the special circumstances discussed later), or a bright light that can be set to automatically signal SOS, which is • • • — — — • • •.

An ordinary flashlight does not count as a visual distress signal. If you do not have an appropriate bright light (USCG-approved number 161.013 marked on it), then you must carry at least three flares. Approved handheld flares are numbered 160.022; aerial flares are numbered 160.066. Check safety manuals on this point, but it is gen-

erally good policy if needing to send off a flare; to send off one, wait a moment or two till that one is out and then send off another immediately. The idea is the first gets their attention, but they might lose sight of the direction, and the second one pins down the direction. Be especially cautious using handheld flares that drip molten metal slag during their burn. The molten slag could set fire to the boat, causing even more of an emergency than you had at hand.

Strobe lights (high-intensity, quick flashing lights) require consideration. They are an effective way to attract attention especially from a large distance, but they must not be used indiscriminately. Strobe lights are legal distress signals only on US *Inland Waters*. Inland Waters is a legal term in this usage, not a geographic one. It specifies those waters upon which the US Inland *Navigation Rules* apply as opposed to the International Rules. The demarcation lines that separate these two types of waters are specified in *Navigation Rules,* as there are no consistent guidelines for judging where they lie. Some coastal bays are international waters; some are inland waters inside a line drawn across the mouth of the bay. All bays, harbors, and inlets of Alaska, for example, are international waters; but major coastal ports of Washington, Oregon, and California are inland waters. Puget Sound and connecting waters, including Lake Union and Lake Washington, are called *inland waters* by the National Weather Service and the Coast Guard's licensing division, but they are international waters according to *Navigation Rules.*

The status of the waters you sail determines the legality of a strobe as a distress signal. This is of interest, for example, if you happen to be inspected for safety equipment by the Coast Guard. More important, on inland waters a strobe can be shown *only as* a distress signal. To show it otherwise, to warn of your position, for example, is illegal with large fines prescribed. On international waters, showing a strobe light would not violate the law against false distress signals, but neither would it bring assistance from neighboring vessels, as it should, in principle, on inland waters, because the law requires all vessels to respond to distress signals.

Any nonemergency use of strobe lights must be restricted to international waters, but even there they are explicitly illegal (Rule 36 specifically states that strobe lights should not be used to attract attention). In actual practice, however, strobe lights often are used on coastal waters by fishing vessels and sailboats to attract attention. We will not pursue this unusual conflict between law and frequent practice.

Beyond their value as warning lights in coastal waters, strobe lights are especially valuable aids to nighttime search and rescue in any waters, once someone is looking for you in response to a distress call by radio or EPIRB. Carried for this purpose, strobe lights should be attached high on the shoulder of a life jacket. On the other hand, flares are much more effective than strobe lights for informing passing ves-

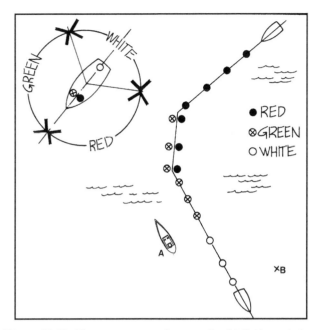

Figure 11-13. *The appearance of a vessel's sidelights and stern light from position A as it passes on the course shown. From position B, you would see a single red light throughout the passing. A power-driven vessel also would show a single white masthead light or two masthead lights if more than 50 meters long.*

type, direction of motion, or special activities. Running lights are stipulated in *Navigation Rules;* they are precise and as a whole fairly complicated. It is neither practical nor necessary, however, to cover these in any detail in this text beyond the basics, and even the basics must be simplified for practical usage in the following discussion—some exceptions and optional lights are not covered. Please refer to the *Navigation Rules* for precise requirements. Light details are in the Appendix to the Rules.

Except for muscle-powered craft and boats less than 7 meters long that cannot exceed 7 kts, all vessels carry sidelights (red on the port side, green on the starboard side) and a single white stern light. If you see a green light in the darkness, you are looking at the right-hand side of a vessel that is moving to your right (although the light would still be on if it were not moving); a red light marks the left side of a boat moving to the left. If you see both red and green, the vessel is pointed straight at you. A single white light marks a vessel headed away from you. Although a single view of a single red or green light tells the general direction of motion of that vessel, it does not tell the angle at which the vessel is moving toward or away from you (see Figure 11-13). These sidelights tell more specific directions only at the moment they change. When a red or green light changes to a white light, the vessel either turned away from you, or has gone by. A red or green light that turns to both red and green means the vessel turned toward you, or you have sailed across its path.

The *Navigation Rules* separate vessels into three categories according to length: more than 50 meters; 50 to 12 meters; and less than 12 meters. Sidelights are required to be visible for 3 nmi for the large vessels, 2 nmi for middle-sized vessels, and 1 nmi for small vessels. In practice, however, it is not always possible to see sidelights from these limits without binoculars. Sidelights are most useful for interpreting vessel traffic when they are at closer range.

The size and type of a vessel is specified by the presence or absence of additional lights. A sidelight alone marks a sailboat under sail; a sidelight and one white light above it marks a mid-sized boat under power; and a sidelight and two white masthead lights above it with one lower than the other mark a ship (vessel over 50 meters long). A ship's masthead lights deserve special attention. They are well-

sels that you are in trouble, even on inland waters. Many boaters on inland waters do not know that strobe lights are distress signals, whereas every boater recognizes flares as such—except possibly around July 4th in American waters, July 14th in French waters, or near New Year's Eve on any waters.

If you must be towed at night, Rule 24 (h) requires that your boat be illuminated when other vessels are present, preferably with a white light from your boat that is visible in all directions (all around light). When this is not possible, the boat towing you must shine a white light on you to identify the tow to approaching vessels using, for example, your bright warning light, which you would always have at night. According to Rule 24 (i), the towing boat need not show the usual lights required of towboats, because it is (presumably) providing assistance, but it does share the legal responsibility that you be properly illuminated. These are not academic details; rules on tow illumination exist for a towed log as well as for a towed aircraft carrier. Any tow inhibits the maneuverability and legal status of the towing vessel. Should a collision occur that results in serious injury or property damage, infractions of the Rules would be pursued relentlessly in Admiralty Court.

Vessel Lights

Nighttime application of the Rules and guidelines presented there begins with the identification of vessels from the appearance of their lights. It is obviously fundamental that a ship's lights not be confused with those of a lighthouse. Every vessel carries running lights to identify its

...In Depth

12.24 Sailboat Lights

The Rules on running lights for sailboats involve more complexities than their counterparts for power-driven vessels. For safety as well as legality, it is important to understand the requirements.

separated lights, with the forward one lower than the aft one, similar to a navigational range. They are required to be visible from 6 nmi off, which means they are always seen long before the sidelights are. These "range lights" are much better than sidelights for telling the direction of a ship. The ship is moving toward its lower light. Furthermore, the separation of the lights changes with the course of the ship. A ship turning toward you is clearly indicated by range lights moving closer together. When headed straight toward you, they are aligned one above the other (see Figure 11-14). Put another way, when the lights are closing, it is turning toward you; when they are opening, it is turning away from you. Range lights are not visible from the stern, which shows a single white light for all vessels not engaged in work. The *Queen Mary* looks just the same as a 25-ft sailboat when viewed from the stern at night.

The name "range lights" is a common nickname, but is not an official term. These lights are the required *masthead lights* for vessels over 50 meters long.

Vessels unique in nature or activity are identified with still more lights. A tug towing or pushing shows two or three white lights in a column, with an additional one or two yellow lights on the stern. Vessels engaged in fishing show two all-round lights in a column, either red over white or green over white. Small craft at anchor show either no light, or a single white light, whereas anchored ships are kept lighted with fore and aft white lights and many deck lights between them. Anchored vessels do not show sidelights. *Navigation Rules* explain these and other lights in

detail for any craft from floating restaurants to minesweepers. Remember that it can be as dangerous to yourself and to others to show illegal lights as to show none at all. With much traffic around, you could cause and be liable for a collision between two other vessels well away from you.

Because of precise light specifications, sailing in traffic at night can actually be safer than in the daytime. Vessel lights often can be seen at night from farther off than you could see the vessel itself during the day, and a small boat's bright warning light (used as needed) could definitely be more conspicuous to approaching ships than its daytime appearance could be. In some cases, even piloting is easier at night. A low point of land with a lighthouse on it, for example, is easier to identify at night than during the day. The first appearance of a bright navigational light also provides a unique piloting opportunity to estimate approximate distance from the light, as mentioned in Chapter 6.

We have to be especially careful on identifying vessel lights in the presence of a lot of background light on the shoreline behind it. Binoculars are usually helpful, but special care is always called for. I recall a case where it was the absence of the background lights that became a sudden warning that there was a ship close abeam whose hull was blocking out the horizon.

Navigation Lights

Characteristics of navigation lights were presented in Sections 2.12. Use of the all-important *Light List* is in Section 3.3. The visible range of elevated landmarks was introduced in Section 6.5.

Piloting at night is often limited to compass bearings to lighted aids (lighthouses, secondary lights, and buoys). The crucial element in planning nighttime navigation is predicting how far a particular light can be seen. If no lights can be seen along a specific leg of a trip, this should be known in advance and planned for. Likewise, if you do not see a light when you thought you should, it is time to stop and figure out why. With changing tidal currents, for example, it could be important to decide as soon as possible whether you have turned into the wrong bay, or have simply not proceeded far enough into it to see the light you are looking for. Most nighttime navigation questions reduce to deciding where particular lights can and cannot be seen in the prevailing conditions.

The visible range of a light is determined by the height of the light, the brightness of the light, and the atmospheric visibility. From the low perspective of a small vessel, the visible range of a light in clear weather is usually limited by the light's height, not its brightness. A light described on the chart as "Fl 4s 25ft 13M" is one that flashes on every 4 seconds, is positioned 25 ft above the mean high water tide level, and has a *nominal range* of 13 nmi. Nominal range specifies a light's brightness by telling how far the light can be seen when its view is not limited by the curvature of the earth—that is, how far it might be seen from an airplane or the bridge of a large ship. From lower perspective, a

Figure 11-14. *The appearance of the two white masthead lights (range lights) and later the single stern light of a power-driven vessel more than 50 meters long passing on the course shown. Red and green sidelights also would be shown, but the white masthead lights can be seen from much farther off.*

RANGE LIGHTS ARE NOT VISIBLE FROM ASTERN

light often cannot be seen from this distance because its view is blocked by the curvature of the earth (see Figure 11-15). The *geographic range* of a light is how far it can be seen over the horizon. As explained in Section 6.5, the geographic range of a light is *approximated* by:

$$\text{geo range (nmi)} = \sqrt{\text{light height (ft)}} + \sqrt{\text{eye height (ft)}}$$

A light cannot be seen from farther off than its geographic range, nor from farther off than its nominal range—assuming average "clear weather," which is defined as atmospheric visibility of 10 nmi. (For exceptionally clear skies, we should replace the nominal range with the luminous range.)

For each light in question, it is the smaller of these ranges that determines the *visible range* of the light. In the example above, the light shines 13 nmi out into space (its nominal range), but from an eye height of 9 ft, it can only be seen out to a distance of 8 nmi (sqrt 25 + sqrt 9). Geographic range must always be calculated (or figured from tables); nominal range is charted or listed in the *Light List*. Recall from Section 6.5 that we are approximating the geographic range to make it easier to remember. The theoretical distance (found in tables) for ideal conditions is 1.17 times larger.

When planning nighttime navigation, determine the visible ranges of all lights to be used and sketch these limits on the chart, as shown in Figure 11-16. Also mark where lights are blocked by local terrain and, when applicable, when they switch from white to red. Some lights have red sectors that mark rocks or other hazards in the vicinity. The boundaries of red sectors are charted as dotted lines, but it

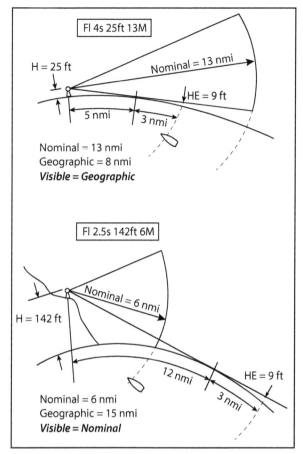

Figure 11-15. *The approximate visible range of a light as determined from the smaller of its nominal range and geographic ranges. The visible range of the top light (low but bright) is limited by geographic range; the bottom light (high but not so bright) is limited by nominal range.*

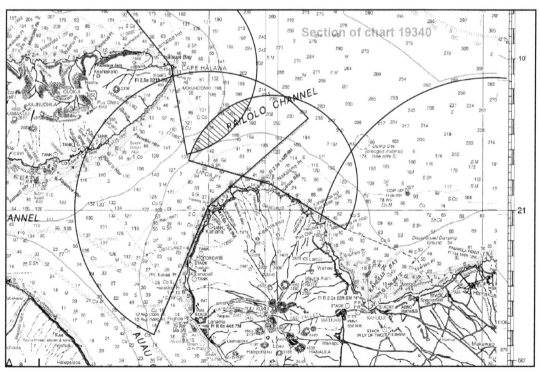

Figure 11-16. *Planning nighttime navigation by determining the visible ranges of lights to be used and sketching these limits on the chart. This is the ocean approach to NW side of Maui, HI. The shaded area marks the only place where three of the major lights can be seen at once. When anticipating reduced visibility or exceptionally clear skies, we should replace the nominal range with the luminous range.*

141

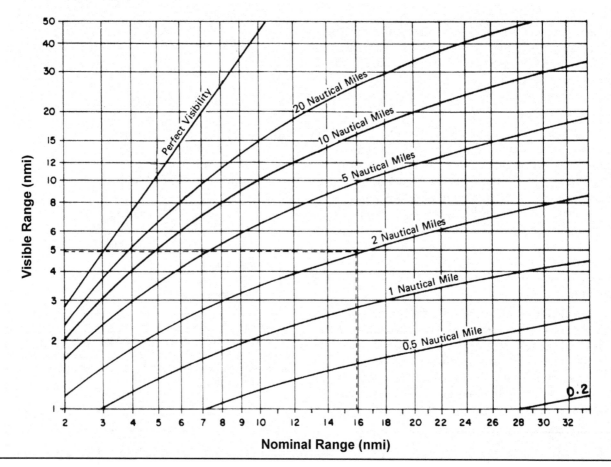

Luminous Range Diagram

The nominal range given in this Light List is the maximum distance a given light can be seen when the meteorological visibility is 10 nautical miles. If the existing visibility is less than 10 NM, the range at which the light can be seen will be reduced below its nominal range. And, if the visibility is greater than 10 NM, the light can be seen at greater distances. The distance at which a light may be expected to be seen in the prevailing visibility is called its luminous range.

Figure 11-17. *Luminous Range Diagram. Example. The* Light List *gives the nominal range 16 nmi. The weather report gives the meteorological visibility 2 nmi (same as atmospheric visibility). The point on the bottom of the diagram marked 16 is followed upwards until it intersects the curve marked 2 nmi. Follow that height horizontally to the left margin to find that the visibility of the light is 5 nmi.*

This diagram enables the mariner to determine the approximate luminous range of a light when the nominal range and the prevailing meteorological visibility are known. The diagram is entered from the bottom border using the nominal range. The intersection of the nominal range with the appropriate visibility curve (or, more often, a point between two curves) yields, by moving horizontally to the left border, the luminous range.

CAUTION
When using this diagram it must be remembered that:

1. The ranges obtained are approximate;
2. The transparency of the atmosphere may vary between the observer and the light;
3. Glare from background lighting will considerably reduce the range at which lights are sighted;
4. The rolling motion of the mariner and/or of a lighted aid to navigation may reduce the distance at which lights can be detected and identified.

is always best to check the *Light List* for all lights you plan to use. Then draw in your intended route across these arcs of visible range so that you can note the locations where the lights would first appear and what their bearings should be from that point. The first appearance of a light is a check of your approximate position; the boundary of a red sector provides an approximate line of position when the color first changes.

The visible range of lighted buoys is more difficult to predict, because their heights and nominal ranges are not always available. When they are available, they are more often in the *Light List* or Local Notice to Mariners than on charts; an example is given in Figures 2-12 and 2-13. When specific data are not available, it is usually safe to assume that buoy lights are limited by nominal range to about 3 or 4 nmi for buoys along the main channels. Binoculars are valuable to nighttime navigation for finding lighted buoys.

During periods of reduced visibility due to fog or rain, the brightness of a light (nominal range) becomes just as important as its height in determining visible range. Visible range is always limited to geographic range, but if the light does not reach that far through the fog, it cannot be seen. The distance a light can be seen through fog is called its *luminous range*. This depends on its nominal range and the prevailing atmospheric visibility. With some guess of the atmospheric visibility in hand, luminous range can be found from the Luminous Range Diagram in the *Light List* and in some *Coast Pilots* (Figure 11-17). In most cases, however, a simple approximation to the tabulated results is adequate. The following formula is one example:

Luminous Range =

(Atmospheric Visibility/10) × Nominal Range +1 nmi

Charted nominal ranges assume a visibility of 10 nmi; so the first term of the formula simply scales the nominal range according to the visibility; the additional 1 nmi is a fudge factor that makes the results more accurate for lower visibilities. This formula works well for atmospheric visibilities down to about one half mile. When the visibility is less than that, it is best to refer to the Luminous Range Diagram.

In the last example (nominal range of 13 nmi, geographic range for your eye height of 8.0 nmi), if the atmospheric visibility were 2 nmi, the luminous range would be 3.6 nmi (2 divided by 10, times 13, plus 1); so you would have to be that close to the light to see it, even though it was over the horizon at 8.0 nmi off. Check Figure 11-17 to see that the proper table value was 4.0, so the approximation is close, but not exact.

Whenever your visibility is less than 10 nmi at sunset, it is necessary to calculate the luminous range of each light before you can plot on the chart the arc of its expected visible range. The problem is arriving at some reasonable guess of the visibility. Because it is defined as how far unlighted objects can be seen during daylight, it is obviously difficult to estimate at night. Some VHF weather radio broadcasts include visibilities, but even these must be used with caution. Visibility changes with time, direction, and elevation. You might see a hill clearly, but not the shoreline just below it where the lights are located. Radar is of course very useful for evaluating the visible range of land or buoys.

Nevertheless, it is important to account for luminous range even if it must be based on crude estimates of the visibility (0.5 nmi, 2.5 nmi, or 5 nmi). If at sunset you can see an island that is 3 nmi off, but not a prominent headland behind it that is 8 nmi off, then the visibility is somewhere between 3 and 8 nmi. If you can barely discern a shore that is 5 nmi off, the visibility is about 5 nmi.

One trick that works during the night is to estimate the visibility based on the observed luminous range to a light that can be seen; then use that visibility to predict the visible ranges to other lights. The distance to a light is the same as its luminous range whenever it first comes into view from a distance off that is less than geographic range (8.0 nmi) and nominal range (13 nmi). For example, suppose we first see a "13-nmi light" only when we get to within 5 nmi of it—lights are often referred to by their nominal range in that manner. Working the luminous range formula backward, the visibility must be about 3.1 nmi (5 minus 1, times 10, divided by 13 = 3.1).

Another trick (mentioned in Section 6.5) is to recognize that the visibility must be at least 3 nmi if you can see a line between the sky and water from an elevation of 9 ft, as this is about the distance to the horizon viewed from that eye height. This has to be looking toward open water, or at least the land in that direction has to be out of sight. These are each crude estimates of the visibility, but they are usually better than unaided guesses. With an understanding of luminous range, piloting in the fog is easier at night than it is during daylight without lighted aids, although this does not alleviate the problem of traffic in fog. Vessel lights have such a low nominal range that they are always difficult to see in reduced visibility. As on foggy days, you will likely hear traffic before you see it; so it is best to avoid traffic in the fog, night or day, unless your vessel has radar and you are fully competent in its use.

When possible, plan nighttime routes with a full moon. Moon phases are given in the *Nautical Almanac,* as are the times of sunrise and sunset, moonrise and moonset. Times listed in these tables are local mean times, which must be corrected for your longitude as explained in the tables. They also must be corrected for daylight saving time when in effect, although the tables do not include emphatic warnings of this. Depending on latitude and season, twilight times extend the useful daylight in the mornings and evenings by 30 minutes to 1 hour or more. To plan the next day's voyage, it is helpful to note the time of day when true darkness sets in or when first light appears. This can be compared to sunset or sunrise time to estimate the duration of twilight. Twilight times are the same in the morning as they are in the evening. To plan future trips, twilight times for any date can be found in *Nautical Almanacs,* even outdated ones. These times change very little over the 4-year leap cycle, and then they repeat.

Remember that some navigation lights are presented in sectors, with the light appearing white from some locations and red from others. The red sector is usually marking a hazard. The transition from white to red and back to white are marks of *very crude* lines of position, because the transitions are rarely sharp. But with solid colors finally showing, you do at least have "sector of position." The *Light List* is very important for working with sector lights, because the nominal range of the two colors is usually different.

For extra protection at night, use reflective tape on your clothing and equipment. This tape is remarkably effective. Search and rescue studies have shown that victims are often detected by reflected light from these tapes before their life jacket lights could be seen.

11.8 Navigation in the Fog

In this section, as in others of this chapter, we are covering the techniques one would use to backup or confirm primary data from your electronics. GPS, radar, and a good depth sounder are the basic instruments of fog navigation. Here we cover general concerns of navigation in reduced visibility. Later in Section 12.22, we cover more specific issues of interacting with traffic in the fog.

From a practical marine point of view, there are two kinds of fog: sea fog and radiation fog. It is fundamental to safety to know the distinctions between them. Radiation fog comes with no wind, and it burns off as the day heats up; sea fog can come with strong winds and last for days. All fog is formed the same way. When the air temperature drops to the dew point, water vapor in the air condenses to fog. It is impossible to tell the difference between a jar of sea fog and a jar of radiation fog. Distinctions between the two types of fog lie only in the way the air is cooled and in the subsequent behavior of the fog mass and associated weather. Sea fog (also called advection fog) presents a more serious hazard to sailors than radiation fog.

As the name implies, sea fog is formed over offshore waters, although with an onshore wind it can penetrate far into long coastal embayments. The most common way it is formed is when warm moist air flows over cold coastal waters brought to the surface by upwelling of deep currents. Areas of dense sea fog can extend over hundreds of miles and persist for several days or longer. It moves with the prevailing winds, which is the main source of its potential danger. A calm, sunny day of pleasant coastal sailing can change within hours to hazardous conditions when a wall of cold sea fog arrives with winds up to 25 kts or more. When sailing in coastal waters prone to sea fog, do not bury your rain gear just because you are starting off in a swim-

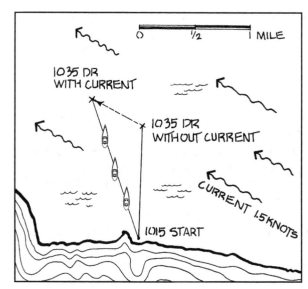

Figure 11-18. *A current-corrected DR plot. In 20 minutes the drift due to a 1.5-kt current would be 0.5 nmi. To adjust for current, move the DR position down-current by 0.5 nmi for every 20 minutes spent in the current, assumed constant.*

suit. Sea fog along coastal waters is common in middle and high latitudes during spring and summer. Check climate data in the *Coast Pilot* for specific statistics.

Sea fog is easily seen in satellite photos; so weather radio forecasts of its presence are reliable, although details of its motion are difficult to forecast. For example, when sea fog penetrates into inland waters or onto land, it often begins to dissipate when the land heats up during the morning. This heating, however, also generates an onshore sea breeze, which in turn brings more fog to the shore. Thus, an important distinction between sea fog and radiation fog is that sea fog does not burn off. In contrast to sailing through radiation fog on inland waters, you cannot set off on a morning sail in sea fog and count on it lifting as the day progresses. Even if you see the fog retreating offshore during the night or morning, you cannot count on it to stay offshore. If the wind develops in the onshore direction, it could move right back in. Also, in contrast to radiation fog, you cannot assume that when you see fog approaching along coastal waters there will be no wind with it. Calm air is characteristic of radiation fog, not sea fog. Sea fog is usually accompanied by wind, although not always. Thick sea fog can occur in calm air, but areas and seasons with prevalent sea fog usually do not have many days of calm air.

Radiation fog is formed over land on clear, calm nights whenever the relative humidity is high at sunset. The lack of cloud cover allows the heat of the land to radiate away overnight, which cools the air near the ground. Winds stronger than 10 kts, however, will usually prevent the formation of radiation fog because it continuously mixes the cool ground air with warmer air above it. The ideal wind for the formation of radiation fog is a light breeze of less than 3 kts, just enough to lift and transport the fog without mixing it. In absolutely calm air, radiation fog will be patchy and only waist deep. Fog is unlikely on cloudy days because the blanket of clouds prevents heat loss by radiation. Although it is formed on land, radiation fog is a concern to boaters because the cool, dense fog descends to fill valleys and spill out over the water. It also can obscure shoreside aids to navigation, even when the air is clear over the water. Radiation fog typically burns off as the day heats up; it rarely lasts more than 3 or 4 hours past sunrise. It is most common during fall (moist months) and winter (long nights). When camping, look for radiation fog to form a few hours after dew first appears on metal objects.

It is not uncommon to begin an inland voyage during a morning (radiation) fog with confidence that the fog will lift. Nevertheless, it is always prudent to check the weather radio forecasts. Clouds might move in during the early morning, blocking the sun and keeping the day cool enough to maintain the fog much longer than usual. Also, if the afternoon forecasts call for fog (reduced visibility) during the night, they are likely to be right, even if the day is warm and clear at the time, and even if the forecasts are completely wrong about the wind speed or direction at the time. Temperature trends needed for fog forecasts are more dependable than the atmospheric pressure trends needed for wind forecasts.

Except for obvious potential hazards of strong winds and long duration that characterize sea fog, navigation in the fog does not depend on the type of fog. The same procedures and safety concerns apply in any type of reduced visibility, such as heavy rain or snow (or sandstorm or smoke). If you anticipate losing visibility while still underway, the first thing to do is establish your position as carefully as possible while landmarks are still in sight. If you are very far offshore, it might be best to head in closer to the beach, but this depends on the beach and the likelihood of ship traffic offshore. In some cases, it might be best to avoid rocky shorelines or coastlines with breaking waves by staying offshore. This decision depends on the circumstances, but in any event you must know where you are. Navigation without visibility is either pure dead reckoning (assuming you have no electronic aids) or "flying by instruments" (using GPS, radar, and depth sounder). Without instruments, no matter how good you are at DR, your position uncertainty is only going to get worse with time once you start relying on dead reckoning alone. If your position is uncertain to begin with, you will soon be lost. If there is any doubt about your compass accuracy, check it while you can. When you are traveling with a group and anticipate fog, it would be useful to compare compass headings as you motor along on the same course.

Needless to say, when traveling in fog, a practiced use of radar, GPS, depth sounder, and marine radio protocol is the key to safe navigation. Throughout this book, we are discussing the basics that would be used to support such instrumentation if you have it, or what to do if you do not have it. Keep in mind, however, that if you do travel in the fog without the proper instrumentation, you are creating problems not just for yourself but for other vessels as well.

When offshore and choosing a compass course to a destination onshore in the fog, it is important to not aim straight toward your target. Instead, aim well off to one side of it by more than enough to compensate for any current or leeway you anticipate. Then when you reach land, you will know which way to turn—something you would not know had you aimed for it and not found it when you arrived. Whether to aim toward the upwind or up-current side depends on the shoreline and lay of the land you are approaching. Finding a small island in the fog, on the other hand, is a challenge to be considered carefully. Potential hazards of the waterway and its traffic must be balanced against the need to go there at that specific time. If currents are involved, recall the rules of thumb given in Chapter 9 for quick estimates of set and ferry angles when currents must be crossed.

Fog calls for careful chart work. After finding your position and choosing a route, plot them both on the chart labeled with the watch time of the fix. Estimate your speed made good, and from this figure how long it should take to reach land or the first audible aid to navigation, such as a foghorn or buoy. Recall that bell buoys sound the same tone and gong buoys have several tones; but both are activated by wave action and consequently they might be quiet in flat, calm water. If you must stop or change compass course underway, note it promptly on the chart. An example of a current-connected DR plot is shown in Figure 11-18 (see also Figure 9-12 and another in 12.13-3).

Your dead reckoning track across the chart is all you have to go by in the fog, but with good record keeping it will do the job. This is the time that all your practice with dead reckoning in clear weather starts to pay off, and be sure to keep an eye on the depth sounder if there is any information to be gained from it.

It is also the time to appreciate that the ultimate goal of dead reckoning is not a *point* on the chart where you *think* you are, but an *area* on the chart where you *know* you are. The difference between good dead reckoning and poor dead reckoning is just the size of this area of uncertainty. Regardless of skill, experience, or conditions, however, the size of the area of uncertainty always increases with time and distance underway when navigating by pure dead reckoning. In the fog, knowing that your average boat speed is 6.0 kts, for example, is not enough. You also must know how well you know it. If you are confident that this average speed is right to within 0.5 kts—you think it is 6.0, but you would not bet the farm that under these circumstances it is not 5.5 or 6.5—then you must consider that your position along any proposed course line will grow uncertain by 0.5 nmi each hour. After 2 hours of sailing without other navigational data, you must consider that you have traveled 12 nmi ± 1.0 nmi.

Chances are, the distance you travel will be fairly close to 12 nmi, because you did your homework to come up with

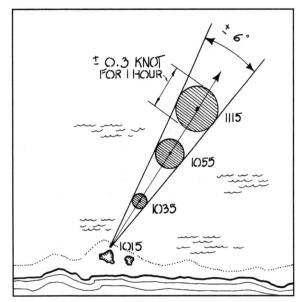

Figure 11-19. *Position uncertainty (shaded areas) increase with time and distance when navigating by DR alone. The example shown is for an average boat speed of 3 kts with an uncertainty of ± 0.3 kts, on a course with uncertainty of ± 6°, which would not be uncommon for a smaller sailing yacht in light air.*

a good estimated speed made good. Nevertheless, in planning when you should reach land, or see a light, or hear a buoy, this uncertainty of 1.0 nmi must be taken into account in order to know when to worry and when not to worry. At 6.0 kts (10 minutes per mile) your target at 12 nmi off could be reached anywhere within a sailing time of 2 hours ± 10 minutes (at 6 kts your uncertain mile will take 10 minutes). A realistic estimate of your time window for arrival is fundamental to safe navigation in the fog. If you do not arrive by the end of the time window, it is time to stop and figure out why.

Another, maybe easier way to think of the uncertainty is this: you have an uncertainty in speed of 0.5 kts out of 6.0 kts, which is an 8.3% uncertainty (0.5/6.0). Consequently, everything you compute with your base average value of 6.0 will be uncertain by 8.3%. At 6 kts, your time run is 120 minutes, and 8.3% of 120 = 10 minutes (0.083 × 120 = 10), which is your uncertainty in arrival times.

Remember, when predicting when you should first see a light in the fog, you must first figure its luminous range from an estimate of the prevailing visibility (Section 11.7).

It is easier to estimate the effect and associated uncertainty of traveling with or against current than it is to estimate the effects of cross currents. Running parallel to current, you might be quite confident, for example, that the current strength is 1.5 kts ± 0.75 kts. As shown in the last example, the effect on your arrival time of a 0.75-kt uncertainty in speed made good depends on your average speed. You can figure the percentage as previously demonstrated, or you can estimate the time window by simply computing the transit times for the extreme possible speeds: for 6 + 1.5

- 0.75 kt = 6.75 kts and 6 + 1.5 + 0.75 = 8.25 kt. Do this for a 20-nmi run to find that at 6.75 kts, the time is 2 hours 58 minutes; at the estimated speed of 7.5 kts, it is 2 hours and 40 minutes, and at the maximum speed of 6+1.5+0.75 = 8.25 it is 2 hours 25 minutes. Your time window is 2 hours 58 minutes - 2 hours 25 minutes = 33 minutes.

The other method would be 0.75/7.5 = 0.10 = 10%. The estimated time is 2 hours 40 minutes = 160 minutes, and 10% of that is 16 minutes, so the window is ± 16 minutes which is 32 minutes, which counting rounding errors is the same we get the other way.

Crossing strong current in the fog should be avoided when possible if you do not have GPS or radar. When it must be done, recall that an uncertainty in compass course of 6° causes an uncertainty in lateral position of 10% of the distance run (Small Angle Rule, Figure 4-4). After sailing 5 nmi with an uncertainty of ± 6° in heading, your area of uncertainty will have spread out to 0.5 nmi on either side of your course line. This lateral position uncertainty must be taken into account in route planning just as your speed uncertainty is (see Figure 11-19). If the lay of the land on the other side of the crossing allows it, it might be safer to let yourself get set downstream of your target, rather than try to ferry upstream of the target without the advantage of range marks to check progress. Crossing wind presents the same concerns. As always, though, go for one side of the target, not straight toward it. Sailing in current in the fog is clearly a case where GPS is a blessing.

One advantage sailboat navigators have when sailing in the fog (in light to moderate wind) is the silence of their vessels. Distant sounds can often be heard under sail at low speeds, and although it is true that sound directions can be misleading in the fog, the problem is sometimes overstated. If a foghorn appears to be first one place then another, it could be a moving ship. On the other hand, the apparent distance to the source of a sound in the fog is, indeed, often misleading. Some sounds might even grow fainter as you approach the source, especially if any land lies between you and the source. Or a sound might vary between loud and faint with changes in wind direction, even though its distance off has not changed. Keep this potential problem in mind when trying to identify or locate sounds in the fog.

...In Depth

12.23 Sound Signals

Sound signals are used to identify vessels in the fog and to clarify maneuvers, signal intent, or issue a warning when two vessels are in sight of one another. The Rules on the latter are the main thing that changes between the International Rules and the US Inland Rules. This note goes over these issues...

Ships and all other vessels are required by law to sound specific signals in reduced visibility, day or night. Although you might on rare occasions hear other specialized signals from ships in the fog, by far the most common fog signal for a moving vessel is one prolonged blast (4 to 6 seconds long) given at intervals of not more than 2 minutes. Although this is technically a limit, not a specific value, most ship sounds will be repeated right at 2 minutes. The interval will usually be constant because the horns are often automatically operated. This sound warns of the presence of a moving ship (the usual source) or other power-driven vessel more than 12 meters long. The other common signal you might hear is one prolonged blast followed immediately by two short blasts (each 1 second long), again at intervals of not more than 2 minutes. This sound warns of the presence of a moving vessel more that 12 meters long that is somehow limited in its ability to maneuver. It could be a ship following a narrow channel or restricted to a region of deep water, a towboat pulling a barge, commercial fishing boats at work, or a sailboat under sail. Two prolonged blasts, a second apart, repeated every 2 minutes is the sound of a vessel that has stopped and is not moving at all, meaning not making way through the water, but it may be drifting with the current.

Sound signals from ships are supposed to be audible in calm air from 2 nmi off in their forward direction.

Let us pause for some math: if the ship is going 15 kts and you are going 5 kts, then you are closing at 20 kts, which is 3 minutes per mile; so at 2 nmi off, you have 6 minutes to passing time.

More generally, when you are in front of a ship, you will have only 3 or 4 such signals to choose and execute some course of action—we are assuming no working radar for the moment. To proceed, check your compass to maintain orientation; remember the 2-minute limit on the interval, and listen carefully for the next signal. Obviously, in the fog it is best not to end up anywhere near the probable path of large ships, which should be easier to do if there are charted shipping lanes present. If you do end up anywhere near traffic lanes when fog sets in, the immediate goal is to get well away from them. When the wind is blowing, ships to weather of you might be heard from farther than 2 nmi off, but ships to leeward might not be heard until much closer. The sound signals of vessels less than 20 meters long are only required to extend out to 0.5 nmi, although in practice many smaller vessels do not sound any signals at all—contrary to the Rules.

Fog signals on aids to navigation (usually at lighthouses or other primary lights) have sounds that cannot be confused with those from ships. Typical sounds include one 2-second blast every 20 seconds, one 3-second blast every 30 seconds, or multiples such as two 3-second blasts every 60 seconds, or three 2-second blasts every 60 seconds. Some foghorns are shielded and oriented to focus the sound in specific directions. This detail is not always on the chart; so it is important to check the *Light List*. When foghorns from both ships and lighthouses are in the background, the difference in their tones often helps identify them.

Other sounds are equally or sometimes more important in the fog. Dogs, people, cars, trains, and factories can often be heard from the water and used to locate land. When sailing along or toward steep cliffs (which is only safe in calm seas), you might try using echoes. Make a loud sound and count seconds until the echo is heard. Your distance off the reflective wall in miles is just this number of seconds divided by 10 (the speed of sound is about 5 seconds per mile, but you must allow for the sound to travel out and back). In coastal waters, the sounds of swells breaking over rocks (boomers) or the sounds of surf are obvious things to listen for carefully. In some circumstances, the smells of land indicate its presence to windward.

If you are in an area with suspected traffic, or you hear a boat in the distance, then it is probably a good time to practice sounding your own fog horn once in a while, meaning at least every 2 minutes. It would be improbable for larger ships to hear the sound over their own engines and apparent wind, but others might hear you. Canned air horns are fairly effective for this type of signaling, but they are not dependable over long periods in a saltwater environment. Mouth-operated air horns are another option. Some of these are very effective, such as British models called railroad horns or coach's horns. Your VHF radio (using channel 16 on low power) is the safest approach to letting the other vessel know of your presence. Some modern versions have hailers that can also sound fog signals at regular intervals.

The value of radar reflectors is often not fully appreciated. In US waters, they are not required by the *Navigation Rules* or federal regulations, but in Canadian waters they are (Canadian Rule 40). These are metal devices designed to reflect a ship's radar and thus give the ship warning of your position. Without a reflector, nonmetal vessels do not show up well on some radar screens and may be weak signals to all types of radar in some conditions. These devices work well for sailboats, because they can be positioned high in the rigging, and the height of the reflector is critical to its effectiveness. There are various models, some rather expensive; but most studies have shown that the simple, inexpensive metal-disk style (a popular model is from Davis Instruments) do essentially as good a job as the expensive ones. Read the instructions, and mount in the "rain catcher" mode, assuming you will probably not be heeled over in most cases in the fog.

When you must sail in waters near traffic lanes, it pays to have a portable VHF marine radio, so you can be on the radio while still at the helm—power-driven vessels can of course use their console model from the pilot house. By monitoring the traffic control frequency (channel 13 or 14, depending on the region) in addition to the safety channel 16, you will have a good idea of the locations of ship traffic in the lanes. Ships report their positions frequently along with their speeds and estimated arrival times at various way points. In some cases, you can actually learn where you are from hearing over the radio where a ship is that you have recently seen or eventually do see or hear. The traffic reports also include frequent reports of the visibility at various locations along the lanes, which is often more valuable data than the weather radio reports, sometimes given only every three hours at specific points.

Here we have to stress again, that it is radar that is your main aid in the fog. With it you can discover the presence of ships that are many miles off, and then communicate with them while there is still plenty of time to assess the situation and maneuver. There is relatively slimmer chances of benefiting by VHF communications with a vessel that you detect bearing down on you as it emerges from the fog. Ships often cannot maneuver fast enough to do anything about a situation like that. Nevertheless, one would certainly have to try. There is a hope that they could quickly tune their radar to close range and higher gain and look for you on the screen and maneuver accordingly.

If you do hear a ship's foghorn or engine apparently very close but cannot see the vessel, it might be best to head straight toward the sound (slowed to bare steerage) in preparation for its appearance. This orientation puts both ears of the lookout or helmsman onto the job equally, gives you a compass course to the sound to monitor its motion, and leaves you ready to turn right or left as called for. See Rule 19e. Start the stopwatch on your wristwatch when you hear its horn, and if you do not hear the horn again within 2 minutes, the ship is probably headed away from you. Remember that faint sounds can be significantly amplified by cupping your hands over your ears.

Away from the hazards of traffic and dangerous waters or coastlines, sailing in the fog is quite a pleasant experience. It is similar to walking through the silence of a snowy forest. If the opportunity arises in safe waters, take a trip in the fog. It is good practice in learning to follow a compass when disoriented.

Again, remember your depth sounder for position navigation and route planning without radar. I have used this many times to achieve confident navigation, one prominent bottom feature to the next, or to follow a safe depth contour along the shoreline. This is discussed in Chapter 6.

11.9 High Seas Navigation

Long trips out of the sight of land are outside of the scope of this book. We cover ocean navigation in our text *Celestial Navigation—A Complete Home Study Course*. Much of the navigation reduces to the same fundamentals discussed throughout this book: compass use, dead reckoning, current crossing, and navigation planning. The main difference lies in the area of piloting, as there are no landmarks at sea to use for reference. GPS electronic navigation and celestial navigation are the primary means for this

application. For background only, here are a few notes on some of the topics involved.

Celestial navigation uses the positions of the sun, moon, stars, and planets to locate a position on earth. It requires a sextant and accurate UTC, along with several special tables including the *Nautical Almanac*. With care and good procedures, we can achieve a position accuracy of about 1 nmi, maybe half that in the very best conditions with extra care. This level of accuracy is not often much help for inland navigation, but it could be useful for a long coastal trip.

One skill we learn in celestial navigation can be used routinely on inland waters and that is checking a compass with the sun. It is described in Section 12.9.

Satellite phones become more attractive for ocean communications, as does some form of tracking system, which could be of interest for some local sailing. Relatively inexpensive options are available from companies such as yellowbrick-tracking.com and findmespot.com, to mention only two. Most HF (SSB) radio and satellite phone email programs also offer a way to read the GPS and track your progress with each email sent.

As noted in our piloting discussions, we can do fast and highly accurate inland piloting using an inexpensive plastic sextant; so if you do try some of those methods you will have the main tool you need to try your hand at celestial navigation. If so, take a look at our book *How to Use Plastic Sextants*. It is your guide not only to plastic sextants but also how to do the best work with any sextant.

All and all, celestial navigation is an easier subject to learn than inland and coastal navigation. For one thing, it is always the same. Learn it here and now, and it will be exactly the same later and somewhere else. This is in marked contrast to the evolving challenges of inland and coastal navigation, where almost every encounter brings new or varied conditions to be resolved. And in the ocean you have plenty of time to track down your errors, whereas in many inland water situations you must respond with the right answer much more quickly.

The role of celestial navigation as a backup to the GPS in ocean sailing is very much like what we cover in this book to backup the GPS on inland sailing. In fact, if you rely on GPS alone to cross an ocean, you will not know if it was right until the last day. On inland waters, you only have to worry about such things for a few hours or so in most cases before any consequences present themselves, but in the ocean you get to worry about this for weeks or more.

Chapter 11 Glossary

Canadian Sailing Directions. A set of several volumes that provide thorough data similar to the US Coast Pilots.

celestial navigation. The process of finding position at sea from timed sextant sights of celestial bodies.

COGOW (Climatology of Global Ocean Winds). An Oregon State University compilation of satellite wind data, which is now the best source of climatic wind predictions available anywhere.

EPIRB (emergency position indicating radio beacon). A device that sends signals to satellites when activated in an emergency. Units are made for the vessel and for individual use on life jackets. Response is confirmed and rescue actions initiated usually within 1 hour.

float plan. The good advice of being sure someone knows your destination, crew, and estimated return time for any day sail or cruise.

HF (SSB). High frequency, single-sideband. The common name of the marine radio using this frequency mode for long-distance communications. Ranges of several thousand miles are possible.

luminous range. The visible range of a light in restricted visibility, based on the nominal range of the light and the atmospheric visibility. It is determined from the Luminous Range Diagram in the Light List or from an approximation developed at Starpath.

National Data Buoy Center (NDBC). Main source for live and archived weather observations. ndbc.noaa.gov

Ocean Prediction Center (OPC). Main source of NWS weather forecasts, analysis and related information for mariners. opc.ncep.noaa.gov.

rain catcher mode. The proper orientation of a basic radar reflector made from two intersecting circular metal plates, so that the radar reflection is maximized.

river bar. The shoaling at the mouth of a river, often some distance off the coastline, which can be dangerous to cross due to breaking waves when an onshore swell meets the ebb from the river.

sea breeze. A wind blowing from an area of mostly water (ocean coast or inland waterway) toward an area that is mostly land. It builds in the morning and dies off at sunset.

CHAPTER 12

IN DEPTH...

Here we present various special topics or fine points in marine navigation. Some are details not previously covered in the text, while others are examples of applying information from earlier chapters. There is no particular order to their presentation here. They are referenced in the text in the areas they relate to. Some articles may mention topics not yet covered at the time you are referred here. Marine navigation is a broad field, with many interrelated subjects. Please treat these instances as an insight into how things are related, with the knowledge that full details will be presented in due course.

12.1 Traditional Skills in the Satellite Age

There is a tendency in these modern times to think that GPS and other high tech electronics have taken all the vinegar out of navigation. We can just push a button now to get our position accurate to within a boat length or so, and push another button to see that position marked on a video chart—which we can zoom in on to view details within a small bay, or zoom out to locate this bay along the coast of a continent. Our charted position is even marked with an arrow showing the direction we are moving and a digital report of our speed over ground that accounts for current, leeway, and compass error. A precise record of everywhere we have been is clearly laid out before us and stored for future use. Check another screen for a beautiful record of the depth contours we are crossing, and check another monitor to see the radar echoes of nearby land masses and any vessels on the waterway.

But there is much more to navigation—and both maritime law and commonsense require us to know it. Navigation means directing the motion of a vessel. This process almost always involves two distinct operations. First, you must know where you are, or how to determine this if you don't, and then from there choose a safe, efficient, legal course to where you want to go. The legal aspect here means your route or maneuver must obey the *Navigation Rules* ("Rules of the Road") as well as local, federal, or foreign regulations. I haven't navigated a good course into Canada, for example, if that route doesn't take me to a Customs Office straight away; and the most efficient route into a major port could well be neither safe nor legal in the presence of Vessel Traffic Service lanes; and so on.

Modern electronics do indeed help tremendously with the first part of navigation, finding and keeping track of position, but this is not at all the main challenge of navigation. It takes more knowledge and practice to set a good course than it does to find out where you are. You can buy equipment that tells you where you are, but you can't buy equipment to tell you which way to go. And there is little consolation in knowing exactly where you were when you got into trouble!

Besides basic chart reading and plotting skills, shaping a proper course requires practical knowledge of wind and seas and currents, as well as traffic patterns and the *Navigation Rules*. On longer voyages, the proper route depends on the capabilities and limitations of vessel and crew, the locations of facilities, and the present policies and regulations of the ports of call. It takes more study and practice to take these factors into account properly in the planning of a voyage (short or long) than it does to master the various ways of finding out where you are underway, even with nothing more than a compass and log to go by.

Part of the task is learning the references, which include the NGA's *Planning Guides* and *Sailing Directions* for international voyages, and NOAA's *Coast Pilots* and Marine Weather Services Charts (or equivalent) for U.S. waters, along with tide and current tables and charts, and the Coast Guard's *Navigation Rules*, *Light Lists*, Notices to Mariners, and so forth.

Unfortunately, to be a good navigator (efficient, effective, and versatile), we can't even leave the easy part to the electronics alone. We must know basic position navigation (piloting and dead reckoning) in the old-fashioned way, regardless of what wonders of the space age we have on board. And it isn't just because the electronics might fail—which for sure they will at some point, maybe even some crucial point—but also because we need the basic understanding of charting, bearings, distance calculations, vectors, and so on just to interpret what the electronics tell us. In other words, we can't sensibly take advantage of what they can do for us if we don't truly understand what they are telling us.

Consequently, a reasonable approach to learning navigation these days is to start out with those topics that best help us take advantage of the electronics. This doesn't change the content of the learning, even if we don't plan to use electronics; it just rearranges the syllabus. Direct use, for example, of latitude and longitude coordinates for inland sailing was not only rare but generally unwise a few years ago. Now, in the space age of GPS, you are likely to see a Lat-Lon position, specified to six digits, posted in 8-inch letters at gas docks. Waypoint guides that list Lat-Lon coordinates for the turning points along routes from anywhere to everywhere are commonplace. In short, the precise meaning of a Lat-Lon position and how to plot it carefully and quickly are more preeminent subject matter these days than they were before electronics dominated.

An alternative guideline to nearly the same syllabus is to concentrate on those topics and methods that we can use to check the electronics. In other words, if the GPS says I am at this point on the chart, what are the best and quickest ways for me to confirm that this is probably true, or to conclude that something is wrong. There are extensive examples of accidents traced to GPS errors or errors in the electronic charts they used.

On either syllabus, we start with charts and plotting; and go on to piloting with ranges, bearings, and depths; and then on to dead reckoning with log and compass. After that, we add currents, darkness, fog, and traffic. The goal here is to cover traditional methods, with an eye toward how this relates to electronics we might have on board. Another goal is to present and discuss more general guidelines that will contribute to good navigation—made into rules of thumb that are easy to remember. For example, the most important rule for good navigation is to plot your position on the chart frequently and label it with the time. This will generally tell you at a glance what you need for quick decisions: where you are, which way you are going, and how fast.

The most important book in navigation is the *Navigation Rules*. These are the laws designed to prevent collisions—collisions with vessels underway, or with vessels at anchor, or with buoys, or with ice bergs, or with islands. The Rules are more than a list of who has right of way and what lights and sounds are legal. They provide sound practical advice for safe navigation in all circumstances.

Good chart practice starts with knowing the symbols and conventions. These are defined in the NOAA booklet *Chart No. 1*. Most are clear from this booklet, but a few—such as all-important rock symbols—can benefit from further clarification. Figure 2-6 (in Chapter 2) shows rock symbols schematically, relative to the tide levels implicit in the definitions. Two tide levels are important to chart reading; zero tide and mean high water. Zero is easy; it is when the tide height at a specific place and time is at (or, for practical purposes, near) 0 ft according to the tide books. This happens for about a two-hour period once a day on the west coast and twice a day on the east coast. Both coasts have two highs and two lows daily, but on the west coast, the peak highs and lows are usually quite different, which ties careful chart reading a little closer to the tide books.

On any chart, at zero tide, the charted depths are the actual depths to expect there. If the tide were 7 ft, you would expect an extra 7 ft of depth in that region; likewise, at a tide of -2 ft, you would have 2 ft less water than shown.

Mean high water is the average of all high waters at a given location, but somewhat surprisingly it is not a number listed directly in tide books. Since it is required for chart reading, it is listed on the chart itself. Look around at the various notes on the chart to find it. Another rule of thumb: when you get a new chart, spend a few minutes and read all the notes on it and mark ones of interest with a highlight marker. Some restricted areas are more restricted than others; sometimes, standard conventions are changed on particular charts; unusual markings or grids are explained; and so forth. If the need should arise, mean high water can be figured from NOAA tide books by adding one half of the tabulated mean range to the tabulated mean tide level.

Charted elevations of land and lights, as well as bridge clearances are usually given as heights above the water when the tide is at mean high water. When the tide equals or exceeds the mean high water level, all the green foreshore is covered by water and all "asterisk rocks" (rocks that cover and uncover) are underwater. A bridge with charted clearance of 50 ft in a region with a mean high water of 10 ft will have an extra 6 ft of clearance when the tide has only risen to 4 ft.

A good way to develop insight into the perspective of charted lands and other prominent features is to read the *Coast Pilot* description of the charted region with the chart at hand. The *Coast Pilot* contains a wealth of navigational information that supplements charted data, including weather and current information, along with special regulations that apply in the regions covered. The same applies to international charts using the *Sailing Directions*.

U.S. and international charts, *Coast Pilots*, *Sailing Directions*, and various special publications like *Chart No. 1* are all available online as free pdf downloads. Links to free echart downloads are at starpath.com/navpubs.

Careful plotting is a hallmark of good navigation. In the age of electronics, it is the opportunity for error that we meet most often—transferring the GPS position to the chart. One way to get practice ashore is to plot light and buoy positions taken from a recent *Light List* onto a chart that shows their positions. When a plotted position agrees with the charted position, you know you have done it right; when they disagree significantly after double checking, you learn why the *Light List* is such an important aid.

Another good rule: memorize: 1 nautical mile = 6,000 ft. It is actually 6,076.12 ft, but the details don't matter in the many practical applications of this relationship, and they distract from memorizing it. Since 1' of latitude equals 1 nautical mile, 0.01' of latitude (0.6") equals 60 ft. When a buoy's latitude in a Notice to Mariners is given as, say, 45° 38' 11.7", they are specifying the position of the buoy to a precision of 10 ft (0.1"). Most buoys move around much more than that with the changing tides—in fact, it is safer to consider charted and tabulated buoy positions as where they were put, not where they are. Furthermore, on a 1:40,000 chart, a 1-mm pencil dot spans 40,000 mm (40 meters) on the chart, which is some 130 ft. When your latitude indicated on the GPS changes from, say, 32° 45.16' to 32° 45.17', it is implying a shift in position of some 60 ft. If the 45.16' changed to 45.26', it would imply a shift of 600 ft, and so forth.

There is really no safe way to avoid this numerical nitpicking in the electronic age of navigation. A modern nav station glows with digital data. It is obviously important to keep in mind what the numbers mean.

One way to expedite routine plotting and avoid repeated angle conversions is to construct customized plotting cards as shown in Figure 7-3 of Chapter 7. A separate card (or corner of the same card) is required for each chart, and the chart must be prepared with extra latitude and longitude lines, but after a few minutes preparation, these are very handy for quick position plotting. Regardless of how it's done, if the plotting process is not quick and easy, one tends to violate the most important rule in navigation: plot your position on the chart frequently, labeled with the time.

12.2 Keeping Track of Course and Position

To direct the motion of a vessel, we must first know where we are and then select a safe and efficient course to where we want to go. Once underway, the task reduces to monitoring and recording progress—to be certain we are doing what we intended—and to interacting with traffic we meet according to the *Navigation Rules*. The process is more or less the same for crossing an ocean as it is for crossing a bay.

There is a valid distinction, however, to be made between the type of navigation called for in cruising and deliveries compared with that best suited for competitive racing. Sometimes in racing, the line between fast and safe is a thin one, but off the race course, there is no call for risk—and there is no call for continual fine course adjustments to the wind, nor continual computations of the favored jibe or tack, nor continual anticipation of the wind ahead and how to set up for it. In racing, the wind is our master; in cruising, the wind is our engine. Obviously, we still want to sail efficiently when cruising, so we always have the wind on our minds, but comfort and safety have more priority in course selection than raw speed. By the same token, the attitudes and techniques of prudent navigation we cover here belong on the race course as well whenever possible. In any event, racing navigation as such is not the topic of this review. For now, we assume we are reaching or under power and have some choice over our course. Later, we go to weather, as eventually we must.

The question at hand now is, what is the best way to do this monitoring of progress underway? After selecting a course and heading off in that direction, the first step, always, is to check that we are making good what we intended—and here, the electronics shine brightest. GPS can tell us our COG and SOG (course and speed over ground), so after just a few minutes on a constant compass heading, we know which way and how fast we are really moving, independent of current, leeway, compass errors, log errors, or steering errors. In many situations, this feature of the instrumentation is much more valuable than the actual position report. Remember, the compass only tells us which way the boat is pointed, not which way it is moving. With a measure of the actual COG, we can fine tune our compass heading to make good the desired course.

If we want course 200, for example, and we are steering 200, but are making good a course of 205 according to plotted track of our past positions, then try 195 for a while to see if that makes 200. It doesn't really matter for the moment what causes the difference between what we steer and what we get, as long as we end up with what we want. We will eventually discover the problem. If current or wind is the cause, 195 will no longer get us 200 since these factors inevitably change. If the water is still and the air is calm, and we continually need this 5° or so on southerly headings, but we need some other correction or no correction on other headings, then we likely have a compass error, which we can track down more precisely if needed later on.

As a rule, the COG is the most important factor to monitor. We usually have some control over our course, and going the wrong direction is usually what leads to trouble. Gradations in the SOG are less important. In other words, in prudent navigation, we choose the course and take the speed that comes with it, assuming it is a safe speed, whereas in sailboat racing, you choose the speed and take the course that comes with it, and hope it is a safe course.

To help with thinking about courses and course errors, and for many other practical applications in navigation, it pays to memorize a simple relationship: a 6° right triangle has a 10 to 1 ratio of its sides. In other words, 6° is 10% (Small Angle Rule). If I travel 14 nmi with a constant course error of 6°, I will end up 1.4 nmi off course. Or use it this way: with 0.7 kts of current on the beam as I travel at 7 kts (current 10% of my speed), I know I will get set about 6°. This is a valuable trick for quick estimates, and it can be scaled up or down a few times: 12° is 20%, 3° is 5%.

Without GPS on board, we still have to make this important initial assessment of the COG. Natural ranges are the best bet for checking course alignment visually—that is, look for anything dead ahead or astern that lines up, and watch that it stays lined up as you proceed. More often than not, you must look back for these ranges as you set off. An island just barely showing behind a headland should stay in the same place as both fade into the distance. If the island starts moving out from the headland or sliding farther back behind it (Figure 12.2-1), then you are being set off course. With a good range, it is easy to set your heading to make your course. Binoculars are often helpful.

Without ranges in sight, we are left to plotting a sequence of position fixes to determine course and speed made good. Crossed bearing lines, or distance off measurements, or some combination of the two will do the job when you have suitable landmarks nearby; but even at their best, it will be difficult to do as well as the GPS can do in determining COG, and it will definitely take longer.

Radar, on the other hand, can often serve very nicely for checking course made good (CMG). A direct approach is to plot a sequence of fixes from range and bearing to some prominent target, or check for natural ranges between radar targets ahead or astern that are not visible by eye. Sailing parallel to a shore is well suited to radar course monitoring by just setting a variable range marker (VRM) on the shore line and watching that the ring does not leave the land as you proceed on a constant compass course.

The idea of sailing a range to ensure your COG is especially valuable when following a buoyed channel. There is a temptation in such cases to simply drive from buoy to buoy when they are all laid out like that for you. But in many such cases, this can be a far too relaxed approach. The buoys are usually there for a reason—it is dangerous to get outside of them. You could stay pointed right at the next buoy as you get set out of the channel by current. It is often mandatory that you keep an eye on the range between the buoy behind you and the one in front of you, and sail this line, not just head to the next one. This will also help you avoid cutting corners, which can lead to trouble. It is usually best to lay out ahead of time exactly where you will turn, and the best route to follow: red to green, close abeam, then green to green, etc, depending on the hazards the buoys mark and your present conditions of wind, current, and traffic. Also confirm the buoy numbers as you pass to minimize surprises. At night, this calls for a good spotlight. Again, radar is ideal for this operation, since buoys will generally show up nicely on the radar.

Regardless of how the course is checked, if the wind won't allow the course you wanted, then choose another that you can make. It is fundamental to navigation to always have an assigned course, as opposed to just wandering along the coastline, headland to headland or buoy to buoy, or following the wind wherever it takes you. On long voyages, it is even good practice to display the course in some prominent place in the cockpit, so all can see it. With a lot of swinging around in the waves, especially at night or with helmsmen changing frequently, or with courses changing as weather patterns change, it is easy to forget the new course and come back automatically to the one you steered all day yesterday. Fatigued and in big waves, this can be dangerous as well as inefficient.

It is, in fact, good procedure to navigate by waypoints in *all* circumstances, not just in buoyed channels, as mentioned above. This approach, moreover, is not limited to electronic waypoints stored in the GPS—although this use (from Loran days) gave popularity to the term—it can be applied to any route, using any method of position fixing. In other words, rather than just sail around an island, following the shore, set up a segmented path of specific courses, with turning (or tacking or jibing) points at specific places, the waypoints. The waypoints could be defined by bearings to landmarks, a certain depth contour when sailing toward some mark, or at the first alignment with some natural range. It doesn't have to be when the electronics start beeping that you have arrived within some preset range of a programmed position. Short of doing this, it is easy to get disoriented when rounding a broad curve. Sailing by waypoints is just one more way to keep in charge of what is going on.

Once we are settled in and tracking the way we want to, attention should turn to various ways of checking off our location along the line. Without this check, we could be making good exactly the course we want, but have slipped off to the side of our desired track. The simplest approach would be to just read the position (or a cross-track error) from a GPS periodically and plot it on the chart. Simple enough, and better than nothing, but this procedure alone is not prudent navigation. We need some verification of any electronic position, and the quicker and easier it is to come by, the more we will use it.

There is no way around it; in the end, we have to navigate the old-fashioned way, and the basis for this is to plot your position on the chart frequently, labeled with the time. But before getting out the compass or sextant for piloting checks, there is other instrumentation we can call on for quick confirmations of GPS position fixes, and we can do a lot by just looking around.

Our trail of position fixes plotted across the chart gives a quick perspective on what we should see where. What should lie dead ahead, for example, when making for land, or what ranges we might pick out on the horizon for an

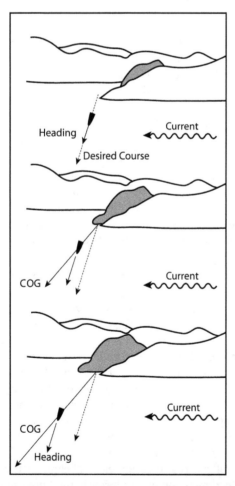

Figure 12.2-1. *Watching back bearings or ranges to see if we are getting set. With no set, the island would stay obscured, just as it was when we rounded the corner onto our new course. As we get set downstream, we see more and more of the island.*

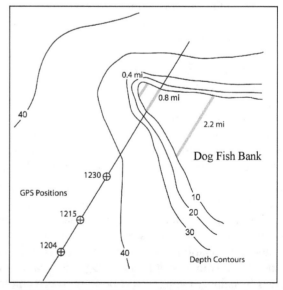

Figure 12.2-2. *At about 1250, we should cross a bank about 0.8 nmi across, which should show a very prominent 4 to 1 rise on the depth sounder trace.*

accurate line of position, or the location of buoys or islets relative to the bow—we can make reasonable estimates of relative bow angles without actually getting out a compass. None of these observations constitute a fix or actual confirmation of our position, but they are checks that could let us know if something is going wrong.

Whenever there is a uniform slope to the bottom, or over a bottom with prominent structure, the depth sounder provides quick and often valuable support of a plotted GPS position—the chart says we should be in 72 ft of water; are we? Sometimes, the tide must be reckoned into this comparison, and in these cases, it is convenient to be sailing with tide books that show daily graphs of the tide height. These days, we might even have made these graphs ourselves at home or underway with software or online resources that plot out the tides and currents anywhere, anytime. There are also numerous smartphone apps.

Even without tide corrections, with a charted trench or bank just ahead, an accurate position check can often be made by logging the distance across it on a known heading (Figure 12.2-2). This is standard procedure in traditional depth sounding navigation (called a *line of soundings*), in use long before electronic navigation came on board. Remember, the depth sounder is more than just an alarm against going aground. It is a crucial navigation aid, especially in the fog.

The most reassuring position check of all, however, goes back again to the radar. The GPS says I am here on the chart, and if this is so, then that point of land should be 65° on the port bow at 3.8 nmi off, and so on. Turn to the radar and see if that is true. This operation not only confirms your position, but also helps identify that radar target, from which you can then identify other radar targets. With this process, the radar screen becomes a more meaningful picture of what you are sailing by. Naturally, we want to be careful not to misinterpret what we see on the radar, but there are not many better ways to learn about radar use than to adopt this style of navigation. Plot the GPS position, read off ranges and bearings to probable radar targets, then identify them. Then when setting up your waypoints for the next turn, you can use the radar more confidently when approaching them.

There is still another value to this approach: it encourages us to learn the names of the points or places we are sailing by, either along a coast or along an inland waterway. With our latitude and longitude continually flashing about the nav station to a boat length's accuracy these days, it is easy to forget the value of knowing where we really are, i.e., 5 nmi west of Jefferson Head or Cabo Correntes or Kealaikahiki Point. For the sake of safety in communications with traffic or in an emergency, it always pays to have in mind a verbal description of your location. In some parts of the world, place names are not readily assimilated at a glance, so choosing the best description of your location and a quick shot at a likely pronunciation can prove useful.

These days, an ideal nav station includes GPS, radar, and a good depth sounder, with one of these capable of showing a plot of tracks between waypoints and past positions en route. A plotter display that can be zoomed out to show an entire route of waypoints, or zoomed in to show when we slip a few boat lengths off the track, is a tremendous convenience, indeed. Nevertheless, all these wonderful aids will not lead to true peace of mind—not to mention safety—without the basic knowledge of what they are talking about and how to check them.

In the long run, confidence and quality in navigation comes from practiced good habits, but even with that, peace of mind underway will eventually boil down to one's ability to do dead reckoning (DR)—pure log and compass navigation, folding in our knowledge of leeway, currents, and steering biases. The reason is simple: some time, some place, for some reason, we will be left with nothing more to go by, and deep in our hearts we know it. Consequently, one of the best uses of GPS is for training in DR. In other words, to see how well we can determine our position from our own basic shipboard tools—log, to say how far we went, and compass, to say which way we went. This type of position reckoning is rightfully distinguished from piloting, which is the determination of a true position fix from charted landmarks or satellites. A DR position is a deduced position, as opposed to a measured position.

To practice with DR, keep a careful record of course and speed (or course and log) and then plot out this track to determine your DR position periodically and compare it with the GPS position. Keep a record of the differences (so many miles off, in such and such a direction, after traveling so far, in so much time) and look for trends or patterns that might help to understand what is causing the discrepancies. Besides keeping track of your DR error in terms of a percentage of the distance run (I was off 0.4 nmi after 10 for an error of 4%), it often helps to think of the DR error as a current—divide the distance between final DR and corresponding fix by the time underway since the last fix to get the drift of the *error current,* and call the direction from fix to DR the set of the error current.

With practice, you learn about your DR errors in various circumstances and can correct for them, or at least understand how they increase the uncertainty of your position with time and distance when navigating by DR alone. It is definitely an exercise that will encourage you to calibrate your instruments. These ideas are pursued in the next section.

12.3 Dead Reckoning Procedures and Uncertainties

If we were guaranteed our GPS would always work, we would not have to do much more for ocean navigation. Unfortunately, relying on GPS alone, we never know whether the GPS was right until the last day of the voyage—and we would be rightfully anxious about that throughout the voyage, because we know this cannot be guaranteed. On the other hand, we can guarantee that the sun will rise tomorrow and the stars will come out tonight, so if we learn celestial navigation, we remove much of this anxiety, as well as learning other valuable skills such as how to check a compass offshore.

But there is always some luck involved in ocean voyaging, just as there is when going to the store to buy a loaf of bread. We cannot guarantee that our own atmosphere won't get in the way of our seeing the sun and stars when we need them most. We could wait out the overcast to find position and figure the next course, but that is not prudent policy. It could well be that this overcast is the forerunner of a storm we very much want to avoid, so we must keep moving. There are numerous reasons that days of delay could be detrimental.

The way we navigate between true position fixes (from cel nav, GPS, or any piloting fix) is called dead reckoning (DR). It is an unusual name, but it has been used by mariners since the early 1600s. It means navigation by compass and log, aided by your knowledge of your boat and the waters you sail. Without actual position fixes, this is the way you carry on. In many senses, the highest goal of navigation training should be learning the skill of accurate DR.

The only way to learn how well you can do DR is to practice it. For this we need a log (odometer), a compass, and a logbook. In the learning process, we can check our DR with the GPS on any waterway, since many of us do not get to sail in the ocean very often. But that is just to get started. The training must ultimately extend into the ocean because the crucial effect of big waves cannot be learned on inland waters. Also, if your local waterway has much tidal current flow, it will have a notable effect on this exercise, but the practice remains invaluable.

The idea is, simply, whenever sailing, keep a careful logbook, and periodically compare your DR position with your GPS position, make a note of the differences (as explained below), then start over again. The more practice you get in various conditions, the more you learn.

Your compass should be checked and deviation removed. A typical binnacle-mounted compass on a nonsteel vessel should have no deviation if adjusted properly, but it has to be checked. Your log and knotmeter should be calibrated (in calm air and still water) along a known distance run. The trip log is just another output from the knotmeter. Magnets in the impeller create a pulse each time it turns. The rate of the pulses is converted to speed in knots; the sum of the pulses is converted to distance run in nmi. Usually, the knotmeter circuitry is such that the same calibration process corrects both.

Using a log for distance run is much more accurate than speed multiplied by time since our speed changes continually, especially in big waves. If you want to know your average speed, record the log every hour, then subtract consecutive log readings.

The other key component to DR is the logbook. Make an entry (Time, Course, and Log) anytime something changes, and if nothing changes, make an entry every 4 hours (minimum)—with an understood policy that no entry means nothing changed. The logbook will include much information, but the only data we need for DR are: the Time of a course change, the Course we changed to at that time, and the Distance Run on that course, which we get from subtracting successive log entries.

As an example, let us assume we are headed off into the ocean and want to start this voyage with careful monitoring of our DR—the good policy we are recommending here. It is 1535 in the afternoon, and we have our GPS position for that time plotted on the chart (see Figures 12.3-1 and 12.3-2). The last recorded position was at 1120 (4h 15m earlier). Then we update the DR track on the chart by plotting out all recorded course changes starting from the 1120 fix position, followed by the final run up to 1535 along the latest course line, and mark that DR position (usually a dot with a half circle). Now measure the range and bearing from the 1535 DR position to the 1535 fix position. Let's say it was 2.0 nmi in direction 150 T. This is how much our DR was in error.

We now come to the main question at hand. Is this a big error or not? In other words, how well can we hope to do DR in the ocean? This is the key factor we need to know so we understand how our position uncertainty is increasing with time, which it inevitably will, when we are out of sight of land. The best next route to follow obviously depends on where we are now, but the best choice could also depend on how uncertain this starting point is. The more uncertain our present position, the more conservative our next route must be.

There are various ways to approach this. We studied this subject in depth when preparing the book *Emergency Navigation* (1980 to 1986). We are talking log and compass here, so nothing has really changed in the intervening

Table 12.3-1					
Sample Logbook				Computed values	
Time	Log	Course	Run	Total run	Total time
1120	606.8	045	0.0	0	0h 00m
1150	610.3	310	3.5	3.5	0h 30m
1259	618.4	289	8.1	11.6	1h 39m
1330	621.6	022	3.2	14.8	2h 10m
1535	638.4	022	16.8	31.6	4h 15m

Figure 12.3-1. *Sample logbook. This 4.25-hour run (1535-1120) had an average speed of 31.6/4.25 = 7.4 kts, after which we found the DR wrong by 2.0 nmi. This is well within the suggested guidelines of 2.8 nmi in this example: 5% of total run (0.05 × 31.6) = 1.6 nmi, and an error current of 0.5 kts for 4.25 hours contributes 2.1 nmi. With time and distance errors about the same, they combine as 1.5 x the average = 2.8 nmi.*

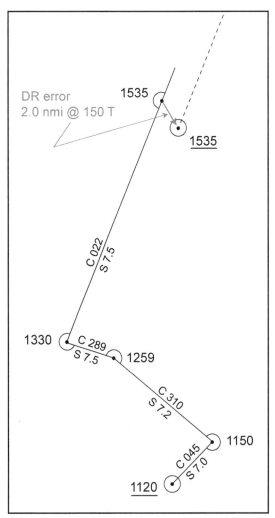

DR error
2.0 nmi @ 150 T

1535

1535

C 022
S 7.5

1330
C 289
S 7.5

1259

C 310
S 7.2

1150

C 045
S 7.0

1120

Figure 12.3-2. *Sample DR track plot. Based on the sample logbook, we start from our 1120 fix and plot all course changes recorded in the logbook until the next fix at 1535. The difference between 1535 DR and fix is the DR error, 2.0 nmi in direction 150. By standard convention, fixes are plotted with full circles, DR positions with half circles. Each leg is labeled with course and speed. After 1535, the old DR track is abandoned, and a new one started (dotted line).*

30 years, except we started out with nothing but cel nav for a reference, then we had Loran, then we had Transit Sat-Nav, and now we have GPS, but the key to good navigation and record keeping has not changed. In fact, the notable thing about Christopher Columbus—other than being a charlatan and one of the few nominally educated people of the time who did not know the radius of the earth—was his exceptional ability at DR. With nothing more than a chip log for speed, a sandglass for time, and a compass he did not understand at all, he still knew remarkably well where he was at all times (relative to his departure) based on his DR skills.

The rules of thumb we came up with in that study were based on two things: how far you traveled and how long it took. Assuming your instruments are calibrated and you do everything right, you still have to assume that your DR position is growing uncertain in time by some 5% of the total

distance run and the effect of an unknown error current of some 0.5 kts. We must consider both factors when estimating our DR uncertainty. Often, one factor will dominate the other, and we can then focus on it. If they are about the same, then we might consider the total error as about 1.5 times their average.

This guideline says that if you go out in the ocean, turn the engine off, and take all sails down, your position will become as uncertain as if you were in a current of some 0.5 kts in a direction you do not know. After 24 hours, you have to assume you could be anywhere within 12 nmi of where you think you are—maybe worse in some cases, maybe not so bad in others. This conclusion is based on wind drift studies, along with noting that the average ocean surface current flow around the world is some 0.5 kts as well.

Note that Pilot Chart current data should be interpreted as about ± 50%. A reported drift of 12 nmi a day could be anywhere between 6 and 18, with the higher estimate more likely if the wind has blown in the predicated current direction for several days, and the lower estimate if the wind has blown the opposite direction for several days.

Likewise, if you zoom off at 30 kts, after you go 100 nmi your DR position will be uncertain by some 5 nmi or so—again, maybe a bit more or a bit less, depending on many factors. In this case, the current drift of 1.7 nmi (0.5 × 3.3h) is small enough (compared to 5 nmi from the distance error) to be neglected, because the errors add as the square root of the sum of the squares.

In other words, the final error in *any* quantity B × C, where the uncertainty in B is b and in C is c, is equal to

$$\text{Final error} = \text{Sqrt }[b^2 + c^2].$$

This accounts for the fact that one error could be plus while the other is minus, or both could be plus or minus; it also shows that if one is small compared to the other it can be neglected, i.e., Sqrt $[5^2]$ = 5, compared to Sqrt $[5^2 + 1.7^2]$ = 5.28.

Although developed for ocean navigation, the limits given here are a good guideline for all navigation, even across a large lake. Namely, without a real position fix, your DR position becomes uncertain by 5% of distance run within an error current of 0.5 kts.

In your practice underway, if you consistently do better than that, you are doing fine. If you cannot achieve that on average, then you are not optimized on your procedures or equipment.

To get a sense of the magnitudes of these limits, note that a 6° right triangle has sides in the ratio of 1 to 10, and this proportion scales down forever and up to some 18°. That is, a 3° triangle has sides of about 1 to 20, a 12° triangle has sides of about 1 to 5, and so on. This Small-Angle Rule is a powerful trick for navigators to know, with numerous applications.

Put into the context at hand, after you sail 100 nmi with a compass that is wrong by 6°, you will be off your intended track by 10 nmi. This is a 10% error; in our DR error estimates, we are talking about 5%. So you can see that 5% DR is quite a good goal, namely, it means you are steering what you record to within 3°, with a log that is exactly right.

As for the log, when we strive for 5%, we imply an indicated knotmeter speed of 7.0 is guaranteed to be right to within about 0.35 kts. This is a conservative goal, which is easy to achieve with calibration, so we see the main factor in DR accuracy is usually CMG. Keep in mind that leeway, which pushes you off course to leeward, also increases your speed, but that speed shows up on the knotmeter.

The saving grace, meaning why this is not quite as difficult as it might appear, is we are assuming we have taken all systematic errors into account, i.e., we correct for compass error, current, leeway, and helm bias as best we can. In this case, the remaining errors are likely to be random, just as well to the left as to the right, so they tend to cancel.

Those errors that do not cancel, but in fact show up consistently, provide valuable information. If we find, for example, that regardless of tack or jibe, we find ourselves set to the south as if we were in a current of 0.3 kts, then we have learned that whatever estimates we have made for the current were off by that amount. Then we can add this to our subsequent corrections. Likewise, compass or log errors will show up as a consistent offset, which can likewise then be accounted for.

Sailing into the wind, you will find that your progress to weather will not be what you expect. The logged distance run will be about right, but your track will be offset downwind some 5° to 10° from what you expected, even with an estimated leeway correction—and it might not be the same on each tack, depending on the waves.

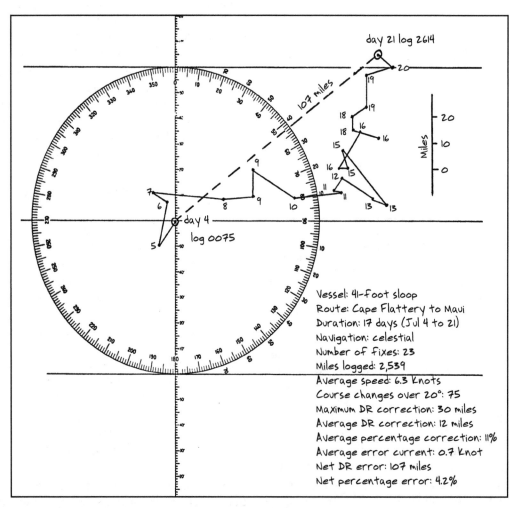

Vessel: 41-foot sloop
Route: Cape Flattery to Maui
Duration: 17 days (Jul 4 to 21)
Navigation: celestial
Number of fixes: 23
Miles logged: 2,539

Average speed: 6.3 knots
Course changes over 20°: 75
Maximum DR correction: 30 miles
Average DR correction: 12 miles
Average percentage correction: 11%
Average error current: 0.7 knot
Net DR error: 107 miles
Net percentage error: 4.2%

Figure 12.3-3. *Vector plot of DR errors for an ocean passage made by cel nav alone in 1982. Individual DR errors are plotted sequentially to show how the vessel would progressively have gone off course if these corrections had not been made. Starting from day 4, the error on day 5 was 11 nmi in direction 215, then on day 6 it was 17 nmi in direction 012, and so on. If no fixes had been taken on this voyage, the boat would have been 107 nmi off position at log reading 2614. Even though the individual errors averaged some 11% (taking into account distance covered on each leg), the net error was only 4%, which shows how random DR errors tend to cancel out over a long run—in part because these DR errors also reflect errors in the celestial fixes. The average DR error current was 0.7 kts (taking into account time spent on each leg), which is somewhat higher than is typical for a sailboat keeping a careful DR log—the winds were unusually erratic for this trip. Error logs like this one are analyzed and discussed in detail in* Emergency Navigation, *and the actual celestial navigation of the whole voyage in presented as a training exercise in the forthcoming* Hawaii by Sextant *(Starpath Publications, 2013).*

In any event, this type of analysis of comparing your fix positions with the corresponding DR positions and thinking in terms of both percentage of distance run and an error current, will help you unravel what is ailing your DR and prepare you for a time when you might not have the fixes to fall back on. An example is shown in Figure 12.3-3.

12.4 Navigation Tools

It is very frustrating business in navigation to return to the chart table and discover you can't find a pencil. When it comes right down to getting the job done, our basic plotting tools and how we store them is vital to good work. I have often stated, and still maintain, that the most important aid to navigation, barring none, is a well-designed tool holder located outside of the chart table—but let's come back to this important, but easily solved problem after a quick look at the basic tools themselves and what they are used for.

Of the many tools and gadgets intended to aid our navigation, only a few will generally survive the test of time and varied circumstances of small craft navigation. These are (1) pencils and erasers, (2) parallel rulers, or some other way to transfer parallel lines across the chart, and (3) dividers. Note that we are differentiating here between plotting tools and other instruments or aids—a handheld bearing compass is a vital instrument; charts, *Coast Pilots*, *Light Lists*, and such are vital aids. For now we concentrate on the actual tools we use to read and put lines onto the chart.

Pencils are your key tool at the nav station. It will take some experience underway in your specific sailing conditions to decide what is best for you. I just stress that this is a very important issue to be resolved. In some conditions, thin-lined (0.5 mm) mechanical pencils serve well, if tested, with lead hardness to match your needs. No. 1 lead (also called 2B) might work best when charts are more exposed to getting damp. But more generally, No. 2 lead is recommended as a compromise between the harder No. 3 that is difficult to see and erase and the softer No. 1 that smears too easily. But this all depends on your conditions. The No. 1 lines are also easier to see in dim light. If using mechanical pencils, the ones with the lead advance down near the tip are convenient because you don't need to interrupt your writing much when the lead breaks.

For standard pencils, the main task is keeping them sharp. A knife will do the job, but it's not efficient. Of the small pencil sharpeners, choose the kind with replaceable blades, and tape a few extras inside the can. Also use good pencils. Poor sharpening behavior (points break before getting sharp) can often be traced to the quality of the pencil rather than the sharpener.

If you have adequate room for it, an electric pencil sharpener and a handful of quality No. 2 pencils are a good solution—it is the same choice the Russian astronauts made while NASA was developing the Space Pen.

For erasers, I prefer two—one pencil-style, for smaller work, and a larger one for bigger jobs. The pencil type is handy because it fits in the pencil holder and is readily available. The larger one is used less often—for example, in cleaning grease pencil notes off plastic-coated current charts or forms for recording VHF wind reports, or for erasing notes that somehow got written on the chart table or bulkhead in a hurry.

Parallel rulers are two regular rulers (usually without scales on them) attached together by two arms that pivot about points attached to the rulers. Regardless of how you separate the rulers, they stay parallel to each other. With this tool, you can draw one line on the chart that is parallel to another line some distance away. This operation is done frequently in navigation. We do it, for example, to read a compass bearing from one buoy to another by aligning the rulers with the buoy-to-buoy line and then transferring this line with the parallel rulers to the nearest compass rose. With a line drawn through the center of the compass rose that is parallel to the direction we want to go, we can read what the magnetic heading should be from the magnetic scale on the rose. A similar operation is necessary when finding our position from several magnetic bearings to charted landmarks or when plotting the layline to a mark when racing.

Parallel rulers all look pretty much the same, but there are some options. For length, I have found that 15-inch ones are about optimum for typical chart tables. I also prefer the clear ones over the black ones since you can see what's under them. Also, they should have small cork feet to keep them from slipping. Most do, but a few models don't, and these are definitely harder to use. In any event, it takes some practice at first to learn to walk parallel rulers very far across the chart without slipping, though it soon becomes second nature. Nevertheless, it is good practice to always walk them back to where you started from to check that you haven't slipped.

Parallel rulers, however, are not the only way to solve this common task of navigation plotting. It can also be done with roller plotters or with two 45° triangles. Roller plotters (sometimes called a Weems Plotter) are a device designed to roll without slipping. They work well on large chart tables and are standard equipment on larger vessels. They have a protractor printed on them, so you can read true bearings from the nearest longitude meridian or latitude parallel without going to a compass rose. But this in turn requires use of true bearings, which is inconvenient in small craft (magnetic) navigation—larger vessels use true bearings from gyrocompasses more than magnetic bearings. These plotters, however, are not so reliable on typical small chart tables since we must fold the charts and these things slip when going over a fold, even when it's underneath the chart. Also you can't use them close to the edge of the chart tables as you can with parallel rulers. In rough weather, we need to tape down the charts, so this limitation is often a frustration. Furthermore, they cost more and break more often. The rollers can corrode if not maintained, at which point they are useless.

Triangles don't have any of these draw backs, but they take a bit more practice to learn and you have two things to keep track of instead of one. Good ones with handles are also rather expensive. Those who are used to triangles will swear by them, but starting from scratch, parallel rulers are probably the best bet.

Dividers are a common draftsman's tool for measuring the distance between two points—or more precisely, for transferring the distance between two points from one place on the chart to another place that has the miles scale on it. You could do the same job with two marks on a piece of paper, but dividers are more convenient. They come in many styles and prices. We prefer ones called ultralight speed bow, about 7 inches long, made of plated alloy to prevent corrosions. Look for those that come with sharp points on each end of the replacement needles .

There is also a style called one-hand dividers that have a large loop on top which you squeeze to open them up. But I find these rather awkward to use and have had no trouble in working conventional dividers with one hand. Also, the points on one-hand dividers are not replaceable, though they could be sharpened with a file. The thick shape of the points renders them not so convenient for using dividers to align parallel rulers, which is another drawback.

The variation that has now become standard equipment in most professional nav stations is called a speed bow. These have an adjustment screw in the center that keeps them from moving once set to a separation, and the speed part means you can override the wheel by pulling or pushing the arms. Years ago, they were very expensive, but for several years now, thanks to a company in Denmark, they are readily available from most distributors at an economical price. They are shown in Figure 12.4-1. This type of divers can be found on all commercial vessels and are clearly the divider of choice among professional navigators.

Now, the important part: a place to keep this stuff outside of the chart table, within quick reach. A simple rack for parallel rulers will do, with a separate deep cup or tube for dividers and pencils—a tissue stuffed in the tube saves the divider points. Both should be straight ahead, within easy reach. Then you have a place to put things when done with them, and you always know where to find them. The inside of a chart table is not a practical place to store things you need often and in a hurry, primarily because it is such a convenient place to put things in a hurry—your navigation tools get buried. Also, at night it is hard to find anything in the chart table since the lid usually blocks the light when you lift it. Without these proper holders, your tools will eventually fall off the table, or behind something, and get lost or broken. We follow up on this point in the next section on the Nav Station.

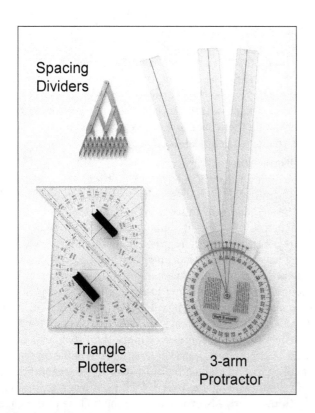

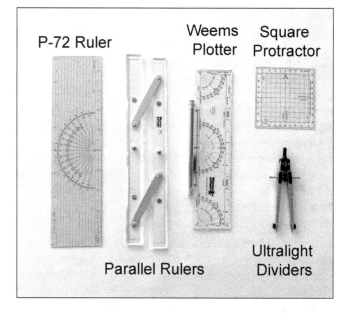

Figure 12.4-1. *Navigation plotting tools. The five items on the right (plotter, parallels, protractor, dividers, and ruler) make up a standard tools kit. The 3-arm protractor is used for 3-body fixes (Section 6-13). The 10-point dividers are a luxury item that is indeed useful in several applications. Triangles are an alternative to parallels or Weems plotter. The very basics are parallel rulers and dividers.*

For completeness, I should mention several other tools that one often hears about. These include multiarmed protractors used for finding position from small angle measurements or other horizontal sextant-angle measurements. They mostly work as intended, but are required only for rather specialized piloting procedures. Their design and use are better saved for a discussion of these special methods. They are especially important on steel hulls where a bearing compass is not reliable. Three-armed protractors are the special ones with a special value; the two-armed and one-armed ones are only dubious options to parallel rulers.

Other proposed alternatives to parallel rulers are large transparent mats with uniform grids printed on them. In some cases, they work nicely, but their main objective is to alleviate the use of parallel rulers and thereby alleviate practice with parallel rulers. And since you can't replace parallel rulers for all jobs with these mats, they are in this sense misguided efficiency. And the list go on... In short, it is hard to replace conventional parallel rulers and dividers for the routine and even specialized tasks of small craft navigation.

12.5 Notes on the Nav Station

Every practicing navigator has an ideal nav station in mind—the place of work, its location, its layout, its tools. The ideal usually comes about the hard way, by ruling out, piece by piece, systems, locations, and things that don't work well. Somehow, things that don't work make a bigger impression than things that do. As it is with learning any aspect of navigation, the best way to find your own ideal is to navigate on different boats. At least with navigation, it won't take too long to find out what works well for you.

Here are a few personal preferences, some more important than others. Having done both, I prefer, for example, to sit facing forward because it is easier for me to think through course changes, tacking angles, wind shifts, and so on when I am facing the way I am going. Chart table work in rough seas is not much different in any direction, if the seat is well designed, and I suspect that if I did it always one way, regardless of what way it was, I would also learn to think more easily in that orientation.

First the seat. A comfortable seat is important because you sit a lot when navigating. Or, rather, you should sit if you can. It's hard to think standing up, as the old saying goes—especially if your back aches, and even the strongest backs ache leaning over a chart table for an hour or more. Luckily it's a rare stand-up chart table that won't accommodate some form of temporary seat. With ingenuity, you can design one that can be removed when not in use to free up the space the stand-up table was intended to provide.

One kind of chart table seat I found very comfortable was cut on an arc so that (when facing forward) you are always sitting straight up-and-down regardless of the boat's heel (Figure 12.5-1). The seat is easy to make from 3/4-inch plywood front and back plates cut with an arc, and then the seat itself made from 1 × 2 slats screwed into the plywood.

The other end of the problem is the feet. For rough going you need some way to get wedged into the chart table seat. One nice solution is a small foot stool built into the sole under the table, or a ledge on the bulkhead in front of the table. These can be custom-made to your leg length so that when in use, your legs are pinned against the bottom of the chart table, holding you in place with hands free. It's best to arrange the design so you can sit comfortably without using this brace since you only need it in rough conditions. Without a curved seat and foot brace, you may need to rig some form of seat belt system that will keep you in place when heeled over or when bouncing about for any reason.

The location of the nav station doesn't matter much. They usually get placed next to the companionway, which is good since you can talk back and forth to the cockpit from there. But this is also a very wet place, so it pays to have a spray curtain built that hangs between you and the

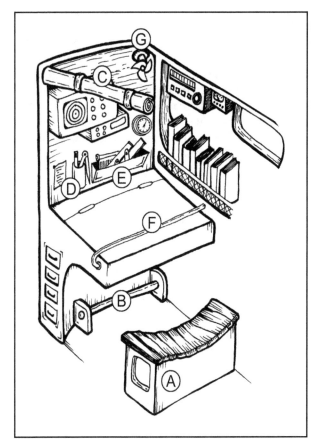

Figure 12.5-1. *An ocean-going nav station. A. Curved seat helps you stay vertical when heeled. B. Footrest so knees can be wedged up under the table to hold you in place in the waves. C. Spray Curtain to keep light in at night, and water out always. Some boats use two; one clear for daylight, one opaque for night. D. Pencil holder, also holds dividers and flashlight. E. Holder for parallel rulers and plotters. F. Bungee to hold chart table lid down. It also holds charts and books in place when underway. G. Fan for navigator's comfort!*

companionway. This serves two purposes. First, it keeps your gear dry—or, more precisely, limits the water on your charts to that which runs off your own rain gear. Second, it blocks out the light, so your work at night does not interfere with the helmsman.

This last point is an important one. The navigator has to work at night, but it is equally important that no light *at all* get out to the cockpit. As you know, even the faintest light makes steering at night very difficult. Going fast in big waves on a dark night, the helmsman has very little for orientation, and it can be dangerous to interfere with that. Often, even stock steering compass lights are too bright in these cases. In short, it pays to think this through so you don't end up duct taping yourself into a cocoon.

As for the nav table lights themselves, I have never seen a specialized nav table light that found its way onto the ideal list. I refer here to the special ones of various designs intended to emit focused light or dim light or red light and so on. The famous, standard goose neck light, for example, is near useless since, goose neck or not, you can't see the whole chart with them. Lift the chart table lid, and you can't see anything. A different, more expensive type that comes close to solving the problem is mounted on a pivot and is detachable for hand use. It has variable intensity and a red light option. Perhaps two or three of these—one stored in a bag for hand use, since they can be difficult to get in and out of the pivot—might do the job, but it is not just a matter of buying one of these fancy lights and screwing it into wherever it seems to fit best. In any event, a small flashlight in the tools holder is a must for special use, such as reading dials, corners of a chart, etc.

For longer stints at the nav station, I prefer a fixed white light over the table and then cover the entire area someway. For shorter tasks, a handheld flashlight does the job providing it has a permanent home near the table so you can always find it when you need it. Individuals will likely differ on this, but I find it difficult to see pencil lines in red light. Also, the coloring on charts looks different in red light and takes some getting used to. Red light, by the way, has no special significance to protecting night vision. The main factor is intensity, and red lights are not bright; hence their value. A low-level white light is just as good, and to me much preferable.

Seat and light are important, but not the most important. The most important aids to navigation, without doubt, are a pencil holder (for pencils, dividers, and flashlight) and a holder for your parallel rulers or plotter that is within arm's reach, *outside of the chart table*. With these holders, you can always find your tools when you need them and you always have a place to put them between uses. Otherwise, they will get lost or broken. Without these holders, sometime in life you will want to draw a line, can't find a pencil, won't draw the line, and later regret it.

My favorite pencil holder is a short tube attached to a shelf or bulkhead. The tube from an empty toilet paper roll does the job in a pinch—duct taped over the bottom, with tissue stuffed inside to protect the bottom from divider points, then taped to the wall. This elegant design has made it across oceans more than once. It holds pencils, pencil-type erasers, and dividers. As soon as engine keys, sunglasses, and various other things start appearing in it, remind people what the chart table is for! A tall square plastic fruit juice bottle is ideal for this type of pencil holder, and this is the type I have used for years, always having a few on hand and taking one onto each new boat. Some time ago, in a magazine story about Volvo Ocean Race boats, they showed the nav station of one boat that had more than $75,000 worth of electronic nav gear, and right in the middle of this stuff, taped to the bulkhead, was this exact type of juice bottle used for a pencil holder. Needless to say, this vessel won my heart immediately.

The space inside the chart table, under the lid, is essentially useless space to navigation. This may seem surprising, but check under the lids of a few chart tables to get the point—and you may get just that, the point of the dividers! The chart table is simply too convenient a place to store what ever has to be put down in a hurry. My standard advice is this: Make an absolute rule that nothing at all gets put into the chart table. Then, when it fills to overflowing, just forget about it. You will not be counting on that space.

Nevertheless, you still have a chart table lid to deal with, which must be secured for a 180° roll. We forgot that once during a pre-race inspection, and we were cited for it. But during the time the inspector checked the rest of the boat, we drilled a hole in the side of the chart table and one in the board beside it and stretched a bungee cord between them secured with figure eights inside to hold down the lid. To lift the lid, just pull the cord toward you; then put it back when you close the lid. This passed muster, and off we went. However, this rule-beater solution actually turned out to be excellent. The cord not only does not get in the way, but serves very nicely for holding down charts and books while underway. I have since used this same system on every ocean voyage with this type of standard chart table lid. You can remove the bungee in calm waters, and the holes are barely noticeable. Or use bails underneath the table.

If you carry a backup steering compass, the chart table top is a good place to store it, so it can be used for navigation reference at the table. When mounting it, keep in mind what might be stored under it in drawers. Check it occasionally with the steering compass, and if they disagree, start pulling drawers open to see whether the compass needle moves. If it does, you found the villain.

Some handheld bearing compasses can be mounted on or near the chart table and used for reference, but a dedicated, adjustable compass is the best bet. These days, a digital fluxgate compass or an electronic repeater from a remote heading sensor is the more likely option for a magnetic heading reference at the nav station. It is generally best to mount the handheld bearing compass just inside the companionway so it can be reached from the cockpit without going below. Again, it will be used more often if it is easy to get to. Needless to say, an independent compass at the nav station has to be adjusted and its calibration monitored.

Besides the compass, it is very convenient to have electronic readouts at the nav station for all navigation instruments. This makes logbook entries easier for everyone and makes the tactics easier for the navigator. Several of the navigator's tasks require knowing compass heading and knotmeter speed—such as solving true wind computations, figuring set and drift from GPS values of COG and SOG—and if you have speed and heading at hand, you do not have to keep asking for it from the cockpit. The never-ending question of the navigator "What is our course?" can then be answered without disturbing anyone. (In most cases like this, you want to know what they are steering, not the actual COG at the moment or the CMG displayed on the echart.)

Keeping the desired course in print in view of the helmsman is another (sort of) nav station issue to be solved. The value of having this written down on deck for quick reference cannot be over emphasized. When the course changes, cross out the old and write in the new. This will help everyone stay on course and be a quick reference if forgotten in fatigue or tension of quick steering in waves. In the old days of sailing, they had elaborate mechanical or manual devices for recording the course called a *course box*, always posted in direct view of the helmsman (Figure 12.5-2).

A modern solution is ScotchBlue Painter's Tape from 3M. It is a remarkable tape that stays in place, even if wet, and comes off cleanly after weeks of exposure. You can write on it with a Sharpie pen for quick notes to yourself or use it for reminders to the helm, such as course to steer or notes on the next leg. An example is shown in Figure 12.5-3. You can also use it to annotate charts or books you do not want to write on—a definite must-have for the nav station.

Unless it is intended for decoration, the barometer should be mounted in the nav station in clear view of someone standing next to the chart table—this is where most crew stand when filling in the logbook. To be of any value

at all, you must be able to look straight onto the barometer dial to minimize parallax, and many aneroid devices must be tapped gently to get an accurate reading, though the higher quality units should be friction free and not need this—though we would likely do it anyway because of tradition. Generally, we are looking for small changes in pressure, and you simply can't gauge these from an angle, leaning over obstructions. It should also have a flashlight mounted next to it for nighttime reading. Again, if it is not convenient to get readings from it, logbook entries of pressure will be of little value. A well-positioned barometer can be valuable even for inland day sailing or racing. New developments in electronic barometers offer another potentially more accurate and convenient option, though good ones might cost as much as a high-quality aneroid.

For offshore sailing, an easily accessible rack for the sextant case is crucial. It can also be very valuable for inland and coastal sailing as well. Distance off and precision position fixing from vertical and horizontal sextant angles are important practical techniques in navigation that do not get used much, in part because most boats don't have a sextant handy (we cover the methods in Chapter 6). Some vessels that do carry a sextant have it so buried that it rarely gets used.

One solution is a convenient rack for the box, or better still, some arrangement that mounts the box itself to the bulkhead. I have often found that the bulkhead between nav station and quarter berth is a good place to mount such a rack. The sextant is then inside the quarter berth, but high enough not to take up useful space, and easy to reach standing next to the nav station.

With the box mounted, after you take the sextant out, you do not have to worry about storing the box with only one hand free. A sextant sight to measure the angular height of a hill is then just as convenient as taking a bear-

Figure 12.5-3. *ScotchBlue Painter's Tape from 3M. A boater's friend; it has many uses for notes and temporary labeling onboard. Photo courtesy of Starpath instructor Larry Brandt on a trip from Portland to Seattle. Such notes are especially helpful when navigating shorthanded.*

Figure 12.5-2. *Russian course box seen on eBay.*

ing to it. A bearing and a sextant height gives you a fix. If this hill is the only thing in sight, you have just done a nice piece of navigation. As noted in the discussion of the sextant methods, a simple plastic sextant will do the job quite adequately, and these would be even easier to mount in a convenient location.

For extended sailing, it pays to have headphone adaptors on all radios. This way the navigator can listen to weather reports without disturbing the off watch. It's also very helpful to have a built-in tape recorder, or a rack for your personal tape recorder, smartphone, or digital recorder near the radios. You can then record weather broadcasts. If reception is poor, you need the recording to replay several times to get the message. Other times, you may be busy or needed on deck. You can have the recorder set up and the radio tuned, and then just turn things on when your wrist alarm goes off, and go back to whatever duty calls. Or you can ask someone to turn on the recorder and radio at a particular time and let you sleep.

Although many of us get by these days without a wristwatch on land, using the cellphone for time, once we set off in a boat, it might be time to reconsider wearing a watch. You don't want to endanger your expensive mobile device, when your need of the time and timer while navigating can be met easily with an inexpensive watch. A list of items to be considered for the nav station is given in Table 12.5-1.

One thing I learned the hard way a long time ago was the value of a small, battery-operated nav station fan. Its purpose is simply to help cool off the navigator in hot weather. And before you start thinking "wimp," let me give an ocean racing scenario from back in the days when we actually navigated by cel nav. It is 90° on deck in the tropics with a nice breeze, but it is well over 100° below decks with no breeze. Eight sailors have been living in a 9 × 25 × 6-foot space for 12 days with no laundry service and a forgotten can of frozen orange juice that somehow fell behind a locker and exploded one week ago. The boat is pitching and rolling in the Trades. The other seven crew are on deck having a great time in the fresh air, on their way to setting an elapsed-time record that will last 20 years—but the navigator is below decks with head spinning in the wooze, working out sun sights that must be done in an hour for the afternoon position report. Now wouldn't you grant this poor soul a small fan?

12.6 Tacking DR and Progress to Weather

The key to long-term success in navigation is good DR. In its broadest sense, it means figuring the best estimate of your present and future positions without piloting or electronic aids, using all other information available to you.

Your log and compass readings are the starting points, but then there are many corrections and adjustments to make, not the least of which are tied to the strength and direction of the wind.

Table 12.5-1 Nav Station Supplies
Penlight style flashlight (for the pencil holder)
Pencils and sharpener (well tested ahead of time)
Dividers (ultralight speed bow is top choice by far)
Parallel Rules (15" clear plastic is popular)
360° square protractor
Large ruler (for extending lines and more, P72)
Weems rolling plotter (when it works, it works well)
Erasers (pencil type and larger gum type)
Large post-office rubber bands (for organizing things)
Industrial Velcro (for improvised mounting of things)
Highlight markers (several colors)
Sharpie pens (fine point and bold, several colors)
ScotchBlue Painter's Tape roll (for notes and labels)
Navigation notebook (for personal records)
Some form of course box

Before looking at how strong winds affect our navigation to weather, let us back up and review some basics about tacking.

Tacking

When sailing into the wind over a completely uniform waterway, your progress forward is measured entirely relative to the wind direction. Two destinations that are the

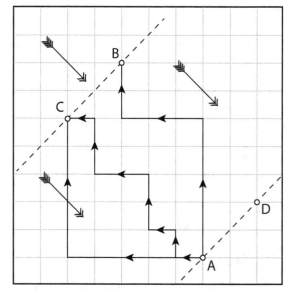

Figure 12.6-1. *Tacking distances. C is closer to A than is B, but it is not closer in time when tacking to weather. Assuming a 45° true wind angle, we must follow the 1-mile grid shown. Start at A and count the miles from A to B and A to C by any route. They are all 10 nmi long. A couple of options are shown. Likewise, in a yacht race, the two boats A and D are equally far from either mark B or C, because they each have the same distance to travel upwind. In practice, however, it could be one was favored over the other based on anticipated wind or current changes. Also, each tack costs some speed and time, so we have to balance out minimum tacks with getting farther off the rhumb line, which has greater exposure to changes in conditions.*

same distance upwind, are the same distance from you regardless of the direct (rhumbline) distance to either. This is a fundamental point in sailing, which is easy to overlook. Referring to Figure 12.6-1, destination C is closer to vessel A than is B, but A and B are the same distance upwind, so it will take the same time to tack to either one.

The key to figuring precise tacking times is knowing the true wind angle (TWA) you are tacking through, but this is not always an easy computation. It varies from boat to boat and from one wind speed to another, and it requires carefully calibrated instruments to determine. Thus we have much to gain for our planning by having a simple approximation.

The estimate starts by figuring the distance to weather (upwind) that you must travel. If your destination is directly upwind, this is just the rhumbline distance to the destination (like A to C in Figure 12.6-1), but if the destination is not directly upwind (like B in Figure 12.6-1) you still have to use the distance upwind, and not the true rhumbline distance. Then we just multiply this upwind distance by 1.5 to estimate the total distance we have to sail, either to a point like C or to one like B. So we can write:

Tacking Distance = 1.5 × Upwind Distance.

The 1.5 factor is an approximation. The exact factor should be something like: Tacking distance = (upwind distance) × [1/cos(TWA)] + about 10%, where TWA is the true wind angle. Here, we assume TWA = 45°, so 1/cos(45) = 1.414, and we add 0.14 to get about 1.58, which we call 1.5! A high-performance yacht might do 40°, so that is 1.10 × [1/cos(40)] = 1.4, whereas a cruising yacht may do 50°, and the factor then is 1.10 × [1/cos(50)] = 1.7. Note the fudge factor of 1.10 is just our truth meter to account for tacking times, and we do not always sail a perfect leg, etc.

The factor of 1.5 is easy to remember, and we also know that things change, so fine-tuning might not always be justified. The very best would be 1.4, but a more typical or conservative estimate might be 1.7, thus we just use 1.5 and accept some uncertainties.

Leeway

Tacking or motoring into strong persistent headwinds brings a new twist to navigation that has a serious affect on DR if not accounted for. Three factors that don't come to mind much in light air now matter a lot. These are wind-driven current, helm bias, and leeway—though we should keep leeway in mind in light air as well. They are each fairly small effects, even in strong winds, but they all cause error in the same direction, so their sum is not small. They cause navigational error because they are invisible—they take us off course, and we have no way of knowing it until the next position fix. In short, we must simply make an educated guess of their individual sets and drifts and correct our DR accordingly.

Leeway is how much a boat slips to leeward on a windward course. It is a function of the boat's draft, the point of

sail (angle into the wind), and the wind speed. Under sail, it is only a navigational factor when going to weather close-hauled in strong winds—or very light wind, but that is not the subject here. The effect is distinctly different from current set because we can in principle measure leeway underway (even without electronics in some cases), so it is not strictly invisible as implied above. A typical keel boat of 6-foot draft might slip as much as 10° to leeward in a solid 15 kts of true wind. Yacht design specs might have this number as just a few degrees, but here we are discussing the reality of navigation, not a design parameter that may have a more complex interpretation.

Leeway is equally, if not sometimes more, important in a powerboat, but it is difficult to predict because the boats and conditions are so varied. A shallow-draft, low-powered, high-freeboard vessel might travel almost sideways in a strong wind, as would a sailboat without a keel under power. The same is true in a kayak or rowboat. Understanding leeway for your specific vessel is a matter of experience.

Leeway can be discerned in your GPS-derived data in special cases. For example, if the wind has just started to blow (so it has not had time to generate any surface current) and there are no other sources of current in the waterway, then when headed upwind, you will find your average COG to be some degrees to leeward of your average compass heading when steering a steady course on the wind, whereas your average SOG will match your average knotmeter speed. When this happens symmetrically on both tacks (wind on either side of the vessel), you have a nice snapshot of your leeway. Sometimes, you can actually see your wake bent to windward (Figure 12.6-2), which is the same effect. Yacht designers have developed underwater gimbaled vanes that measure the angle of motion through the water relative to the centerline for an accurate measurement of leeway versus wind speed and heeling angle.

With WAAS-enabled GPS, leeway shows up very nicely on units that directly compute current based on SOG and

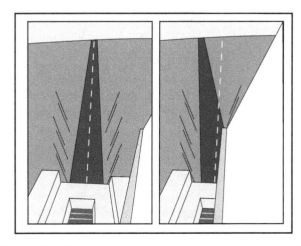

Figure 12.6-2. *Leeway seen in wake angle. Left no leeway; right with leeway. In old days, the sailing masters would trim their sails to keep the "wake straight astern."*

COG compared with accurate inputs of knotmeter speed and vessel heading. Going to weather in still water, you will have current on your windward beam regardless of your tack.

From a practical point of view, you can ignore leeway as soon as you fall off the wind in a typical sailboat. Above some 45° apparent you can forget it unless you are still well heeled over or have other evidence that you might be slipping. This large reduction in leeway with a relatively small course change is not likely to apply to powerboats with notable leeway. Remember that leeway, unlike current, adds uncertainty only to your course direction, not your speed. In slack water, your knotmeter speed is your SOG even as you are slipping with leeway.

Leeway depends on wind speed for all vessels, but its behavior is easier to anticipate under sail. If your optimum sailing wind speed is 10 kts true, then leeway increases going both up and down from there. In one sense, this is how optimum wind speeds are defined for sailing vessels. If it is, say, 6° at optimum, then by the time you get to 20 kts, it might be as high as 15°. In practice, however, it doesn't get much higher than this in normal operations because by then you start to fall off—except in some well designed race boats, it just doesn't pay to pound into the waves in very strong winds. And once you fall off, the slipping stops. Likewise, at very low winds (a knot or two), you will also slip a lot, but again at some point, you fall off and it goes away.

Leeway also depends on keel depth—keel depth is more important than keel shape, which is important for powerboaters and paddlers as well as sailors to keep in mind. Sailing a kayak, for example, just a paddle down in the water makes a world of difference. Likewise, to first approximation, a fin-type racing keel and a full-length cruising keel are about the same in this regard for a given depth. The high-tech fin keel, however, can make up a lot by the actual lift it adds as water flows over it as wind does on airplane wings. We have recently seen amazing sailing performance of AC72 "keels" in the 2013 America's Cup catamarans. They actually used leeway (pointing angle) versus speed as a tuning parameter depending on the wind speed.

Wind-driven Current

Leeway occurs in all waters, regardless of actual current flow. In strong winds, however, no water (ocean or lake) will remain still for long. When the wind blows steadily for half a day or longer, it generates a surface current in any body of water. This new wind-driven current (wind drift) must be added vectorially to the prevailing ocean or tidal current, or treated as a new issue in areas with no natural currents.

As a rule of thumb, the strength of the wind drift is some 2.5% of the wind strength, directed 15° to 30° to the right of the wind in higher northern latitudes and to the left of the wind in higher southern latitudes. In central latitudes, the set is more in line with the wind. In Puget Sound or

Juan de Fuca Strait and similar confined waterways where the land constrains the wind to flow along the waterway, wind drift here can be figured as essentially parallel to the waterways—with or against the tidal flow. In any waters, though, a 25-kt steady wind for a day or so will generate a current flowing downwind of up to 0.6 kts.

In long, heavy rains, the wind-driven current tends to be larger, since the brackish surface layer slips more easily over the denser salt water below. In extreme cases, you might expect surface wind drift of over 3% in long, strong winds with much rain. Estimates of wind-driven currents are shown in Figure 12.6-3.

Helm Bias

Helm bias is even more evasive in our navigation reckoning, under power or sail. Strong winds bring high seas (at least in the ocean) and with them the problem of steering over them. It is usually possible in these circumstances to detect a persistent course alteration at each wave. A common tendency going to weather is to fall off or get pushed off slightly at each wave. The only way to gauge this effect on the average course manually is to stand and watch the helm and compass for some time, and then make a guess at an average offset.

Or simply look at a GPS track of past positions, which is what one would do in a normal situation—although it would still be difficult to pull out the helm bias from leeway and wind-driven current in some cases.

We are discussing DR here, however, and that means we are assuming we don't have electronic aids to look at. But it does bring up the important point that the best use of such wonderful nav aids is to use them to teach us about DR. In other words, when the waves start to build, confirm with the helmsman what course is being steered, and then watch the plot of positions to see what is being made good

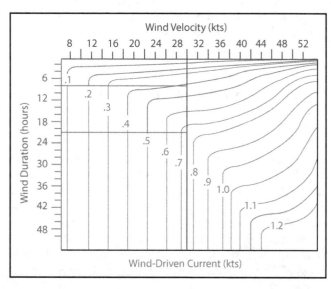

Figure 12.6-3. *Wind-driven current as a function of wind speed and duration. For 30 kts of wind, we expect 0.4 kts current in 8 hours, building to just over 0.7 kts in 21 hours.*

(CMG). There can, of course, be other influences (the subject at hand), but by noting what is being made good and then just standing there and watching the compass and the helm for a while, you can see what is taking place.

We are looking at going to weather here, which won't happen much in strong winds unless you are racing or trying to claw off a coast after getting in too close, but this same helm bias occurs going downwind as well. The bias headed downwind tends to be to leeward in big waves and fresh air, but under sail in light air, it might tend to be upwind in big waves as you try to keep the boat moving. So the summary is going to weather helm bias will most likely be to leeward, but going downwind, it could be either way. Again, helm bias means we end up steering on average a different course than we intended to. It has been a known factor needed for accurate DR since at least the 1600s.

If you are navigating a race boat, there can be numerous types of helm bias to watch out for, and they might be personality driven. Some drivers like to go fast regardless of what the course is supposed to be. Others might choose a more conservative course than called for to avoid the risk of rounding up.

Here's an example to sum up these invisible problems. Going to weather across a 0.6 knot wind drift at 6 kts would set you off course some 5°, your leeway might be some 10°, and a helm bias account for another 5°. In this case, the overall off-course set is about 20°. In the ocean, after 100 nmi, you would be 30 to 40 nmi off course to leeward if you did not figure these factors into your DR. Summarized another way, going to weather in a steady 20 to 25 kts of wind, will most likely cost you at least 20° of CMG.

When sailing to weather in strong winds, you will always be slipping downwind more than you might guess. While the GPS is still working, keep a record of what angles you actually tack through in big waves and strong winds—not compass headings, but the actual angle between the two track lines on the echart plot. If you end up having to DR in these conditions without electronics, then it is usually a reasonable first guess to assume you did indeed cover the miles your log indicates, but then simply set the CMG some 20° to leeward.

When racing or cruising, there is an obvious advantage to tacking at the right time. If the electronics take a hike when you need them, these are the basics to fall back on. The compass headings alone won't help. In the above example, it would mean overstanding the windward mark by 20°.

12.7 Sailing the US West Coast

We include this very specific route planning discussion knowing full well that not all readers anticipate this particular voyage, because it shows the type of reasoning and planning that can be carried out for any extended coastal voyage, in any part of the world.

From Point Conception, CA, to Cape Flattery, WA, is some 900 nmi, northwest then north along the coast. Another 70 nmi inland along the 12-nmi wide Strait of Juan de Fuca between Canada and Washington puts you in the San Juan Islands, and just beyond them lie the Canadian Gulf Islands. Together, these island groups offer some of the best cruising in the world, with good weather extending from early May to the end of September.

At 7 kts on the rhumbline, one could (in principle) get from Point Conception to the Islands in 6 days—tacking the whole way would extend this (again, in principle) to some 10 days. This trip, however, is not a straightforward matter of geometric navigation along or across a rhumbline. It has been remarked more than once by Northwest sailors who went on to circumnavigate the globe that their biggest challenge underway was getting down the coast to southern California. This voyage, in either direction—even at the best times—calls for careful planning and prudent seamanship. West Coast weather changes at Point Conception. The challenge of the US West Coast is usually north of this point.

There is no inside passage along this leg; it is open water, often at the business end of Pacific weather patterns. Although there are indeed a number of beautiful harbors along the coasts of Northern California, Oregon, and Washington, they can't be counted on for refuge—it could be more dangerous to attempt an entry than to stay offshore. The best reference for the voyage is the *US Coast Pilot, Vol 7*, and for these harbors in particular, a Coast Guard publication called *Guide to the Hazardous Bars on the Pacific Coast* listed in the references. These ports are at the mouths of rivers, and the river bars are dangerous to even large high-powered vessels when strong ebbs meet deep ocean swells. In these conditions, you are faced with steep breaking waves, strong cross currents, and narrow entrances—and, as often as not, in the fog.

This passage does not lend itself to gunkholing up or down the coast. In favorable conditions, there are places to stop, but the full trip under sail or power is long enough that there is no way (even in midsummer) to be guaranteed favorable wind and seas farther along. The trip must be shaped as an ocean passage without planned stops, and then see what develops as far as stopping goes. It is a voyage better thought of as a delivery rather than a cruise. When conditions are good, make miles, rather than dally in the pretty places.

As a purely practical matter, if the primary goal is to cruise your own vessel in the Northwest, as opposed to the broader goal of getting there and back on your own bottom, then it is worth considering shipping the boat by truck. In the end, unless your vessel and crew are already ocean ready, the cost (in time and dollars) will be about the same or less by truck.

Now with why and how to avoid it safely behind us, we can get on with how to do it. After all, there is to be had a certain satisfaction, pondering a map of North America, recollecting a voyage from this point here, clear around to that point there, in the summer of such and such, knowing what it's really like in the blue part just off that point, and so on. And there is no way to get into that state of mind without putting in the miles.

First, this is a late spring or summertime trip. Statistics for strong wind, big seas, and fog are shown in Figure 12.7-1. Prevailing summer weather is dominated by the Pacific High, typically centered some 1,000 nmi west of San Francisco. The clockwise circulation around the High, brings north-northwest winds off the coast that peak in late July and August. These are usually light winds of some 15 kts, but they can build to a sustained 30 kts in special circumstances.

The origin of these stronger winds is a trough of low pressure that periodically builds over the deserts of California and Nevada. The trough packs up the isobars along the coast, forming a tight gradient along the California coast. These are stable weather patterns that can last for days, resulting in strong steady northerly winds over a fetch of 500 nmi. Consequently, the real problem is the sea state. Combine these big wind waves with a northwesterly swell from some far-off storm in the North Pacific, and you end up with steep chaotic seas, especially along the edge of the continental shelf.

In these special circumstances, it is difficult going at night headed south and nearly impossible to make progress northward, night or day. These patterns are well forecasted, however, and easy to detect on weather maps. And again, this is a potential pattern, not the most likely one. More typically, one is dealing with light to fresh northerly winds and their associated seas. Generally, May or June is a good time to head north, before the high firms up offshore.

How far offshore to make the passage? Some cruising guides recommend traveling far offshore (100 nmi or more); others argue for running right along the coast. The distinction between far offshore and close inshore, in this case, however, is not really a matter of how many miles from the coastline. The key reference here is the location of the continental shelf, which occurs at some 100 fathoms. Inside of 100 fathoms, the depth gradually diminishes as you proceed inshore; outside of the shelf, it falls off rapidly to the deep ocean bottom. South of Monterey Bay, the shelf is only some 5 nmi offshore; farther north, the shelf extends out 20 to 40 nmi. Along the entire coast, at 60 nmi offshore, you are definitely in the ocean. It is unlikely that you would experience much different conditions at 100 nmi off than you would at 60 nmi off.

As a rule, the sea state changes at the shelf. Offshore, the waves are bigger, but longer and more organized. At the shelf they are steeper and more confused, and as you proceed farther inshore, they eventually diminish. It is a good idea to draw in the shelf on the chart with a highlight marker and then keep track of where you are relative to it, along with notes on the sea state. Tacking north offshore,

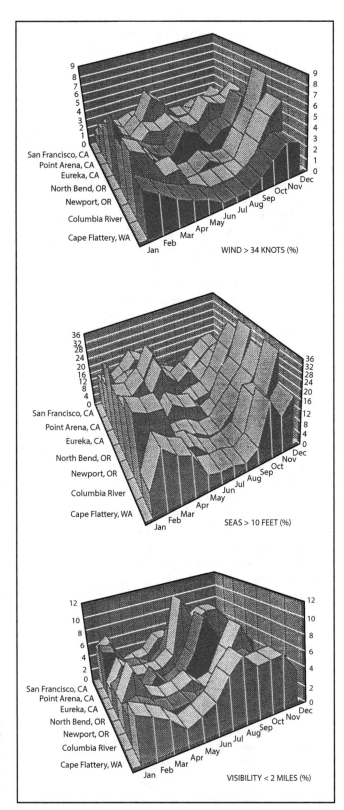

Figure 12.7-1. *Data adapted from the* US Coast Pilot, Vol. 7, *based on ship reports. Since vessels tend to avoid bad weather when possible, these data underestimate the percent frequencies listed, but the seasonal variations and relative distributions along the coast remain valuable guidelines. Notice the window for lower wind and seas does not coincide with the window for less fog. Figure from the Starpath Weather Trainer Live.*

you should be able to detect the steepening of the waves as you get into the shelf region on your inbound tack, which should help plan how far in to carry the next tack.

My own definite bias (north or south bound), however, is to take the inshore road, traveling point to point along the coast and even heading inshore of this line if the seas or adverse winds build. But there are pros and cons and some provisos involved.

The all-important seas are definitely better close inshore than they are offshore. To check this from anywhere in the US, you can use the online data from the National Buoy Center or call the Dial-a-Buoy service to get live data from a particular buoy or lighthouse (888-701-8992).

When you have 6 to 8 ft significant wave heights offshore, you can have 1 to 3 ft inshore, which for some vessels is go versus no-go when you must go against it. With a computer modem available, the offshore and inshore coastal reports can be compared at home easily and inexpensively by using one of the various sources listed in the references. These computerized data are sometimes more current than even the latest VHF radio broadcasts.

Now back to the fog. The point-to-point route has better seas but puts you in traffic. Shipping traffic takes this route and there are fishing fleets to work through, and throughout July and August, this coast is famous for fog. Consequently, to take advantage of calmer seas inshore, one needs radar and some practice in using it for collision avoidance. Again, May is a good time for heading north because the fog is also less likely then. May or June is not an optimum time for heading south, however, because if the winds do build then, they are just as likely to be from the south.

On the inshore route, you have VHF coverage the entire time for NOAA weather, Coast Guard information on bar conditions and relays of coastal weather, and periodically some cell phone connections. A satellite phone is an obvious bonus for communications. They are available as rentals, weekly or monthly.

You can also check with passing traffic for weather conditions ahead. Sometimes, there are areas of significant local winds that are not yet reported on the weather broadcasts. One time headed south, a northbound fisherman we met at about 90 fathoms volunteered that the wind 10 nmi farther south was already at 30 kts, but that if we headed in to 30 fathoms, we would be OK. He was right.

In any event, a continual watch on channel 16 is crucial for this passage (not to mention required by law). You will use it to clarify passing arrangements with traffic when needed and get updates on lights and buoys from the Coast Guard. It will remind you to listen to the Coast Guard weather relays (which give information farther along your route than you can pick up from the local VHF stations) and you can (and should) monitor Vessel Traffic Service broadcasts near the approaches to San Francisco and Cape Flattery. Coastal weather services are explained in detail on NOAA's Marine Weather Services Charts 9 (Point Conception to Point St. George) and 10 (Point St. George to Canadian Border).

Besides avoiding traffic, the standard argument for sailing offshore is to have plenty of sea room in bad conditions, which is, of course, good reasoning, because refuge inside a harbor at a river bar is unlikely once conditions have deteriorated—Crescent City, at the CA-OR border, could be the only open harbor between San Francisco and Cape Flattery, and sometimes San Francisco, itself, is a challenge to get into for a low-powered vessel. If I were close enough to shore, however, to check on inshore conditions by radio, I would still check them and consider hanging out at the sea buoy (first buoy at the channel entrance to a harbor from the sea) as one possibility. It could be that the bar is too rough to cross, but conditions at the sea buoy could be much moderated over what they are out in deeper water. The Coast Guard will tell you when it is not safe to cross a bar, but I have never heard them say it is safe to cross a bar; they only report conditions. Likewise, they will report conditions at the sea buoy if they know them, but my guess is they would rarely say it is better to be one place rather than another. These are decisions we must make. Also remember if you are at the entrance to a large harbor there could be a lot of traffic coming by, so a careful watch and proper lights are crucial. We are choosing between a rock and a hard place in tough conditions. (If you are confident of your GPS you might not need the visual reference of the buoy and choose to wait some distance from the buoy. With radar you can keep an eye on the buoy location without being in visual sight of it.)

The sea room argument definitely applies to storms and severe fronts (certain in winter, possible in early spring and fall), but these are not the typical problems in a summertime trip along the coast. Summer storms are possible, but the more typical problem here is strong north winds and big seas in otherwise good weather—clear sunny skies and warm temperatures (when not in pea soup fog!)—caused by the Pacific High-California Trough interaction. These conditions usually moderate inshore, and often significantly moderate at night inshore while seas and winds are still piped up offshore. The strong gradient winds are more northerly than the lay of the coast line below Cape Mendocino, so there is some blocking that takes place inshore in that area, as happens on a smaller scale at each indentation of the coast.

Currents are usually not a major factor in the overall passage. Off the shelf, the current averages some half knot or so to the south. On the shelf, the current is primarily wind driven, running north in the winter from prevailing south wind, and running south in the summer from prevailing north wind. Again, speeds of much more than half a knot or so would be rare, except for the enhanced tidal flow near major headlands and at harbor entrances, which rotate directions with the tides. Approaching any harbor, careful monitoring is required to correct for sideways sets.

Summary

In many circumstances, heading way offshore to make this coastal route is simply adding a few days to the passage in order to get into rougher conditions.

Radar is somewhere between very desirable and mandatory for a trip along the coast. At any time of year, the trip should be planned as an open ocean, heavy-weather voyage, without planned stops. High seas communications are valuable for the offshore route. Headed in either direction, if a storm or bad front were forecasted once underway (usually bringing southerly winds), I would figure the ETA to the nearest harbor and check by radio for estimated conditions at the bar and sea buoy at that time and balance that information with forecasted offshore conditions. Intentions to get across a bar must be activated early before swells from the storm close the bar. I would assure that there were at least two people on board that could run the vessel, because strenuous conditions could develop and last for several days. I would have the engine in good condition and plenty of fuel.

Headed south by sail from WA, consider July or August. I would plan an inshore, point-to-point route down the coast—or with no strong winds off CA forecast after a day or so, I would go more directly south, ending up farther offshore with bigger waves to surf in. If the reported seas off CA from the Trough-High interaction start to build significantly, I would head inshore for a more sheltered run. In any event, plan on giving the several major headlands along the route a wide passing.

Headed north from CA, consider May or June, again planning an inshore route, heading farther out only if you are assured of favorable winds there with none inshore. With no real wind either place, I would motor the whole way and not wait for it. With strong winds developing from the north, consider heading more inshore at each opportunity, but still giving the headlands a wide clearing coming out from behind them.

USCG References

NGA and NOAA products on navigation and weather are available from several sources. For paper charts, see nauticalcharts.noaa.gov, which includes a list of regional chart dealers. For echarts, we maintain an updated link at starpath.com/getcharts. *US Coast Pilot Volume 7: Pacific Coast,* California, Oregon, *Washington, and Hawaii* is a primary reference for the route. It includes monthly weather and sea state statistics as well as descriptions of the harbors en route. A list of Coast Guard stations along the coast is in the *Coast Pilot* appendix. *USCG Special Notices to Mariners* is published annually but available throughout the year online. It includes a summary of information unique to the waters covered as well as general information on seamanship and regulations. The 13th District edition includes a section called *Guide to Hazardous Bars.* It can be downloaded along with other valuable information at uscg.mil/d13.

Marine Weather Services Charts

These handy publications are no longer supported by NOAA, except No. 15 for Alaskan waters. This NOAA link has it and other related publications: www.weather.gov/marine/pub. Because they are so valuable, we have an article on how you can make your own "MSC," meaning compile the same information, described at this link: davidburchnavigation.blogspot.com/2015/03/marine-weather-services-chart-how-to.html. MSC data includes all radio sources of marine weather along the coast with descriptions and schedules of the products.

Internet and SatPhone Sources of Weather

There are numerous sources of weather including hourly satellite cloud photos as well as weather maps every six hours. Start with National Data Buoy Center (ndbc.noaa.gov) for the latest observations and recent past conditions. Weather maps are at the Ocean Prediction Center (ocean.weather.gov). For coastal routes check out the Unified Analysis maps. OPC provides these every 6 hours, but they are actually updated every 3 hours at the Weather Prediction Center (www.wpc.ncep.noaa.gov). The best climatic wind data are at the COGOW site (numbat.coas.oregonstate.edu/cogow).

Further References

To learn about modern resources and their application, see *Modern Marine Weather* (starpath.com/weatherbook). To learn or refresh radar usage, see *Radar for Mariners* (starpath.com/radarbook). Both books are available in various ebook formats convenient for reference underway.

Charlie's Charts of the U.S. Pacific Coast by Charles and Margo Wood, include notes and sketches of harbors from San Diego to Seattle, with general notes on the route. They are available at nautical bookstores or from the publisher, and are a valuable supplement to the *Coast Pilot* information for small craft boaters.

12.8 How to Check a Compass

The steering compass is a fundamental aid to navigation. It tells us which way we are going. Out of sight of known landmarks, it is our primary means of orientation. It is important that the compass works right, and equally important that we know some way to check that it works right.

There are standard ways of doing this that we won't get into now, except for this: They all involve sailing a known magnetic course (read from a chart) and comparing this magnetic course with the compass reading. If the two agree, you have no compass error (deviation) on that course, and if they don't, your error is the difference between the two. The standard reference for this topic is the *Handbook of Magnetic Compass Adjustment*, which is available online.

Figure 12.10-1 is a sample of a charted option useful for this type of compass. Another example of a convenient place for this type of check is the breakwater at the Shilshole Bay Marina (Figure 12.10-2), which can be readily seen online in Google Earth. It is oriented at 021.2 True, so with a 16.0° E variation, the magnetic bearing headed north is 005.2 M. Sailing north parallel to the breakwater, your compass should read 005.2 C; sailing south along the breakwater, the compass should read 185.2 C. Similar locations or charted ranges are available in most waterways.

Or, as a quick check anywhere, compare your steering compass with a handheld bearing compass, held well away from iron rigging, some eye-glass frames, etc. If these two compasses disagree after careful comparisons, the error is probably in the steering compass. (Careful means you should take a handheld bearing to a distant object continuously as you swing ship to be sure you are standing in a magnetic disturbance-free place. If the distant bearing does not change, your location is good.)

Instead, we will discuss another, more versatile method. It may not get you a fraction of a degree accuracy, but it could save the day in a pinch.

With the following trick, you can check your compass anytime, without any aids at all, even if you don't know where you are and don't have a chart, or even in the middle of the ocean with no knowledge of celestial navigation. In short, this is a good trick. It deserves a niche near the top of your bag of tricks.

The trick is based on the principle that a compass with error on one compass heading should have an equal and opposite error on the opposite compass heading, which is a good assumption for nonsteel boats. We then make an approximation to this principle that allows us to use it in a practical way, as explained later on. First, the procedure:

STEP 1. Pick a distant landmark that is near dead ahead on the compass heading you wish to check. Sail straight toward it, and note the compass reading. Example: A prominent peak on the horizon, 5 or 6 nmi away, lies dead ahead, and the compass reads 220 C (the letter C labels the heading as read from the compass; the letter M labels magnetic headings read from the chart).

STEP 2. Now figure the compass heading that is directly opposite your landmark. Example: 220-180=040 C.

STEP 3. Now turn and sail directly away from the distant landmark, and note the new compass heading. If the compass heading sailing away from the landmark is exactly 180° off of the compass heading sailing toward the landmark, then your compass has no error on the toward or away headings. If the away compass heading is not exactly 180° different from the toward compass heading, then your compass has error on both headings, toward and away.

Example: If the compass reads 040 as we sail away, then we have verified that the compass works right on compass headings 040 C and 220 C. In other words, when the compass reads 220 C, we are indeed sailing a magnetic course 220 M, which we can read from or plot directly on the chart using the magnetic rose scale printed on all nautical charts. Remember, though, that a compass with error on any heading will have different errors, or no error, on other headings. So this check has only verified that the compass is right when it reads 040 or 220. This same compass could still be off 20° or more on some other headings.

If the compass does not read 040 as we sail away from the landmark, then we have error on these compass headings, and our next step is to figure out how much error and what is the direction of the error. For our example, we will assume the compass read 020 C when it should have read 040 C.

STEP 4. Figuring the error. This step has two parts: finding the size of the error and finding the direction of the error. The first part is easy. The error is one half the difference between the compass course we expected to get (toward course plus 180°) and the compass course we got. In the example, we expected to get 040 C for no error and we got 020 C. The difference is 20°, so the error is 10°. This error applies to both the toward and away compass readings. When the compass read 040, it was wrong by 10°, and when the compass read 220, it was wrong by 10°. These errors, however, will be in opposite directions. One of these compass readings is too high by 10°; the other is too low by 10°.

Figure the direction of the errors as follows. The proper magnetic heading of the away course is halfway between the compass course you expected and the compass course you got. In the example, we expected 040 C and got 020 C, so the correct magnetic course away from the landmark is 030 M. Since we read 020 C on the compass when we were sailing on course 030 M, the compass reading was 10° low on compass course 020 C. Since the opposite course must have the opposite error, this compass reads 10° high when it reads 220 C—it should read 210 C.

If the compass had read 060 C when we expected 040 C, we would still have a 10° error on each heading, but now the directions of the errors would be reversed. And so on.

The away course is harder to hold than the toward course, so it helps to align the landmark with parts of the boat—sighting the mark along the boom tied to centerline, for example. Or better still, instead of a single landmark, use two in a line (a range), like a nearby buoy and a hill on the shore behind it. Keeping these objects in line will guarantee you are sailing reciprocal courses.

When out-of-sight of landmarks, you can throw a jerry can or some such thing overboard and use it for your mark. The only additional concern here is drift. This method assumes the leeway of the boat and the object are the same. With no wind, this is no problem. Currents have no effect on this method.

This means of compass checking is an approximation because the principle used applies to reciprocal compass headings and in the procedure we sail reciprocal magnetic headings. For compass errors of less than 20° or so, however, this distinction is not important, and the method works fine—meaning within a couple degrees at worst, if all else is done right.

For larger errors, say 30° or so, this method is only an approximation. The large error you find won't be right to the degree, but it for sure will be better than not knowing the error at all. Fortunately, errors this large are rare on a well-positioned compass. If you find something this big, first look for some obvious magnetic disturbance near the compass.

If you are comfortable adjusting your own compass, however, you can use this method to do it accurately, regardless of how big the initial error is. The first correction you make won't be exactly right, but the next one will be small, and for small errors, the method is accurate. Most compass manuals explain the adjustment procedure adequately, and how to apply it using this method should be apparent.

12.9 Compass Checks with the Sun

This shortcut method of accurate compass checking works on sunny days for binnacle-mounted compasses that have a shadow pin in the center—which most do, although they are often overlooked or not thought of as such. It is a vertical pin, usually about a half inch tall, mounted in the center of the card. The pin is there as a guide to taking bearings, as well as for use with the sun, as explained here. This method can be used on any waters, even in confined docking areas, and it does not require a chart, knowledge of the local variation, or any special knowledge of celestial navigation.

When the sun shines across the card, the pin casts a shadow on the card, and the bearing of this shadow can be used as a reference for compass checks. See Figure 12.9-1. This method is best done early in the morning or late in the afternoon when the sun is low enough that the shadow reaches the numbers on the perimeter of the compass card. When the sun is higher, the shadow is short, and you must use a ruler and some patience to project the line of the shadow out to the numbers, as shown in the illustrations. In any event, you need to read this shadow bearing

as accurately as possible, which with little practice in calm conditions is about 1° precision even on cards marked only every 5°.

Although the magnetic bearing of the sun is changing continuously throughout the day as it moves westward across the sky, this bearing change is slow enough in most cases that you can assume it is constant over a period of a few minutes, and that is all it takes to swing ship and check the sun's bearing as you go around. If there is no error in the compass (no deviation), then the shadow bearing will be the same regardless of the boat's heading. With deviation in the compass, the shadow bearing will be different on different headings, and this difference can be used to determine the deviation on any heading.

On non-steel hulls, it is adequate to check the compass only on the cardinal compass headings (N, S, E, and W). If these are right, you can be confident that the intermediate headings are also right. The procedure is to head North according to the compass, read the shadow's bearing from the compass card and record it, then proceed on around, to the left or right, reading the shadow bearing while holding steady compass courses on E, S, W, and N again. The second shadow bearing headed North should be the same as it was when you started if you got around in time. If off a degree or two, it won't matter for this first check to see what the overall errors look like.

The second approximation used in this method is that any errors you find will be equal and opposite on reciprocal compass headings. Translated into practical terms, this means that if the shadow bearing was 250 when headed North and 270 when headed South, its proper bearing should have been 260 on both headings. In other words, your compass read 10° low when headed North (deviation 10° East) and 10° high when headed South (deviation 10° West).

With any deviation in the compass, the errors you find in the North-South direction must be different from the ones you find in the East-West direction. In the last example, you might have also found that when headed East, the shadow bearing was 255 (dev 5° E) and when headed West, it was 265 (dev 5° W). The N-S errors must be removed from the compass separately from the E-W errors.

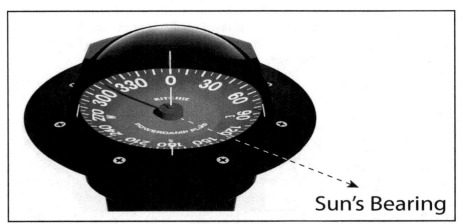

Sun's Bearing

Figure 12.9-1. *Reading the sun's bearing from the reciprocal of the shadow pin bearing. Here the shadow is at 315 C, so the sun's bearing at the moment is 135 C, when the vessel was headed 000 C. From convenient resources online, we can determine the true bearing of the sun at this time, and from this and the known variation for our location, we compute the magnetic bearing of the sun. The difference is then the deviation of the compass on our present heading.*

To remove the errors with the internal adjustment magnets, first do another check of the N and S errors, and from this you can figure what the proper shadow bearing should be now that some time has passed. The 10° error should be the same, if the measurements were good, but the bearings will be centered around a slightly different value, say by now, at 265, meaning you actually read 275 and 255. Head North on the compass, and pick a reference mark to steer toward during the adjustment. Use either of the side screws (running athwartships through the compass) to shift the compass heading 10°. The compass was low on a North heading, so you would turn the adjustment screw until your heading read 010, without altering the actual heading of the boat. To double check the direction, watch the shadow bearing; it should move to 265 as you adjust the card.

This will be a very small turn of the screw, just a few degrees rotation typically, and generally, the direction is toward neutral on the adjustment magnets, meaning toward a direction that makes the screw slots more parallel to the waterline. The adjustments must be made with a nonmagnetic screwdriver or with the brass key provided with many compasses for this purpose.

Next, remeasure the E-W errors, because correcting the N-S errors could have changed the E-W values. This is especially likely if the errors you removed were over 15° or so. Then remove the E-W errors in the same manner, but this time you head East or West, and use the fore or aft adjusting screw.

Note that some French and English compasses do not have internal magnets for this adjustment. These compasses typically have empty tubes lying along each side of the compass, into which separate magnets must be inserted for compensation. This job is best done by a professional, as it will take more time and money to track down the right magnets to use than it will cost to have them do it for you.

An Even Better Method

The sun method just described uses several approximations and also calls for changing course to make the checks. Often we are underway and just need to be sure the compass is right on our present heading, and then we will worry about other headings when we can. This comes up, for example, in an ocean yacht race, where some doubt about the steering compass might arise because all of the electronic heading sensors are reporting other headings; in a race, you do not want to stop and swing the ship.

But we do not have to. Here is a quick and easy solution that you can use in the ocean or in your local lake. We are relying now on celestial navigation in a sense, but we do not need any of the details if we are on land and have access to the internet. We just assume if you are in the ocean, you have the full tools to solve this with conventional cel nav methods.

We start with the measurement of Figure 12.9-1 where we learned that the compass bearing to the sun was 135 C when the vessel was headed 000 C. Note that this heading does not matter for this application. We just happen to have a nice picture with the compass in that direction. For this method, you measure the sun bearing on whatever heading you happen to be on.

But we do now need more information. We need to know the time accurate to within a minute or so, and we need to know our location. You can get both from the GPS. Now we need to look up or compute what the true bearing of the sun was at this moment based on cel nav principles, or we just go online and look it up.

Go to starpath.com/usno for a quick link to the right place at the US Naval Observatory. Then type in the time of the bearing and your Lat-Lon. An example is in Figure 12.9-2, which assumes we were headed north in Chesapeake Bay on October 14, 2013, and we recorded the bearing at 0930 EDT, which is 1330 UTC. The true bearing to the sun at the time was 123.5°.

Next, we need the local magnetic variation. We could get it from a chart, but for this type of precise compass check, we might want to go back online and get the most accurate and up-to-date value. This you find at the National Geodetic Center (see starpath.com/navbook) for specific dates and locations. For our example date and location, the correct value is 11° 05.3' W, or about 11.1° W. See Figure 12.9-3.

So the proper magnetic bearing of the sun is 123.5 + 11.1 = 134.6 M. The compass showed 135 C, so the deviation on heading 000 C is -0.4° which would be called 0.4° W.

Object	GHA		Dec		Hc		Zn	Refr	SD	P
	°	'	°	'	°	'	°	'	'	
SUN	26	00.8	S 8	19.9	+24	29.5	123.5	-2.2	16.0	0
MARS	73	41.0	N12	58.0	+65	16.3	~~174.4~~	-0.5	0.0	0
JUPITER	114	33.0	N21	57.2	+53	28.5	255.7	-0.7	0.3	0
SATURN	5	59.5	S13	15.1	+ 7	02.3	112.7	-7.3	0.1	0
ADHARA	120	57.8	S28	59.4	+11	16.4	219.0	-4.8	0.0	0
ALDEBARA	156	34.4	N16	32.1	+17	25.1	277.8	-3.1	0.0	0

Celestial Navigation Data for 2013 Oct 14 at 13:30:00 UT

For Assumed Position: Latitude N 37 36.0
Longitude W 76 06.0

Almanac Data — Altitude Corr

Figure 12.9-2. *Data from the USNO. The true bearing of the sun (Zn) is 123.5° at 0930 EDT from this location in Chesapeake Bay, VA. We also see that the height of the sun at this time (called Hc) was 24° 29.5' above the horizon, along with other data we are not using. We can convert this true bearing to a magnetic bearing using the local magnetic variation.*

Calculate Declination

Location

* Latitude: `37.5`   ○ S ⊙ N

* Longitude: `76.1`   ⊙ W ○ E

Model

* Model: ○ IGRF 11   ⊙ WMM 2010

Date

* Date: Year `2013` ⬍   Month `10` ⬍   Day `14` ⬍

Result

* Result format: ⊙ HTML   ○ XML   ○ CSV   ○ PDF

[Calculate]

Latitude:	37.5° N
Longitude:	76.1° W
Date	Declination
2013-10-14	11.07° W changing by 0.02° W per year

Figure 12.9-3. *Input and output screens from the online geomag computation. A nice graphic confirms the location and displays varia-tion. Land navigators call variation "declination," but this term is not used on the water. There is a Windows version of this program that you can download to your PC for a convenient backup to check older charts. They only claim an accuracy of ±0.5°, which is a reminder of the accuracies involved, because the charts are not any more accurate than this output.*

We have learned that this compass is essentially correct at this heading, as it is difficult to be confident we have read the shadow bearing to this precision. But the main point is that this method has no other approximations in it. The result you get is as accurate as you can read the shadow bearing on the compass card.

This is a very powerful method. It would be instructive to try it once or twice whenever you see a nice shadow on your compass card, no matter where you are. Just write down the shadow bearing, the time, and the location, and your actual compass heading at the time. Then you can check the compass for that heading when you get back home. If convenient, record the data headed roughly north or south by compass and also roughly east or west by compass, and then you will have a pretty good analysis of your compass with a few minutes of paperwork at home.

12.10 Log and Knotmeter Calibrations

In this section, we use locations from the Seattle area for doing the testing, but it should be clear how to select similar places for testing in your own area. We can also learn even more about areas not familiar to us by viewing them on Google Earth (or any internet mapping service) and then imagine similar places in local waters.

An accurate log and knotmeter are fundamental to good navigation. Too often, we live with what we know is wrong. We may start off knowing our instruments are about 10% low, but as time goes by and the crud grows thicker on the paddle wheel, knowledge of their accuracy deteriorates into just knowing they are low, and eventually into not even bothering to look at them. Navigation in the fog is more exciting than it should be when you don't have an accurate log. Furthermore, true wind instruments will not calculate the proper wind angles and speeds if the knot-meter is wrong.

Most knotmeter and log systems are electronically tied together. If your knotmeter reads 10% low, your log reads 10% low. If you fix one, you fix both. They work off the same paddle wheel: the log just counts the signals from the knotmeter to figure miles traveled through the water. The calibration procedure we present here assumes these two instruments are tied together in this way, one calibration knob or set of switches for both instruments.

The standard way to calibrate these instruments is to sail or motor along a known distance and see whether your log records the proper run. You can also time the run, and divide the distance covered by the time run to see whether your knotmeter read the proper speed during the run—assuming you can hold a near constant speed over the run.

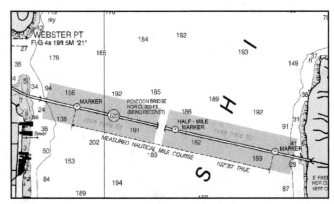

Figure 12.10-1. *Sample of a charted measured mile to use for knotmeter and log calibrations.*

The best Seattle area location to make this simplest type of knotmeter check is in Lake Washington using the charted mile and half-mile markers along the Evergreen Point Floating Bridge (Figure 12.10-1). The advantage there is the lack of current and the well-established distance. But for many boaters, it is inconvenient to make the trip through the Ballard Locks (just south of the Starpath HQ!) and over to the Lake. Furthermore, an accurate calibration is rarely as easy as this simplest method might imply. Even without current, however, headwinds will slow you down and tailwinds will speed you up, so you must go both ways and average the results. Instrument manuals often give instructions on the procedures. The following method applies to any brand of instruments, although it was adapted from a Brookes and Gatehouse manual many years ago.

The advantage of this method is it can be done in changing winds and changing currents, all accomplished over a fairly short run. This allows you to repeat it several times to check your results after adjusting the calibration. One Seattle area place to try this without going through the Locks is inside the Shilshole Bay Marina breakwater (Figure 12.10-2). Using the south end of the "I" docks, just opposite the bend in the breakwater, as a range marking one end of the run, and the fishing pier (called a breakwater on the chart) just short of the north end of the main breakwater as another range to mark the other end of the run, you have a distance of 0.40 nmi for your checks. In the work form shown in Figure 12.10-2, this would be M = 0.40 in this case.

You can also check your compass during this run since the breakwater is oriented very near 005 magnetic. Your compass should read 005 headed north parallel to the breakwater and 185 when headed south. This should be done *inside* the breakwater as shown, because there is a dangerous shoaling just near the breakwater on the outer side. The speed limit inside is 4 kts, so adding turning times, count on about 10 minutes a run. Doing it the required three times, adjusting the calibration and then another three times as a check, you are looking at about an hour of time to do the job at this site. If you can find a comparable or even shorter well-marked distance in open water where you can go faster, the calibration is quicker.

This procedure includes a double average so it doesn't matter that wind and currents are likely to be present during the measurement time, so long as they are either steady or changing uniformly during the test. Your speed can also change during the test; it won't affect the calibration. If traffic gets in the way, slow down to let it by, and the run is still good.

Before calibration, pull the paddle wheel to be sure it is clean and spins freely. Also, if you have the option to rotate its orientation when in place, do this while underway (after cleaning) to find the orientation that gives maximum speed. Depending on the water flow over the hull, the optimum orientation may not be strictly parallel to the centerline.

Figure 12.10-2. *Shilshole Bay Marina. Inside the breakwater is a good example of a place to check the log, as well as the compass. The line shown is 0.40 nmi long in direction 005 Magnetic. The variation is about 16.2 E at this time. From Google Earth.*

Refer to Figure 12.10-3 for the form that might be used. There is also a numerical example in the figure.

Step 1. Use a chart to find a well marked straight line running at least 0.25 nmi. Measure this distance carefully and call it "M," and record it in space (1). Wind and current may vary during these tests providing it is steadily increasing or decreasing in the same direction. Your own boat speed may change during the tests, but you should go in a straight line while covering the distance of "M" miles. At the start of a run along this distance, record your log reading in space (3) , and also start a stopwatch.

Step 2. At the end of the run along the known distance, stop the watch, and record the time run in space (5) and the final log reading in space (2).

Step 3. Figure the logged run by subtracting (3) from (2), and record it in space (4). Use the table provided to convert the time run in minutes and seconds to decimal hours, and record it in space (6).

Step 4. Figure your velocity made good (V1) for run 1 by dividing M by T1, i.e. (1)/(6), and record it in space (7). Also figure your speed through the water (SI) by dividing D1 by T1, i.e. (4)/(6), and record it in space (8).

Step 5. Now repeat the process headed in the other direction along the known distance "M", and fill in the form as above. Then do it once more headed back in the original direction to get the numbers for the third run.

Step 6. Using the three values of Vn from the three runs, figure "A" as the sum of the first and third values plus twice the second value, and figure "B" using the three Sn values in the same way. Then find the calibration factor "K" by dividing A by B. Your proper speed is your knotmeter reading multiplied by K. If K = 1.0, your log and knotmeter are correct; if K is bigger than 1.0, your instruments read low; if less than 1.0, your instruments read high. The value (K - 1.0) × 100 is your percentage error. If a knotmeter reads 6.0 kts with a K of 1.10, the actual boat speed is 6.6 kts. If you logged 20 nmi with these instruments, you would have actually covered 22 nmi.

Figure 12.10-3 shows an example of a knotmeter calibration done in an apparent wind that increased from about 15 to 20 kts during the test, in a current of about 0.2 kts. The measurements show that the knotmeter was 9% low.

Run Number	n = 1	n = 2	n = 3
(1) True Distance, M (nmi)			
(2) Log reading at finish			
(3) Log reading at start			
(4) Logged run, Dn (end-start)	D1	D2	D3
(5) Time Run, Tn (min. & sec.)			
(6) Time Run, Tn (decimal hr.)	T1	T2	T3
(7) VMG Vn = M/Tn	V1	V2	V3
(8) Speed Sn = Dn/Tn	S1	S2	S3

To find time (T) in decimal hours from h:m:s use:

$$T = h + [\, m + (\, s / 60 \,)\,] / 60.$$

A = V1 + 2 x V2 + V3	K = A/B
B = S1 + 2 x S2 + S3	

Run Number	n = 1	n = 2	n = 3
(1) True Distance, M (nmi)	0.40	0.40	0.40
(2) Log reading at finish	69.30	69.84	70.38
(3) Log reading at start	68.94	69.46	70.03
(4) Logged run, Dn (end-start)	D1 0.36	D2 0.38	D3 0.35
(5) Time Run, Tn (min. & sec.)	3m 58s	4m 57s	3m 57s
(6) Time Run, Tn (decimal hr.)	T1 0.066	T2 0.083	T3 0.066
(7) VMG Vn = M/Tn	V1 6.06	V2 4.82	V3 6.06
(8) Speed Sn = Dn/Tn	S1 5.45	S2 4.58	S3 5.30

A = V1 + 2 x V2 + V3	K = A/B
21.76	1.09
B = S1 + 2 x S2 + S3	
19.91	

Figure 12.10-3. *Log and knotmeter calibration form. Instructions are in the text, as well as discussion of the example shown.*

12.11 When Will We Get There?

I'm going 5 kts; my destination is 10 miles off; how long will it take me to get there? Answer: 2 hours. This is a pretty easy problem—all we need to know is we mean 10 nmi when we say 10 miles, and we need to know a knot is a speed of 1 nmi per hour. At a speed of 5 kts, we go 5 nmi each hour, so it takes 2 hours to go 10 nmi—but that is more of a practice problem than a practical problem.

The more realistic problem the navigator faces is a knotmeter that reads, say, 5.6 kts and a destination distance that must be figured from a crooked course across a chart—up to that island, around it, through that pass, and then into the harbor, or some such course equally different from a simple straight line. Then there might be currents along the course, and the currents might be different on different legs of the course. And the destination might lie to windward on part of the course, so you couldn't sail the direct-line course on that leg anyway—you would have to tack back and forth across it. And finally, if the wind is strong, other factors (including leeway, waves, and wind-driven currents) will cause your windward progress to be much less than you figure from your compass, current predictions, and knotmeter alone.

In short, accurately figuring when you will get there, even on a typical daysail, is rarely a simple exercise of dividing the straight-line distance by your knotmeter speed. To solve this common problem in the mathematically correct manner is not easy (current vectors, apparent-to-true wind conversions for tacking angles, leeway, and such things all enter into it). Fortunately, it doesn't really matter. Even if you did do it all exactly right, you would rarely get the exactly right answer... unless, of course, you were a Predicted Log racer. These folks are the experts at this type of precise navigation, because that is the very basis of their sport. Many powerboat yacht clubs take part. Many offer lessons and opportunities to ride along as observers.

But barring that worthy activity, in most practical navigation, you rarely even need to know that time equals distance divided by speed. To do this calculation, after all, you need to know the distance, and you get the distance by walking your dividers along the course with their separation set to some distance interval that you get from the miles scale on the chart. If you simply set the dividers' separation (in nmi) equal to your boat speed (in kts), then each step you take is one hour along the course. Count the hours, and you've got the time. Chances are you will do this more often than you will divide numbers.

That works well for longer runs, distances that take more than an hour at your present speed. For shorter runs, it helps to know your boat speed in minutes per mile. For example, at 6 kts it takes 10 minutes to go 1 mile. To figure time on course at 6 kts, use dividers to find the distance in nmi from the chart, and then multiply that distance by 10 to get the total minutes. At 6 kts, 4 nmi take 40 minutes— or think of it as 10 minutes per step with your dividers set

to 1 nmi. The 6-knot time is the one I remember, and more often than not, I just estimate times at other speeds from this, but it's not hard to figure that 5 kts means 12 minutes per mile, and so forth.

Minutes per mile = 60/speed.

These shortcut time calculations are, still, for straight-line, constant-speed courses—meaning on a reach or run or under power. When tacking to windward from point A to point B you must sail farther than the straight-line distance between the two points, and we need a way to estimate how much farther if we are to estimate the time to get there. Again, to do this right is complicated and usually not worth it because the wind and boat performance may, and likely will, change along the course. Instead, a simple rule of thumb will usually do as well as can be done, and that was outlined in Section 12.6. Namely:

Tacking Distance = 1.5 × Upwind Distance.

Figure the distance upwind (to weather) that you need to go, and multiply that by 1.5. Refer back to Section 12.6 to see that the upwind distance could be less than the rhumbline distance to your destination, but the total tacking distance will be longer.

Sailing a rhumbline course with a current pushing you along, just add that current to your knotmeter speed to get your speed made good (SMG), and use this SMG to figure time on course.

When tacking through a current that runs parallel to the wind, you can estimate your SMG by adding ±0.7 times the current speed to your knotmeter speed to get your SMG, and then use the tacking-time method described earlier with this new speed.

12.12 Wrinkles in Practical ECS

The use of ECS (electronic chart systems) is fundamental to modern navigation, just as much as it is fundamental that we know how to navigate without it. The term means connecting a GPS to an echart display and navigating by moving map technology. An icon representing the boat shows where you are at all times on an electronic version of a nautical chart. You can view the chart in dedicated echart plotters or in the chart display of a GPS unit, or in your smart phone, but the most functionality comes with viewing the charts in a computer program dedicated to the task, running (usually) in a laptop.

The acronym ECDIS (electronic chart display and information system, pronounced ek-dis) means essentially the same thing, but it refers to the official system of the International Maritime Organization (IMO) that has strict standards on the types of charts, the hardware, and the format of the display. Ships must use ECDIS; yachts can use anything they like and call it ECS.

The types of GPS units and the types of echart display devices we can choose from are changing rapidly. A Bluetooth GPS running one of several excellent programs in a small laptop offers excellent mobility if you sail on different boats. The full package, including a few custom echarts, is around $900 or so.

About 10 years ago, when we were asked, "Should I take a computer along on my cruise?" the answer was, "Yes, if you need one for your work and entertainment, but otherwise the hassle might not be worth the reward in navigation and communication." Now if we get the same question, the answer is, "No, you should not take *a* computer along; you should take two!" Build two of these laptops with all of your navigation, communications, and weather software installed and running, so you have a mirror-image backup. It takes some tweaking to get a PC dependably communicating with several external devices and then sharing this input with several programs running at once, so there is no point in having to do it twice if one fails on an extended ocean voyage.

The hassle of protecting a PC and its even more vulnerable attachments when underway in the ocean has not changed at all over the years, but the reward you get from the system is so very much higher. For now we are discussing just navigation, but modern high seas communications and weather data gathering and analysis requires a computer. Notice this still says PC in a world that is evolving toward Macs, but we will leave this as is for now because for this maritime application, the PC is still probably the best bet. There are more and varied marine applications for PCs than for Macs, especially in ECS. This will likely change, and Mac fans (like ourselves) will be keeping an eye on it, but it will be some time before we see them in the discount warehouses where we can pick up a matching pair for half the price of one Mac.

Needless to say, there are sailors who successfully sail around the world without computers, but in doing so, they give up tremendous resources for safety and efficiency.

ECS is perhaps more immediately important on inland and coastal waters, but even in the ocean the same basic procedures and advantages apply. Here is a brief outline, which we might call "How to Navigate Today," keeping in mind all the tools and procedures we have covered in this book to support and backup these procedures.

Start with Waypoints

Every voyage, 2 nmi or 2,000 nmi, proceeds by waypoints. Spend the time to choose the best way to go, taking all factors into account.

Generally, we do this selection with the echart program, zoomed out to see an overview of most of the route. Use the route tool to quickly set the approximate location of each of the main turning points, then zoom in to drag the waypoints to the best position, and add more as needed. Then give them each a real name and lock their position. The real name should be preceded by a number, so you can order them, and know where you are along a route. Just numbers or just names is not good.

Then make a printed voyage plan table or spreadsheet with the names and Lat, Lon of each point, and the course and distance between them. Also add estimated speeds for each leg of the route. Most echart programs will format this data for you and figure the times at each way point and then export or print this record directly for you. Somehow, we should end up with a printed record. We are dealing with computers after all, and we don't want to do this twice.

For inland waters, the waypoints are best when in view of a prominent radar target or other way to uniquely identify the location by visual means. In broad terms, it is a goal of good navigation training to choose optimum waypoints.

If you are planning for a yacht race, or if any part of your cruising voyage calls for crucial navigation, then you should immediately export these waypoints from the PC program into your handheld GPS. It takes some instruction manual reading to learn the process of transferring waypoints, routes, or actual tracks between PC and handheld, but the effort is well worth it. If anything goes wrong at a crucial moment, you will then be ready instantly with a solution. As navigator, you can also be monitoring progress along the route as you sit on deck when you have your handheld GPS programmed. When using an echart app in a smartphone, you can just export from the computer the route of waypoints to a gpx file, and then email that file to yourself, then open it in the smartphone app. Many new smartphone or tablet nav apps also let you do the reverse, that is, sail a route and then share the route or actual track of past positions to an email address. Check your mail on the computer, and then open the attachment in your computer nav program.

Then the job is to follow the waypoints. If you cut corners or skip waypoints, then the setup was wrong. There will be discoveries along the way that call for waypoint changes, but if so, change the waypoint and then sail the new waypoints you now have. Remember, you might be sailing the route again someday, so you can record it properly now for the next time. In a sense, if you do not follow the waypoints, you are not navigating to your destination; you are just sailing there.

Set up Routes

Successive waypoints define the line between them. Our job is to stay on that line as best we can. When under sail, we will have obvious limitations on our route, but we still must keep that line in mind at all times. Let's look at the simplest case first, under power or reaching so we have control over our heading.

The waypoints have been compiled into a route, which is made of legs between successive waypoints. We start by activating the route, which will draw lines for each leg, and also display the range and bearing to the second waypoint, assuming we started at the first. Leaving the first waypoint, head the boat in the direction of the next waypoint, say it is

300 M, and steer that course as accurately as you can for some time, and watch your track on the echart—the breadcrumb trail of your past positions.

Watching the track is usually done best with a dual display of the same chart. Open a second window showing the boat, and zoom one display in and the other display out. The close view can show within boat lengths if you wander off the desired course line to the next waypoint. The higher view keeps you in perspective of where you are along the route.

Another tool of most echart programs that can expedite safe, efficient navigation is the predictor line that can be set on the vessel icon. This line shows the instantaneous direction of the COG, along with marking where you will be at a user-selected look-ahead time. The time projection can be minutes or hours, depending on the circumstances, but it is always a valuable addition to the display.

Some ECS also allow the vessel heading to be projected forward from the vessel icon, which shows clearly you are getting set when it does not line up with the COG predictor line. This valuable optional display requires a separate electronic heading sensor. In some cases, you may already have a heading sensor for the autopilot or radar, in which case it might just be a matter of getting that output into your ECS system. I have seen cases where it is a simple one-wire connection.

Stay on Track

Now monitor your progress as shown in the steps of Figure 12.12-1. If you see you are getting set, meaning your actual track is diverging from the desired course line for any reason (we do not care what is causing it), then it is a call for action.

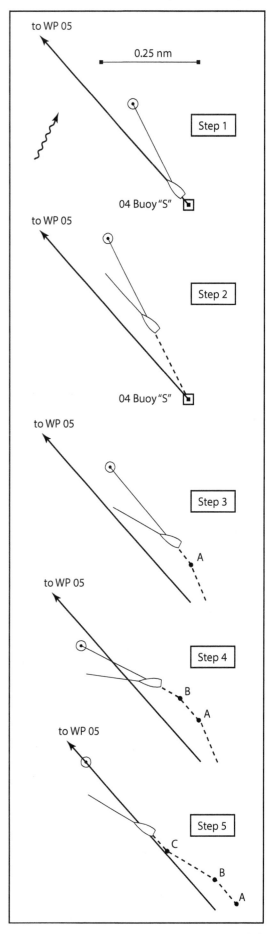

Figure 12.12-1. *Getting back on track after being set off by current or any other reason.*

Step 3-1. *Head the boat in the direction of the next waypoint, and steer that course as steady as possible as you watch the track behind you on the plot.*

Step 3-2. *Spot the set. The course to next mark (WP 05) is 300 M. Knot-meter speed is 6 kts. A current of about 2 kts is flowing N-NE, causing a set of about 15°. The thin line on the vessel icon is the heading line (at 300 M), which shows what you are steering. The line with circle on the end shows the COG (at 315 M) and predicted location of the boat in 2 minutes. Notice that in less than 2 minutes, we have a good idea of our set when zoomed in to this scale.*

Step 3-3. *Correct the course, and check the results. After turning into the current by 15° (to heading 285 M), we watch the track and notice we need a bit more, and at point A, we find that heading 283 M tracks parallel to the desired course with COG = 300 M. The COG line is now parallel to the desired course line.*

Step 3-4. *But we want more than the right course; we also want to be on the right line, so we need to over correct, and at point B, we turn to heading 260 M to get back on the desired track.*

Step 3-5. *Once back on the track at Point C, we can turn to the proper course that we know corrects for current, namely 283 M, and we are now tracking right down the line as desired.*

This is an easy maneuver to carry out, and with all these tools available, we should not accept less than what we want.

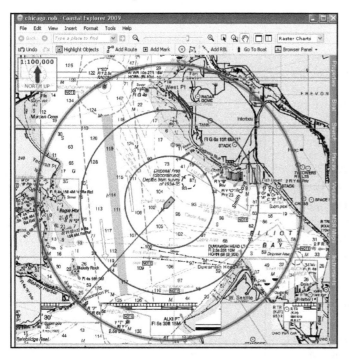

Figure 12.12-2. *Echart display (left) with range rings on the vessel icon set to match those on the radar (right) for a quick ID of the targets and our relative location. This is a North Up radar display, which shows the ship's heading line (SHL) toward the SW matching the echart heading line. The radar shows 3 electronic bearing lines, 2 marking the tangents to the headland shown, and one to the right of the SHL. The fourth ring showing on the radar is a variable range marker, being pulled into position with the plus-sign cursor. Notice the unambiguous dah-dit radar signal of the RACON just aft of the starboard beam, nicely correlated with the echart rings. Echart from* Coastal Explorer. *Radar image from* Radar for Mariners.

Zoomed way in on the echart display, it will be obvious in a short time provided you are steering a steady course. The navigator needs the helmsman's help at this stage. If the COG turns out to be 315 M, for example, as you steer and desire to make good 300 M, then you are getting set 15° to the right. We speak of this in water currents terminology, but it is actually an *error current*, whose source is not important at this stage. It could just as well be due to a compass error as to moving water, but in many waterways, it is indeed the tidal or coastal current setting you off course.

To correct for this offset, turn left into the current by this 15°, and monitor your COG and track. If you are now making good 300, then fine; if not, tweak the heading till you get exactly what you want. But as shown in the example, you are not done yet. You found the right course, but you are off the track you wanted, so you need to overcorrect long enough to get back on the desired track. This is not always crucial, but it could be, so it is good policy to practice doing exactly what you intended to do when you laid out the waypoints. Then keep an eye on your track, and adjust as needed. At the next waypoint, turn to the new course and do it all again.

Monitor Progress

The hallmark of good navigation is not relying on any single navigation aid, and that includes GPS. A versatile

ECS can facilitate quick checks of your GPS position and rate of travel. The depth sounder and radar are often the first instruments to check.

Using raster echarts (graphic images of paper charts, called raster navigation charts, RNC), you can read or interpolate the depth at your position from the printed soundings, correct for tide height, and compare it with your depth sounder. Or easier still, note when the echart display shows you crossing a prominent ledge within soundings, and watch to see the depth sounder confirms the crossing. This method is less sensitive to your sounder's calibration. Vector echarts on the other hand, since they are rendered images of digitized chart data (called electronic navigation charts, ENC), can actually interpolate and display the active charted depth at your location to compare with your depth sounder. Many echart programs include digital tide predictions, which expedite the process.

Radar is usually the strongest supplement to GPS—or vice versa! Several echart programs allow the user to set multiple range rings on the vessel icon, which turns out to be a very handy feature for coordinating ECS with radar use. You can set these range rings to match the range rings on your present radar display and also set the display mode (head-up or north-up) to match, and then use the echart display for an instant interpretation of the radar screen. This comparison is one of the best ways possible to confirm your position—or when disoriented, it is a quick way to regain what is formally called "situational awareness," a worthy goal at all times, on the water and off. See Figure 12.12-2.

Some ECS models can overlay the actual radar image on the echart to execute this comparison, which serves well in many cases, but sometimes the combined images are very complex or at least require special tuning. If you do not have that bonus, you will find the range rings on the ECS vessel icon serve well for this purpose.

When all radar targets are clearly identified, we can get by for position checks just using the range and bearing to good radar targets. Both values are obtained digitally from the radar and the ECS display.

Without radar, you can set the ECS to magnetic bearings and use compass bearings to check your position. Keeping a sharp eye out for natural ranges will always be a bonus to checking positions as well.

Calling the Layline when Sailing

For sailors, there is a fundamental use of ECS that almost justifies its use by itself, but it is probably not used as much as it could be. It is the important task of deciding when to tack or jibe, which is usually the key decision to make underway under sail. Tack too early, and you have to tack again; tack too late in a race, and you may lose the race.

With GPS trails showing on the screen, we can see exactly what we need to know to make this decision. As soon as we have established trails from both tacks (namely the

CMG of each), we can copy one and move it to the mark to see the layline we need to reach for the next tack. The process is illustrated in Figure 12.12-3.

The way you draw and then move the line that is parallel to your track will differ from one program to the next, but they all have some way to do this. If you do not have the function to move a line on the screen, then measure the CMG of the tack line, and just create a reversed line emanating from the mark.

If you see your track curving rather than being a straight line, then you know immediately that something is changing. Either the wind is changing or the current is. We have to look at other data from the GPS to decide which, but in any event, we can project what we are seeing to the next tack.

Solve Vector Problems

A hidden (golden) wrinkle in ECS is its very convenient ability to solve any of the common vector problems we run across in navigation. The process is illustrated in Figure 12.12-4. Problems that otherwise require protractors, rulers, dividers, and much careful plotting can be mastered in seconds with this method. Again, you have to practice with the program you have to determine the best approach, but any program will do this, and it is a very good trick to know.

Tides and Currents Display

Unless you sail in an area with no significant tides or currents, this is another feature of ECS that makes it worth the cost and learning curve. Most ECS programs offer a convenient integrated display of both tides and tidal cur-

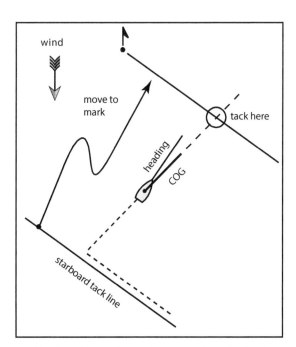

Figure 12.12-3. *ECS is the best way to call the layline in strong current or leeway. Assuming things stay the same, once you have tacked and got your tracks on each board, you can plot bearing lines to match them, and then move the tack line to the mark. Then project your COG line to know when to tack to lay the mark. .*

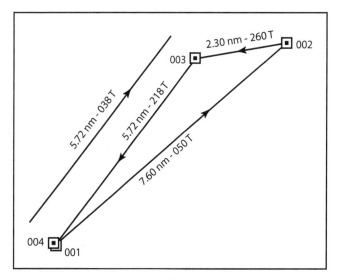

Figure 12.12-4. *ESC programs are very convenient for solving vector problems in navigation. A simple CMG in current example is shown. Steering 050 T at 7.6 kts, what will we make good in current of 2.3 kts at 260 T? At any location on any chart, make a 3-leg route of the vector triangle for a one-hour period, then reverse the last leg to learn it is SMG=5.72 at CMG=038. Even the most complex vector problems are easily solved in this manner. True wind from apparent, or relative motion diagrams in radar can be solved the same way.*

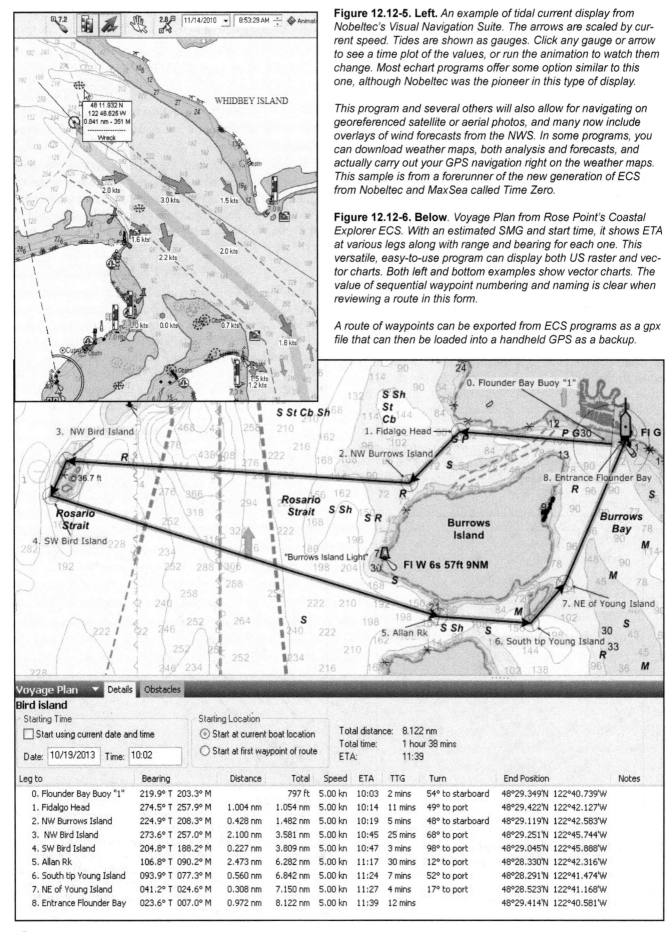

Figure 12.12-5. Left. *An example of tidal current display from Nobeltec's Visual Navigation Suite. The arrows are scaled by current speed. Tides are shown as gauges. Click any gauge or arrow to see a time plot of the values, or run the animation to watch them change. Most echart programs offer some option similar to this one, although Nobeltec was the pioneer in this type of display.*

This program and several others will also allow for navigating on georeferenced satellite or aerial photos, and many now include overlays of wind forecasts from the NWS. In some programs, you can download weather maps, both analysis and forecasts, and actually carry out your GPS navigation right on the weather maps. This sample is from a forerunner of the new generation of ECS from Nobeltec and MaxSea called Time Zero.

Figure 12.12-6. Below. *Voyage Plan from Rose Point's Coastal Explorer ECS. With an estimated SMG and start time, it shows ETA at various legs along with range and bearing for each one. This versatile, easy-to-use program can display both US raster and vector charts. Both left and bottom examples show vector charts. The value of sequential waypoint numbering and naming is clear when reviewing a route in this form.*

A route of waypoints can be exported from ECS programs as a gpx file that can then be loaded into a handheld GPS as a backup.

Voyage Plan ▼ Details | Obstacles

Bird island

Starting Time
☐ Start using current date and time
Date: 10/19/2013 Time: 10:02

Starting Location
◉ Start at current boat location
◯ Start at first waypoint of route

Total distance: 8.122 nm
Total time: 1 hour 38 mins
ETA: 11:39

Leg to	Bearing	Distance	Total	Speed	ETA	TTG	Turn	End Position	Notes
0. Flounder Bay Buoy "1"	219.9° T 203.3° M		797 ft	5.00 kn	10:03	2 mins	54° to starboard	48°29.349'N 122°40.739'W	
1. Fidalgo Head	274.5° T 257.9° M	1.004 nm	1.054 nm	5.00 kn	10:14	11 mins	49° to port	48°29.422'N 122°42.127'W	
2. NW Burrows Island	224.9° T 208.3° M	0.428 nm	1.482 nm	5.00 kn	10:19	5 mins	48° to starboard	48°29.119'N 122°42.583'W	
3. NW Bird Island	273.6° T 257.0° M	2.100 nm	3.581 nm	5.00 kn	10:45	25 mins	68° to port	48°29.251'N 122°45.744'W	
4. SW Bird Island	204.8° T 188.2° M	0.227 nm	3.809 nm	5.00 kn	10:47	3 mins	98° to port	48°29.045'N 122°45.888'W	
5. Allan Rk	106.8° T 090.2° M	2.473 nm	6.282 nm	5.00 kn	11:17	30 mins	12° to port	48°28.330'N 122°42.316'W	
6. South tip Young Island	093.9° T 077.3° M	0.560 nm	6.842 nm	5.00 kn	11:24	7 mins	52° to port	48°28.291'N 122°41.474'W	
7. NE of Young Island	041.2° T 024.6° M	0.308 nm	7.150 nm	5.00 kn	11:27	4 mins	17° to port	48°28.523'N 122°41.168'W	
8. Entrance Flounder Bay	023.6° T 007.0° M	0.972 nm	8.122 nm	5.00 kn	11:39	12 mins		48°29.414'N 122°40.581'W	

rents. Just click a button, and all the local tidal data show on the screen, usually with arrows showing the current speed and direction, and often with an animation option to show how these vary with time. This way you can easily plan a route that takes best advantage of favorable currents, or you choose one that lets you avoid adverse current. In areas like the Pacific Northwest where currents dominate much of our navigation, this is a feature that saves enormous amounts of time. An example is shown in Figure 12.12-5.

Voyage Plans

Another valuable feature of many ECS programs is the option to print out an organized log of any route. This way you have an independent written record of the waypoints, along with course and distance between each one. Some even offer snapshot chart views of each leg of the route for quick reference underway. If anything should happen to the electronics underway, these printouts then become very good backups. A sample is shown in Figure 12.12-6. This is such a valuable feature that it might be included in your checklist when comparing programs. Some let you add a current correction to each leg, change speeds, or add delays. Some include a chartlet for the route on export; others can export direct to spreadsheet format. They have various names including Voyage Plan, Route Plan, Plan Book, etc.

Free Echarts and Software

Most ECS programs offer a free demo version, some of which can be used indefinitely with limitations. Even those demos that do not offer live GPS navigation do offer a way to study charts and lay out a route—though it might require a purchase to print a route plan or export a route in gpx format.

Echarts of US waters are free from NOAA (starpath.com/getcharts), so it is free and easy to learn the ropes of ECS to discover which system best meets your needs.

12.13 Running Fix and DR Corrections

We often say in class that the transition from prudent skipper to navigator takes place with the mastering of the running fix. Most basic navigation prior to that involves finding a fix from two separate objects, whereas the running fix lets you find a fix from a single object. We can also do the same by finding distance off one object and the bearing to it, but those piloting methods are not as universally applicable as is the running fix.

The technique is not so often learned because it is not so often needed on inland waters—but when it is needed, you need a navigator. Now in the age of GPS, it is even less called upon, and consequently such skills are almost doomed in the eyes of many skippers. On the other hand, when it is needed now, the need for a navigator is even more pronounced.

If you go on to learn celestial navigation, you will be glad you know how to do a running fix. Although it might be rare to need a running fix in sight of land, it is a routine daily procedure of celestial navigation, where we do running fixes between successive sextant sights of the sun.

One of the important challenges a navigator faces is finding position from a single landmark. On inland and coastal waters, the problem occurs in the fog whenever a single light is the only reference. It also occurs on clear days when only one coastal feature (peak, tower, rock) can be identified. You then do a running fix, find out where you are, and from there take bearings to identify the other peaks, and from then on you can take simple cross bearings for a fix.

Depending on the circumstances, there are several ways to find position from a single reference (both inshore and offshore), but a running fix is the most reliable and versatile method. It is a plotting technique that combines piloting and DR.

When done with compass bearings, the procedure boils down to taking one bearing, proceeding far enough along that this bearing changes notably, at which time you take another bearing. Then you figure out where you must be in order to see what you saw, after doing what you did.

With the two lines of position (LOPs) plotted on the chart, the chart work is equivalent to finding the one place along the first LOP that you could leave from, sail the distance you did in the direction you did, and end up on the second LOP.

The standard running-fix procedure with no current and no course changes is shown in Figure 12.13-1.

Step 1. Take a magnetic bearing to the light, and plot the LOP on the chart labeled with time of the sight. Notice that after plotting this one bearing line we know two things: (1) we are located somewhere on the line we just plotted and (2) we know our DR is wrong—but we do not know how wrong. If the line had gone right through the DR position, we would then have known that our DR *might* be right, but this one line going through one corresponding DR position does not prove the DR is right. We only know from this bearing line that we are on the LOP.

Step 2. Hold a steady course and speed until the magnetic bearing to the light has changed by at least 30°, preferably more. Smaller bearing changes give weaker fixes, but there is little to be gained by waiting beyond a bearing change of 60°. With a log available to count miles run, it is not necessary to keep a constant boat speed.

Next take a second magnetic bearing to the light, and plot this LOP, labeled with the second watch time.

We now need to figure how far we traveled between these two bearing sights. You can subtract the two log readings or figure distance run from average speed multiplied by the time between sights. Once you have the distance run, you can update your DR plot to mark where you think you

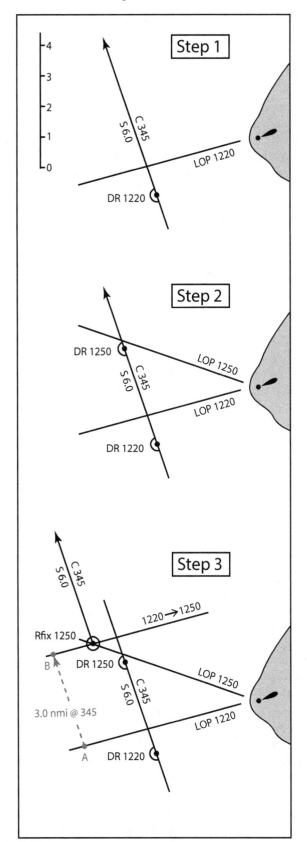

Figure 12.13-1. *A running fix without current or course changes. The distance between points A and B is the difference in log readings at the bearing times; the direction A to B is the course steered between bearings, which is just what we have already plotted on the DR track.*

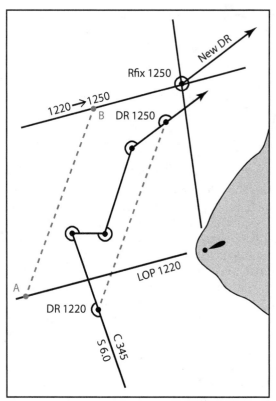

Figure 12.13-2. *A running fix corrected for course changes. The LOP should be advanced along the course made good between sights (1220 to 1250), starting from any point A on the first LOP. This is the key to then later correcting for current and leeway.*

were at the time of the second bearing line. The distance between these two DR positions is how far you traveled between sights and the direction you traveled, but this is still just a DR plot, so we do not know whether this is really the line we were on.

Notice in this case that the second LOP (1250) was even closer to the DR, which might encourage (deceive) us more; we cannot conclude any more than we did at the first time we made this comparison.

Step 3. Now we *advance* the first LOP to the time of the second to see where we really are, and where we were at the time of the first sight as well. Starting from any point A on the first LOP, draw a line in the direction sailed between sights, and mark off the distance run between sights along that line. Then use parallel rules to move (advance) the first LOP to the point B, which marks the end of the run between sights. Label the advanced LOP with both times joined by an arrow. Your position at the time of the second LOP is the place where the advanced LOP crosses the second LOP. If you care to know where you were at the first bearing, just project this Rfix position back to the first LOP. In this example, we were passing this light almost a mile farther off than our original DR track indicated.

Once you have an Rfix, you start a new DR track from that position, and just abandon the other. We might just keep in mind that we were off to the left, and so we can see how that compares with what we find at the next fix.

A running fix is as accurate as a conventional bearing fix from near-simultaneous bearings to two separated objects provided the DR between the two sights of the running fix is accurate. This requires a calibrated log or knotmeter, a corrected compass, and careful records between sights. It also requires that you know the currents present. Leeway should also be included when sailing to windward in very strong wind or very light wind.

To carry out a running fix in the presence of current and leeway, and also with course changes between sights, refer to Figure 12.13-2. All such corrections are accounted for by just advancing the LOP along the CMG that was accomplished between the two sight times. In other words, plot your DR track as best you can during the time period between the two bearing sights, then plot the DR positions along that track that correspond to the two sight times, and then draw a line between those two positions. That straight line track is what you use to advance the first LOP to the second, just as if that is what you actually sailed.

Again, you just move that line segment to any point A on the first LOP and then move the first LOP to the point B at the end of it, and the intersection of that with the second LOP is your running fix.

Remember, the object sighted must be close enough that its bearing changes significantly in a reasonable time. If the object is too far away, or too near the bow or stern, the time required between sights will be so long that small uncertainties in the DR will accumulate, and the accuracy of the fix will suffer. As a rule of thumb, consider the uncer-

tainty in the final running fix will be slightly larger than the uncertainty in the DR between sights.

Now we proceed to correct for leeway and current. We do this by just correcting the DR plot for these factors and then use the starting and ending points to find the CMG, and we advance along that line.

Correcting DR for Leeway

Leeway rotates your course line downwind by the leeway angle. It is your job to figure out or estimate how big this angle is. It could be anywhere from 5° to 20°, but as noted elsewhere, not likely to be larger. Once you have this estimate, it is an easy job to correct a DR track for this, as illustrated in Figure 12.13-3 .

Unless you had specific information to the contrary, we can assume that a leeway correction applies only when close-hauled, sailing to weather. Even falling off to a close reach reduces the leeway dramatically in most vessels. On the other hand, it is not out of the question that even a powerboat with much windage might slip to leeward as well, and in these cases, you would just apply whatever correction you detect or estimate. It is even possible that a powerboat might have to tack across strong winds in big seas for the safest course.

Correcting DR for Current

We can correct the DR for offsets by tidal or coastal current, but only with crucial assumptions. First, we must have some estimate of the current direction and speed, and second, we have to assume that both remain constant over

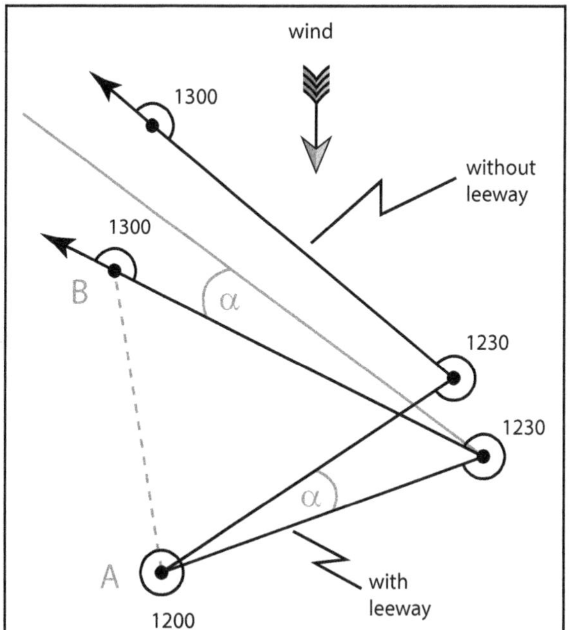

Figure 12.13-3. *Correcting tacking DR for leeway angle α. The distance run from 1200 to 1230 is the same as without leeway, the course angle is just plotted α° downwind. Doing a running fix from 1200 to 1300, you would advance the 1200 LOP by the line A-B.*

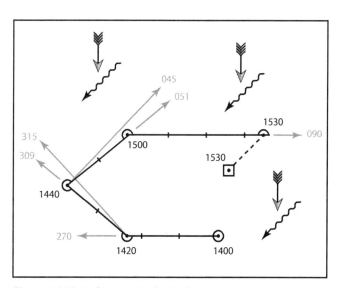

Figure 12.13-4. *Correcting DR for 6° leeway sailing in a current of 0.8 kts to the SW. We assume no leeway on the two reaching legs, and 6° to leeward when tacking. We need logged runs or good average speeds to make the DR plot, but the current correction depends only on the time spent in the current. This example was scaled for 7 kts reaching and 6 kts tacking. The square symbol marks out best account of our position at 1530. We can call this a corrected DR or an estimated position.*

the region and time period we are considering. If we know things are changing in time or location, then the corrections have to be done piecemeal, over areas of constant conditions.

Nevertheless, even with rough estimates of the current and its persistence, we do much better by making the corrections than we do by ignoring them. Furthermore, within the assumptions made, the correction is very easy.

All that needs to be done is to plot out the DR track over the time period of interest with course changes and leeway if present, and then move the final DR position by the total drift of the current during the time we were in it. For example, sailing in a north wind, you could reach 20 minutes. west (no leeway), come up on the wind, and tack northwest for 20 minutes (with 6° leeway), tack again to the NE for 20 minutes (again 6° leeway), then fall off to the E and sail 30 minutes more (no leeway). With this information, you can make a DR plot for this run, correcting for leeway on the two weather legs. You will get something like Figure 12.13-4.

You need to know the speeds on each of the legs, or better still, the log readings at each course change, in order to make the DR plot, but we actually do not need this information to correct the final plot for the current. For the current correction, all we need to know is how long we were in the current, and the answer is 1 hour 30 minutes, or 1.5 hours. To correct our DR position for current, we just have to correct it by how much the water has moved during this 1.5 hours.

If the current during this time was 1.0 kt to the south, we would just take the final DR position and move it 1.5 nmi to the south. If the current were flowing southwest at 0.8 kts (as shown in Figure 12.13-4), we would move the final DR position 1.2 nmi to the southwest (1.5 × 0.8). You plot what you do, then correct it for what the water does. That is all there is to it.

You can sail many miles on inshore waters and never need a running fix, but if you sail long enough in varied conditions, eventually you will run across a situation where a running fix is the only way to find out where you are. A navigator should be prepared for all conditions, so practice with running fixes is fundamental to good navigation preparation.

12.14 Meaning of COG, SOG, and SO ON

The jargon and acronyms of modern electronic navigation are complex and still evolving. Concise communication has always been important in navigation. Expedient abbreviations are not new. What is new are the many on-board electronic aids that can derive important navigational parameters directly, relieving the navigator of the traditional vector math. Consequently, more parameters are used these days to judge performance than in the past. The challenge is that manufacturers of the electronics that calculate

these things do not always agree on what to call the results. VMG (velocity made good) means quite different things, depending on which brand of which black box you read it from.

The following terms pretty much follow the Bowditch Glossary, but these days the National Marine Electronics Association (NMEA) as well as various publications of the International Maritime Organization (IMO) have ultimate control on what we use—or should use. The results do not match those of any one particular brand of electronics, but as no two brands agree, I step on no toes (or all toes). The terms are illustrated in Figure 12.14-1.

The Terms

Heading (H). The actual direction the boat is pointed, read from a compass. This heading, however, does not tell which way the boat is moving. With no way on, a boat drifts in whatever direction the wind blows or the current sets it, regardless of which way it is pointed.

Course Over Ground (COG). The actual direction the boat is moving in relative to land. It is the direction of one position fix to the next. Difference between average values of COG and H is caused by current, leeway, and biased helmsmanship in waves or shifting winds, or heading sensor errors.

Course (C). The direction to a desired destination (the next mark or some favorable spot on the race course, or a waypoint on a route) measured from your present position. This destination can be stored in the GPS, which in turn calculates C and displays it continuously. If boat speed were the same in every direction, C would be the direction to go. However, sailboat speed—and often powerboat speed—is not the same in every direction, so C is not often

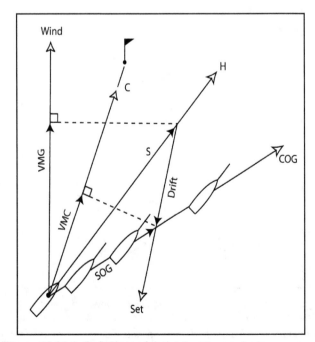

Figure 12.14-1. *Definitions of derived vector products.*

TW	000°		
C	023°		
Set	190°		
Drift	2.1 kts		
H	041°	051°	061°
S	4.50 kts	5.00	5.50
COG	062°	072°	082°
SOG	2.90 kts	3.70	4.50
VMC	2.25 kts	2.40	2.30
VMG	3.40 kts	3.15	2.67

Figure 12.14-2. *Sailing in current, VMC is more important than VMG, which is relative to the wind direction.*

the optimum course to steer. In many cases under sail it is not even a possible course to steer.

Speed (S). Speed of the boat, relative to the water, in the direction of the heading (H) of the boat. The knotmeter speed. In one sense, S is the least important speed of all since a boat can sail against current with S reading 3 kts while the boat is not moving at all. In another sense, S is the most important speed because it is the only fast check on sail trim and helm.

Speed Over Ground (SOG). Speed of the boat, relative to the land, in the direction of COG that the boat is actually moving. It is derived from the distance between two sequential GPS position fixes divided by the time between the two fixes. It is the speed used to figure how long it will take to go another mile in the actual direction the boat is moving. On a straight course at roughly constant speed (steady conditions without erratic helmsmanship), current is the only thing that can make SOG much different than S. When SOG is bigger than S, the current is helping; when SOG is smaller than S, the current is hurting. Note that leeway actually increases your knotmeter speed, so it is rather different than current in this regard.

Speed Made Good (SMG). This is distinguished from SOG in that SOG is an active live value read from the GPS, whereas SMG is a speed you might predict based on estimated courses and times, or it could be the value of the average speed you accomplished after a run over some period of time, with or without course changes. Both SOG and SMG are computed the same way, namely, the distance between two positions divided by the time between them, but the SOG time intervals are very small (maybe 1 second or less, or you can force an average that is a bit longer in some instruments) and it is a dynamic value, potentially changing continuously, whereas SMG is a static value determined from static locations and times.

Course Made Good (CMG). The difference between CMG and COG is the same as that between SMG and SOG.

Thus, we can end up saying things like: "My COG varied between 200 and 150, but at the end of the day our CMG was 170." Or, for example, "Sailing in and out of the wind and current our knotmeter speed varied from 4 to 7, with sometimes a great current ride getting the SOG up to 8 kts, but for the full trip across the bay our SMG was only 5.3 kts."

Another distinction is this. Your COG is shown on the echart as a live projection from the boat icon, showing the direction you will be proceeding in if nothing changes. But once you have a track of past positions displayed behind the boat icon, the direction of that track would be called a CMG.

Velocity Made Course (VMC). Speed of the boat, relative to the land, in the direction of the desired waypoint. This is the speed that tells how fast you are getting to where you want to go. It is the projection of SOG onto the course direction (C). You can have a great SOG, but if the COG is not toward your destination, you are not making the progress you want. The VMC is the truth meter to watch (Figure 12.14-2). To follow up on the introduction, this parameter is still called VMG on some units, but we should reserve VMG for SMG relative to the true wind. The NMEA counterpart is called *waypoint closing velocity* (WCV), but this term is not often used in modern electronics, so we defer to VMC, which is used.

Velocity Made Good (VMG). Speed of the boat, relative to the water, in the direction of true wind. This speed is unique among the above. It is calculated by wind instruments, not navigation instruments, and is a measure of sailing performance, as opposed to the others which measure navigation performance. For more details see Section 12.30.

12.15 Sailboat Racing with GPS and Radar

The trick to racing with GPS is learning to take advantage of it without letting it take advantage of you. I can think back to when true wind instruments first appeared. Many of us chased the VMG meters of our new toys all over the race course, while less sophisticated boats sailed right by us watching their telltales. It took practice to turn true wind instruments into required equipment on the race course. The same transition is still underway to some extent with GPS, and with radar, strangely enough, it has barely gotten underway. GPS is obviously required equipment for competitive yachts, especially in current, but at the same time, it can be tactically misleading or outright dangerous if used improperly.

When racing, navigation reduces to knowing where you are and what course you are making good on each tack or jibe. Everything else the navigator does to figure the fastest route from A to B is really tactics. GPS, more than anything else, aids racing by giving the navigator more time for tactics, because it dramatically reduces the time it takes to navigate. Nevertheless, good navigation remains the key to good tactics. You can't pick the best route to some place else without knowing where you are now (in a lake or in the ocean), and you also need to know how fast your progress is on each board in present conditions—not to mention the key factor of having some guess of conditions on other parts of the race course or ocean.

So the first step to racing with GPS is learning how to navigate with GPS. This is especially important in racing, where sometimes the line between safe and fast is a thin one that must often be drawn quickly.

Navigating with GPS requires knowing how accurate it is at any given time and place. We tend to take this for granted, but this is not as easy to know or to test as it might seem, since it is not always easy to know where you are to a precision good enough to test the GPS, especially when moving. A good first step to learning about GPS accuracy is to leave the unit turned on and recording and plotting positions every minute or so overnight when you are tied up at the dock. Then maybe do the same thing at home with the device sitting in a window that sees only half the horizon. An example is shown in Figure 12.15-1.

More often than not, we end up very impressed with the accuracy, but it takes just an example or two of statistical excursions to keep us alert to potential hazards, and to remind us of the basic tenet of navigation: do not ever rely on one aid alone for position information in a crucial situation.

If the displayed accuracy parameter is 30 ft or less, you probably have conditions as good as they get. If this number is 60 to 160 ft, the position is not reliable. But these are still a statistical measurement of the distributions of any one reading of the dial, which you learn by recording the positions overnight. These values are best considered as the radius of the uncertainty, not the diameter. Thus, you could get consecutive readings that vary by twice the indicated amount, or even more. In short, if an accurate position is required, we must do some time averaging on the data.

These uncertainties must also be considered when entering the waypoints of the marks on the course. The standard procedure is to enter the marks as soon as you know them, then save the actual location as waypoints as you go by them to use for a second rounding.

If there is a narrow pass you must go through, and you might have to return through it in the fog, then it is best to have it entered as a permanent waypoint from a stored position during an actual transit of the pass. Likewise, if there is an off-lying submerged rock that it pays to go inside of (from a racing point of view—we are not talking prudent sailing here), it is best to find it someday when not racing and enter its true position by sitting very near it for some time. Then you can go inside it at night or in fog with somewhat more confidence. The same applies to cutting corners on spits and headlands. But in all cases, keep in mind that we need to have other checks on our navigation. It is not prudent, racing or not, to rely solely on GPS.

With the hazard entered as a waypoint, you can let the GPS do the piloting around it by monitoring the GPS outputs of range and bearing to the hazard waypoint, keeping in mind what you may have learned about the accuracy. Obviously, we must be confident the GPS is working right if we are to use it this way. And the only way to do this is to watch it continuously whenever in use, even after having checked it carefully during the past. If you are not using ECS to record your trail, plot your GPS position frequently (every couple of minutes or so, depending on the circumstances) on large-scale charts and check this position visually at each opportunity. The problem, as always in racing navigation, is doing it fast. We can often get by with the echart plots, but if it really matters, you want to be sure you have the printed chart set up and ready to use if needed.

The fastest way to plot that I have come up with is the method shown in Figure 7.3. It was developed for racing with GPS without echarts. It takes some chart preparation, but once done, you are ready for an efficient backup as needed.

The charted track of these positions can then be compared with the GPS COG output as a double check. Another fast situation check is to note what lies dead ahead looking over the bow compared with what your echart or paper chart CMG claims is dead ahead. If these two views do not match, then you may be getting set or slipping with leeway. Also check your position whenever passing close abeam of any prominent landmark—as you see the landmark approaching, recall its waypoint (entered as a potential candidate or mark before the race), and then watch range and bearing as you pass. None of these checks is as good as a fix, but they are fast and can be done frequently. Remember too that in many cases, the depth of the water is another check of your position.

Getting there fastest

GPS can aid in choosing the favored tack, but typically, you must sail each tack for some time to get this help. Enter the windward mark as a waypoint, and monitor the VMC (velocity made course) to this waypoint—also still called VMG (velocity made good) on some units, but I will use VMC for this speed here to avoid confusion with wind-instrument outputs of VMG along the true wind direction.

The VMC is your true speed toward the mark, taking into account course angle, leeway, current, and heading (helm) variations due to the wind and sea state. One approach is to make frequent entries into a logbook of COG, SOG, VMC, along with the true wind speed (TWS). Then watch the VMC on each tack. If one is faster than the other, and nothing else has changed, then you are getting there faster on the tack with the faster VMC.

But we must be careful here. The GPS can't compute an accurate value of this very quickly; it does not know what lies ahead, and it does not know what is happening on the other tack as you sail into new conditions. A combined change in wind and current, for example, might improve your present VMC and make you happy, not knowing that it has improved the VMC on the other tack even more. In short, when considering the favored tack or jibe, one has to watch all parameters on all instruments, not just the VMC.

In some conditions, you might just have to sail the other tack in the new conditions before you can make this call. It can be difficult to gauge the effect of the sea state on your VMC.

Choosing the favored downwind reaching angle is often a more transparent operation. It's also an important one, especially on long legs through current when the mark is not in sight. If you reach harder, you go faster but must sail farther, so there is an optimum reaching angle that maximizes VMC. In some circumstances, the angle between current set and rhumb line will have a greater effect on optimum heading to steer than the polar diagrams of speed versus reaching angle, but even so, in light air you generally must reach harder than in heavy air.

The practical approach is just to pick the apparent wind angle that seems about right (or that everyone else is sailing), record VMC to the mark, come up 5°, trim, wait a few minutes for the GPS to think about it, and record the new VMC. If it is better and the true wind is still the same, then you are doing better. Then hunt around this way for the optimum reaching angle. But also monitor everything else. With wind or current changes, you may have to fall back off to optimize VMC even though it is increasing as you watch it. It might increase faster falling off.

In steady conditions, especially with strong current, knowing the CMG for each tack (that is, keeping a plot or logbook of this data) helps predict the layline, since it is just the CMG of the opposite tack or jibe that will take you to the mark at the same apparent wind angle—in the present conditions of wind, current, and leeway. If you do not

have ECS to do this as shown in Figure 12.12-3, you can use parallel rulers to plot the reciprocal of the opposite-tack's CMG from the next mark. Then project your COG forward to where it intersects that line. Measure the distance to go, and then use your SOG to compute how long it will be until the next tack.

One of the more challenging problems in GPS racing, however, is figuring how this call should be altered after you made it, once you detect from GPS that conditions have significantly changed. This boils down to guessing what the new opposite-tack CMG will be now that the present one has changed for some reason.

Another, sometimes valuable use of derived parameters is determining how long to carry a headsail reach around an island before setting the spinnaker. But this is just one of many good examples of how GPS only contributes to a decision (by giving, in this case, important COG and current data) that usually must be made from instantaneous wind data rather than averaged navigation data—not to mention a good guess of conditions farther up the course. It is an example of a decision that must often be made faster than the GPS can think.

Any use of derived parameters like VMC, COG, and SOG must be done with some patience—a clear conflict with racing principles. Zooming in on a plotted track display can help speed up the evaluation. Put another way, sometimes we simply can't use these data because decisions they aid must be made before the GPS has time to provide the answers. Figuratively speaking, the GPS determines each of these derived values by remembering where it was some time ago, and then calculating what the course and speed must have been to get from there and here. It then carries out a sliding average of these results for a preset averaging period, which is adjustable in some units. But each of

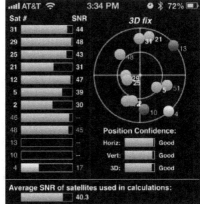
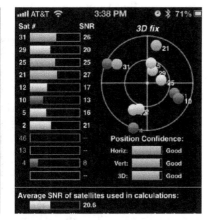

Figure 12.15-1. *Two GPS tracks for 30 minutes each. Red track (smaller pattern) had good reception (top left) with two WAAS satellites (46 and 48) in view, though only one is needed; the green (larger) pattern had poor reception (top right), and looking out the window, it could not see either WAAS satellite. In each case, the centroid of the GPS positions did not coincide with the true location of the receiver, but they were within the reported accuracy level. This was an X150 BlueTooth GPS connected to opencpn.org software running in a Mac, then moved to Google Earth as gpx files for plotting.*

these positions has some uncertainty in it, so if we are to get a good speed, given that we have precise times, we must travel enough that this uncertainty is small compared with the distance between them. If my GPS position is bouncing around by 100 ft, and I am moving at 1 knot (100 ft per minute), then I must travel longer than 1 minute just to move out of the noise. Recall that a latitude increment of 0.01' is 60 ft.

On the other hand, if I am moving at 10 kts, then I will move 1,000 ft in 1 minute, so the 100-foot uncertainty causes only a (roughly) 10% uncertainty in my speed.

Here, again, is a place where practice helps, since the time we must wait to get a tactically useful COG and SOG depends not only on the magnitude and uniformity of our speed and course, but also on the present accuracy of our position determined by geometric factors such as the view of the horizon and satellite angles. You might be able to test this by varying the averaging times. Again, some units display an accuracy factor that is at least a quick hint to the quality of the fixes. Periodically checking the satellite status display for your unit (similar to those shown in Figure 12.15-1) will be a good reminder of your satellite health.

GPS receivers for mariners have made much progress over the past few years. They are locking onto the signals faster and doing a better job of evaluating them. But we still benefit from a guideline on how long we should wait for dependable data after a prominent maneuver, such as a tack or jibe. A starting point (from my own records, which might actually be too conservative these days) is to average for a number of minutes equal to 10 divided by SOG. After this time period, I hope that the SOG is right to within a few percent, and that the COG is right to within a few degrees—assuming, of course, that we are indeed sailing a straight line at constant speed. By right I mean that what I read is within a few percent of what it would be if I averaged much longer, and that I would not see variations larger than that on the dials. If this is not the case when you do the tests, then change the averaging time accordingly. If they stabilize sooner, choose a shorter averaging time; if still bouncing around at an averaging time near (10/SOG) minutes, then lengthen the time.

These tests, with some cooperation from the helm, can be made during the tune up before the start (if you get onto the course early enough) and should be checked periodically throughout the race, especially if your average speed changes significantly. This is a perfect study for the navigator to make during practice sails. In other words, hold a steady course and speed, then tack as efficiently as possible and monitor the COG and SOG to see how long they take to stabilize. In fact, you end up learning more about your tacking performance than the GPS in these studies, but you will also be able to compare the knotmeter and compass with the COG and SOG to see how they correlate in stability as you maneuver. Compare, for example, how much speed you lose on the knotmeter compared with that displayed in

the SOG, and measure how long it takes the COG to stabilize compared with the compass heading.

We need a guideline for averaging times because on the race course the SOG and COG will bounce around because they are actually changing as we sail—when racing, we are not trying to hold a steady course; we are trying to go fast. The goal is to have some minimum averaging time after which we know the changes are real, and not just the GPS trying to sort itself out after a large change in course and speed. Be sure to check the manual to see whether there is any preset averaging time in effect and whether you have control over this.

Then if you have a tested average time, try to adhere to it. If you look at the answers too early, it is hard to overcome the temptation to believe them. And , of course, try not to tack again (if not needed) before good numbers are established. The measured COG and VMC on that tack can be valuable data, even if there is no particular advantage to sailing it right now.

If the numbers are still changing past your known averaging time, then chances are something has changed on the race course or the boat. You may have sailed into new current, but you can't be sure till you give it some time.

In some sailing areas, a main virtue of the GPS is its ability to tell us the current we are in. If the COG differs from your heading (H) and the SOG differs from the knotmeter speed (S), then you are in current—or in current with leeway, when going to weather in very strong or very light air. Pure leeway without current can be detected since SOG will be very near S, but COG will be some degrees to leeward of H, and these conditions will be the same on both tacks—a circumstance that is not possible with current present. Actual set and drift are valuable data, in large part because they test your current predictions, which lets you know whether you or pure chance is in control of this factor.

With most GPSs, however, it is much easier to know we are in current than to know the current we are in. Only top-line ECS will accept knotmeter and heading sensor inputs and use these with SOG and COG to output set and drift. Generally, we must figure this ourselves as outlined in Section 12.20—or input the data into a dedicated mobile app, and let it do the calculations.

This brings up the point of sophisticated ECS developed for yacht racing. The full system has to include high quality instruments and software. These systems not only figure the current and fold this in with the wind data and your own boat's polar diagrams for best performance, they will also make all predictions you might care about on the race course, and equally important, before the race at the start line. It is standard equipment on high-end racing yachts. During the America's Cup when you saw the navigator looking at a huge wrist display, or folding down a tablet mounted on their chest, it was a program like this they were looking at. Everything you want to know laid out in big numbers in front of you.

There are many options with various levels of racing information. Popular software includes: *Expedition, Deckman, Adrena, qtVlm*, among others, and instruments with associated software popular with racing sailors include B&G, Garmin, NKE, and again, many others. Besides requiring top quality instrumentation, however, success with these systems requires very careful calibration and maintenance. Even a relatively small error in the input can make a large error in the derived output. This is not plug and play.

One of the key features of all of these racing ECS is the ability to store *all* the data from *all* of the instruments and display them as a strip chart in any combination, such as wind speed, boat speed, and pointing angle. Or current set and drift as a function of time, or distance. This gives the navigator a complete graphic picture of what is going on. This is ideal for testing and training, as well as developing target boat speeds and sailing angles. It is also direct display of the GPS performance discussed above.

Radar in Racing

We do not cover details of radar navigation in this book, but we must mention in the present context the extreme value of radar on the race course. Even local racing with boats large enough for radar can benefit from a careful use of this important tool. We still see racers on deck (leaning against a radar post) trying to determine whether or not a certain boat nearby is going faster or slower, or is it pointed higher or lower, "making trees or not making trees." A trip to the radar screen below could answer those questions in minutes, very quantitatively. It involves unfolding the relative motion diagram with some quick screen measurements, or with a calibrated heading sensor and knotmeter, it can sometimes be read right from the screen with what is often called a "mini ARPA" function (automatic radar plotting aid). Even without the mini ARPA option, a stabilized display using a heading sensor greatly improves the process.

Needless to say, in any form of navigation, we often care to know the relative speed and heading of a nearby vessel, so this radar exercise is not restricted to racing. For details of the several steps involved, see *Radar for Mariners*.

12.16 Marine Radios

Radios are fundamental to marine navigation. They are used for vessel-to-vessel communications for safety and communications, as well as for calling the USCG in an emergency, or talking with harbor masters to arrange docking and checking on facilities. The radios and their usage are completely standardized and controlled by national and international rules.

The most common, and essentially required, radio is used for short-range communications, which span the line of sight distance from antenna to antenna. These are called VHF radios, named after their frequency range (very high frequency, ~156 to 162 MHz), a signal frequency similar to those of commercial FM radio stations, which are also short-range line-of-sight, but from very much higher antennas. In most situations, once on the water, the VHF radio replaces your cellphone as the primary means of communications.

There are extensive resources online that cover VHF radio usage. In principle, the most fundamental is fcc.gov, but this is not a user-friendly site. The basics we need on procedures are all laid out nicely at the USCG Navigation Center site (navcen.uscg.gov), which is a fundamental resource for all of marine navigation and communications. Find the link called "Radio Information for Boaters." For equipment options, pricing, and in-depth operations, the West Marine website does a nice job explaining various radio options. As with all electronics, we learn a lot from downloading manuals from several companies.

There are console units with external antennas that have optimum performance (with a good installation), and there are also handheld units, which are invaluable on any size vessel. The console units should be installed and tested by professional electronics technicians.

In contrast to masthead antennas in console units (up to 25 watts output), the low output power of portable units (6 watts) and the greater electrical attenuation of signals so close to the water can cause even greater electronic limits. Handheld radios used from the deck or dinghy often do not reach the theoretical line-of-sight ranges.

VHF radios differ from cellphones in that you do not just turn them on and call; you must first select the proper channel to communicate on, depending on the nature of the communication. The Navigation Center link has a list of channels. Figure 12.16-1 is a card that can be handy if you do not use the radio often and need a quick reference of which channel to use.

Usually, you can communicate with large ships or sailboats (with antennas on the masthead) that are within 10 nmi off—meaning, as a practical guide, when in sight on a clear day—but you might not be able to reach a fishing boat or other small powerboat that is more than 5 or so miles off, even when clearly in sight. The Coast Guard has very good VHF radio coverage throughout US coastal and inland waters; they use repeater antennas, so you need not be near an actual Coast Guard station to communicate with them. Except for a few blind spots between islands or inside of deep coves, the Coast Guard can usually be reached with a VHF radio within and along most American coastal and connecting waters. On the other hand, their antennas are so high and the power so large that when sailing farther offshore, you might easily hear them from a distance off that you cannot call back from .

Weather radio broadcasts on VHF can be received from anywhere within the geographic limits of the broadcast antennas, but any VHF transmission can be shut off completely by intervening terrain. The locations and heights of NOAA weather radio broadcast antennas are given on

Marine Weather Services Charts, and although they are no longer supported by NOAA, the heights and locations of these antennas are an example of valuable data they contain.

Because most vessels equipped with VHF radios continuously monitor the watch channel 16—an official requirement, although one that is not strictly adhered to by all small craft—an emergency call might well be received by other vessels even when the Coast Guard cannot receive the transmission from your location deep inside a sheltered cove along a steep shore. Standard procedures for sending or relaying emergency messages are covered in official and commercial publications on radio use, and it is not legal or practical to use these radios without first studying these references.

It is important be aware of the rules on radio usage. If you loan or rent boats or radios, it could be important to note that the laws presented in *Navigation Rules* clearly state that the owner of the vessel shares the responsibility for any violation of the Rules, regardless of who actually made the violation; some Federal Communications Commission (FCC) rules on radio usage are contained in *Navigation Rules*, but not all. Sailboat owners who have chartered their boats have been fined and the fines upheld for violations they knew nothing at all about until they received the violation notice.

Published battery life on handheld units varies from 8 to 20 hours; based on 90-05-05 usage: 90% standby, 5% receive, and 5% transmit at high power. A fully charged 10-hour battery charge could be used for about 30 minutes of total talk time. Calls must be brief and to the point. Backup battery packs and telescoping antennas (which significantly increase radio range) are valuable options. Most units are now waterproof—but does it float? Some do, some don't.

Modern VHF radios offer many options, reflected in a price range of $150 to $1500. Emergency broadcasts with a built-in GPS or a link to your GPS is one of the enhanced features. Some can also be rigged as a loud hailer. Most let you monitor multiple channels at once, with numerous configurations. Ironically, the more features you get, the harder it might be to place a simple call. Marine VHF radios have grown up to the point that we now need to read the manuals—gone are the days with just three knobs: volume, squelch, and channel selector, with a high-low output power switch... but to be fair, gone also are the days when a fisherman needed three VHF radios to meet his needs.

Uses of a VHF Marine Radio

You can receive weather broadcasts on the weather channels WX1 to WX7. Adjacent stations used different channels. In some areas, you can receive more than one. You can also hear the reports online for many stations, which is good practice (see starpath.com/navbook for an updated link). The broadcasts are continuous, twenty-four hours a day, with updates of actual reports every three hours, and new forecasts every six hours. American coastal

weather broadcasts are given by the Coast Guard at specific times on channel 22A. For schedules and more details, see NOAA Weather Radio (nws.noaa.gov/nwr). Other countries, including Canada, use channels 67, 26, 25, and 19 for these special broadcasts.

Use channel 16 to call for emergency help from any vessel or the Coast Guard. Nonemergency calls to the Coast Guard are made first on channel 16, then switched to channel 22A. The Coast Guard broadcast Notices to Mariners (i.e., that a lighthouse is temporarily not working) and special weather broadcasts are first announced on channel 16, then broadcast on channel 22A.

To contact other vessels for weather or sea state information, or to check that they see you (in some special circumstances of collision risk) or to talk to other boaters equipped with radios, make initial contact on channel 16 or 9. Once contact is made, switch to one of the unused working channels: 68, 69, 71, 72, or 78A. Channel 70 is not in this list. That channel is strictly reserved for digital transmissions between automated equipment and related distress or safety calls, which are most effective if your radio has a GPS connection.

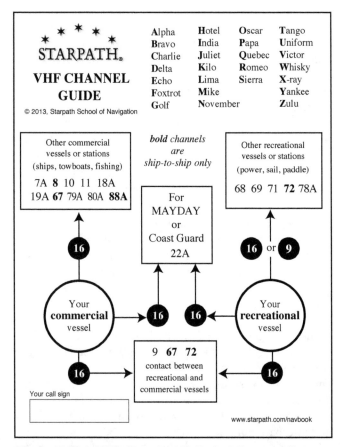

Figure 12.16-1. *VHF channel guide. Dark circles are calling channels; boxed channels are the switch-to channels once a communication link has been established. Older radios may not have the "A" labels, pronounced alpha, i.e., 22-alpha. Use only low power when calling vessels near you. A pdf version for printing is at starpath.com/navbook.*

The alpha (A) designation to some channels means they are for US waters only, and they might not work properly in Canada, for example. If your radio has a US-International switch somewhere, be sure it is set properly for the waters you are in. Older radios might not show this distinction, in which case they will work in US waters but maybe not on international waters.

For planned communications within a group, one of the working channels can be chosen ahead to avoid the extra contact through channel 16 (provided that someone else is not using it when you want to call; only one party can use a channel at one time within a given geographic area, and you may not interrupt except in emergencies).

Channel 9 is an alternative to channel 16 for calling between recreational vessels. Its use is encouraged in areas with high traffic where extensive use of channel 16 by non-commercial vessels has interfered with operations. Channel 16 remains the best choice for emergency calling, however, even where 9 is actively used for calling.

Channels 13 or 14 (and in some places 11) are available for monitoring (listening only) ship traffic discussions, often with their locations, port operations, and the visibility reports they frequently provide. Although you could make contact with ships or the Coast Guard Traffic Control on these channels, it should be strongly avoided. These are busy channels intended only for navigational matters of large vessels. Channels 11, 12, 74, and others also are used for this purpose in some areas. (Channel 13 or 67 is often the main working frequency of drawbridges and locks, although they could be called on 16 for initial contact.)

Before the rise of cellphones, it was common to use the VHF to place phone calls to land lines through the local marine operator, but this service is essentially replaced by extended cellphone coverage. In the last printing of the book we cited what was to turn out to be the last station to offer this. In an emergency situation that has left you in an unknown location in thick fog (without a phone or smartwatch!), the Coast Guard can locate you by radio direction finding on your transmitted signal. This service should be reserved for real emergencies.

Practice with your radio before setting off on a trip that might depend on its use. Contact other vessels to test its range; talk to passing fishing vessels or recreational craft. Also, whenever you are near the water or in VHF range of vessel communications, turn on your radio and eavesdrop on the various channels to learn the protocol—which is also a reminder that VHF calls are not at all private. Many people will be listening to everything you say.

It also pays to have everyone on board familiar with the radio usage. The VHF is easy to use, but there is no point in having to figure it out for the first time in an emergency.

Again, cellphones are not an alternative to VHF. Every vessel on the water should carry at least a portable VHF. But obviously we should take our cellphones with us on the boat. Chances are they will have apps we need for computa-tion or weather work, even if not for marine communications. And, sure enough, there have been numerous cases where they were used to call the USCG in an emergency. At one point, *cg was a way to call the USCG in some districts, but that has long been discontinued. In an emergency, call 9-1-1 with your location services turned on, then they know where you are as well.

Also keep in mind, that you might get better cellphone reception from a higher elevation, so if a remote call is crucial, consider going as high in the boat as possible—on some coastal tugs, they call the crow's nest the "phone booth." If your chart shows any drilling platforms nearby, you might also head toward them, as they might have a cellphone tower on them.

Once you travel outside of VHF range, communications are restricted to HF (SSB) radios or to satellite phones. These are beyond the scope of this book, although long coastal cruising would call for one of these options . There are pros and cons to consider when making a choice between these. Satellite phones can be rented by the week or month.

A recent change that affects HF (SSB) usage in coastal waters is the USCG decision to discontinue HF frequencies 2182 and 2670. These were the offshore equivalents of VHF channel 16 for calling and channel 22A for communications with the USCG on the low end of the HF (SSB) radio's frequency range. Replacement protocols are covered at the Navigation Center. My own experience would support that decision; there are other HF options that are much more dependable, and these were not often used, largely because many radio installations did not perform well at these lower HF frequencies.

12.17 POD and NCC Printed Charts

NOAA discontinued printing the traditional lithographic paper charts in April, 2014. The reasons given included the rising popularity of echarts, and (more to the point) the wide acceptance of NOAA print-on-demand (POD) charts. Agents who sold both types of charts sold 80% more POD charts than litho charts, in large part because when they get back to the ship, the navigators know the charts are up to date. "Federal budget realities" were also mentioned, but this was not a predominantly economic decision, even though traditional litho charts have been heavily subsidized.

POD charts have become the standard for most nations, but we note this now, in early 2023, just as the POD chart era itself is coming to a close! NOAA is well into its 5-year program of discontinuing traditional paper charts and all chart products related to them. By the end of 2024 all such charts and products will no longer exist. These traditional chart products are intended to be replaced by electronic navigational charts (ENC) supplemented by a new concept in paper charts called NOAA Custom Charts (NCC). Just as POD charts eventually outpaced the use of litho charts,

ENC usage has long outpaced the use of paper charts, so this major policy change is in large part a response to that.

Viewed in an electronic chart system (ECS), ENC include much more navigational information than a paper chart can display, and they are updated weekly, plus they are easy to download and install.

The new NCC paper charts are based on the ENC chart data, and how we obtain the NCC is an all new concept in charting. Each mariner custom designs the charts they want with an online NOAA app, covering just the region they want. It does not have to follow the boundaries of existing paper charts, nor of existing ENC. Choose the area you want charted, the scale you want to use, and an appropriate paper size, and the app creates a hi-res PDF file of that chart, along with all the notes that would appear on charts of your selected region. It is then the mariner's task to find a place to print the chart, which they do at their own expense.

There are many printing options. Existing POD chart outlets will print them in standard chart sizes on standard chart paper, but these will end up costing about the same as traditional POD charts. Alternatively, they can be printed at Office Depot, Staples, or other outlets, at the paper size and quality of your choice, often at notable savings. Since you can make charts of any region, you might choose sets of smaller ones that can be printed on smaller paper, better suited for small craft navigation. A portal to NCC related links is at starpath.com/NCC, which includes details on print options.

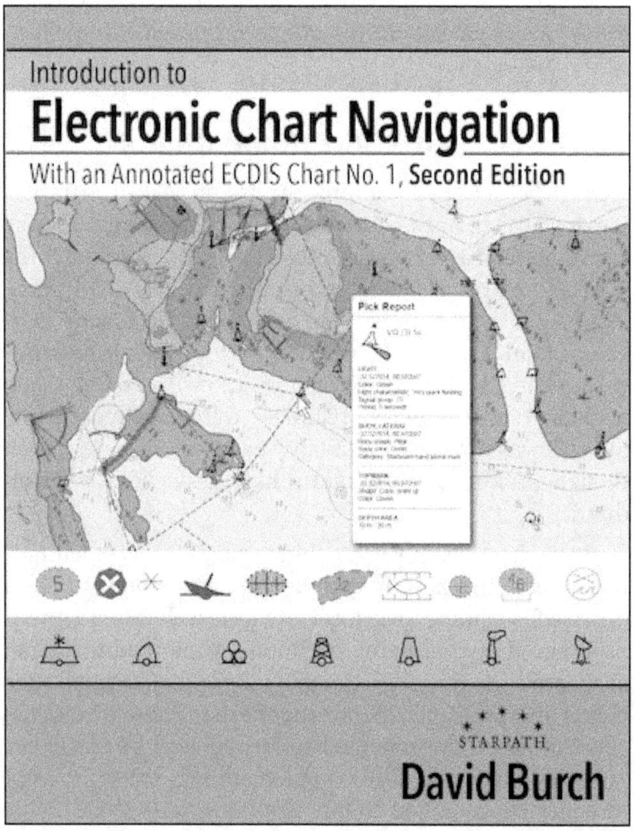

We recommend that all mariners experiment with these new style paper charts by creating and printing ones that cover areas you sail in. The NCC app is still in development stage; the link above lists challenges still to be solved. But we are confident that eventually these new paper charts will be superior to the traditional versions we have used for years. An update to the app is expected in early 2023, which includes among other improvements a way to save your chart set up, so you can just reload it to create a new PDF that has all the latest updates installed.

For the time being, the NCC are effectively considered as backup to the primary, official charts which are the ENC that must be viewed in an ECS. Any suspected deficiency in an NCC could be checked with the corresponding ENC, viewed, for example, in one of the free ECS such as OpenCPN or qtVlm. Both have Mac and PC versions. The former has an Android version; the latter has both Android and iOS versions, but in both cases the mobile versions are not free. The US ENC are all free downloads. See starpath.com/getcharts for a portal to all related products.

As noted, ENC contain much more navigation information than paper charts, but how this information is presented, and how we interact with ENC in general when navigating is quite different than we are used to with paper charts. These topics are not within the scope of this text, but our book *Introduction to Electronic Chart Navigation* (Figure 12.17-1) covers these charts and the new type of "chart reading" they call for.

12.18 Accuracy of Current Predictions

Our best efforts at navigation planning are going to be disappointing if we are sailing in water that is moving and we don't know about it.

In the Pacific Northwest, this is a common problem. Much of Puget Sound, the Strait of Georgia, and the Strait of Juan de Fuca, have tidal currents over 1 knot, and currents of 3 to 4 kts are not uncommon over some large areas like Admiralty Inlet. Even stronger currents occur in narrow passes (7 kts in Deception Pass or 15 kts in Seymour Narrows, BC), but these—though definitely a concern for the safe navigation of the passes—are less trouble to our overall navigation because they are confined to the limited region of the passes. The more insidious problem is the 1 or 2 kts current over a large region, especially when that current is changing continuously.

If I must go through Deception Pass, it is important that I know the current is strong there and how to look up when the current occurs; but it is a more important navigational challenge to know the currents between where I am now and Deception Pass, so I can figure how long it will take me to get there. If I do this part wrong and miss the minimum current at the Pass, knowing the current in the Pass doesn't do me much good!

Introduction to
Electronic Chart Navigation
With an Annotated ECDIS Chart No. 1, **Second Edition**

STARPATH
David Burch

Figure 12.17-1. *Text on use of ENC and related navigation.*

The problem with tidal currents is they change with the tides. Very broadly speaking, the flood current flows in as the water rises; the ebb current flows out as the water falls. Ebb currents are usually stronger than the floods because of river runoff. River runoff adds outgoing volume, but more important, it adds fresh water to the ebbs which makes the outgoing water slippier than the more dense incoming water.

Water with no current is called slack water. There is typically a slack period between flood and ebb, because tidal currents typically weaken as they change direction. But the slack can be very short lived, especially in narrow channels where currents are strong. A general rule for all waterways is: if the water can move at all, it is more likely to be moving than to be slack. Put another way, slack water is rarely still water.

To plan routes in currents, we must predict their strengths and directions at various locations and times. Predicting tidal currents in a complex estuary like Puget Sound—or even worse, in the San Juan Islands of Washington state—is a tough job. We can't hope to get it right to the tenth of a knot at a given time specified to the minute. Although current predictions appear to do just that, they are not intended to be interpreted quite that literally. In the real world, our goal must be less ambitious—more likely predicting the direction of the current, and then, with luck, whether or not it is large (2 to 3 kts or more), significant (0.5 to 2 kts), or essentially negligible (less than 0.5 kts), meaning small enough that we wouldn't go out of our way to get in or out of it.

Suppose the current predictions say the maximum strength of the morning ebb at a particular point on a particular day is 3.1 kts. It is predicted to occur at 0820. Now how much can we count on these values?

That answer depends on the winds, atmospheric conditions, and river runoff—and probably a few other things, but those are the main ones. Nevertheless, as a rule of thumb, we probably won't be surprised too often if we consider the NOAA predictions accurate to within about 20% on the strength and about 20 minutes on the time. Since 20% of 3.1 is 0.6, expect the maximum ebb current at that point to be somewhere between 2.5 kts and 3.7 kts, and expect maximum flow at somewhere between 0800 and 0840 in the morning.

In special conditions, we might make a guess at what side of this uncertainty to lean on. If the wind is strong and steady (say, 20 kts for half a day or longer), then you might add about 0.5 kts (2.5% of wind speed) of wind-driven current to the NOAA predictions in the direction of the wind. With a day-long 20 knot southerly in the region, the predicted 3.1 ebb might be closer to 3.6 kts. The floods for that day are predicted to be about 0.6 kts, but in this wind, that flood might be wiped out completely, with the water weakly ebbing or slack throughout the predicted flood period.

The times of maximum flow—based on a simple addition of the wind current and tidal current would not be changed by strong winds, but the times the current changes the directions would be. A wind in the direction of the current will make that cycle longer (meaning it starts earlier and lasts longer), leaving the maximum flow at about the predicted time. In the above example, the ebb might start some 30 minutes to an hour earlier and last about that much longer. The size of the time shift depends on the strength of the floods on either side of the ebb. The turn to a strong flood would be little affected, whereas a weak one might not show up at all.

The effect of excessive river runoff is similar to that of strong winds. It increases the strength and duration of the cycle, but in this case, the added current is always in the direction of the ebb. If it has been raining hard for a week or so, expect the ebbs to be stronger and longer and the floods to be weaker than predicted. Even rules of thumb would be hard to come by for this effect, but it can be strong—strong enough to reverse a 2-kt flood in some areas. The key is often the color of the water. Brown or gray water is usually a sign of river runoff. "If the water is brown or gray, it could be going the wrong way." Or here's a better jingle: "Brown water is yellow snow as far as currents go."

Unseasonable high or low pressure also affects the currents because it affects the tides through what is called the *inverse barometer effect*. This effect was known to mariners in the 1800s, when they came up with the jingle "The fog nips the tide." They had it almost right, but it was not the fog suppressing the tide range. It was high atmospheric pressure, which often enough leads to clear skies and cool nights that bring fog. The effect is small; we get only 10 cm of tide change with a pressure deviation of 10 mb, but for deep lows you can have tides rising well over a foot higher than expected due to pressure alone. (This was an important factor in the flooding from Storm Sandy on the NE coast in 2012.)

In regard to numerical estimates from pressure alone, you can get a rough feeling for the magnitude by scaling the currents from the normal tidal range with that for a range about 1 ft higher to estimate this component of the correction. That is, if the predicted range is 5 ft with a predicted 2 kts of current, then a 980 mb low (about 30 mb below average) could raise the HW by 1 ft (30 cm), so we might expect a peak current of $(6/5) \times 2 = 2.4$ kts. That is just to show that this effect is not huge, but it is also not zero. There are a lot of data on tide height versus pressure (storm tides), but not much on the resulting currents, primarily because it is difficult to separate out the contribution from more dominant wind-driven currents that come with the high winds associated with deep low pressure. On the other hand, a very high pressure will tend to inhibit the tide range, with proportionally less current flow.

12.19 AIS

The Automatic Identification System (AIS) is a worldwide electronic navigation system designed to prevent collisions and to facilitate maritime traffic control and security. It was developed for commercial vessels, but any vessel can take advantage of this important service on some level. It is now a key component of the electronic instrumentation of all vessels, recreational and commercial.

AIS shows where all ships and other commercial vessels within VHF radio range are located—they are required to have AIS—as well as all of the other vessels who have chosen to add optional AIS transmitters. AIS signals include the vessel's dynamic data: Lat-Lon, COG-SOG, and true heading (requires a separate heading sensor), as well as certain static data such as name, MMSI (Maritime Mobile Service Identity), call sign, vessel type, length and breadth, and GPS antenna location. Signals from Class A broadcasts (discussed below) also include voyage data including destination, ETA, cargo, rate of turn, present draft, navigation status (moored, underway, restricted maneuverability, constrained by draft, etc).

You have two ways to take part: You can install a receiver alone to learn about traffic around you, or you can install a transceiver, to both see AIS traffic and broadcast your own AIS information as well. Both are optional for recreational mariners, but transceivers are mandatory for commercial traffic. Receivers alone cost $60-$300, whereas transceivers are in the $800 to $3,000 range. At minimum, an AIS receiver should be considered standard electronic navigation equipment on all recreational vessels. Reception alone is very easy to set up; some new VHF radios include AIS output as an option, sharing the same antenna. Transceiver set-up is required to be assisted by a certified technician.

There are a few simple, but important, basics: First, we need a way to display the targets. The higher end receivers include a display of text data—which is not so convenient if that is all you set up—but all receivers have an output in NMEA format. The simplest solution is input the NMEA signals to your electronic chart system (ECS). This might be some integrated package of instruments and displays, or without that, you can run echarts on a laptop. AIS receivers have a USB output that goes directly into your computer. The free OpenCPN and qtVlm, for example, has many convenient AIS display options, as do all commercial echart programs.

Next, there are two classes of AIS signal transmission: Class-A transmission is the higher-end type required on ships and other commercial vessels, and Class-B transmission, available to vessels not required to carry Class A. All AIS receivers display both A and B signals, so the equipment decision is mostly receive only or transmit and receive. Recreational mariners can choose Class-A or Class-B transmission. Class A transceivers offer higher

performance, but they cost more, so Class-B transceivers are more popular with vessels not required to carry Class-A.

Vessels required to carry AIS Class A include: all commercial vessels over 65 ft, towing vessels over 26 ft with horsepower over 600, vessels certificated to carry more than 150 passengers, most dredging vessels, and all vessels with dangerous cargo.

Vessels required to carry AIS Class B if they do not carry Class A include: fishing industry vessels, and some passenger vessels that do not use traffic lanes nor have speeds over 14 kts. Vessels that would otherwise be required to carry AIS, but whose operations are restricted to a 1-nmi radius, can apply for an exemption to the AIS requirement. Other previous exemptions to the carriage rules all end on Mar 1, 2016. Vessels required to carry AIS must turn them on not later than 15 minutes before getting underway.

In short, ships, tow boats, and most larger commercial vessels use Class A, as do some fishing vessels, but most fishing vessels and most recreational vessels will be using Class B. Table 12.19-1 compares the specifications of Class A and Class B, and an enhanced B called B-SO or B+.

AIS can also be of great assistance in basic chart navigation in that prominent aids to navigation (buoys, lights, bridge pillar marks, etc) often send out AIS signals that show up on your echart display in the proper locations (labeled ATON).

Collision avoidance is also greatly enhanced by AIS because most echart programs read the AIS dynamic data of the targets and they know your own COG and SOG, so they can compute and display for you the closest point of approach (CPA) and the time to the CPA (TCPA) based on present conditions. Then as either of you alter course, you watch how this changes.

Search and rescue operations have special AIS modes that locate vessels and aircraft involved. There are even small, personal AIS transmitters that you can carry and activate if overboard so you show up on all local AIS receivers.

Table 12.19-1 AIS Class-A Compared to Class-B		
	Class A	Class B / B+
Transmit Power (watt)	12.5W / 2W* (low power)	2W* / 5W
Dynamic data reports Underway**	0 - 2 kt 10s 2 - 14 kt 10s 14 - 23 kt 6s >23 kt 2s	3m / 3m 30s / 30s 30s / 15s 30s / 5s
Anchored or moored	3m	—
Static data reports	6m	6m
Voyage data reports	6m or when changed	——

* This low power implies for typical installations an effective range of 5 to 7 nmi, compared to 25 nmi or more for Class A.
** Class A reporting rate increased to 2 or 3 seconds when turning. Class B does not include rate of turn information.

AIS reception also enhances your radar watch in the ways listed below.

AIS Synergy with Radar

1. AIS can find and communicate with targets hidden behind land or around corners that radar cannot see, and then plots them on an echart as if seen by conventional radar.

2. A radar echo can be identified or contacted by vessel name and vessel class rather than using a generic hail.

3. Target interactions (CPA, TCPA) can be improved because the target vessel is broadcasting performance data such COG and SOG and even a rate of turn when turning.

4. Extended tracking range is obtained since VHF communications reach out farther than typical radar ranges and thus passing arrangements can be made long before the vessels meet.

5. Ship target intentions will be more clear, and will help with maneuvering decisions, because the target's destination, ETA, cargo, draft limitations, etc. are broadcast along with other AIS data.

6. Some ECS radar displays and all commercial vessel radars have an input for AIS signals so they can display the AIS targets overlaid on top of the radar targets.

There are numerous AIS sources online and in mobile apps that present near-live AIS signals for most waters of the world. In principle we could use our smartphone with a 4G connection to actually see the AIS targets around us when we are underway. This however, is not at all a dependable or safe approach. There is often a large delay between actual AIS reports and the ones we see in these apps, and this could lead to serious navigational errors.

Check www.starpath.com/navbook, where we will try to keep a link to live, accurate AIS transmissions that you can input to your echart program for practice. A sample of AIS targets shown in an echart program is in Figure 12.19-1, with a detailed view in Figure 12.19-2.

12.20 Currents from GPS

GPS tells us where we are and which way we are moving (COG), and how fast we are moving (SOG). If our COG and SOG do not agree with our heading (H) and knotmeter speed (S), then we are likely being set by a current.

If we had H and S inputs into the right kind of electronic chart system (ECS), it could combine these data with COG and SOG and report to us directly the set and drift of the current. Some ECS are set up to do this (discussed in Section 12.15), but most are not.

Figuring current is a vector problem. Our motion through the water (H, S) is one vector; the way we end up moving (COG, SOG) is another vector. The difference between these two is the vector we want (Set, Drift).

It doesn't take fancy calculations to tell simply whether we are in favorable or adverse current. If SOG is bigger than S, the current is helping us; if not, it is hurting us. We even know the current strength and direction without special calculations when we happen to be sailing directly with or against the current. If COG is about the same as H, but SOG is less than S, then the current is on the nose with a strength equal to the difference between S and SOG. Current on the stern will also give a COG equal to H, but now SOG will be larger than S.

But when COG and H are different, life is not so simple. We are then sailing across the current and we can't figure current strength or direction without solving the vector problem. This could be solved by plotting or by direct computation using basic vector formulas, or by a dedicated app in your computer or smartphone. The latter is clearly the easiest solution, though not the most dependable—that is, it takes batteries and may not be waterproof.

The procedure is this. After spending a few minutes on a given course, watch that H, S, COG, and SOG have reached steady values. For an example, let's say that compass heading H = 045, knotmeter speed S = 5.0, COG = 070, and SOG = 6.0. Record these in your logbook, and then run your program or do your plotting, and you should learn that the current is 2.6 kts, setting toward direction 125, as shown in Figure 12.20-1. The current direction is magnetic if H and COG were magnetic, and true if the inputs were true.

Bear in mind that what we get this way won't necessarily be all water current. When headed upwind, there could be leeway as well. In these cases, we must be careful when interpreting what we get. If SOG and S are similar in these conditions, but COG is some 10° or so to leeward, then we are probably looking at leeway alone. This is almost certain if the same thing occurs on the other tack.

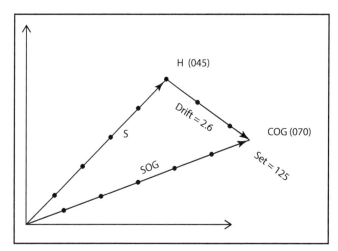

Figure 12.20-1. *Plotting solution for set and drift. Step 1, using any convenient units (i.e., 1 cm = 1 kt), draw a line in the direction of H with length S. Step 2, draw a line for SOG in the direction of COG using the same speed scale. Step 3, Drift is the length of the line from H to COG, and the set is the direction of that line. Example given is the first example from Table 12.20-1.*

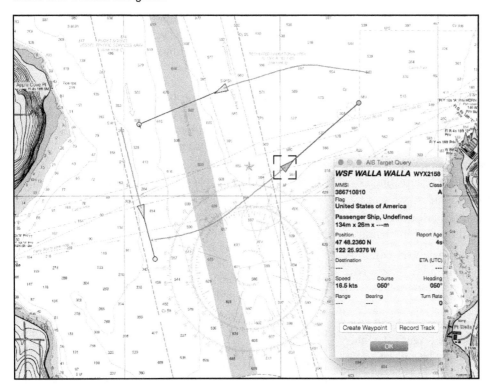

Figure 12.19-1. *AIS targets viewed in OpenCPN. Active or selected target is the one whose information is being displayed (marked with a square box), else the targets are called sleeping targets, which is misleading—they are sleeping only in that you have not chosen to read the data. Echart programs often have ways to annotate or color the symbols beyond the standard format. Projected vector lines show COG and SOG. The above are set to show 3-minute projected positions. Sometimes we can detect current when the true heading line is different from the COG. Destination information when present is more often wrong than right. This has to be manually updated and often gets overlooked.*

you will generally know pretty much what is going on from just comparing COG with H and SOG with S from their digital values.

Of course, it still pays to look out the window once in a while. If headed downwind, across a line from smooth water into white-capped water, and the knotmeter pulses up briefly, we have entered adverse current. We can compute away all we want, but generally, that old pre-GPS trick works pretty well, namely, watch the knotmeter dial very carefully at the instant you cross a potential current line. It will either pulse up or down as you cross into adverse or favorable current. The bigger the pulse, the bigger the current. It is just a quick pulse as the paddlewheel hits new current; once in it, the knotmeter will resume the steady value it had.

These days of GPS, we can detect the presence of current and correct for it without knowing its actual set and drift. The virtue of solving for set and drift is to confirm that our pre-voyage planning was correct or to check that the current predictions for the region are useful. It often pays to figure out what actual current you are in and compare it with what your resources predicted you should see. A few practice problems are given in Table 12.20-1.

Remember that if the input directions are Magnetic, the current set will be a Magnetic direction, but all current predictions from tables or charts will give the set as a True direction. Needless to say, the current results for actual water flow—as opposed to a generic *error current*—will be accurate only if the knotmeter and compass are properly calibrated.

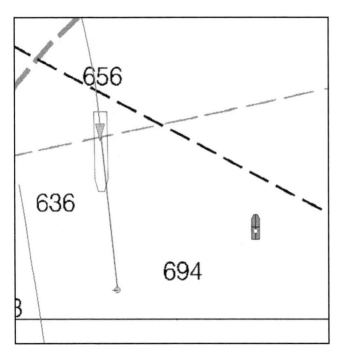

Figure 12.19-2. *ECS display can be set to show actual target size and precise location when zoomed in. On the right is our vessel, also scaled to right dimensions and precise location. We can see that the target heading and COG are different. This is viewed with OpenCPN.*

Current vectors should be independent of relative wind direction, S, or H—assuming we haven't entered into new current. This is another problem. You often want to know the current fast, before you move out of it, but we can't do this type of reckoning any faster than it takes the GPS to get good numbers and we process them. On the other hand,

Table 12.20-1. Practice Finding Set and Drift					
Input		Output		Current	
H	S	COG	SOG	Drift	Set
045	5.0	070	6.0	2.6	125
135	5.0	125	3.5	1.7	336
180	7.5	193	9.2	2.5	235
315	4.8	330	5.5	1.5	025
355	7.0	350	4.7	2.4	185
(Speeds in kts, directions in true or magnetic)					

12.21 Traffic in the Fog

Picture this: you are cruising through a thick fog, a long way from land, and out of the gray silence, you suddenly hear a loud prolonged blast from a fog horn. It sounds close, and it seems to come from somewhere on the port bow. What do you do?

That, in a nutshell, is the subject at hand. And as we will see, we need to know more about the situation before we can answer this question, and it will help to review the background. The key point is whether or not we have radar available. If we did, we were presumably using it for some time leading up to this moment. In any event, we are going to be careful.

There are distinctly different rules on how vessels are supposed to interact with each other in clear weather (day or night), as opposed to how they interact in restricted visibility, when they cannot see each other visually. The laws and guidelines are presented in the *Navigation Rules*. A fundamental tenet in clear weather is that when two vessels approach each other in clear sight of each other, one has right of way over the other. The only exception in clear weather is when two vessels under power approach head to head, on reciprocal courses, in which case both must turn right. The Rules do not say who goes first or why, because it does not matter. Both must turn.

Also fundamental to the Rules—in all conditions of visibility—are the concepts of *risk of collision* and *close quarters*, neither of which is defined explicitly in the Rules themselves. A working definition of close quarters, which can withstand the scrutiny of the courts, is to think of it as that space around you that is required for your own maneuver to avoid a collision (in the circumstances at hand), regardless of what the other vessel might do, suddenly and unexpectedly. This is your space; as long as you have this you are safe. If you anticipate a vessel entering this space with any doubt at all that it will pass safely, then the Rules give you the right and indeed the obligation to maneuver to get back your space, regardless of what other Rules might be in effect at the time. The extent and the shape of the close-quarters space depend on the circumstance. Passing another vessel at slow speed in a narrow cut, it could be a matter of yards; interacting with full-speed ships in the ocean, it is more often a matter of miles.

In the fog, an understanding of the concepts of collision risk and close quarters becomes even more crucial because the Rules change when you are interacting with vessels you cannot see visually—that is, with vessels you hear, or detect by radar alone. You must then rely more often and more heavily on your personal definition of these key concepts. In the fog, there is no stand-on vessel and no give-way vessel.

No one (sail, power, or paddle) has right of way in the fog. All vessels are given the same instructions, which appear in Rule 19, Conduct of Vessels in Restricted Visibility. This is the key rule, although fundamental Rules 5 to 8 on Proper Look-out, Safe Speed, Risk of Collision, and Action to Avoid Collision still apply, as they are specified as valid in *all* conditions of visibility.

How you comply with Rule 19 depends on whether or not you have radar on board and working. Rule 7(a), by the way, says that if you have radar, you must use it, and Rule 7(c) says, specifically, that you should use it properly, which implies a basic understanding of how to use radar to detect risk of collision and related observations, such as how to tell if a target moving toward you on the radar screen is one you are overtaking or one that is headed toward you.

Radar is, undoubtedly, the most important electronic aid to collision avoidance and perhaps to navigation in general, but there is a clear obligation to learn its use that follows it onto the boat. It is a small price to pay, however, for the safety and efficiency it affords. The Starpath text *Radar for Mariners* and PC radar simulator Radar Trainer are proven ways to master these skills.

Without Radar

When traveling in the fog without radar, you can only know of approaching traffic from their fog signals (one prolonged blast every 2 minutes for a ship making way), or by hearing their engines. In principle, you could also hear a ship calling an "unidentified vessel" on your VHF, but that is not you detecting them.

According to Rule 19 (e), if we hear a fog signal "apparently forward of the beam," we are instructed to slow to the minimum speed needed to hold course, and if necessary, take all way off, and in any event navigate with extreme caution. Clearly, though, in a small vessel, which is a poor radar target, we must consider any noise we hear as a call for extreme caution.

Note there are no instructions for altering course in these circumstances, nor any justification for it. Turning away from a fog signal is not helpful, and would just confuse anyone watching you on radar. "Extreme caution" clearly suggests using the VHF radio immediately to try to reach the signaling vessel, and here an accurate GPS position could be very helpful. The prudence of a handheld VHF at the wheel in such conditions is obvious.

There is not much else you can do, other than repeat your own fog signal (one prolonged under power, one prolonged and two shorts under sail) aimed in the apparent direction you heard from. It is unlikely this would be heard from a ship, unless they were moving slowly with a bow watch, but it could be heard from smaller vessels. Then you wait, and listen, and be ready to maneuver immediately. Drifting along in the fog in an area of known traffic without wind and without your engine on and no way for a ready maneuver is prohibited in 19(b).

One advantage a sailboat has in light air in the fog is you can hear very well. Ship signals are often on timers, so they will sound precisely every two minutes, or whatever smaller interval they are using. Check your watch to know when to listen for the next one. Keep in mind that the apparent distance off of sounds is not very reliable in the fog, and the directions to them are not much better, but the directions can in some cases be useful—why else would they word the Rules to include that observation. A good radar reflector is a must. Ask a passing vessel to check your radar echo some time in clear weather.

In the most frightening situation, when the signal we hear from any direction is obviously very close, we can anticipate being *in extremis*, meaning that at this point, collision avoidance is going to be up to our maneuver alone.

RULE 19. Conduct of Vessels in Restricted Visibility

(19a) This Rule applies to vessels not in sight of one another when navigating in or near an area of restricted visibility.

(19b) Every vessel shall proceed at a safe speed adapted to the prevailing circumstances and conditions of restricted visibility. A power-driven vessel shall have her engines ready for immediate maneuver.

(19c) Every vessel shall have due regard to the prevailing circumstances and conditions of restricted visibility when complying with the Rules of Section I of this Part.

(19d) A vessel which detects by radar alone the presence of another vessel shall determine if a close-quarters situation is developing and/or risk of collision exists. If so, she shall take avoiding action in ample time, provided that when such action consists of an alteration of course, so far as possible the following shall be avoided:

(i) an alteration of course to port for a vessel forward of the beam, other than for a vessel being overtaken;

(ii) an alteration of course toward a vessel abeam or abaft the beam.

(19e) Except where it has been determined that a risk of collision does not exist, every vessel which hears apparently forward of her beam the fog signal of another vessel, or which cannot avoid a close-quarters situation with another vessel forward of her beam, shall reduce her speed to the minimum at which she can be kept on her course. She shall if necessary take all her way off and in any event navigate with extreme caution until danger of collision is over.

Figure 12.21-1. *Rule 19 from the* Navigation Rules

The *Navigation Rules* (Figure 12.21-1) instruct us to slow to bare steerage as quickly as possible and navigate with extreme caution, which to me would mean turn toward the apparent direction of the danger we hear. A head-on approach presents a smaller target and gives us the best chance for a quick maneuver to either side, and if we should collide near head to head, we have a better chance of getting pushed aside rather than smashed.

Clearly, if much travel must be made in the fog in the presence of traffic, radar is definitely called for. One does not have to go through many encounters like this to agree. I get nervous just writing about it. And raw fatalism has no role in prudent seamanship. The problem we face if unprepared with our own equipment is the misjudgment too often made by ship captains that the sophistication of their own radar justifies high speed in the fog. The courts never agree, but that is beside the point.

When we put ourselves in position to hear the Charon call of a fog signal bearing down on us from a mile or so off in an uncertain direction, giving us 3 or 4 minutes to get our lives in order, when we could have known half an hour ago that something was coming, and not long after that where it was going, then we have pumped more adrenaline into our sailing than need be—and have probably misallocated our equipment budget.

With Radar

With radar on board, the instructions of Rule 19(d) are more specific (Figure 12.21-1), and a great deal more reassuring to work with. When we first detect a radar target moving toward us from any direction (right, left, front or back) our first assignment is:

Step (1). Watch it to see if a risk of collision or a close-quarters situation is developing.

We do this by marking it on the radar screen with pen or using the electronic bearing line (EBL) and variable range marker (VRM). An erasable overhead projector marker is a good choice for on-the-screen marks. Or we record the target's range, bearing, and time on the border of a chart. In the language of Rule 7(b), use some "systematic observation." Any fast ship in open water that is headed toward a passing of within 2 or 3 nmi of you is headed toward a potential risk of collision. And if you have been watching a target at all on a small boat radar from some 10 or so miles off, then it is definitely a ship—or a drilling platform.

Step (2). If so (i.e., collision risk developing), "take avoiding action in ample time."

Note the big difference here between the instructions of this rule and the other rules covering interactions of vessels in sight of one another. In-sight rules tell us what to do when already within the risk of collision or close quarters in order to avoid a collision. Here, we are instructed to avoid the risk itself. "In ample time" means maneuver before the risk of collision or close quarters occurs. There is no holding course and speed by anyone during an interaction in the fog, even if you are being overtaken. Your job—the job of both vessels observing each other on radar—is to maneuver so that you do not get into a situation where there is risk of collision. In other words, we are to stay farther apart than when passing in clear weather, and the burden of seeing to this separation lies on both vessels, not on just one as in the case of clear weather.

Step (3). If you alter course as part of your maneuver—which is not necessarily the best thing to do in all circumstances—the direction that you turn depends on where the targets are on the radar screen. For targets forward of the beam (on either side), you turn right. For targets on the beam or aft of the beam, you turn away from the target. In other words, if we are to turn, we are instructed to turn right for all approaching vessels except those on the quadrant of the starboard quarter. See Figure 12.21-2. Or, for an easier way to remember it:

Forward of the beam turn right,
aft of the beam turn away.

The only situation where it might not be clear immediately what direction your ultimate maneuver should take is when a target is approaching on the starboard beam and it is not clear whether it is slightly forward or slightly aft or right on the beam. In this case, you might want to consider slowing down. If you slow down, the subsequent change in relative motion will take its track forward of the beam. In any event, the instructions go on:

Step (4). If for any reason you cannot avoid a close-quarters situation with a vessel forward of your beam (by slowing or with a course alteration), then slow down to bare steerageway, and if necessary, take all way off and navigate with extreme caution—the same as if you had heard a fog signal forward of the beam.

It is, however, very unlikely that you would get into this situation with a competently operated radar. In almost all such cases, if you are on a collision course with a vessel according to the radar and you are still moving, then stopping alone will pull his radar track "up-screen" enough to remove the immediate risk and give you time to further evaluate the situation. More generally, if the target is already going to pass forward of you, then slowing will open up the passing distance. It pays to remember that the other vessel may not be watching its radar at all, or may not even have one.

Rule 19 is explicit in all circumstances on what turns should be made when choosing to turn—although slowing down for targets that are already going to pass in front of you may be the better call. There are only two optional maneuvers that might come into play involving overtaking from dead astern. When you are certain the target approaching from forward of the beam is one you are overtaking, then you have the option to pass on either side, which could involve a turn to the left to open the distance. Once he sees what side you are on (as a target approaching from aft of his beam), he should move the other way to

open the passing distance farther. A vessel would show up on the radar screen as one you are overtaking if his radar target is moving down your screen at a relative speed distinctly slower than your own speed. A radio contact would clarify this.

The other option also occurs in overtaking, when a target approaches overtaking you from exactly astern, in which case you could turn either way if you think it is getting too close on this course. He is overtaking you, so he has the option to go either side, although it is clearly not good seamanship on his part to run up the stern of a vessel he is watching on the radar, assuming he is watching you on radar. Your 90° turn at some point should solve the problem.

In all such maneuvers, Rule 8(b) applies: maneuvers should be large enough to be readily apparent on the other's radar—which calls for big turns, 60° or more. And so does Rule 7(c): assumptions about risk of collision should not be made on the basis of scanty radar information—often meaning when the target is too far away, or when your course is varying so much that you can't establish a clear radar-screen trace of the approaching target. If you can't figure out what is going on while you are moving, then you must slow down or stop to figure it out (Rule 8(e)). As mentioned earlier, Rules 5 to 8 all apply in the fog as well

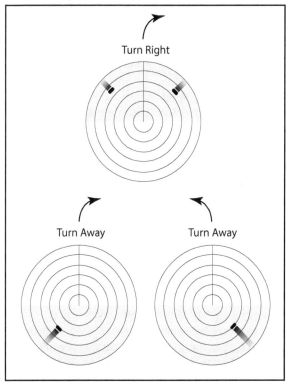

Figure 12.21-2. *Radar maneuvering in the fog according to Rule 19d. Turn right for all targets approaching from forward of the beam as soon as your know their trails, usually by the 4 to 6 nmi range, and turn away from targets approaching from aft of the beam. All turns should be prominent enough that they are readily detected on the other vessel's radar. Small changes in course and speed should not be used.*

as in clear weather and are worth reviewing. These, along with Rule 19, in their official wording, should be referred to for study. Paraphrasing the Rules as done here is always a risky business.

Once a vessel emerges from the fog and you can see each other visually, the operative rules revert to the standard steering and sailing rules, wherein one vessel will be obligated to stay clear of the other. Consequently, it pays to estimate the range of visibility and, from the present range and bearing of radar targets, estimate when and at what bearing they should emerge from the fog, thinking ahead on what your response will be at that time. Near Vessel Traffic Service lanes, where the services include regularly scheduled or periodic broadcasts of ship locations, it is crucial to monitor these broadcasts, plot the ship positions, and figure the ETA of your vessels' passing.

12.22 Navigation in Traffic

When interacting with traffic, it is always important to find a vessel visually with binoculars and at night to identify its lights as soon as possible after detecting it on radar or after first spotting some indication of light on the horizon. Often times, the bearing of a vessel can be more accurately determined and then watched for changes earlier with a good bearing compass (in binoculars, for example) than it can with the radar's electronic bearing line. Rule 7(d) requires us to watch the compass bearing of approaching traffic to evaluate risk of collision; it is not an option.

It is also important not to assume that what appears to be a safe passing course at first observation will remain that way. Watch the traffic continuously until safely past. If there is any doubt at all about a safe passing, then try to reach them on VHF radio to confirm that they see you. Use low power, as you are calling a vessel in sight and do not want to clutter up the radio channel, or want everyone who might hear you to be alerted.

Radar is, as for many aspects of collision avoidance, especially valuable for clarifying this communication. "Deep sea vessel, 4.8 nmi on my starboard bow, this is the sailing vessel…" They now know at what range to look for a vessel on their radar. Then try to establish when they see you visually, which may not be until within a mile or two or even closer, depending on conditions. Shorthanded, a portable VHF radio is very convenient for this.

In any event, night or day, clear or fog, it is always important that one does not maneuver without knowing what is going on. It is more dangerous to guess what is taking place when the traffic is far off than to wait until it gets close enough to be certain. This is particularly true and at the same time particularly difficult when first detecting traffic approaching dead ahead. Once you get close enough that risk of collision exists, more often than not, the burden of the stand-on vessel (i.e., a sailboat with an approaching ship in open water) is really higher than that of the vessel that must give way—especially when the give-way vessel is

a tank and the stand-on vessel is an ant. Nevertheless, the Rules specify clearly what actions are to be taken once risk of collision exists, and to violate these definitely increases the chances of misfortune. The Rules do, however, tell us when we can and should maneuver on our own to avoid a collision.

In the meantime, the goal is to stay alert and evaluate the situation as carefully as possible while checking lines, trim, mustering crew if need be, discussing options, checking the spotlight, and so forth to be ready to maneuver when the time comes. Some vessels have an all-hands alarm rigged near the wheel for such eventualities. Remember, in strong winds, especially when you slow down, it can become very noisy. You may not be able to yell to people at the mast, let alone to those in the cabin below. In some cases, it could pay to turn the engine on and have it ready—when racing, it could be a good time to charge the batteries.

In most cases, as the encounter develops, it will be clear that the vessel is going to pass off to one side or the other, although it may be closer than you might hope for. I have seen many ships pass us, under sail in mid-ocean, at full speed well within a mile (on one occasion, it was a quarter of a mile, at night). In most of these cases, we were in radio contact with the vessels, and as such, the passing was safe, although well within the realm of risk of collision. On another occasion, in mid-ocean on a clear, sunny day, flying a bright-colored gigantic spinnaker and blooper, we had to drop the blooper and alter course to avoid a ship that did not respond to the radio or alter its course or speed in the slightest. It was a totally unmarked rust bucket some 300 ft long, without a soul in sight anywhere, and it still passed close enough to recognize faces on board, had there been any.

This brings up an important issue, namely, when do you maneuver on your own to avoid collision? With the traffic in sight visually, the pertinent reference is Rule 17 (Figure 12.22-1), along with key points from Rule 7 and others. In a nutshell (though not the best place to keep such rules), you may do so as soon as you know what is taking place (Rule 7c) and are convinced that the approaching give-way vessel is not taking appropriate action for a safe passing (Rule 17a-ii). You could, for example, be certain he is going to pass to windward, but you are uncomfortable with how close it will be. In that case you are justified in falling off to open up the passing distance. Again, though, that maneuver must be reserved until you are certain of what he is doing. If he had actually been going to pass to leeward, this premature maneuver would have caused trouble for both of you. Radio contact is always best when possible.

Or there could be simpler cases that call for your maneuver; for instance, you are looking into the wheel house of a crossing vessel with binoculars, and there is no one driving the boat. Whenever you have doubts about what the other vessel is doing, the law requires that you sound the doubt or danger signal (5 short blasts on your air horn).

Rule 17 Action by Stand-on Vessel

(a-i) Where one of two vessels is to keep out of the way the other shall keep her course and speed.

(a-ii) The latter vessel may however take action to avoid collision by her maneuver alone, as soon as it becomes apparent to her that the vessel required to keep out of the way is not taking appropriate action in compliance with these Rules.

(b) When, from any cause, the vessel required to keep her course and speed finds herself so close that collision cannot be avoided by the action of the give-way vessel alone, she shall take such action as will best aid to avoid collision.

(c) A power-driven vessel which takes action in a crossing situation in accordance with subparagraph (a)(ii) of this Rule to avoid collision with another power-driven vessel shall, if the circumstances of the case admit, not alter course to port for a vessel on her own port side.

(d) This Rule does not relieve the give-way vessel of her obligation to keep out of the way.

Figure 12.22-1. *Rule 17 from the* Navigation Rules. *The full set of the Rules is online. References are listed in Section 10.9*

For crossing sailboats or interactions with smaller power-driven vessels, this may get some results, but it is wishful thinking that a ship will hear such sounds. A ship could, however, see a spotlight, and 5 or more flashes on a spotlight has the same meaning. In any event, you should be stopping by then or very shortly thereafter. It would be hard to justify barreling on into a situation that you have just announced on your whistle that you do not understand and consider dangerous.

Your option to maneuver in such circumstances, however, changes to an obligation (Rule 17b) once the traffic approaches so close that a collision cannot be avoided by the other vessels maneuver alone. This is obviously the extreme situation; it is called *in extremis*. It is also obviously a situation to avoid, which is probably best done by clarifying in one's own mind how to apply Rule 17a.

The key here is your personal definition of *close quarters*, and then not let any vessel approach closer than that whenever risk of collision exists. A workable definition for this purpose is to assume close quarters is that region about you that is required for your own maneuver to avoid a collision (in the circumstances at hand), regardless of what the other vessel might do, suddenly and unexpectedly. This is your space, and as long as you have this you are safe. With this in mind, if the established path of an approaching vessel is anticipated to pass closer than this, you maneuver to get back your space. This is not a call for arbitrary evaluations and early actions. The first obligation is to hold course and speed so that both you and the approaching traffic can evaluate the situation properly. This is just a means of deciding how close is too close.

12.23 Sound Signals

Every boat operator is required by law to know and obey the *Navigation Rules*, and everyone even remotely related to the boat shares the responsibility of the operator for the consequences of any collision, as every collision involves some violation of the Rules. An important part of the Rules that tends to be under-learned are the rules governing the sound signals all vessels are required by law to make in various circumstances. Part of the neglect of the sound rules stems from the fact that we simply do not hear these sounds nearly as frequently as we should in many parts of the country. Considering the amount of traffic we have in Puget Sound, for example, it is still rare to hear maneuvering signals. Recreational and commercial vessels alike do not make these sounds as often as they should by law. When we don't hear them, we tend to forget they exist. On the East Coast, on the other hand, they are heard much more often, especially in the Intracoastal Waterway.

Nevertheless, if a collision can be traced in any way to a missing signal or to a wrong signal or to the misinterpretation of a signal, then the party guilty of this sound violation will buy some share of the overall collision liability, regardless of being right or wrong in other violations that may have been even more crucial to the collision. In short, regardless of whether or not we choose to sound the proper signals in every circumstance, it remains important to know the Rules and be prepared to make that decision in the light of its potential consequences.

The rules on sound signals are complex as a whole, but less so if we restrict the topic to just a few of the more important signals in the *International Rules (COLREGS)*, as opposed to the *US Inland Rules*—sound signals, by the way, are the only part of the Rules that differ significantly on inland and international waters. The International Rules apply usually to waters on the ocean side of a line drawn point to point across coastal bays, but there are exceptions, notable of which in the Northwest are Puget Sound, Lake Union, and Lake Washington. All Alaskan and Hawaiian waters are international as well. These exceptions are itemized in an Annex to the *Navigation Rules*. On Inland Waters boaters are obligated to know the inland sound rules, which we will not cover here.

There are essentially two kinds of sound signals: *identification signals,* given in or near areas of reduced visibility (fog, rain, smoke) to let unseen vessels know what type of vessel you are and what you are doing, and *maneuvering signals,* given only when in visual sight of other vessels to confirm for them the maneuvers you are in the process of making. The maneuvering signals apply only to power-driven vessels. Sound signals are summarized in Figure 12.23-1.

The two primary identification signals given in the fog are: 1 prolonged blast every two minutes or less given by "regular" power-driven vessels that are moving (whether ships or skiffs), or 1 prolonged blast followed by 2 short blasts every two minutes given by just about every other type of vessel (sailing vessels, tow boats, fishing boats, or power-driven vessels somehow restricted in their maneuverability). The latter signals are given whenever the vessels are underway (i.e., not anchored, moored, or aground) regardless of their motion. A "regular" power-driven vessel, on the other hand, changes from 1 prolonged to 2 prolonged whenever they stop moving (underway, not making way).

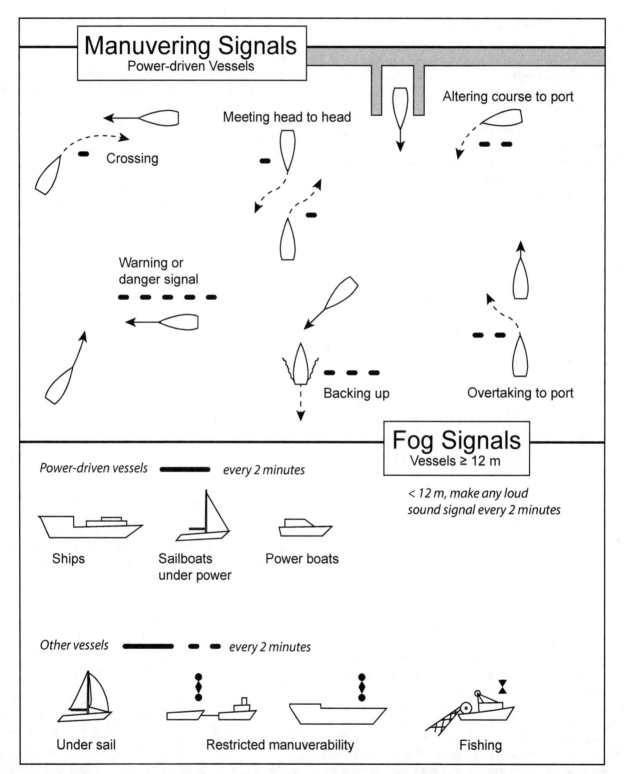

Figure 12.23-1. *Samples of sound signals for vessels maneuvering in sight of one another. These are not used in restricted visibility, or when interacting with a vessel by radar alone. The only signals made in the fog are the standard fog signals characteristic of the vessel class and its activity. All shown are underway. All signals are made up from prolonged blasts (4 to 6 seconds long) and short blasts (1 second long).*

These rules apply to all vessels, there are no exceptions for small boats. A prolonged blast is defined as 4 to 6 seconds long; a short blast is 1 second long. Remember a sailboat with its engine on and in gear is a regular power-driven vessel, regardless of sails set.

As an example, consider a sailboat in the fog. While sailing you sound 1 prolonged and 2 short every 2 minutes. The wind dies, so you turn on the engine and start giving 1 prolonged every 2 minutes, because you are now a power-boat. You feel some vibration and shift to neutral and drift while you investigate the problem. During this period, you should sound 2 prolonged every 2 minutes (power-driven vessel not making way). The engine dies, and you can't get it started, and there is no wind, so as you ponder this situation, you sound 1 prolonged and 2 short every 2 minutes as you are now a power-driven vessel that can't maneuver. If you hear another vessel's signal and wish to warn them of your position, you would use the same signal you have been using, 1 prolonged and 2 short. If you happen to be sinking and in immediate danger, you would lay on the horn, since a long continuous sound is a distress signal for any vessel.

Maneuvering signals are a different matter altogether. First, they are only given by power driven vessels, or sailboats with engines engaged. Second, they are only given when in sight of another vessel. On international waters, the two primary maneuvering signals are rudder signals. Whenever you turn the wheel in the proximity of another vessel in sight, you must sound a signal. One short blast means I am turning to the right; two short blasts mean I am turning to the left. No answer signal is required of the approaching vessel so long as they themselves are not altering course. If they also turn in response to your maneuver, they sound the corresponding signal: 1 to the right; 2 to the left. Whenever you shift into reverse in sight of a nearby vessel, you should sound 3 short blasts; the same signal would be given whenever you wish to convey to another vessel that you are operating astern.

Sailing vessels do not give these maneuvering signals, but powerboats are supposed to give them when maneuvering around sailing vessels on International Waters—this is not required on Inland Waters.

If for any reason, any vessel, including sailboats under sail, fails to understand the maneuvers of an approaching vessel, they are *required* to immediately sound 5 short rapid blasts. This is an important signal to know and be prepared to sound. It is reason enough to have an air horn standing by. At night, you can signal the same warning with 5 one-second flashes of a spotlight.

It is just as important on the receiving end. If a ferry, for example, sounds 1 or 2 long blasts in sight of you (i.e., no fog), he is typically just warning you of his presence. If he sounds 5 short blasts, it is a much more urgent warning that he does not know what you are doing and that there is a potential risk collision.

Although we do not hear them in all cases that we should, according to the law, maneuvering signals are

not optional, nor are there exceptions depending on boat length. If you are boating on Inland Waters, then check the *Navigation Rules* for important modifications to the specific meaning of the maneuvering rules and how to respond to them. The danger-warning signal is the same, however, in all waters, worldwide.

Here is an exercise. What will be the judge's first question to this boater's explanation of the collision? "I had the right of way, but he just kept coming at me. I had no idea what he was doing, so I turned to get out of his way, and that's when he hit me" Answer: Did you sound the danger signal?

Exercise 2, before the judge, in another case. "I sounded the danger signal, but he did not stop, and then I sounded the danger signal again, and he still did not stop, and then within a minute he hit me." Judge's answer: "Do I understand properly that you knew a dangerous situation was developing; you warned him twice about it, but you still kept going?

Summary: Sound the danger signal, and when doing so, be prepared to stop if your sound is not getting the response you anticipate.

12.24 Sailboat Lights

Considering the potential safety hazard in the heavy traffic of many popular sailing areas, it is very important that sailboats show the proper lights when sailing at night. In many cases, skippers have not checked their lights and may not even know what the rules might be. They assume the boat is delivered to them with proper lights. Nevertheless, infractions are widespread and potentially dangerous. You can be certain that if an accident occurs that could be traced even remotely to improper lights, the courts would pursue the details relentlessly. In any collision, improper lights will earn you partial liability regardless of other circumstances of the event.

The laws of lights are presented in the *Navigation Rules*. Sailboat lights are covered in Rule 25, and technical details of the lights are presented in Annex I—every boat over 12 meters long (39 ft) is required to carry a copy of the *Navigation Rules* on board in US Inland Waters, although it is obviously prudent on all waters. Sailboat lights are summarized in Figure 12.24-1.

Every vessel is underway when not anchored, aground, or moored. If you are not attached to land you are underway, regardless of how fast you are going or not going. When underway, lights must be carried from sunset to sunrise, and also during the day in restricted visibility.

When under sail without the engine in gear, the sailboat must show red (port side) and green (starboard side) sidelights and a white stern light. The stern light is visible in the aft 135° sector where the sidelights cannot be seen. When under sail, you may also show from the masthead an all-round red light over an all-round green light. These optional lights, however, are not required and are not often used.

When under power, a sailboat becomes a powerboat regardless of sails set. A powerboat under 50 meters long must show, in addition to sidelights and stern lights, a white masthead light visible from straight ahead to 22.5° aft of the beam. This light is visible from all directions except where the stern light can be seen. Under sail or power, a sailboat shows only a single white light when viewed toward its stern. A masthead light is different from the anchor light, which is also located on the masthead but is visible from all directions.

Now for details. If your boat is under 20 meters long (65.5 ft), you may carry the sidelights and stern light on the masthead in a single light (a tricolor), but only when you are sailing. Also, if you show a tricolor, you cannot show the optional red over green sailing light. Of more interest, however, a tricolor light is not legal when you are under power, regardless of boat size. Furthermore when using a tricolor, you must not show sidelights from the deck at the same time. You can have both kinds of lights on the boat, but you can use only one at a time. You will be stopped for this violation and fined. The value versus hassle of a tricolor must be considered.

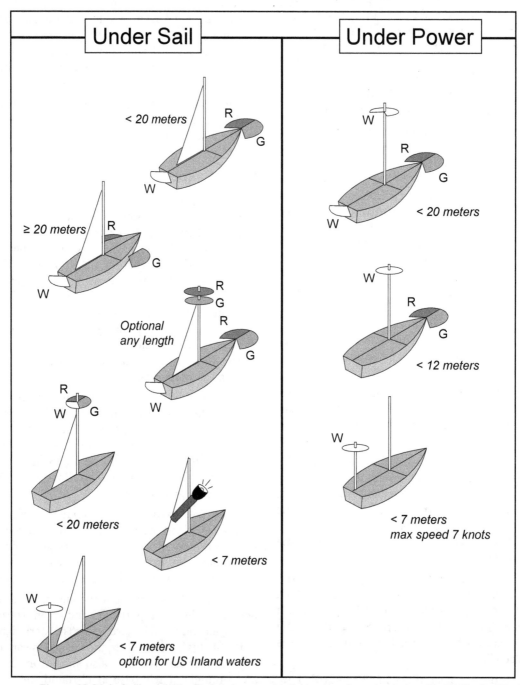

Figure 12.24-1. *Sailboat lights. Red and green sidelights show from dead ahead to 22.5° aft of the beam.*

There is no law (for boats under 20 meters) that says the sidelights cannot be in a single light on the bow (which most are), but they must only be visible in the prescribed sectors. The rules state that sidelights should not be visible more than 3° across the bow or 5° aft of the prescribed arc. This is where many infractions occur. Sidelights often reflect off the bow pulpit (or sails piled on deck) in such a way that they can be seen from all directions (all-round light). The same thing often happens with the stern light reflecting off gear on the transom. So there can be some virtue to a tricolor for use under sail.

If your boat is under 12 meters long (39 ft), you can when under power use a single all-round light (such as an anchor light) in place of a masthead light and stern light. It is illegal and dangerous, however, to show two white lights off the stern.

Some sailors use their masthead light, anchor light, or a special light to illuminate a masthead wind vane when sailing. Such lights are potentially dangerous and illegal. If you use a light for the wind vane, it should be checked at the dock to verify that it cannot be seen from the side of the boat. Usually, a special light is required for this. Another solution—if you don't mind the extra weight aloft—is to carry a tricolor below the wind vane, which will illuminate it nicely. Use this when sailing, then switch to deck-mounted sidelights, a stern light, and a masthead light when under power.

Light intensity is also specified in the Rules. Sternlights must be visible from 2 nmi off for boats over 12 meters (39 ft) long, sidelights must be visible from one mile off for boats under 12 meters, and 2 nmi off for boats over 12 meters. The masthead light must be visible from 3 nmi off for 12- to 20-meter vessels, and 2 nmi off for vessels under 12 meters.

Sailboats under 7 meters long (23 ft) need not carry any of the above lights when sailing, but if they do not, they must have ready a white light that they can shine "in time to prevent a collision." From a practical point of view, this should be a bright light, not just a conventional flashlight, although the required intensity of this light is not specified in the Rules. When under power (outboard) on a boat under 7 meters, however, you must continuously show an all-round white light, not just carry the light on board. This light must be visible for 2 nmi.

The use of strobe lights is covered in Section 11.7. And we should not leave this subject with the impression that it is only sailboats with illegal lights. Illegal lights are a common problem that we see just as often on powerboats, recreational and commercial. It is always important to keep in the back of the mind that the lights we see may not be strictly right according to the rules. Cruise liners lit up like Christmas trees, wandering around on some gambling run, are a prime example.

12.25 How Close is Too Close?

Sailboats that experience close crossings with ships are generally either racing boats or single-handers. Cruising skippers with proper watches and adequate local knowledge usually prudently maneuver to avoid close encounters—not counting, of course, cases of negligence or lack of knowledge, which is dangerous if not negligent. In Puget Sound, for example, if I sail into Eagle Harbor channel as a ferry is leaving the Winslow dock, I am making a bad call, one that risks the safety of my boat and potential fines to boot. Every mariner in these waters must know about ferry traffic.

I should know about the ferry that is preparing to leave, which way it will go, that it is constrained to follow the channel, and that it has the right of way—even though my own boat might also be constrained to the same channel by draft in certain parts once I head in. The right of way rule is No. 9 (b) and (d). I should also know that the ferry is required to announce within 5 minutes of its departure time on VHF channel 14 that it is preparing to leave, and then to sound a single long blast when it does leave. I should also keep watch ahead of time to see whether cars are coming or going and should know roughly how long the loading process takes. This is important local knowledge in this case.

But we are not pursuing special cases now. For now, we want to look at clear-cut cases of not having right of way and what we must do about it. The problem that single-handers have is different. Their right-of-way problem is unique. They have essentially no recourse in any near-collision case when not at the wheel, because the *Navigation Rules* require that every vessel maintain a *proper watch*. The full definition of proper watch is not in the Rules themselves, but it has been established in court cases. Among the many requirements is one that says the watch must have no other duties besides watching. The question of driving the boat *and* watching depends on the conditions; several judgments have acknowledged that as OK in some circumstances, but this might not be the case in severe wind or sea conditions that take full concentration to drive the boat. Furthermore, you most definitely cannot sleep and watch at the same time. This has been tested in court more than once, and single-handers always lose this one, regardless of various radar alarms that might have been in place.

In areas with official USCG traffic lanes, the initial Rule that gives most ships right of ways is Rule 10 (j) "A vessel of less than 20 meters in length or a sailing vessel shall not impede the safe passage of a power-driven vessel following a traffic lane". Essentially all ships and working towboats follow the USCG Vessel Traffic Service (VTS) lanes directed from the VTS Center's radar system. They communicate on specific VHF channels (see navcen.uscg.gov for a channel list). Ferries assume these rights, even though they cross the lanes as much as follow them, because they are participating with the VTS system and have certain Rule 9 rights for the fairways of their routes.

The next rule of interest is Rule 16: "every vessel directed to keep out of the way of another shall, so far as possible, take early and substantial action to keep well clear". *Keeping well clear* has been interpreted in court to mean clear enough that there is no risk of collision, which is defined in Rule 7 (a) to mean there can be no doubt about it; otherwise we have to assume risk of collision exists. Court cases have elaborated on this to the point that it is not even adequate to show that collision was highly improbable; you must show that you kept clear enough that risk of collision could not even have developed on your crossing course.

Ask yourself, for example, "Will I remain clear of that ship if the jib sheet parts, or if someone falls overboard as we converge?" Years ago, I was on a race boat, and the skipper insisted on the tactic of going into the lanes out to the point where we were in line with the ship, then tack, which would then bring us back out its way by the time it got to that point, and with this we got the maximum time out where the wind was best. On one such maneuver like this, on throwing off the sheet for the tack, it got jammed in the winch. A sailboat that tacks without throwing off the sheet, heaves to, i.e., it stops. This experience taught the skipper a good lesson, and cost him one sheet that had to be cut in the emergency and cost him much time in the end.

Rule 8(d) adds that "action taken to avoid collision with another vessel shall be such as to result in passing at a safe distance..." And now we get to the punch line, what is a safe distance? It is not 50 ft. That cost a California sailor $6,000 in fines ($5,000 for right of way violation, $1,000 for negligence). It is not 75 ft either. That cost another California racer the same amount—though it was later dropped to $1,400 + $400.

The answer is closer to 3,000 ft, according to an early printing of the USCG District 13 *VTS Operator's Manual*. It stated in this regard that "A reasonably safe distance between commercial vessels and recreational vessels is considered to be at least one half mile ahead and one fourth mile abeam of the deep draft vessel or vessel with tow." I include this to show how thinking on this has evolved. Latest editions of this manual have removed ferences to specific distances, which probably means their legal staff finally read what they were publishing!

That sounds like a lot, but it's not really. At a freighter speed of 14 kts, that only gives you 2 minutes for prayer if you get stalled somehow in front of it. In short, if you choose to cut much closer than those published guidelines, it might pay to watch the bow angles using your prayer beads instead of compass bearings. It will save fumbling around for them if you're caught in a bind.

The *2013 Puget Sound VTS User's Manual* (online at the nav center), when addressing the issue of staying clear of vessel traffic following Traffic Separation Schemes (TSS = shipping lanes), adds this note exactly as shown below:

"Shall Not Impede" means a vessel MUST NOT navigate in such a way as to risk the development of a collision with another vessel (i.e. when a power driven vessel following a TSS is forced to make an unusual or dangerous maneuver in order to avoid one of the vessels listed above, then the vessel following the TSS has been impeded).

On the other hand, the guidelines mentioned refer to deep-draft vessels in traffic lanes confronting recreational vessels. I have seen racers do some very foolish things with freighters, but I have also seen a very large ship nearly knock down several sailboats and swamp a dozen salmon fishermen that were not in the lanes at all, but just adjacent to them in the *inshore zone*, that region between the shoreline and the traffic lanes. This was in clear violation of Rule 6 (a) and (ii) on safe speed in the presence of heavy traffic, not to mention the potential development of collision risk. The same manual above warns ships not to do that, because, apparently, they have to be told that.

In short, just as with driving on the road, if we are to be safe, we have to drive defensively at all times and not assume everyone we encounter is going to obey the rules.

A sad fact of modern maritime affairs is that now the question of how close is too close is no longer just a matter of collision avoidance. In the wake of the 9/11 attack, the IMO established the International Ship and Port Facility Security Code, which in the US is implemented through the Maritime Transportation Security Act of 2002, which is documented in CFR 33, Parts 101-106. This extensive and very complex law requires ports to monitor the safety of vessels in their waters by enforcing *Protection and Security Zones* around navy vessels, tank vessels, and large passenger vessels. The zones are defined in Figure 12.25-1. The rules on US Navy vessels apply to all waters of the world, and those on tank ship and large passenger vessels are in effect in most large shipping ports. Check with your local USCG district headquarters to see whether your ports are covered by these restrictions.

These are serious laws, strictly enforced. Violations are felonies with up to 6 years in prison. If you ply large commercial waterways like Puget Sound, for example, you will know that the penalties could even be higher—if you get anywhere near the security zone without slowing to bare steerage you will be met by one of the vessels shown in Figure 12.25-2. They may be small, but they are very serious, and very fast, and there are a lot of them.

Traveling within 500 yards of any of these vessels, anchored or underway, you should monitor VHF channel 16. Not just the USCG, but also the Captain of any one of these protected vessels has the authority to tell you how and when to maneuver within 500 yards (0.25 nmi).

Recent yacht racing news also reminds us that the question of how close is too close depends on what you are doing. During the 2013 America's Cup race in San Francisco, the whole world watched 72-ft catamarans cross paths as close at 10 ft with a closing speed of nearly 80 kts! (Figure 12.25-3). Not only was it phenomenal to see sailboats go that fast, but also a notable reminder of the difference between yacht racing rules and the *Navigation Rules* that other vessels must adhere to.

Sailboat racing on the public waters of the world is a bizarre situation. Racing sailors are given permission by the USCG to violate the *Navigation Rules* when interacting with each other, so long as they obey the Rules when interacting with vessels that are not racing. It is rather like the Highway Patrol giving permission to drag race down a main street, with the participating racers setting their own rules.

Racing sailors have their own set of rules called the Racing Rules of Sailing, coordinated by the International Sailing Federation (ISAF, sailing.org). One of their rules is that individual races can change the rules as needed, and the America's Cup race did make several crucial changes. For example, in normal ISAF racing, you must finish with the same crew you started with. In the America's Cup, not only could you lose crew overboard, but you were forbidden to take them back on board if you could—another example of racing rules that can be quite contrary to what is normally considered good seamanship.

One maneuvering rule that differs notably in racing is how close you can pass and still be legal. When racing it al-

most boils down to: if you did not collide, you were not too close. Another is how an overtaken vessel can respond. Off the race course, the overtaken vessel must hold course and speed, but when racing, so long as the overtaking boat does not have its bow past your stern, you can turn right into it and force it away.

Either of these two racing maneuvers could put you in jail if they caused injury off the race course, but they are commonplace, even tactically crucial, while on the race course. So the message is: sailors do not want to learn to maneuver by watching racers interact, and racing sailors want to remember that "keep well clear" and "ample time" have very different meanings when interacting with vessels that are not racing.

12.26 How to Fold Charts

Ask a dozen cruising mariners how best to fold and store charts, and you will likely get a dozen different answers. So with that background, we boldly go on and proclaim what the best method is!

First, though, we should say that if you have only just a few charts, it really does not matter too much. When there are only a few charts, it is easy to find what you want, no matter how you store them. The crucial issue of chart storage comes into play when you have a lot of charts, because then the situation can get very much out of hand in just one long trip or a season of sailing with multiple charts.

The solution is, fold them inside out, chart-side in, blank white paper side out, either once or twice, depending on the chart size. Most charts take two folds. Then label the corner, as shown in Figure 12.26-1, with the chart number. It is best to use a consistent size and style of lettering. We've found that a bold *Sharpie* pen is ideal for this.

Then arrange the charts in numerical order and store them flat somewhere, preferably in a sealed plastic garbage bag or other waterproof wrapping. Under a settee cushion might work, or under a bunk mattress.

WARNING!

Do not approach within 100 yards of any
U.S. naval vessel. If you need to pass within 100 yards of a
U.S. naval vessel in order to ensure a safe passage in accordance with the
Navigation Rules, you must contact the U.S. naval vessel or the Coast Guard
escort vessel on VHF-FM channel 16.

500
Yards

100
Yards KEEP OUT!

OPERATE AT MINIMUM SPEED

You must operate at minimum speed
within 500 yards of any U.S. naval vessel
and proceed as directed by the Commanding Officer or the official patrol.

Figure 12.25-1. *Protection and Security Zones around US Navy Vessels. The same applies to tank vessels and large passenger vessels (ferries and cruise ships) in major US ports. See 33 CFR 165.1321, 165.1313, 165.1317. In Puget Sound, the security zone around submarines is twice as large at 1,000 yards (0.5 nmi).*

Figure 12.25-2. *USCG Defender A-Class response boat employed by the USCG for harbor security and other purposes. They are 29 ft long and make over 46 kts.*

Then get a chart catalog of the region of your charts and mark the catalog with each chart you have. There are two places to mark it: one is the list of charts included in the catalog, and the other is to use a highlight marker to draw in the actual outline of the charts you have. This catalog then becomes your index of charts. For long voyages, it will be referred to frequently.

The virtue of this method of folding and stacking is that when you are looking for a chart in the stack, each chart presents only one corner. Folded this way, you have a crisp uniform presentation for all charts. If you try to fold them right side out and use the nice large chart numbers printed in each corner, then each chart will present four sheets to you as you search the stack, and they will not be uniform at all. Oftentimes, charts must be found in a hurry, and this is the method that best solves the problem.

On a long run, you might use your catalog to find the ones you need for the day, pull them all out, and stack them on the chart table. When done, they can be refolded and inserted in proper numerical sequence back into your main stack.

For a boat with a lot of charts, I cannot stress how important this operation is. On most new boats I travel on, the very first thing that must be done is to spend the afternoon organizing the charts. This procedure usually reveals multiple copies of identical charts, as well as important ones that are way outdated. If you find duplicates, you might want to note the chart date in the label, and then decide what to do about them later on. In any event, they will be easy to find after this operation.

If you ever visit any Navy, NOAA, or USCG vessel that does not have a 4 by 5 foot chart locker, which can store them all unfolded, then you will almost certainly see the charts folded in the manner described above. In fact, even ships with chart lockers often use this system, which is how

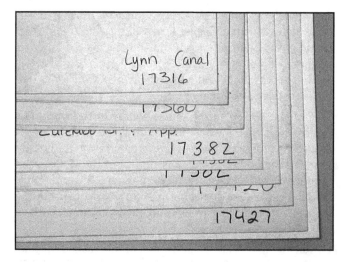

Figure 12.26-1. *Best method for folding charts: inside out, labeled on the single-sheet corner with chart number and perhaps name. Stacked in numerical order.*

I first learned of this technique buying a stack of old charts from a Navy shipyard. The technique has since been confirmed from other sources and personally tested for many years.

In some cases (fewer now than some years ago), charts have printing on both sides. Choose the side you are least likely to use, and call that the back to write on. Folding and labeling POD charts would be the same as for the traditional lithographic printed versions.

12.27 Magic Circle for Speed, Time, and Distance

Throughout all navigation we are confronted with problems of Speed, Time, and Distance: we know two of these, and we need to figure the third. There are several ways to solve these problems, and it doesn't matter at all which

Figure 12.25-3. *A close encounter at very high speed in the 2013 America's Cup between two AC72 racing catamarans, Emirates Team New Zealand (on port) and Oracle Team USA (on starboard, at the crossing). This one turned out to be even too close for the Racing Rules. ETNZ did save the day and carried on racing, but was penalized. The saving grace in this type of sailing is the remarkable skill of the sailors. As the saying goes, don't do this at home.*
Image © ACEA/PHOTO ABNER KINGMAN.

method we use. But we need to know some method well enough that we would never put off doing a calculation simply because we felt uncomfortable doing it. Here are the typical problems:

(1) Port Townsend is 37 nmi away, and I can travel at 5 kts. How long will it take to get there? Speed and Distance are known; what is the Time?

(2) I have sailed 165 nmi from noon to noon. What was my average speed? Or, I want to check my knotmeter by timing the run along a measured mile. The mile takes 7 minutes and 20 seconds, what was my speed? Time and Distance are known; what is the Speed?

(3) The sun sets in 2 hours and 50 minutes. I can make 8.0 kts. How far can I get before sunset? Speed and Time are known; what is the Distance?

One way to solve these problems is to use a nautical slide rule like the one shown in Figure 12.27-1. Common kinds are concentric plastic disks with speed, time, and distance scales printed along the rims. You rotate the disks to set the two known values on the proper index marks, and read the solution from another index mark. These slide rules are rugged, inexpensive, and easy to use.

Another approach is to solve the problem with a calculator directly from the definition of speed: Speed = Distance/Time. The formulas for Time and Distance come from inverting this formula. In this approach, we must remember the right formulas, and we must keep the hours and minutes straight, usually by expressing all times in decimal hours. That is, 1h 22m = 1h + (22/60) h = 1h + 0.367 = 1.367 h.

The *Magic Circle,* shown in Figure 12.27-2, is one way to do this. The figure shows how to apply the circle to remember the formulas. Some mariners remember the trick

with an address: *60 "D" Street*, which will be apparent from the presentation.

Practice examples are shown in Table 12.27-1. Choose any two, and solve for the third. If you prefer to use decimal hours (Figure 12.27-3), just change the address to 1 "D" Street! Figure 12.27-4 is a reminder of how we can solve such quick computations these days in a smartphone app.

Oftentimes, we can solve our Time and Distance problems without resorting to slide rules or formulas. One way to figure how long it will take to get somewhere is to set your speed on your dividers, and just walk them along your route. If my speed is 6 kts, I set 6 nmi on the dividers—the distance I travel in 1 hour—and count the hours as I walk the dividers to my destination.

Another shortcut is to figure the minutes per mile at your typical cruising speed. At 6 kts, a mile takes 10 minutes, so a 5-nmi run would take 50 minutes, and so on. For

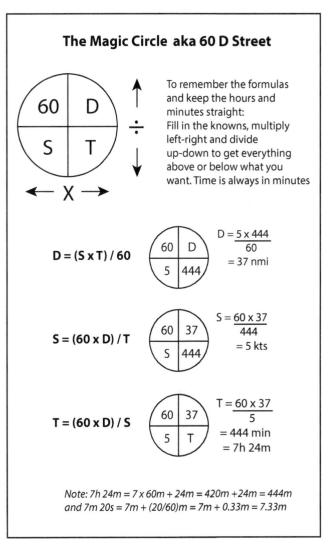

Figure 12.27-2. *Magic Circle aka 60 "D" Street as a way to remember the algebra of speed, time, and distance problems. The example shown is the first one from Table 12.27-1. You can use the reminder diagram with decimal hours by changing the 60 to 1.*

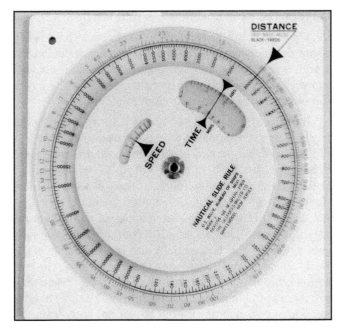

Figure 12.27-1. *A nautical slide rule, showing that 6.0 kts is 10 minutes per mile.*

docking or figuring the drift of currents, note that 1 knot is 100 ft per minute.

If you lose your knotmeter and want to figure your speed from the time it takes to pass some floating debris, use the following: Speed (in kts) = 0.6 × Speed (in ft/second). Your speed in feet per second is the length of the boat in feet divided by the number of seconds it takes for the object to pass from bow to stern.

12.28 Limitations of GPS

If you rely solely on GPS to navigate in the fog, you will not know whether it was right until the fog lifts—or some other, maybe abrupt, event lets you know.

This is just as true navigating in clear skies of unknown waters. You do not know whether you are right till you get there... or do not. If you don't reach out of the boat

Table 12.27-1 Practice with S,T, & D		
Speed	*Time*	*Distance*
5.00 kts	7h 24m	37.0 nmi
6.88 kts	24h	165 nmi
8.18 kts	7m 20s	1.00 nmi
8.00 kts	2h 50m	22.7 nmi

Figure 12.27-4. *Two views of the standard iPhone calculator. Rotating the phone changes from basic to advanced modes.*

SPEED, TIME, and DISTANCE CALCULATIONS

S = Speed in knots	S = D/T
T = Time in *decimal hours*	T = D/S
D = Distance in nautical miles	D = SxT

Note: 3h 15m = 3h + (15/60)h = 3h + 0.25h = 3.25h

Figure 12.27-3. *The basic formulas using decimal hours.*

for orientation and confirmation by other means, you are putting all of your navigational fate into a single piece of electronics—a clear violation of a major tenet of good seamanship: do not rely on any single source for navigation. Relying solely on GPS is a quintessential example of what engineers call a single point of failure.

On the other hand, GPS is usually very dependable, and with all the options for backup handheld units and bags of batteries, we are fairly well assured that we will usually know our latitude and longitude to a high degree of accuracy from this tool in normal circumstances.

It is prudent, nevertheless, to remain mindful of its limitations in normal circumstances, and especially in unique situations. Numerical values of our latitude and longitude, for example, will not be enough in some cases. Without a plotted position on a chart, Lat-Lon coordinates are not much help in knowing where we really are. Even with precise Lat-Lon values at hand, the crucial piece of navigation knowledge is usually where we are relative to landmarks or underwater hazards around us. Dependence on GPS presumes we are practiced at transferring these numerical coordinates to a valid chart... or having some echart software doing this for us on a chart we can trust is right.

The availability and quality of the charts we have is key to our dependence on GPS. In many cruising waters of the world, we can end up in a small bay or inlet that is not well represented on the only chart scales available. The bay is too small to show up the only chart available.

In the past, we could say at this point that maybe the bay is shown adequately on the best chart available; we just did not have that particular chart on board. But now there is no real excuse for that. Echarts of all US waters are free, and digital storage is very cheap, so there is no reason now not to have all charts available for any location. We might not choose to buy the printed versions of all of them (at about $20 each), but we should have the echarts for such contingencies. This is essentially also true for waters of the world outside of the US where echarts are not free. The reason is other countries or agencies selling the charts only sell them as full bundles of entire regions. The cost of buying one or two echarts (if even an option) is the same as buying all of them for a given region.

In areas with limited charting, knowing Lat and Lon is not much help, because the chart is not much help. We must navigate these isolated waters with traditional methods that rely only on what we see and measure from the boat. We have ways to find distance off an uncharted feature, and we can tell from natural ranges whether we are dragging anchor, and we can map out the bay with our own depth sounder and tide books.

And we should keep in mind that GPS, even where it is working fine, is not as fail-safe as we might wish. For one thing, GPS is notoriously easy to jam, either maliciously or accidentally. Just google "jam GPS" or "GPS failures" to find many examples. They vary from a hacker trying to prevent being tracked actually shutting down an airport GPS facility he was driving by, to military exercises shutting down GPS access to large sections of the ocean for testing purposes. If you rely on your boat as a backup to doomsday, be assured that GPS will be the first thing to go in any major conflict.

But aside from this romance, the results of GPS positions and the derived data it provides must definitely be monitored. In the presence of steep cliffs, the satellites can be blocked, which can at least deteriorate the accuracy if not cause complete loss of a fix. Many beautiful waterways of Alaska, for example, have such fjord-like passages. But this, too, is a specialized scenario. Modern receivers offer usable fixes with just 3 satellites, which are available in all but the tightest quarters, though the fixes may bounce in and out as the satellite geometry changes.

In a sense, the real risk of "relying on GPS" is not so much the GPS itself, but the full system of electronics, input power, antennas, networking, display screens, and often proprietary echarts that bring us the final results. Any one of these crucial components can fail. You might push a button in, and it does not come back out, and all is locked up. Or some microscopic knife nick in an antenna cable made when rerouting the cable leads to a corroded mush inside the cable in a matter of weeks of saltwater baths. Or we rely on a computer to plot the positions, and the computer crashes. (You might guess that computer experts would be less concerned about that, but indeed they will be the first to identify the computer as the weakest link in the system.)

Failures of some component of an ECS are not rare at all on a long voyage. For such long trips, backup handheld GPS units or a complete redundancy of your system is mandatory if you are going to depend on this.

My guess is there are not nearly as many marine accidents due to actual GPS signal errors as you will find claimed in the literature. Many of these reports are more likely cockpit errors in assigning waypoints incorrectly or simply reading some dials incorrectly or losing power or a good satellite geometry temporarily at a crucial time—or most likely of all, the position was plotted on a proprietary echart that was in error. Nevertheless, the number of accidents due to GPS-dependent operation is nowhere near

zero. If it were near zero, we would not need the warnings we get in essentially every GPS manual and start-up screen that warn us specifically not to depend on this system— which includes the custom charts they are using in place of official NOAA charts. See Figure 12.28-1.

Nor would we need questions like this one on the USCG license exam for deck officers:

724. Which statement concerning GPS is TRUE?

    A. It cannot be used in all parts of the world.

    B. There are 12 functioning GPS satellites at present.

    C. It may be suspended without warning.

    D. Two position lines are used to give a 2D fix.

ANSWER: C

But the question of relying on GPS for navigation is much more basic in the maritime world. Mariners are rightfully a very conservative group. They know that once they pull away from the dock they must be self-reliant. If you choose a life on a small boat at sea, then a fundamental rule that has been proven so many times we don't have to go over it is you must be prepared to take care of yourself in any contingency. Murphy's Law was invented on a

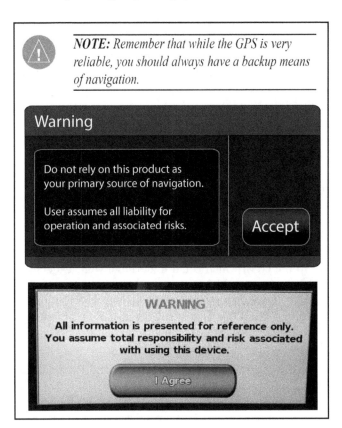

Figure 12.28-1. *Warnings not to depend on GPS based chart plotters as sole source of navigation. Top from a manual; bottom two from start-up screens. These are also an unspoken warning about the unofficial charts being used, which could be more of an issue than the GPS, which is inherently pretty dependable. .*

small boat at sea. Anything electrical is vulnerable after some time in the salt air, especially when it is being jarred, bumped, banged, and dropped and very likely getting wet as well.

To be self-reliant, we need dependable means of navigation. A handheld GPS and spare batteries stuffed into a well-protected vacuum sealed bag is a pretty good backup, but it is not at all bulletproof. Batteries of any kind are not bulletproof. One could even argue that the durability of handheld GPS units is not improving with time. They are getting cheaper, and they do have more functions, but the more they evolve toward consumer products, the less dependable they become.

But we can go beyond the numerical likelihood of not having it when we need it, and look at how it affects us when we do have it. The main hazard of depending on GPS routinely is we soon lose practice at basic piloting skills, or worse still, we decide we do not need to learn these skills at all any more. In short, we forget why we are in a boat in the first place.

The history of modern civilization can be tied to the history of boats and navigation. There is a reason that all great scientists throughout recorded history devoted much of their energies to solving problems of navigation. Good navigation practice is a key to progress—on an international scale and on a very local scale. Confirming our location by bearings, or depth soundings, or natural ranges, or carrying out an accurate DR run is an intellectually satisfying experience. Relying only on own hands and mind and basic tools like a compass and log, we accomplish something both tangible and useful. Sound navigation is a part of maritime tradition.

Besides that, learning basic navigation makes us better mariners in a more abstract sense, because whether we show it or not, we will be anxious about our navigation if we are depending on something that we (most of us) cannot hope to understand. GPS is a black box. With nothing else to check it with, you can just hope that it works right—and, again, you will only know that when you get there or do not. And when you are anxious, you are more likely to make a mistake. You risk the chance of exposing your anxiety to the crew, which could undermine your leadership, which in turn could lead to all sorts of unpleasantness. None of that will happen of course so long as everything is going fine, but if things start to get stressed for any reason (bad weather, broken gear), this factor will just add to the challenge.

In the long run, it is best to learn the traditional navigation skills and use them often, at least to confirm the GPS position. You will then know you can fall back on these skills for primary navigation if you need to, and that alone will make it worthwhile. If you plan to crew on other vessels, then knowing how to navigate will be an important part of your credentials and will certainly help you find a good crew position. Many skippers do not themselves believe this is necessary, but they will be happy to have someone on board who knows how to navigate.

GPS is certainly one of the most significant engineering achievements of modern times. It has, maybe more than any other single technology, dramatically influenced so many diverse activities. You can argue it is even negligent to leave the dock without it—but it is equally negligent to go to sea without knowing how to navigate without it. We can see this sentiment in the minds of the IMO experts that coordinate the standards for the licensing of ship's officers worldwide. Not only do they still require an extensive demonstration of piloting and DR skills, they also require celestial navigation for ocean routes. The ongoing requirement for celestial navigation is particularly telling. Out of sight of land, celestial is the only backup to GPS, and clearly there is no authority who feels we are ready to rely on GPS without a backup.

12.29 WAAS-Enhanced GPS

In very broad terms, GPS determines a position from intersecting ranges to satellites at known locations. The GPS unit measures the ranges by precise timing of radio signals from the satellites. Position errors are in large part due to small errors in this timing process. One way to improve accuracy is to measure the GPS position from a receiver located at a very well-known location, and then compare that with the actual location. The difference (GPS error) can then be broadcast to other GPS units in radio range so they can correct their positions by a corresponding amount to achieve an enhanced accuracy. This process is called *differential GPS*, and it is in use by various government agencies and private companies for super high accuracies—as good as ±10 cm in some cases.

The Federal Aviation Administration (FAA) has coordinated a variation of that concept using multiple land-based reference stations along with several geostationary satellites used to broadcast the corrections to the public. The system is called the Wide Area Augmentation System, WAAS. Most modern marine GPS receivers are WAAS enabled and offer this enhanced accuracy, taking a typical uncertainty of 15 to 40 meters (45 to 120 ft) and reducing it to 5 to 10 meters (16 to 33 ft) accuracy. The units will consume more power with WAAS on. Often more important is that this enhanced accuracy leads to more accurate COG and SOG values, both computed more quickly after a large change in course or speed. It also makes the elevation output of the GPS into a sometimes usable value. Without WAAS, the elevation is often quite wrong; with WAAS, it can be on average quite close, but it will still bounce around proportionally more than the horizontal position does.

The key practical factor in taking advantage of this system is seeing the geostationary satellites that broadcast the corrections. For US usage, these are located over the Equator at 129° W (#46); 125° W (#48); and 117° W (#44), where the numbers indicated are the NMEA identification

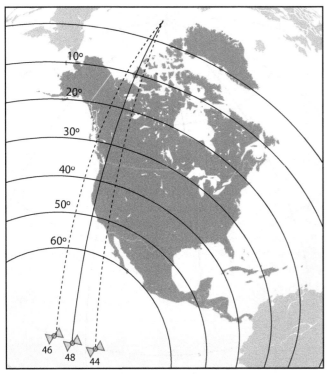

Figure 12.29-1. *Approximate elevations of WAAS satellite #48, from which rough estimates of the other two can be made. Online apps give precise elevations and bearings to each of them.*

Figure 12.29-2 shows the coverage of the WAAS system along with that of similar systems available in Europe (EG-NOS) and in Japan (MSAS). Some GPS units advertise that they can use more than one of these systems, which would be of interest only if you plan to travel to one of these other coverage areas.

To follow up on earlier mention of the role of navigation in the history of civilization and related international relations, we note the new debate in the US Congress about allowing Russia to establish land-based reference stations in the US to augment their version of GPS called GLONASS. Some US instruments use GLONASS to improve GPS performance, but so far, WAAS-level accuracy is not available to these signals. The question is one of improving overall accuracy for consumers versus the security risks that might accompany such a system.

12.30 Velocity Made Good (VMG)

As noted in Section 12.14 on terminology, some instrument companies use VMG to mean progress to the next waypoint, which we would propose is better called velocity made course (VMC). If your instruments do that, then refer back to that section for that interpretation.

VMG is more of a sailing performance term these days, and most instruments chosen for sailboats (at least the wind instrumentation) will use it that way. It could be that you have wind instruments using VMG one way, and a GPS system using it another way. That makes communications trickier, which is something we try to avoid in navigation.

As a sailing performance term, it means the speed of the boat, relative to the water, in the direction of true wind, as shown in Figure 12.30-1. This computed speed is unique among the other derived quantities we use in navigation (COG, SOG, etc), because it is calculated by wind instruments and knotmeter, not GPS and knotmeter, and it is a measure of sailing performance as opposed to the others that measure navigation performance.

numbers that are listed in your GPS for each satellite it sees. Figure 12.29-1 shows the elevation of #48 from the continental US. If your view to the horizon is blocked in a WAAS satellite direction you will not be able to get the WAAS-enhanced accuracy. Knowing this limitation could affect some planning or navigational decisions if high accuracy is required. If your hobby is geocaching, then knowing the elevation and bearing to WAAS satellites is crucial to pinpointing locations on land, where these views are more commonly blocked by buildings or hills. Back in Figure 12.15-1, there is a comparison of two GPS position distributions, with and without the help of a WAAS satellite.

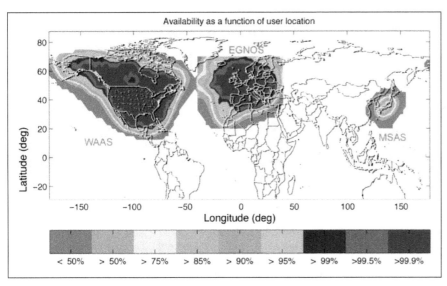

Figure 12.29-2. *Worldwide GPS augmentation systems along with the along with their regions of overage with percentage availability. There is no enhanced GPS services in the low and southern latitudes.*

There is a link to detailed description of WAAS and EGNOS systems included on the resources page: starpath.com/navboook

The true wind direction that is used for VMG reference must be computed by the instruments from the wind measured on the boat, which is the apparent wind. The vector relationship between these is shown in Figure 12.30-2, which also shows the VMG vector as well.

VMG can be used tactically sailing upwind or downwind. The principle of its value is the same in either direction, although the reference direction is reversed. When you fall off sailing upwind (turn away from the wind direction), or come up sailing downwind (turn toward the wind direction), you go faster, but you are sailing more off the wind direction so you have farther to go. Consequently, there is an optimum combination of heading (H) and knotmeter speed (S) that will maximize VMG. This information is, in principle, all included in the boat's *polar diagram* for each sail combination and wind speed. A sample is shown in Figure 12.30-3. Such diagrams are sometimes provided by the yacht designer, but they can also be measured directly with various levels of sophistication. There is special software dedicated to this job, which facilitates the measurements and analysis, but every sailor has some idea of these results in their mind for their boat, with or without actual diagrams.

Optimizing VMG is often thought of as finding the best apparent wind angle (AWA) to sail, as opposed to best compass heading to sail, but if the wind is constant, these are the same. The tacit assumption here is that when sailing to windward, you want to maximize your speed in the direction the wind comes from, and when sailing downwind, you want to maximize your speed in the direction the wind is blowing. The former is always the case (by definition), while the latter is not always so clear, but it is the case where finding optimum VMG comes into play most often.

Sailing to weather, VMG tells if you are *pinching* (sailing too close to the wind) or *footing* (sailing too far off the wind). Although often of most value in the first stages of learning to sail a particular boat, sail, and wind combination, VMG to weather can still be important to watch as wind and waves begin to change—particularly if these changes call for sails that are not used often. The optimum AWA will likely change with wind speed and sail.

The more frequent tactical use of VMG comes when sailing downwind in light to moderate air toward a mark that lies dead downwind in no current. Here the task is to choose the optimum downwind reaching angle, since reaching is faster than sailing dead downwind (Figure 12.30-3). In principle, the optimum reaching angle could be read from a polar diagram, but I venture to guess that this is not done very often. The more dependable approach—in these somewhat special circumstances—is to just watch VMG as you come up, continuously trimming to the new AWA. VMG will get bigger and then get smaller as you go through the peak. A sample is shown in Table 12.30-1.

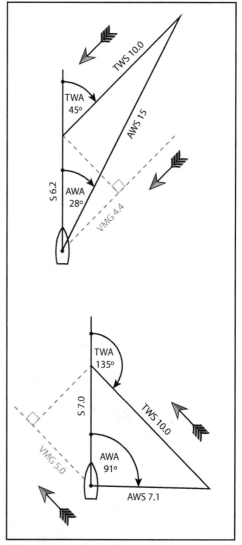

Figure 12.30-2. *Finding true wind speed and true wind angle from apparent wind measurements. The true wind is always aft of the apparent wind. All instruments must be accurate to get useful information from this analysis.*

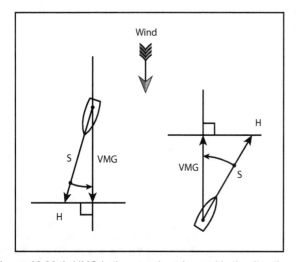

Figure 12.30-1. *VMG is the speed made good in the direction of the wind. It is the knotmeter speed (in the direction of the vessel heading H) projected onto the true wind direction, which must be determined from the apparent wind speed, apparent wind angle, and knotmeter speed.*

The virtue of this downwind VMG measured from wind instruments, as opposed to the VMC measured with GPS—*which is truly what you want to optimize in all cases*—is the time it takes to get the answer. Even with the necessary trim at each new AWA, VMG is often faster than a realistic average of VMC from the GPS. The VMG is essentially instantaneous, although there can be time averaging constants set on each of the inputs. When the wind changes, VMG can tell you what is happening in seconds, as opposed to a minute or so to evaluate an average VMC. One approach is to find optimum VMG downwind and then check the VMC as the final truth meter.

Once you have good polar diagrams or comparable experience with sailing your boat, you can develop a set of *target speeds* going upwind and downwind in various true wind speeds. This list, which is a good blue-tape candidate in view of the helm and trimmers, is the quickest way to

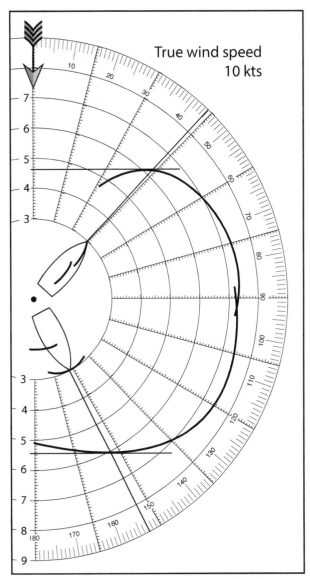

Figure 12.30-3. *A sample polar diagram for a 35 ft sailboat for a true wind speed of 10 kts. The optimum true wind angle downwind is about 153°. A measurement underway is shown in Table 12.30-1.*

confirm that you are doing your best, and if not, to keep looking to figure out why.

On the other hand, the wind and knotmeter data must be accurate if the VMG output is to be of much tactical advantage. The minimum quality you might want, for example, is to have the data mean the same thing on either tack or jibe, and also be true if the boat is heeled over or not, or be the same reaching with a spinnaker or a headsail. There are subtle effects to be reckoned with here, most of which can be traced to how the wind data is measured at the masthead. Frankly, it is a lot of work to get it right, though it can be much assisted by customized software that lets you calibrate the instruments to account for asymmetries in the measurements. Consult manufacturers to get the pros and cons of various systems.

True Wind versus Water Wind

From a navigator's point of view, the derived navigation functions are of more tangible interest than the wind data. It is easy to appreciate, for example, that strong current makes downwind VMG difficult to interpret. For one thing, current affects apparent wind speed, but does not alter knotmeter speed. Consequently the wind direction is not calculated properly, and so the projection of S onto it cannot be right. This is not to say that a maximum VMG won't mean a near optimum reaching angle, but it is by no means clear.

Furthermore, even without current, if the mark is not dead downwind, one jibe is favored over the other, but there is still an optimum reaching angle. This angle, however, cannot be found from a simple maximization of VMG, since this is speed dead downwind. Put current into this problem, and the clear value of choosing the reaching angle by maximizing the GPS's VMC is obvious—if the leg is long enough to permit this. VMG might then be used as a secondary reference to warn of sudden wind changes that call for course alteration. Usually, an echart display that is plotting out your actual track across the chart is the simplest way to choose your jibes or tacks.

If we choose to reach out of the boat and compute the true meteorological wind direction properly, we must be even more careful. The method of computing TWA used for VMG is based on an apparent wind direction measured relative to the bow, in direction H. But if the boat is actually moving in direction COG that is different from H, we cannot apply this TWA to H to get the true wind direction.

We can let the wind instruments do their job as de-

Table 12.30-1 Optimizing Downwind VMG*					
H	033M	028M	023M	018M	012M
S	5.6	5.8	6.2	6.3	6.6
VMG	5.2	5.3	5.4	5.3	5.2

* *Sailing downwind, as we come up on the wind by changing heading H, the knotmeter speed S increases steadily, but the VMG goes through a peak, marking the optimum reaching angle for maximum progress downwind.*

scribed, but when we want to know the true meteorological wind speed and direction for weather routing and shipboard forecasting, we must solve the vector triangle using COG and SOG, as shown in Figure 12.30-4. It is essentially the same, but we first compute the apparent wind direction using AWA and H, and then find the vector difference between the apparent wind and the true motion of the boat relative to the ground. If there is no current or notable helm bias or leeway, these two winds will be the same, but in special cases they can be significantly different.

Thus, we see the value in the terminology distinction between *water wind* (relative to the water, using S and H) versus *true wind* (relative to the ground, using SOG and COG).

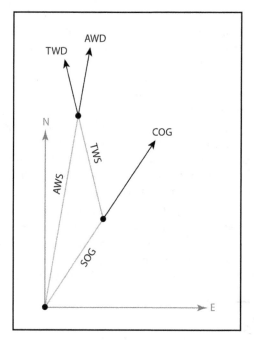

Figure 12.30-4. *Computing true wind direction (TWD) and true wind speed (TWS) based on apparent wind direction (AWD) and apparent wind speed (AWS) for a given SOG and COG. The AWD is determined from the apparent wind angle relative to the bow and the true heading of the vessel. This true wind speed and direction (relative to land) is the meteorological wind, as opposed to the* water *wind (relative to the water) we get from using S and H instead of SOG and COG. The latter is used to evaluate sailing performance with VMG. If there was no current at all, no notable leeway, and no helm bias within the averaging periods used, then these two winds would be the same.*

Chapter 12 Glossary

advanced LOP. An LOP that has been moved (with parallel rulers or plotter) without rotation from one time to a later time, usually to form a running fix.

AIS (Automatic Identification System). An IMO sanctioned collision avoidance system that uses VHF frequencies to broadcast a vessel's COG and SOG, along with other identification information. Recreational mariners can participate by reception alone to monitor commercial traffic, or register for an identification number and broadcast their own information as well to nearby traffic.

ARPA (automatic radar plotting aid). A collision avoidance radar system sanctioned by the IMO that displays target vessel's projected course, along with their true speed and the CPA. It requires a heading sensor and a stabilized radar display. Similar functionalities that do not meet IMO standards are called Mini-ARPA, MARPA, or ATA (for automatic tracking aid) by different manufacturers.

course box. A device rigged to post the present course in view of the helmsman.

Dial-a-Buoy. A service of the NDBC that gives live observations from weather buoys by calling a toll-free number: 888-701-8992.

ECDIS (electronic chart display and information system). The official ECS system sanctioned and specified by the IMO. Pronounced "ek-dis."

error current. The difference between the compass-knotmeter vector and the COG-SOG vector.

falling off. A sailor's term for turning away from the wind direction. The opposite is "coming up."

footing. Falling off of the optimum tacking angle in order to gain speed or alter position to leeward.

GeoMag. A software program that computes magnetic variation from the National Geodetic Center.

GPS satellite status display. A radar-like display showing the angular altitude and azimuth of satellites in use, usually with some measure of the signal strength of each.

head-up radar display. The basic radar display that shows the ship's heading line always oriented straight up, so that all targets are seen on the screen in terms of relative bearings.

helm bias. The tendency of the helmsman to temporarily alter course in the same direction on successive waves of a seaway or when under sail to turn in the same direction with successive wind gusts.

in extremis. The approach of another vessel in a risk of collision that is so close that a collision can be prevented only by a maneuver of your own.

inverse barometer effect. Name of the result that low atmospheric pressure enhances tide height and high pressure diminishes it. A small effect except in extreme cases, known to mariners since the 1800s.

layline. The route that takes a sailboat to a windward destination on one tack.

nautical slide rule. A plastic device that was once common for solving speed, time, and distance problems. Now largely replaced by mobile device apps.

NMEA (National Marine Electronics Association). A trade organization that supports marine electronics development, standards, sales, support, and education. See nmea.org.

NOAA Weather Radio. The NWS program of broadcasting continuous marine weather data on the VHF that includes synopses and forecasts updated every 6 hours and observations updated every 3 hours, or more often in severe weather.

pinching. Sailing closer to the wind than optimum in order to gain progress to windward at the sacrifice of speed.

POD charts. Print-on-demand nautical charts, which will be the only source of printed charts after April 2014. Two companies contracted for the printing are geospatial.com or oceangrafix.com.

prolonged blast. In the *Navigation Rules*, a signal sound or light flash that is 4 to 6 seconds long.

Protection and Security Zones. The areas 100 and 500 yards wide that mark the no-entry zone and the "reduce speed to bare steerage" zones around Navy vessels, tank ships, and large passenger vessels, enforced by the USCG under the authority of the Marine Transportation Security Act.

Racing Rules. The set of rules used in yacht racing established by the International Sailing Federation for racing yachts interacting with each other. The standard *Naviga-tion Rules* apply when racing yachts are interacting with nonracing vessels.

retired LOP. An LOP that is moved backward in time. The opposite of advanced.

route plan. As used in ECS, an output file that lists all legs of a route with the range, bearing, and ETA of each. Some include a labeled chartlet showing the route. Also called voyage plan or plan book.

running fix. A piloting fix obtained by advancing an earlier LOP to one taken at a later time. The accuracy of a running fix is as good as the DR is between the two sight times.

sea buoy. The first buoy at the channel entrance to a harbor from the sea

short blast. In the *Navigation Rules*, a signal sound or light flash that is 1 second long.

storm surge. The excess of water coming ashore as a result of strong winds, onshore currents, and low pressure.

tricolor navigation light. The sidelights and sternlight combined into one lantern carried on the centerline of the vessel, which is a legal option for vessels under 20 meters long.

up-screen. In radar terminology, it is motion of a target toward the top of the ship's heading line, which in the standard head-up display means toward the top of the screen. A target that turns more up-screen is one that is turning more toward the direction you are steering.

US Naval Observatory (USNO). Founded in 1830, it is one of the oldest scientific agencies in the country. Originally, it had the responsibility of nautical charts and all matters of navigation, but now all but celestial navigation has moved to other agencies. Many of our classic references originated there, such as *Bowditch*, once called N.O. Pub No. 9.

VHF channels. Communication on VHF radio is restricted to specific channels, numbered 1 to 99, sometimes with a letter A (alpha), which are selected based on the nature of the communication. The channel usage list is given at navcen.uscg.gov.

VMG (velocity made good). The speed of a vessel projected onto the true wind direction. Some instruments use this term for VMC.

VTS (Vessel Traffic Service). The USCG division that coordinates the use of shipping lanes (TSS).

water wind. Wind speed and direction specified relative to the water.

Turn your textbook into a home study course.

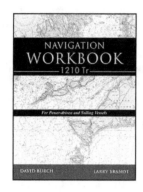 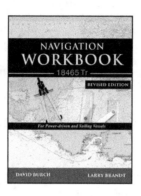 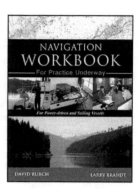

Available at your favorite book outlet or online at www.starpath.com

Three workbooks are available to expand your training with extensive practice exercises covering all aspects of small craft navigation. Each are organized and keyed to the chapters of this text. These are the types of problems all navigators should know how to solve. Two use standard training charts; the other is a unique presentation of practice exercises that you can create when underway using actual circumstances. This book can turn any day on the water into an onboard training seminar. Many can even be done while at anchor. All reference materials needed are included.

The exercises that require a chart use Training Chart No. 18465 Tr (west coast) or 1210 Tr (east coast), which are inexpensive in print and also available as RNC echarts that will run in any program. There are numerous commercial and open source programs that you can use to solve all the plotting and route planning exercises in electronic format, including tides and currents. OpenCPN and qtVlm are popular free versions for Mac and PC.

We encourage navigators to solve the exercises with both traditional paper plotting as well as electronically, using electronic bearing lines and range rings.

Index

Printed in the USA
CPSIA information can be obtained
at www.ICGtesting.com
LVHW080741120724
785245LV00009B/1472

9 780914 025405